Children's Daily Prayer

For the School Year 2000–2001

By Elizabeth McMahon Jeep

A Liturgy of the Hours for the Classroom:
Including an Order of Prayer for Each School Day
Plus Meal and End of the Day Prayers for Each Month
That Reflect the Spirit of the Church's Seasons and Feasts

LTP
LITURGY
TRAINING
PUBLICATIONS

CONTENTS

ACKNOWLEDGMENTS

Readings from the Old Testament and New Testament, except as noted below, are taken from the *Contemporary English Version* of the Bible, copyright © 1991 American Bible Society, 1875 Broadway, New York NY 10023, and are used by permission of the American Bible Society. All rights reserved.

Readings from the books of Esther, Tobit and 2 Maccabees are taken from the *New Revised Standard Version* of the Bible, copyright © 1989, Division of Christian Education of the National Council of the Churches of Christ in the United States of America. Used with permission. All rights reserved.

Excerpts from the English translations of the psalms and canticles from the *Liturgical Psalter,* copyright © 1994 International Committee on English in the Liturgy, Inc. (ICEL); the English translation of the *Angelus* and the *Regina Caeli* from *A Book of Prayers,* copyright © 1982 ICEL; excerpts from the English translation of the *Book of Blessings,* additional blessings for use in the United States, copyright © 1988 ICEL; excerpts from the *Liturgy of the Hours,* copyright © 1970 ICEL. Used with permission. All rights reserved.

English translation of the Glory to the Father by the International Consultation on English Texts (ICET).

Texts taken from *Catholic Household Blessings and Prayers,* copyright © 1988 United States Catholic Conference, Washington, D.C., are used with permission. All rights reserved.

Texts from *Gates of Prayer: The New Union Prayerbook,* copyright © 1975 Central Conference of American Rabbis, New York. Used with permission. All rights reserved.

CHILDREN'S DAILY PRAYER 2000–2001, copyright © 2000 Archdiocese of Chicago: Liturgy Training Publications, 1800 North Hermitage Avenue, Chicago IL 60622-1101. All rights reserved.

Order phone: 1-800-933-1800
Editorial phone: 1-773-486-8970
Fax: 1-800-933-7094
E-mail: orders@ltp.org
Internet: www.ltp.org

CHILDREN'S DAILY PRAYER was illustrated by Carolina Arentsen. The book was edited by Kathy Luty. Audrey Novak Riley was the production editor. The design is by M. Urgo. The book was typeset by Karen Mitchell in Gill Sans and Sabon and printed in Canada by Webcom Limited.

ISBN 1-56854-324-7
CDP01
$15.00

INTRODUCTION

This book is for organizers and leaders of children's communal prayer. While it is likely that the organizer is a catechist or another adult, it is hoped that the children themselves will assume leadership during their times of prayer. This will enable them to take more responsibility for their prayer and to develop skills and a taste for the church's daily worship that can last a lifetime.

A service of prayer is provided for each day of the school year. An additional service of prayer is provided for groups that meet only once a week. Simpler prayers are offered for mealtime and for the end of the school day. The service of prayer for the day or for the week includes an introduction that briefly sketches the saint or feast of the day or some aspect of the liturgical season. Attention is also paid to the natural seasons of the year, important events in other religions, the prophets and peacemakers of our time and civil holidays that have significance for children.

This book covers a school year lasting from August 28, 2000, to June 17, 2001. For schools that remain open past June 17, on pages 326 and 327 there are many suggestions for extending prayers through the month.

On page 7 is an order of prayer for teachers preparing for the opening of school. Teachers who use this book before school begins will have no trouble helping children understand its various elements quickly. The Late Summer section closes with a prayer for faculty meetings that can be used at any time throughout the year.

This book is written both for students in religious education programs and for students in parochial schools. We encourage teachers to help students gain a strong sense of "ownership" of this book. Help them read it, use it and even invent and adapt new ways of putting it to use. We have tried to make suggestions clear and simple so that preparation time will be kept to a minimum.

In this book, Daily Prayer and Weekly Prayer focus on the feasts and seasons of the year and usually include the petitions of the classroom community. Meal Prayer focuses on our gratitude for food and other blessings, and on the needs of others. End of the Day Prayer is focused on dedication and peace.

This pattern should be adapted to serve your needs most effectively. You can, for example, use part of Daily Prayer to begin the day and the rest of it to begin religion class. For a shorter service, just the Psalm or End of the Day Prayer might be used. The blessings and other special prayers in this book can be used when appropriate. In all cases, it is best if students take the roles of Leader and Reader.

It is important that both teacher and students feel comfortable with the routine of prayer. What is printed in this book is a starting point, but if there are readings, prayer forms, special devotions or ethnic feasts that are important to your parish and school community, they certainly should be introduced. Your own creativity and preparation

will be necessary in celebrating your patron saints. You are invited to use the prayer formats found in this book, substituting appropriate psalms, songs, readings and prayers in your local celebrations.

The bibliography on page *xvi* lists the various resources used to prepare *Children's Daily Prayer.* Search here for publications that can provide further information on feasts, seasons, saints and holidays. Note in particular the book *Companion to the Calendar,* published by LTP, which contains information about every season, feast and saint of the church's year. The book was written to be useful to elementary grade students.

In *Children's Daily Prayer,* the material in the Looking Ahead sections provides good background for those who prepare eucharistic liturgies for children. The prayers and readings in this book are not designed for use at Mass; however, the music used daily should be used at the eucharist as well.

Children's celebrations are best done within the context and themes of the church year. For example, the celebration of Halloween should have a clear relationship to the observance of All Saints' Day, All Souls' Day and the month of November. Advent customs have their own character and do not usher in the beginning of the celebration of Christmas. The week of Christmastime in early January deserves a hearty celebration. Saint Patrick can be celebrated as a "Lenten saint" who prepares us for a more robust celebration of Easter. The Paschal Triduum should be experienced as the most important festival of the year.

Special days for which extra prayers and blessings have been supplied include Holy Cross (September 14); Archangels Raphael, Michael and Gabriel (September 29); Guardian Angels (October 2); Saint Francis of Assisi (October 4); Halloween, All Saints and All Souls (October 31 through November 2); Thanksgiving (November 23); the Week of Prayer for Christian Unity (January 18 to 25); the Presentation of the Lord (February 2); Saint Valentine (February 14); the Ascension of the Lord (May 24); and feasts of Our Lady. There are also rituals and blessings to mark the beginning and ending of Advent, Christmastime, Lent and Eastertime, as well as the beginning and ending of the school year.

It is possible, however, to overdo a good thing! When something is added, such as a blessing, something else may be subtracted. This is especially true if the school celebrates the eucharist regularly; you may want to eliminate or shorten other times of prayer on those days.

The Parts of This Book

As the contents pages show, this book is organized by months or seasons, with the long seasons of Lent and Eastertime each divided in two. The 13 main sections of this book each contain five parts: an

introduction called Looking Ahead; a Psalm that is used to begin Daily or Weekly Prayer; a Meal Prayer and an End of the Day Prayer that also will be used throughout the period; and finally, a series of dated pages that contain the orders of Daily and Weekly Prayer.

A selection of optional prayers is offered. A Blessing for Birthdays is printed on the inside of the back cover. There is an order for praying the rosary as a class (page 348). There are prayers for the sick (page 347), psalms suitable for days of sadness or trouble (page 346), the Litany of the Saints (page 89), an End of the Day Prayer for feasts of Mary (page 25), a blessing of gifts for people in need (page 350), a blessing of food for sharing (page 351), and a blessing of those who have celebrated a sacrament of initiation (page 274). New this year is a prayer of farewell on page 345 for a teacher or student who leaves before the school year is over. Use these prayers as the need arises.

Several blessings, such as that of a cross, pets, an image of Mary or an Advent wreath, are printed near the days on which they ordinarily would be celebrated during the year. An index (page 352) includes the saints and feasts celebrated this year.

Looking Ahead

Each section of this book begins with its own introduction, called Looking Ahead. These pages have three parts. *About the Month* or *About the Season* alerts the class to the mood of the month or season and the ways the church hopes sacred time will be celebrated. *Preparation* suggests changes in the classroom worship environment and gives direction concerning the prayers. The section titled *The School of Religion* provides guidance for after-school or weekend religion classes, or for other groups who gather only once a week.

The ideas in the Looking Ahead pages will need to be attended to before the season begins; they should be read to the class and discussed several days in advance.

Students—especially younger students—may need to become involved in discussion and hear explanations before they will appreciate the ideas on these pages. It is a good plan to appoint a student liturgy committee to keep up with these seasonal needs. This way, the teacher is not alone, for instance, in decorating the classroom.

Daily Prayer and Weekly Prayer

Each page of Daily Prayer or Weekly Prayer has a date. The order of prayer begins with an introduction that helps focus the children's attention. It offers a brief look at the saint or feast of the day, the season of the year or the day's scripture reading. Next, the leader is directed to turn to the psalm for the season or the month. After the psalm, the leader turns back to the dated page.

Next, the Reading is proclaimed, with accompanying acclamations.
The Reading is always from the Bible and should be followed by a
short period of silence to allow the words to settle into the hearts of the
children. Allow this silence to become an important part of each gathering. Children who are able to read clearly and respectfully should be
invited to serve as readers. No one, adult or child, would proclaim a
scripture passage without first taking time to prepare it.

The readings in this book are taken primarily from the *Contemporary
English Version* of the Bible and are suitable for the vocabulary and
understanding of children. This is the same translation of the Bible that
is used in the *Lectionary for Masses with Children.*

For the sake of simplicity, all scripture passages are called "readings"
rather than being divided into "readings" and "gospels." However, the
appropriate liturgical acclamation is given in each case. Students may
need to be taught the correct response.

*Reflections for each day encourage students to make the scriptures
their own.* These short questions challenge children to think through
some of the implications of the reading. One or more of these statements can be the foundation of a homily or a statement of faith by a
teacher or student. They can be discussed by the class or reflected on in
silence. In parochial schools, they can be used later in the day if Daily
Prayer is used in the morning.

The Closing ends Daily Prayer and Weekly Prayer. Its form varies,
but it is usually either a collect or intercessions. Intercessions are an
important form of prayer both for children and for the church. When
used well, intercessory prayer offers an opportunity for children to
share some of their own concerns and participate more personally in
the service.

*The blank space in each Closing should be filled in with students'
birthdays, current events and concerns, and other reasons for the
class to offer prayers of thanksgiving or petition.* Time should be
taken at the beginning of the year for each child to write in this space on
the proper day his or her baptismal anniversary, birthday or specially
chosen feast day (the student's name day, perhaps). This is also the place
to write the joys and crises of local, national and world events as the
year progresses and as the students' awareness of these matters expands.

The leader of prayer can simply announce these intentions as something to keep in mind at prayer, for example, "Let us remember these
intentions: For Heather and Roberto on their birthday. For Carl's
uncle, who is sick." Or the leader can present the intentions in the form
of intercessions, for example, "For Heather and Roberto on their birthday, let us pray to the Lord." All would respond: "Lord, have mercy."

Spontaneous petitions from the children can add to or substitute for
those printed in the book. Rules can be made (for example, only three
or five petitions each day) so that the opportunity does not become a

free-for-all and ultimately counterproductive. In any case, the class should have the opportunity to formulate its own petitions.

Meal Prayer and End of the Day Prayer

These are usually short prayers. They change each month or each season and can be found on the pages immediately following the Psalm. These pages are available as a student prayer book, *Blessed Be God!* Students who use that book will be better able to join in the prayer responses. Students also may be able to take a copy home for use at the family meal and at bedtime. If you are not able to use *Blessed Be God!* these pages may be photocopied from *Children's Daily Prayer* and handed out.

Meal Prayer can be done in the classroom or cafeteria before the midday meal. You may want to add or substitute a song. In October, the Meal Prayer is the traditional noontime Angelus, and during May, the Regina Caeli.

End of the Day Prayer also might include a song. Sometimes there is a trinitarian blessing at its conclusion. The leader of prayer will need to learn how to hold out an arm in blessing, and the class may need to learn to make the sign of the cross in response.

The Ways We Pray

Acclamations are short statements of faith and devotion used at regular times. They are often in the form of a dialogue between the leader and the class, and students should be encouraged to memorize them. These short statements often carry the mood of the liturgical season. Most of them can be sung, even on a single note, and should be sung if at all possible.

Silence is sometimes called for, especially after hearing the scriptures. Begin with a period of time the children find comfortable (such as half a minute) and gradually lengthen it. The silence should be preceded by something the children can reflect on.

Ritual and gesture are important aspects of Catholic prayer, along with a sense of the sacramental value of physical objects. This book suggests various gestures, ritual items and decorations for the seasons.

There are no directions to stand or sit during various parts of the prayers; this is a matter for the teacher and class to decide as they become comfortable with this book. However, it is traditional to stand for prayer. We sit to sing the psalms and to listen to scripture readings (except the gospel, for which we stand). These traditions suggest that most prayer be done standing, especially during the Closing of Daily or Weekly Prayer.

Ministers of prayer guide us through Daily and Weekly Prayer, which require at least two ministers: the leader and the reader (although more than that can be accommodated).

It is the role of the leader to find and mark the correct pages, give the signal to begin, set the pace and make sure that the other ministers know when to take their parts. The leader also leads the "Side B" parts of the Psalm.

The chief duty of the reader is to proclaim the scripture, so he or she must prepare in advance in order to read well. That person also leads the "Side A" parts of the Psalm and the congregational parts of the Closing.

Being a good leader or reader takes practice and talent. Rather than changing ministerial roles daily, it's better to change weekly so that ministers become familiar with this book.

Instructions for the leader and reader are printed on the inside of the front cover. Most Meal and End of the Day Prayers can be handled by one minister, but it is advisable to have a second person lead the responses, especially if students do not have copies of the prayers.

Training of ministers should be unthreatening. At the beginning of the year, everyone will need practice; occasional reminders should be sufficient after that. Here are three rules of "liturgical behavior":

1. *Stand up straight.* It gives prayer the dignity it deserves and establishes your ministerial role.
2. *Slow everything down.* Walk slowly to the lectern; read slowly; light the candle slowly.
3. *Exaggerate everything a bit.* Read more loudly than usual; bow more deeply; bless with your arm stretched out as far as it will go.

Scripture Readings

Readings included in Weekly Prayer are based on the Sunday liturgy and are usually taken from the gospel. The use of these readings during the week or on Saturday mornings will help the children prepare or reflect on the parish's Sunday worship.

During the fall, the church follows the readings of Year B, which present key teachings of Jesus from Mark's gospel. With Advent and Christmastime, we begin Year C with readings that emphasize the prophecies of Isaiah, and the figures of John the Baptist and Mary. During winter, readings from Luke lead us through the public ministry of Jesus. During Lent, the readings prepare students for participating in the Paschal Triduum (the three-day celebration of Easter: Holy Thursday evening through Easter Sunday evening). The readings of Eastertime are taken from John's gospel and touch on the saving work of Jesus. In June, we return to the Sunday gospels of Ordinary Time.

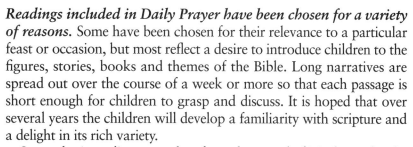

Readings included in Daily Prayer have been chosen for a variety of reasons. Some have been chosen for their relevance to a particular feast or occasion, but most reflect a desire to introduce children to the figures, stories, books and themes of the Bible. Long narratives are spread out over the course of a week or more so that each passage is short enough for children to grasp and discuss. It is hoped that over several years the children will develop a familiarity with scripture and a delight in its rich variety.

September's readings are taken from the gospel of Mark to echo the Sunday gospels of Year B, the current lectionary year.

The book of Genesis provides the readings for October. The first story of creation is followed by the story of the first sin. The figures of Abraham, Sarah, Isaac, Rebekah, Jacob and Joseph have been presented in some depth over the course of the last two years. This year Abraham, Sarah, Isaac and Rebekah are introduced briefly, and then the focus shifts to Jacob.

In November, we read from the book of Exodus, focusing on the struggle with Pharaoh, the events of the Passover and the years in the desert. As Thanksgiving approaches, Ordinary Time ends with the harvest-time story of Ruth and related readings on almsgiving.

Advent introduces readings from the prophecy of Isaiah that describe changes the promised savior will bring about. These readings are followed by familiar stories from Luke's gospel of the annunciations to Zechariah and Mary, the visit of Mary and Elizabeth, and the birth of John. These readings prepare the children for the celebration of Christmas in their homes and parishes. Readings from the first chapter of John's gospel at Christmastime trace the transition from the preaching of John the Baptist to the public ministry of Jesus.

In January we read about the prophet Samuel and the adventures of the first two kings of Israel, Saul and David. During February the focus shifts again to the gospel of Luke, which the church reads on Sundays in Ordinary Time in this lectionary year. Luke's presentation of the words and deeds of Jesus brings us to the beginning of Lent.

During the early weeks of Lent a variety of readings focus on the attitudes of penance and renewal that mark the season. The stories of the Samaritan woman at the well, the cure of the man born blind, and the raising of Lazarus shift our attention to the coming Easter experience of the sacraments. In the last weeks of Lent we return to Luke's gospel for an account of the events on Jesus' final journey to Jerusalem. The events of the night of the Last Supper prepare us for the celebration of the Paschal Triduum.

The readings proclaimed during the first weeks of Eastertime focus on post-resurrection appearances and teachings of Jesus. During May we follow the adventures of the early Christians as portrayed in the Acts of the Apostles. The figures of Stephen, Paul and Barnabas receive attention, and readings about the role of the Holy Spirit in the church prepare us for the celebrations of the Ascension of the Lord and Pentecost, when Eastertime concludes.

In June we hear the stories of holy women mentioned in the Hebrew scriptures or in the New Testament. Readings assigned to the final week of the school year concern the coming glory of the savior's final reign.

Music

As Saint Augustine wrote, to sing one's prayer is to "pray twice." Hymns for each month or season are suggested on the Looking Ahead pages. A hymn can be sung in Daily or Weekly Prayer before the opening Psalm or after the Closing, or as an alternative to reciting the Psalm. Hymns also can be sung at other times of the day (for example, at the conclusion of the End of the Day Prayer).

The hymns have been chosen from GIA/LTP's *Hymnal for Catholic Students*. The songs and psalms in this hymnal were selected as standard repertoire for Christians. Tapes of the songs are available as a teaching aid. If another hymnal or other musical resource will be used at prayer, select from it pieces that are similar in mood and spirit to the ones suggested here. Choose music you believe will still be sung by the church when the students have become adults.

Many of the acclamations and repeated elements in this book, such as the Lord's Prayer and the litanies, can be sung. Schools and parishes with the musical resources may want to replace the recitation of the psalms with sung psalmody, either in the responsorial style used at Mass or in metrical hymn settings.

Don't be afraid of repetition in music. Using the same hymn for several weeks increases the likelihood that the children will learn it by heart and will appropriate it as genuine prayer. The melodies used for the acclamations can stay the same all year. That is how churches known for strong congregational singing do it; they do not change the music all the time. Instead, they gradually introduce the people to good, solid songs—songs to last a lifetime.

Children's Daily Prayer can be used well without any singing, but that is not the most desirable plan. Sung prayer is at the heart of the Christian tradition. Your efforts will be well rewarded if you integrate Daily or Weekly Prayer with the music program of the school or with the music ministry of the parish.

Active Participation

In many schools, prayer is led over the public-address system. While this may be practical for a number of reasons and in a few cases may even be necessary, it is probably not the best way to lead children in prayer. In its essence, common prayer is supposed to be an encounter between the assembly and God. This immediacy is hardly reinforced when prayer is guided by a disembodied voice.

In addition, "long-distance leadership" may not permit the adjustment of the prayers to the age or to the special needs of each class. Spontaneous intercessions, birthday blessings, the lighting of a wreath and the singing of hymns are all aspects of prayer that build up a class into a worshiping community. Prayer leadership exercised over the public address system may short-circuit this development.

Young people should become skillful and comfortable with proclaiming scripture, offering intercessions and blessings, and taking a leadership role among their peers. In many parishes, children see, Sunday after Sunday, a form of worship seemingly "owned" by the priest. Authority over prayer can seem to belong to one person whose distance from the community is underscored by distinctive vesture and seating.

Certainly, contemporary Catholic theology strives to correct this impression, but young children do not know theology. They know what they experience. It is likely that the experience of small groups at prayer, at home and in the classroom, will teach them as no book can that communal prayer is the joy and obligation of every believer.

Student Copies of the Prayers

If possible, give all the children copies of the Psalm. Parochial school students will find it useful to have copies of all three seasonal pages: the Psalm, the Meal Prayer and the End of the Day Prayer. These pages are included in *Blessed Be God!,* a student prayer book that is a companion to *Children's Daily Prayer.* These books are inexpensive and can easily be kept in desks or in the prayer center.

For teachers who prefer to make copies of individual pages as the year goes on, reminders are included in *Children's Daily Prayer* a few days before each change of season or month. Duplicated pages can be kept in desks or in religion folders during the season. Keep extra copies on hand.

When copying the Psalm or other prayers, you might wish to mask the page number and any instructions on the page such as "turn back to Daily Prayer or Weekly Prayer for today" that are meant only for the leader of prayer.

As a purchaser of this book, you are allowed to duplicate only the Psalms, Meal Prayers and End of the Day Prayers; these copies may be used only with your class or group. You may not duplicate the Psalms or Prayers unless you are using them with this book. Other parts of this book may not be duplicated without the permission of Liturgy Training Publications and/or the copyright holders listed on the acknowledgments page.

Scheduling Weekly Prayer

Students who meet only once a week need a consistent format for prayer so that they know what to expect and how to participate. Catechists should plan from the beginning for students to take the roles of leader and reader. Rely on the students' help in carrying out the schedule of prayers and blessings.

This book offers a Weekly Prayer for each week from September 10 to June 17 which is based on one of the readings of the Mass of the Sunday. You can choose to anticipate the Sunday coming or reflect on the Sunday past. However, on important feast days, instead of using Weekly Prayer, it might be better to use that feast's Daily Prayer or a feast day blessing.

Plan ahead! Early in the year, create a schedule that accommodates the church's seasons and feasts. With this in mind, a November prayer schedule for Wednesday evening classes might look like this:

DATE	PRAYER	LEADER	READER	NOTES
Nov. 1	Daily Prayer, p. 87	Erica	Valerie	■ Handout: A Prayer for the Dead, p. 90, for use at home
Nov. 8	Weekly Prayer, p. 98	Valerie	Andy	
Nov. 15	Weekly Prayer, p. 104	Andy	Lupe	
Nov. 22	Thanksgiving Prayer, p. 108	Lupe	Ben	■ bless Thanksgiving donations, p. 350
Nov. 29	Weekly Prayer, p. 122	Ben	Naomi	■ Handout: A Blessing of the Advent Wreath, p. 121

Prayers or blessings that might take the place of Weekly Prayer:

On holy days of obligation (*), many religious education programs schedule the eucharist, and some may cancel classes. Be sure to schedule a celebration for the patronal feast day of your church. Remember also the Farewell Blessing for a Friend (page 345) that might be used when a student or teacher leaves before the school year is over.

Dear Students and Teachers,

This year students in Australia will be using their own version of this book. Please keep them in your prayers.

Have you heard that now there is a *Children's Daily Prayer for Summer* edition? Tell parents about it.

Have a wonderful year! May God's love follow you every day.

This is my address:

Elizabeth McMahon Jeep
Liturgy Training Publications
1800 North Hermitage Avenue
Chicago, IL 60622-1101

Thank you,

Elizabeth McMahon Jeep

Elizabeth McMahon Jeep

Reference Bibliography

The publications listed here were useful in the preparation of *Children's Daily Prayer.*

Ritual Books, Prayer Texts and Other Liturgical Resources:

Book of Blessings. Collegeville, MN: The Liturgical Press, 1988.

The Book of Common Prayer. New York: The Church Hymnal Corporation, 1979.

Catholic Household Blessings and Prayers. Publishing Service, United States Catholic Conference, 1986. Every home (and classroom) should have a copy!

Christian Prayer: The Liturgy of the Hours (Morning Prayer, Evening Prayer, Night Prayer). ICEL. Baltimore: Helicon Press, 1976.

Gates of Prayer: The New Union Prayerbook. New York: Central Conference of American Rabbis, 1975.

Lectionary for Masses with Children. Sunday volumes for Years A, B and C, and a volume for weekdays. Chicago: Liturgy Training Publications, 1993.

General Information:

All Saints: Daily Reflections on Saints, Prophets, and Witnesses for Our Time. Robert Ellsberg. New York: Crossroad Publishing Co., 1998.

Butler's Lives of the Saints, New Full Edition. Collegeville, MN: The Liturgical Press, 1997 and continuing.

Celebrating the Church Year with Young Children. Joan Halmo. Collegeville, MN: The Liturgical Press, 1988.

Chase's Annual Events: Special Days, Weeks and Months. Chicago: Contemporary Books, Inc., annual.

"The Christmas Cycle," *Liturgy,* volume 9, number 3. Washington, DC: The Liturgical Conference, 1991.

The Folklore of World Holidays. Margaret Read McDonald, ed. Detroit: Gale Research, Inc., 1992.

A Guide to the Saints. Kristin E. White. New York: Ivy Books, 1991.

"Liturgy: The Calendar," *Liturgy,* volume 1, number 2. Washington, DC: The Liturgical Conference, 1980.

"Liturgy: Rhythms of Prayer," *Liturgy,* volume 8, number 4. Washington, DC: The Liturgical Conference, 1990.

Modern Saints: Their Lives and Faces. Ann Ball. Rockford, IL: Tan Books and Publishers, Inc., 1983.

The Oxford Dictionary of Saints, fourth edition. David Hugh Farmer. New York: Oxford University Press, 1987.

A Pilgrim's Almanac. Edward Hays. Leavenworth, KS: Forest of Peace Books, Inc., 1989.

LTP Materials Useful to Teachers:

At Home with the Word. Annual. Sunday scriptures with discussion and ideas for living as a Christian.

Bible Stories for the Forty Days. Melissa Musick Nussbaum. 1997. Stories bring to life characters from both testaments whom we all should know.

Blessed Be God! Elizabeth McMahon Jeep. 1994. A companion to *Children's Daily Prayer* prepared for students (and their families), with the Psalms, Meal Prayers and End of the Day Prayers for each month or season.

Children in the Assembly of the Church. Eleanor Bernstein, CSJ, and John Brooks-Leonard, eds. 1993. Essays about liturgy with children.

Children, Liturgy and the Word. A 26-minute video focusing on ways to celebrate children's liturgy of the word.

Children's Prayer Folders. Hold the seasonal prayer sheets handed out from *Children's Daily Prayer,* as well as any other important papers from your religious education program.

Companion to the Calendar. Mary Ellen Hynes. 1993. Information about every season and day of the Christian year.

Fling Wide the Doors! 1992. An Advent calendar that runs till Epiphany. Big and small versions.

Forty Days and Forty Nights. 1995. A Lenten calendar with doors to open from Ash Wednesday until Easter.

A Guide to the Lectionary for Masses with Children. Peter Mazar and Robert Piercy. 1994. Includes suggestions for weekday Masses during the school year.

Paschal Mission. An annual series of weekly handouts for Lent, Triduum and Eastertime.

Preparing Liturgy for Children and Children for Liturgy. Gabe Huck, et.al. 1989. Valuable guide for those who work with children and worship.

The Religious Potential of the Child. Sofia Cavalletti. 1992. A classic book.

Sunday Morning Video. Introduce your early elementary students to Sunday worship with this colorful video.

Take Me Home: Notes on the Church Year for Children. Christine Kenny-Sheputis. 1991. Useful weekly reproducible take-home notes.

Take Me Home, Too. Peter Mazar. 1997. New handouts for seasons and feasts.

Teacher's Guide to Children's Daily Prayer. An audiocassette narrated by Elizabeth Jeep outlining the purpose, value and intent of *Children's Daily Prayer.*

Teaching Christian Children about Judaism. Deborah Levine. 1995.

The Welcome Table: Planning Masses with Children. Elizabeth McMahon Jeep, ed. 1982. Essays for liturgists and catechists.

Welcome, Yule! An annual series of weekly handouts for Advent and Christmastime. Poster available.

The Winter Saints. Melissa Musick Nussbaum. 1998. Stories of the special characters who inhabit our winter calendar.

The Year of Grace: A Liturgical Calendar. Annual. Poster size (26" square!) and notebook size.

LATE SUMMER

ORDINARY TIME
LATE SUMMER 2000

◼ ABOUT THE SEASON

While it may seem as if the rest of the world is enjoying the beach or the pool, you will be unpacking books, decorating bulletin boards and airing out classrooms. For teachers, principals and directors of religious education, late summer is a time of high

LOOKING AHEAD expectations, hard work, good resolutions and perhaps a little bit of anxiety. What will the children be like? Will they like me? Is the faculty going to work well together? Am I going to have a good year?

Volunteer catechists face the same tension and excitement. There are many changes in personnel and programs from one year to the next. Are the teachers' meetings and workshops going to be worthwhile? How will teaching interfere with my other obligations? Should I have agreed to teach this year?

These thoughts visit neophytes and veterans alike, yet that is not the real theme of these weeks. The strongest feeling is one of excitement. It is what keeps teachers coming back year after year. You are starting fresh, with new books, new skills and new ideas. Few professions offer a long summer in which to regenerate one's energy and enthusiasm, followed by a "New Year's Day" in late August or early September.

◾ SOON THERE WILL BE AN ANXIOUS GROUP OF STUDENTS BUBBLING AND TUMBLING OVER YOUR DOORSTEP, bringing youth, enthusiasm, excitement and curiosity. They will look for your smile of welcome. They will see the way you have made the room a place of warmth and hospitality. Desks will shine, windows will sparkle, and neatly lettered name tags will greet new owners of hooks or lockers. The children will notice things you have brought in to mitigate the "institutional" look: a colorful fabric or Navaho rug hung on the wall, shells brought back from summer days at the beach, a kite for recess on a windy day.

◾ AS PART OF YOUR HOUSEKEEPING, YOU WILL WANT TO CREATE A FOCAL POINT FOR CLASSROOM PRAYER. It might be a table or bookshelf set aside as a "prayer corner" where the Bible, this prayer book and other signs of prayer are placed. These might include a candle, a bowl of water, a cross, an image of Mary or an image of the parish's patron.

Some signs will change with the seasons of nature, with the shifting concerns of the children and with the feasts and seasons of the church's calendar. You might begin with the tokens of late summer, such as a glorious sunflower. Religious images, such as a feast day icon or a picture of a saint, might also change throughout the year to help bring the children's attention to the cycle of the church's prayer.

Teachers of day school and teachers of the after-school programs who share the same rooms will have to spend time getting acquainted and discussing some of the housekeeping details that affect prayer. How will after-school students be made to feel at home? Will they be able to bring things to the prayer corner?

Anyone who works with children on a daily basis is wise enough to expect the unexpected. The systems you plan and the programs and regulations you ordain may not last a month. A teacher, after all, can only organize and focus but can never fully control what happens in the classroom. Flexibility is what keeps teachers young.

◾ IT IS APPROPRIATE TO TURN THE LAST WEEKS OF AUGUST INTO A TIME OF PRAYER AS WELL AS PREPARATION. This is your opportunity to proclaim a new year and to set priorities as well as lesson plans in order.

◼ PREPARATION FOR LATE SUMMER

On the following pages, you will find a Daily Prayer to use during the days before the school year begins. This prayer is for teachers. Prayers for the students

begin with the Monday before Labor Day. The introduction to the book and this section for Late Summer are the only parts of this book that have not been prepared for use by students.

On page *xvi* is a bibliography of publications used to prepare *Children's Daily Prayer.* You can use these resources to locate further information about holidays, saints and the liturgical seasons.

• ASIDE FROM THE OBVIOUS VALUE OF OPENING AND CLOSING THE DAYS OF CLASSROOM PREPARATION WITH WORSHIP, using this book during August, either alone or as a faculty, will familiarize you with its format. Once school starts, you will be better able to introduce it to the children and then turn the leadership of daily prayer over to them.

The prayers for Late Summer are different from the prayers for the other times of the year. This section contains only a single page for Daily Prayer to be used as often as needed.

• TO LEARN THE FORMAT FOR PRAYER, PLEASE FOLLOW THE INSTRUCTIONS PRINTED ON THE INSIDE OF THE FRONT COVER. Adapt them as necessary if you will be praying alone. It is suggested that you read the name of each child on your class list as the Closing of Daily Prayer for Late Summer, so you will need that list each day. If you are praying with other faculty members, all should read their students' names in silence. If you are alone, you may read your students' names aloud.

• SUGGESTED HYMNS: Throughout the year, you can sing a hymn to begin Daily or Weekly Prayer. You can also substitute a hymn for the Psalm or sing a hymn to conclude the End of the Day Prayer. In any way you can, try to make song a part of prayer.

"This day God gives me" (page 4 in the *Hymnal for Catholic Students*) is a good choice for this time of year. Based on the Lorica of Saint Patrick, it is set to the popular Irish melody "Bunessan," better known as "Morning has broken." Keep this song in the file for March 17.

■ THE SCHOOL OF RELIGION

There are no Weekly Prayers for the month of August. These begin in September, when religious education classes usually begin.

Please notice, however, that the Weekly Prayers are dated according to the Sundays of the year. The reading for each Weekly Prayer is from one of the Sunday readings, most often the gospel. Some classes may choose to anticipate the Sunday, and others may choose to reflect on the Sunday past.

Volunteer catechists who use this book for their own prayer during the weeks before classes begin will be in a good position to decide how best to use it with their students. It may be that the entire school of religion will use the Weekly Prayer before separating for instruction. In that case, the End of the Day Prayer and a hymn can be used in the classrooms before dismissal.

If the students come immediately to their classrooms, you might begin with a hymn and close with Weekly Prayer. You might prefer to begin with part of the Weekly Prayer (the Introduction and Psalm perhaps) and use the rest of it before dismissal. Once some of these decisions are made, look at page *xiv* for further help in scheduling prayer for the year.

May God bless your preparations and make your classroom, school and parish places of peace, safety, creativity and growth for everyone this year!

A PSALM FOR LATE SUMMER

 all make
the sign
of the cross

Psalm 95:1–2, 4–7

LEADER Lord, open my lips.

ALL **And my mouth will proclaim your praise.**

LEADER Come, sing with joy to God,
shout to our savior, our rock.

ALL **Enter God's presence with praise,
enter with shouting and song.**

SIDE A God cradles the depths of the earth,
holds fast the mountain peaks.

SIDE B God shaped the ocean and owns it,
formed the earth by hand.

SIDE A Come, bow down and worship,
kneel to the Lord our maker.

SIDE B This is our God, our shepherd,
we are the flock led with care.

LEADER Come, sing with joy to God,
shout to our savior, our rock.

ALL **Enter God's presence with praise,
enter with shouting and song.**

**Glory to the Father, and to the Son,
and to the Holy Spirit:
as it was in the beginning, is now,
and will be for ever. Amen. Alleluia.**

turn to
Daily Prayer
on page 7

LATE SUMMER

MEAL
PRAYER

LEADER   Let us offer God praise and thanksgiving:

ALL   ▶ all make
        the sign
        of the cross

LEADER   All the world hopes in you, O Lord,
             that you will give us food in our hunger.

ALL   **You open wide your hand**
        and we are filled with good things.

     Bless us, O Lord, and these your gifts
        which we are about to receive
        from your bounty.
     Through Christ our Lord. Amen.

     ▶ all make
        the sign
        of the cross

LATE SUMMER

END OF THE DAY PRAYER

> all make
> the sign
> of the cross

LEADER God, come to my assistance.
ALL **Lord, make haste to help me.**

> the following words
> can be sung to the melody for
> "Praise God from whom all blessings flow":

ALL **Lord, bless the work that I have done,**
  and bless the evening still to come.
Let my return a blessing be
  to all who share a home with me.
Give us with food and rest and play
  a fitting end to this good day.
From webs of sin grant us release,
  and touch our planet with your peace.

LEADER ▶ hold out one hand
  toward everyone
  in blessing, and say:

May the Lord bless us,
  protect us from all evil,
  and bring us to everlasting life.
ALL **Amen.**

> all make
> the sign
> of the cross

DAILY PRAYER

Before the School Year Begins

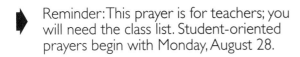 Reminder: This prayer is for teachers; you will need the class list. Student-oriented prayers begin with Monday, August 28.

■ INTRODUCTION

Reflect on some of the memorable teachers in your life. What qualities did they share? Who showed you what it means to be dedicated to exploration and learning? Who showed you that you matter? Who listened to your ideas?

Saint Paul, like us, was both a catechist and a model for his hearers. The reading today carries a message from Paul to each catechist.

■ A PSALM FOR LATE SUMMER

 turn to page 4

■ READING

I Thessalonians 5:10–11, 16–18, 23–24

Listen to the words of the apostle Paul:

Christ died for us, so that we could live with him, whether we are alive or dead when he comes. That's why you must encourage and help each other, just as you are already doing.

Always be joyful and never stop praying. Whatever happens, keep thanking God because of Jesus Christ. This is what God wants you to do. I pray that God, who gives peace, will make you completely holy. And may your spirit, soul, and body be kept healthy and faultless until our Lord Jesus Christ returns. The one who chose you can be trusted, and he will do this.

The word of the Lord.

■ REFLECTION

Is my theology and my catechesis solidly focused on salvation in Christ? What steps can I take this year to nourish my faith and my understanding of the gospel?

■ CLOSING

Let us remember these intentions:

Loving and welcoming God,
  look with steadfast love on the students
  who will soon gather here.
Bless each of us for whom Christ died
  and in whom Christ lives:

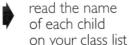 read the name of each child on your class list

Let us pray with the words that Jesus taught us:

Our Father . . .

sing "alleluia"

Al-le-lu-ia,   al-le-lu-ia,   al-le-lu-ia.

A Prayer for Meetings

At any time of the year, parts or all of the day's prayer may be used to begin and conclude a faculty meeting or a parent meeting. The following is an alternative.

Everyone will need a copy of the psalm for the season or month. Provide a candle or an Advent wreath when appropriate.

To Begin the Meeting

LEADER AND ALL

 pray the psalm
for the season or month

READER   Ephesians 2:20–22
Listen to the words of the apostle Paul:

You are like a building with the apostles and prophets as the foundation and with Christ as the most important stone. Christ is the one who holds the building together and makes it grow into a holy temple for the Lord. And you are part of that building Christ has built as a place for God's own Spirit to live.

The word of the Lord.

 keep silence
for a minute or two

LEADER
Holy Spirit of God,
   you call us together as one
   to bring to children
   the message of your love.
Be with us in this gathering.
We ask this in Jesus' name.

ALL **Amen.**

At the Close of the Meeting   Ephesians 3:20–21

LEADER
Let us remember these intentions:

To you, O God,
   who by the power at work in us
can do far more than we dare ask or imagine,
to you be glory in the church
and in Christ Jesus to all generations,
   now and for ever.

ALL **Amen.**

LEADER

 hold one hand out
in blessing
over those gathered, and say:

May the grace of our Lord Jesus Christ,
   and the love of God,
   and the fellowship of the Holy Spirit
   be with us all, now and for ever.

ALL **Amen.**

SEPTEMBER

Monday, August 28, to Friday, September 29

ORDINARY TIME
SEPTEMBER 2000

■ ABOUT THE MONTH

Autumn is the longest school season. In many ways it is the best season, too. It begins with the last hot days of summer and ends with the chilly days at Thanksgiving.

For the first few weeks of school, you may be tense and excited. You may even feel as if you cannot remember anything you learned last year. But don't worry. Soon you will be back in the swing of things.

LOOKING AHEAD

All over the country, teachers, principals, directors of religious education, librarians, custodians and others have been getting ready for students just like you. Many people have been busy making this school beautiful. Have you noticed things around the school that have been done to make you happy to be here?

Are there new things in the building? Are there new teachers? new students? It is a good bet that you have some new things for school, too. Who made sure that you got those new things? Who made sure you were ready for school on time? There are many people who love you. They have worked hard so that you and your friends have a good school year. Those people deserve your thanks.

▪ SOMEONE ELSE DESERVES YOUR THANKS. God has provided the wonderful month of September for all of us. The weather is good. The land is beautiful. It's also a good month for friendship. You can meet the new people at school and make them feel welcome. You can talk to the ones you did not see all summer. Because you are older than you were last year, you can do this more easily.

You are in a higher grade too, so you will learn new things. There are many things you can do now that you could not do before. It is good to give God thanks and praise for all the love poured out on us and for all the good days to come.

▪ THIS BOOK IS A GUIDE FOR YOUR PRAYER. Some of the prayers change each day. Some stay the same. This is the way the church prays.

▪ DIRECTIONS FOR USING THIS BOOK FOR PRAYER ARE PRINTED ON THE INSIDE OF THE FRONT COVER. When it is your turn to lead the prayer, you can read those instructions again. It is a good idea to attach ribbons to the book and to use them to mark your place. You may want to hang bells or other ornaments from the ends of the ribbons. Or, instead of ribbons, you can mark your place with paper clips.

▪ GOD CREATED YOU AND GOD LOVES YOU. So let your thoughts and feelings rise to God in prayer. Let this year of grace be the best school year ever. And let September, like everything you do, begin and end with praise and thanksgiving.

■ PREPARATION FOR SEPTEMBER

On September 3 we remember Pope Gregory the Great. Throughout autumn, we will sing a Gregorian chant "alleluia" at prayer. Gregorian chant is named after Pope Gregory. We will try to sing our prayer often this year.

▪ PLEASE LEARN THE CORRECT RESPONSES TO THE READINGS. After a reading from a gospel, the reader says, "The gospel of the Lord." Everyone replies, "Praise to you, Lord Jesus Christ." But if the reading is not from Matthew, Mark, Luke or John, the reader says, "The word of the Lord," and we answer, "Thanks be to God."

▪ DAILY AND WEEKLY PRAYERS HAVE A BLANK SPACE FOR YOU TO WRITE INTENTIONS. Intentions are things to pray about. For example, "For Lucia's grandmother, who is sick," "For Jonathan on his birthday," and "For people hurt in the earthquake."

During the first week of class, teachers and students should fill in their baptismal anniversaries or birthdays in the blank spaces on the correct pages of this book. That way we will remember to pray for them on those days. Religious education students should mark their special days in the blank space of the Weekly Prayer pages. Remember that these pages represent an entire week or more. If your special day falls on a weekend or during a vacation, select another day for yourself, such as your saint's feast day.

Other happy or sad things that happen, such as the birth of a new brother or sister, the parish feast day, or the sickness of a grandparent, should be added to the list of intentions as the year goes on.

▪ A BLESSING TO USE ON BIRTHDAYS IS ON THE INSIDE OF THE BACK COVER. It can be used at the end of Daily or Weekly Prayer, or at some other time.

▪ THREE SPECIAL BLESSINGS CAN BE USED DURING SEPTEMBER. The first is a blessing of the school year, on page 15. This can be used during the first week of school or at the first gathering of the school of religion.

The second is a blessing of the cross. On the feast of the Holy Cross, September 14, or on a day near the feast, we can bless the classroom crucifix and crosses brought from home. This blessing is on page 31.

The third is a blessing of flower bulbs for planting. This is a traditional way of observing the feast of the angels Michael, Gabriel and Raphael, on September 29, or the feast of the Guardian Angels, on October 2. This blessing is on page 53.

▪ SUGGESTED HYMNS: "Let all things now living" (page 150 in the *Hymnal for Catholic Students*) has a beautiful Welsh tune. The word "Welsh" means "from Wales." The Welsh people are famous for their melodies. Another song that seems to go with Labor Day and the start of a new school year is "God, who stretched the spangled heavens" (page 130 in the hymnal). These words are set to an American tune that can be sung as a round.

"Lift high the cross" (page 154 in the hymnal) is worth learning in honor of the feast of the Holy Cross (September 14).

■ THE SCHOOL OF RELIGION

You will find that the Weekly Prayers help you prepare for the Sunday eucharist. The readings come from the Masses of the Twenty-third, Twenty-fourth, and Twenty-fifth Sundays in Ordinary Time.

▪ SEPTEMBER 17 IS CATECHETICAL SUNDAY. In many parishes, teachers receive a blessing on that Sunday. The theme for that day's celebration is "A Year of Favor: Making All Things New." Be sure to greet your teachers and pray for them on that day.

If you meet on weekdays, you might want to use that day's Daily Prayer instead of the Weekly Prayer, especially if you will be meeting on a feast day.

A PSALM FOR SEPTEMBER

> all make
> the sign
> of the cross

Psalm 145:1–2, 8–9, 13–14, 17–18

LEADER Great is the Lord, highly to be praised.

ALL **Age to age proclaims your works.**

SIDE A I will exalt you, God my king,
for ever bless your name.
I will bless you every day,
for ever praise your name.

SIDE B Gracious and merciful is the Lord,
slow to anger, full of love.
The Lord is good in every way,
merciful to every creature.

SIDE A The Lord is faithful in every word
and gracious in every work.
The Lord supports the fallen,
raises those bowed down.

SIDE B The Lord is just in every way,
loving in every deed.
The Lord is near to those who call,
who cry out from their hearts.

LEADER Great is the Lord, highly to be praised.

ALL **Age to age proclaims your works.**

**Glory to the Father, and to the Son
and to the Holy Spirit:
as it was in the beginning, is now,
and will be for ever. Amen. Alleluia.**

> turn back to
> Daily Prayer or Weekly Prayer
> for today

SEPTEMBER

LEADER   Let us offer God praise and thanksgiving:

ALL ▶ all make
the sign
of the cross

**In the name of the Father, and of the Son,
and of the Holy Spirit. Amen.**

LEADER   Loving God,
you set a table before us
and fill it with good things.
Teach us to share what we have
so that no one who comes to eat
finds an empty table.
We ask this through Christ our Lord.

ALL   **Amen.**

LEADER   For the food we are about to eat
and for the life that it nourishes,
let us offer thanks to God:

ALL ▶ all make
the sign
of the cross

**In the name of the Father, and of the Son,
and of the Holy Spirit. Amen.**

SEPTEMBER

ALL  all make
the sign
of the cross

**In the name of the Father, and of the Son,
and of the Holy Spirit. Amen.**

LEADER Be our shining light, O Lord,
during the rest of this day
and all through the night.
Show us the good that surrounds us
so that we might praise you.
Protect us from all dangers
that we might give you thanks
through Jesus,
who is Lord for ever and ever.

ALL **Amen.**

LEADER ▶ hold out one hand
toward everyone
in blessing, and say:

May the Lord bless us,
protect us from all evil,
and bring us to everlasting life:

ALL ▶ all make
the sign
of the cross

**In the name of the Father, and of the Son,
and of the Holy Spirit. Amen.**

END OF THE DAY PRAYER

A Blessing of the School Year

Bring apples, grapes or other fruit; enough to be cut up and shared. Bring a basket and a knife or other equipment to help share the fruit. Begin and end with a simple song, such as "Taste and see" in the Hymnal for Catholic Students, *page 59.*

LEADER
Let us begin this year as we begin each day,
by signing ourselves with the cross of Jesus.

 all make
the sign
of the cross

LEADER   Psalm 34:2–3, 6, 9
Let us all say:
I will praise your name for ever:
My Lord and my God!

ALL
I will praise your name for ever:
My Lord and my God!

LEADER
I will never stop thanking God,
with constant words of praise.
My soul will boast of God;
the poor will hear me and be glad.

Turn to God, be bright with joy;
you shall never be let down.
Drink in the richness of God,
enjoy the strength of the Lord.

Let us all say:
I will praise your name for ever:
My Lord and my God!

ALL
I will praise your name for ever:
My Lord and my God!

LEADER
It is good to begin our season of study
in the autumn,
when farmers are bringing in
their harvest of good things to eat.

 hold up the fruit,
and say:

Just as the work of the farmer
has produced this fruit,
so our work in this class will bring us
the nourishment of God's word.

 extend a hand
over the fruit,
and say:

God our Creator,
you provide food for our bodies,
ideas for our minds,
and your love for our hearts.
Bless this fruit that we share
as a symbol of the time and friendship
we will share during the coming school year.
Be with us now and for ever.

ALL
Amen.

 all make
the sign
of the cross

pass the fruit
among the group

MONDAY PRAYER

August 28, 2000

▶ Reminder: September's Psalm, Meal and End of the Day Prayers are on pages 6 to 8 of *Blessed Be God!* Pray the Blessing of the School Year, on page 15, sometime this week.

■ INTRODUCTION

Today we remember Saint Augustine *(uh-GUSS-tin),* one of the greatest bishops of the church in Africa. He wrote many books about God's love for us. He wrote about our strong desire to be close to God. When he taught the people about prayer, he told them to rejoice and to sing God's praises. "Remember," he said, "when you sing, you pray twice."

During this new school year we will try to sing well and pray well together.

■ A PSALM FOR SEPTEMBER

▶ turn to page 12

■ READING

Mark 1:4–5, 7–8

Listen to the words of the holy gospel according to Mark:

John the Baptist showed up in the desert and told everyone, "Turn back to God and be baptized! Then your sins will be forgiven."

From all Judea *(joo-DEE-uh)* and Jerusalem *(juh-ROO-suh-lem)* crowds of people went to John. They told how sorry they were for their sins, and he baptized them in the Jordan River.

John also told the people. "Someone more powerful is going to come. And I am not good enough even to stoop down and untie his sandals.

I baptize you with water, but he will baptize you with the Holy Spirit!"

The gospel of the Lord.

■ REFLECTION

John wanted the people to turn their hearts to God. How can we turn our hearts to God this year? How did John's mission help prepare for the coming of Jesus?

■ CLOSING

Blessed be God, Creator of days and seasons. Let us all say: Blessed be God for ever!
Blessed be God for ever!

Let us remember these intentions:

Loving God, you give us this new school year
 and new friends with whom to share it.
Bless all who pray and work
 and learn together.
And grant a happy year to all the world.
We ask this through Christ our Lord. **Amen.**

Let us pray with the words that Jesus taught us:
Our Father . . .

▶ sing "alleluia"

Al - le - lu - ia, al - le - lu - ia, al - le - lu - ia.

TUESDAY PRAYER

■ INTRODUCTION

Today we remember the death of John the Baptist. John was not afraid to tell people when they were doing evil things. Many people who listened to him did turn to God, and John baptized them. But some other people were angry that John told them openly to change their ways. King Herod and his wife were angry with John, so they put him to death.

This is a good day to pray for all people who are brave enough to speak the truth.

■ A PSALM FOR SEPTEMBER

turn to page 12

■ READING

Matthew 11:7–10

Listen to the words of the holy gospel according to Matthew:

Jesus spoke to the crowds about John:

"What sort of person did you go out into the desert to see? Was he like tall grass blown about by the wind? What kind of man did you go out to see? Was he someone dressed in fine clothes? People who dress like that live in the king's palace. What did you really go out to see? Was he a prophet? He certainly was. I tell you that he was more than a prophet. In the Scriptures God says about him, 'I am sending my messenger ahead of you to get things ready for you.'"

The gospel of the Lord.

■ REFLECTION

Do we follow others because they are popular? Because they are exciting? Do I really listen to the teachings of the prophets that God sends into my life? How can we follow the word of God this year?

■ CLOSING

Blessed be God, Creator of days and seasons.
Let us all say: Blessed be God for ever!
Blessed be God for ever!

Let us remember these intentions:

Loving God, you give us this new school year
and new friends with whom to share it.
Bless all who pray and work
and learn together.
And grant a happy year to all the world.
We ask this through Christ our Lord. **Amen.**

Let us pray with the words that Jesus taught us:
Our Father . . .

sing "alleluia"

Al-le-lu-ia, al-le-lu-ia, al-le-lu-ia.

WEDNESDAY PRAYER

August 30, 2000

■ INTRODUCTION

As we begin a new school year, we learn again how to pray well together. When we pray, we pay attention to God who is here with us. We listen to God's word, and we share with God our thoughts, hopes and fears.

But prayer must be more than words. It must come from the heart. So we allow for times of silence in our prayer. Each day, we begin prayer by trying to become still and ready. We try to offer our prayer with Jesus, who pleased his Father very much.

■ A PSALM FOR SEPTEMBER

turn to page 12

■ READING

Mark 1:7–11

Listen to the words of the holy gospel according to Mark:

When John was baptizing people in the Jordan River, he told them, "Someone more powerful is going to come. And I am not good enough even to stoop down and untie his sandals. I baptize you with water, but he will baptize you with the Holy Spirit!"

About that time Jesus came from Nazareth *(NAZ-uh-reth)* in Galilee *(GAL-uh-lee)*. John baptized him in the Jordan River. As soon as Jesus came out of the water, he saw the sky open and the Holy Spirit coming down to him like a dove. A voice from heaven said, "You are my own dear Son, and I am pleased with you."

The gospel of the Lord.

■ REFLECTION

What did God reveal about Jesus at his baptism? How does God let us know that we also are God's dear children?

■ CLOSING

Blessed be God, Creator of days and seasons.
Let us all say: Blessed be God for ever!
Blessed be God for ever!

Let us remember these intentions:

Loving God, you give us this new school year
    and new friends with whom to share it.
Bless all who pray and work
    and learn together.
And grant a happy year to all the world.
We ask this through Christ our Lord. **Amen.**

Let us pray with the words that Jesus taught us:

Our Father . . .

sing "alleluia"

Al-le-lu-ia, al-le-lu-ia, al-le-lu-ia.

THURSDAY PRAYER

August 31, 2000

■ INTRODUCTION

When we gather to pray this year, we will listen to a reading of God's word from the Bible. During September, many of our readings will come from the gospel according to Mark.

When the reader ends with the words, "The gospel of the Lord," we always answer, "Praise to you, Lord Jesus Christ." Then we spend a few minutes in silence, letting the words of the gospel echo in our hearts.

In today's reading we will hear how Jesus began his new work for God. He began by gathering some friends to help him.

■ A PSALM FOR SEPTEMBER

turn to
page 12

■ READING

Mark 1:14–18

Listen to the words of the holy gospel according to Mark:

After John was arrested, Jesus went to Galilee *(GAL-uh-lee)* and told the good news that comes from God. He said, "The time has come! God's kingdom will soon be here. Turn back to God and believe the good news!"

As Jesus was walking along the shore of Lake Galilee, he saw Simon and his brother Andrew. They were fishermen and were casting their nets into the lake. Jesus said to them, "Come with me! I will teach you how to bring in people instead of fish." Right then the two brothers dropped their nets and went with him.

The gospel of the Lord.

■ REFLECTION

What could be the meaning of this message that John and then Jesus proclaimed? What does it mean to fish for people? Why does Jesus want others to join in his work?

■ CLOSING

Blessed be God, Creator of days and seasons.
Let us all say: Blessed be God for ever!
Blessed be God for ever!

Let us remember these intentions:

Loving God, you give us this new school year
    and new friends with whom to share it.
Bless all who pray and work
    and learn together.
And grant a happy year to all the world.
We ask this through Christ our Lord. **Amen.**

Let us pray with the words that Jesus taught us:
Our Father . . .

sing
"alleluia"

Al - le - lu - ia,   al - le - lu - ia,   al - le - lu - ia.

FRIDAY PRAYER

September 1, 2000

■ INTRODUCTION

Monday, September 4, is Labor Day in Canada and the United States. We set aside this day to reflect on the work we do. Some people work in offices or stores, hospitals or homes. Some work on ships or farms or trucks. Some work with other people, and some work alone. Some work with machines, and some work with books. Some work with plants, and some work with animals. And many of us will be working hard at school this year. Each person's work adds to the peace and welfare of the world. Let us remember all workers in our prayers today, and each day this weekend.

■ A PSALM FOR SEPTEMBER

➤ turn to page 12

■ READING

Mark 1:19–22

Listen to the words of the holy gospel according to Mark:

Jesus saw James and John, the sons of Zebedee *(ZEH-beh-dee)*. They were in a boat, mending their nets. At once Jesus asked them to come with him. They left their father in the boat with the hired workers and went with Jesus.

Jesus and his disciples went to the town of Capernaum *(kuh-PER-nee-um)*. Then on the next Sabbath he went into the Jewish meeting place and started teaching. Everyone was amazed at his teaching. He taught with authority.

The gospel of the Lord.

■ REFLECTION

Jesus was sent to do the work of his Father. What work will we do for God this year? Who has God sent to teach me? Who has God sent to teach my parents?

■ CLOSING

Blessed be God, Creator of days and seasons.
Let us all say: Blessed be God for ever!
Blessed be God for ever!

Let us remember these intentions:

Loving God, you give us this new school year
    and new friends with whom to share it.
Bless all who pray and work
    and learn together.
And grant a happy year to all the world.
We ask this through Christ our Lord. **Amen.**

Let us pray with the words that Jesus taught us:
Our Father . . .

➤ sing "alleluia"

Al-le-lu-ia, al-le-lu-ia, al-le-lu-ia.

TUESDAY PRAYER

■ INTRODUCTION

On this date, three years ago, Mother Teresa died in Calcutta, India. Her holiness and her love for the poor were known all over the world. The thousands of men and women who joined in her work are called the Missionaries of Charity. Next month, on October 7, they will celebrate the fiftieth anniversary of their order. Like Mother Teresa, they make a solemn promise to give "wholehearted and free service to the poorest of the poor."

■ A PSALM FOR SEPTEMBER

▶ turn to page 12

■ READING

Mark 1:29–34

Listen to the words of the holy gospel according to Mark:

Jesus left the meeting place with James and John. They went home with Simon and Andrew. When they got there, Jesus was told that Simon's mother-in-law was sick in bed with fever. Jesus went to her. He took hold of her hand and helped her up. The fever left her, and she served them a meal.

That evening after sunset, all who were sick or had demons in them were brought to Jesus. In fact, the whole town gathered around the door of the house. Jesus healed all kinds of terrible diseases and forced out a lot of demons.

The gospel of the Lord.

■ REFLECTION

Jesus was willing to help both strangers and friends. Do I save my smiles for my friends only? Do we help only those who can help us back?

■ CLOSING

Blessed be God, Creator of days and seasons.
Let us all say: Blessed be God for ever!
Blessed be God for ever!

Let us remember these intentions:

Loving God, you give us this new school year
    and new friends with whom to share it.
Bless all who pray and work
    and learn together.
And grant a happy year to all the world.
We ask this through Christ our Lord. **Amen.**

Let us pray with the words that Jesus taught us:

Our Father . . .

▶ sing "alleluia"

Al-le-lu-ia,   al-le-lu-ia,   al-le-lu-ia.

21

■ INTRODUCTION

Many people need our help, and we give help whenever we can. But there are others, all over the world, who need greater help than we can give. Each day we will remember some of them in our prayers.

When we ask God to bless someone we call it an intention or a petition. We can also remember people on days of joy such as their birthday.

■ A PSALM FOR SEPTEMBER

➤ turn to page 12

■ READING

Mark 1:21–28

Listen to the words of the holy gospel according to Mark:

Jesus and his disciples went to the town of Capernaum *(kuh-PER-nee-um)*. Then on the next Sabbath he went into the Jewish meeting place and started teaching. Everyone was amazed at his teaching. He taught with authority. Suddenly a man with an evil spirit in him entered the meeting place and yelled, "Jesus from Nazareth *(NAZ-uh-reth)*, what do you want with us? Have you come to destroy us? I know who you are! You are God's Holy One." Jesus told the evil spirit, "Be quiet and come out of the man!" The spirit shook him. Then it gave a loud shout and left.

Everyone was completely surprised and kept saying to each other, "What is this? It must be some new kind of powerful teaching! Even the evil spirits obey him." News about Jesus quickly spread all over Galilee *(GAL-uh-lee)*.

The gospel of the Lord.

■ REFLECTION

What forms of evil do we see in the world today? Do I sometimes forget that Jesus has power over real evil? Do we sometimes try to fight evil without asking God's help?

■ CLOSING

Blessed be God, Creator of days and seasons.
Let us all say: Blessed be God for ever!
Blessed be God for ever!

Let us remember these intentions:

Loving God, you give us this new school year
    and new friends with whom to share it.
Bless all who pray and work
    and learn together.
And grant a happy year to all the world.
We ask this through Christ our Lord. **Amen.**

Let us pray with the words that Jesus taught us:
Our Father . . .

➤ sing "alleluia"

Al - le - lu - ia,   al - le - lu - ia,   al - le - lu - ia.

THURSDAY PRAYER

September 7, 2000

■ INTRODUCTION

Today we will hear of a sick man who met Jesus. As we listen to the gospel we can ask ourselves, "How can I pray as this man prayed?"

When we put ourselves into the story we discover more about the way Jesus acts toward those who call on him.

■ A PSALM FOR SEPTEMBER

▶ turn to page 12

■ READING

Mark 1:40–44, 45

Listen to the words of the holy gospel according to Mark:

A man with leprosy *(LEP-ruh-see)* came to Jesus and knelt down. He begged, "You have the power to make me well, if only you wanted to." Jesus felt sorry for the man. So he put his hand on him and said, "I want to! Now you are well." At once the man's leprosy disappeared, and he was well.

After Jesus strictly warned the man, he sent him on his way. He said, "Don't tell anyone about this. Just go and show the priest that you are well. Then take a gift to the temple as Moses commanded, and everyone will know that you have been healed."

The man talked about it so much and told so many people that Jesus could no longer go openly into a town. But people still came to him from everywhere.

The gospel of the Lord.

■ REFLECTION

If Jesus had not cured the man, might he have given up his faith in Jesus? Is my faith strong even when Jesus does not do what I ask?

■ CLOSING

Blessed be God, Creator of days and seasons.
Let us all say: Blessed be God for ever!
Blessed be God for ever!

Let us remember these intentions:

Loving God, you give us this new school year
   and new friends with whom to share it.
Bless all who pray and work
   and learn together.
And grant a happy year to all the world.
We ask this through Christ our Lord. **Amen.**

Let us pray with the words that Jesus taught us:
Our Father . . .

▶ sing "alleluia"

Al - le - lu - ia,   al - le - lu - ia,   al - le - lu - ia.

FRIDAY PRAYER

September 8, 2000

▶ Reminder: Today please use October's Meal Prayer, the Angelus, on page 49, and the End of the Day Prayer on page 25.

■ INTRODUCTION

Today we celebrate the birth of Mary, the mother of our savior, Jesus. She is also the mother of all who follow Jesus, so we call her our Blessed Mother. People of every nation and language honor Mary. They have given her many titles of respect.

Today's reading teaches that everyone who obeys God belongs to the family of Jesus.

■ A PSALM FOR SEPTEMBER

▶ turn to page 12

■ READING

Mark 3:31–35

Listen to the words of the holy gospel according to Mark:

Jesus' mother and brothers came and stood outside the house where Jesus was teaching. They sent someone with a message for him to come out to them. The crowd that was sitting around Jesus told him, "Your mother and your brothers and sisters are outside and want to see you."

Jesus asked, "Who is my mother and who are my brothers?" Then he looked at the people sitting around him and said, "Here are my mother and my brothers. Anyone who obeys God is my brother or sister or mother."

The gospel of the Lord.

■ REFLECTION

When I pray, do I speak to Jesus as my brother? If all who do the will of God are brothers and sisters, how should people treat one another?

■ CLOSING

Let us remember these intentions:

Let us pray with the words that Jesus taught us:

Our Father . . .

Mary, our mother,
    you sheltered Jesus in your own body,
    raised him with a mother's care
    and followed him in faith.
With you, we celebrate God's saving love.
Let us all say:

Hail Mary, full of grace,
    the Lord is with you!
Blessed are you among women,
    and blessed is the fruit of your womb, Jesus.
Holy Mary, Mother of God,
    pray for us sinners,
    now and at the hour of our death. Amen.

▶ sing "alleluia"

Al - le - lu - ia,   al - le - lu - ia,   al - le - lu - ia.

24

Prayer on Feasts of the Blessed Virgin Mary

END OF THE DAY PRAYER

▶ all make the sign
of the cross

LEADER Mary said "yes" to the plan of God, alleluia!
ALL **Mary carried in her body
the light of the world, alleluia!**

▶ in Christmastime or Eastertime
light a candle

LEADER Through the grace of our loving God,
Mary became the mother of Jesus
and the mother of all who follow him.

▶ the leader's part is in the left-hand column;
the responses are on the right

Holy Mary,   **pray for us.**
Holy Mother of God,   **pray for us.**
Health of the sick,   **pray for us.**
Shelter for the homeless,   **pray for us.**
Comfort for the troubled,   **pray for us.**
Justice for the victim,   **pray for us.**
Help of Christians,   **pray for us.**

LEADER Pray for us, holy Mother of God.
ALL **That we may become worthy
of the promises of Christ.**

LEADER Holy God,
through the prayers of Mary, our Mother,
make us faithful disciples of Jesus, your Son.
We ask this through Christ our Lord.
ALL **Amen.**

▶ all make the sign
of the cross

▶ in Christmastime or Eastertime
put out the candle

25

WEEKLY PRAYER

With a Reading from the Gospel for Sunday, September 10, 2000

▶ Reminders: A Blessing of the School Year is on page 15. A Blessing of the Cross is on page 31. September's Psalm is on page 6 of the student booklet *Blessed be God!*

■ INTRODUCTION

With the start of the new school year, we again study math, science and reading. And we also take up the study of our Christian faith. During this year we will listen to the gospel of Jesus and try to let it teach us how to live.

■ A PSALM FOR SEPTEMBER

▶ turn to page 12

■ READING

Mark 7:31–37

Listen to the words of the holy gospel according to Mark:

Jesus went through the land near the ten cities known as Decapolis *(de-CAP-uh-lis)*. Some people brought to him a man who was deaf and could hardly talk. They begged Jesus just to touch him.

After Jesus had taken him aside from the crowd, he stuck his fingers in the man's ears. Then he spit and put it on the man's tongue. Jesus looked up toward heaven, and with a groan he said, "Open up!" At once the man could hear, and he had no more trouble talking clearly.

Jesus told the people not to say anything about what he had done. But the more he told them, the more they talked about it. They were completely amazed and said, "Everything he does is good! He even heals people who cannot hear or talk."

The gospel of the Lord.

■ REFLECTION

Selfishness keeps us from hearing people asking for help. It keeps us from hearing God's word in our heart. How can Jesus cure us?

■ CLOSING

Let us remember these intentions:

Holy God, you give us the power to speak
   so we can tell of your wonderful works.
You give us the power to hear
   so we can listen to your word.
We give you thanks for your loving care.
With Christ we give you glory
   now and for ever. **Amen.**

Let us pray with the words that Jesus taught us:
Our Father . . .

▶ sing "alleluia"

Al-le-lu-ia, al-le-lu-ia, al-le-lu-ia.

26

MONDAY PRAYER

September 11, 2000

> Reminder: Thursday we celebrate the feast of the Holy Cross. The Blessing of the Cross on page 31 can be used in class. Talk this over with the teacher.

■ INTRODUCTION

As we read the gospel according to Mark, we learn that Jesus taught in parables. Parables are stories that use symbols to help us understand something. When we hear Jesus' parables we try to see the symbol in our minds, so that our imaginations can help us discover the meanings of the story.

■ A PSALM FOR SEPTEMBER

> turn to
> page 12

■ READING

Mark 4:30–32

Listen to the words of the holy gospel according to Mark:

Jesus said, "What is God's kingdom like? What story can I use to explain it? It is like what happens when a mustard seed is planted in the ground. It is the smallest seed in all the world. But once it is planted, it grows larger than any garden plant. It even puts out branches that are big enough for birds to nest in its shade."

The gospel of the Lord.

■ REFLECTION

How does the kingdom of God begin small, like a tiny seed, and then grow? What could Jesus mean by the birds that nest in its shade? What kind of shade does the kingdom of God provide for me?

■ CLOSING

Let us remember these intentions:

God calls us to work together this year.
We will share our time and ideas.
We will protect and encourage one another.
We begin by learning each other's names.
Please be silent now and pray for each person
    in this class.
Say each person's name in your heart.
If there is a name you do not know,
    learn it sometime today.

> stop;
> give everyone a few moments to pray

Let us pray with the words that Jesus taught us:

Our Father . . .

> sing
> "alleluia"

Al-le-lu-ia,   al - le-lu-ia,   al-le-lu-ia.

TUESDAY PRAYER

■ INTRODUCTION

In today's reading, Jesus helps some people who are in trouble. When we hear the story today, let us try to remember the words that Jesus says. They are meant for us as well as for the disciples in the boat. Jesus wants us to remember those words when we are in trouble.

■ A PSALM FOR SEPTEMBER

➤ turn to page 12

■ READING

Mark 4:36–41

Listen to the words of the holy gospel according to Mark:

The disciples started across the lake with Jesus in the boat. Some other boats followed along. Suddenly a windstorm struck the lake. Waves started splashing into the boat, and it was about to sink.

Jesus was in the back of the boat with his head on a pillow, and he was asleep. His disciples woke him and said, "Teacher, don't you care that we're about to drown?"

Jesus got up and ordered the wind and the waves to be quiet. The wind stopped, and everything was calm.

Jesus asked his disciples, "Why were you afraid? Don't you have any faith?"

Now they were more afraid than ever and said to each other, "Who is this? Even the wind and the waves obey him!"

The gospel of the Lord.

■ REFLECTION

Are there dangerous storms in my life and in the lives of people I know? Do I believe Jesus can help me through the storms? How do we pray during times of sadness or trouble?

■ CLOSING

Let us remember these intentions:

Loving God,
  we seek you in the wind,
  and find you in the storm.
We call to you in faith,
  and trust you in danger.
Be with us always
  when we pass through troubled waters.
We ask this through Christ our Lord. **Amen.**

Let us pray with the words that Jesus taught us:

Our Father . . .

➤ sing "alleluia"

Al - le - lu - ia,   al - le - lu - ia,   al - le - lu - ia.

WEDNESDAY PRAYER

■ INTRODUCTION

Today we remember John Chrysostom *(KRIS-uh-stum),* a famous bishop and teacher of the early church. He was given this name, which means "golden mouth," because he gave beautiful speeches.

The cross is the symbol for the way Jesus defeated sin, hatred and death. From earliest times Christians have treasured it. This is what John Chrysostom wrote about it: "Let the sign of the cross be continually made in the heart, the mouth, on the forehead, at table, in the bath, in bed, coming in and going out, in joy and sadness, sitting, standing, walking."

■ A PSALM FOR SEPTEMBER

➤ turn to
page 12

■ READING

Mark 5:22–24, 35–36, 38–40, 41–42

Listen to the words of the holy gospel according to Mark:

A man named Jairus *(JYE-rus)* knelt at Jesus' feet and started begging him for help. The man said, "My daughter is about to die! Please come and touch her, so she will get well and live." Jesus went with Jairus. Many people followed along with them.

Some men came from Jairus' home and said, "Your daughter has died! Why bother the teacher any more?" Jesus heard what they said, and he said to Jairus, "Don't worry. Just have faith!"

Jesus went home with Jairus and saw the people crying and making a lot of noise. Then Jesus went inside and said to them, "Why are you crying and carrying on like this? The child isn't dead. She is just asleep." But the people laughed at him.

Jesus took the twelve-year-old girl by the hand and said, "Little girl, get up!" The girl got right up and started walking around.

The gospel of the Lord.

■ REFLECTION

What did Jesus ask of Jairus? What did Jairus want for his daughter? How can this reading encourage us and our parents?

■ CLOSING

Let us remember these intentions:

God most holy,
 you have given us life
 and renewed us in your Spirit.
Teach us to rely on you
 even when death is near.
We ask this through Christ our Lord. **Amen.**

Let us pray with the words that Jesus taught us:

Our Father . . .

➤ sing
"alleluia"

Al - le - lu - ia, al - le - lu - ia, al - le - lu - ia.

29

> Reminder: The Blessing of the Cross on page 31 may be used today.

■ INTRODUCTION

Today Christians celebrate the Holy Cross. The cross is the symbol for the way Jesus defeated sin, hatred and death. Christians are signed with the cross when they are baptized and also when they are buried. The sign of the cross shows our willingness to follow Jesus and our joy at being part of his family.

Today's reading reminds us of a story in the Bible. God told Moses to make a metal snake and to put it up on a pole. When people looked at it, poisonous snakes could not harm them.

■ A PSALM FOR SEPTEMBER

> turn to page 12

■ READING

John 3:14–16

Listen to the words of the holy gospel according to John:

Jesus said, "The Son of Man must be lifted up, just as that metal snake was lifted up by Moses in the desert. Then everyone who has faith in the Son of Man will have eternal life.

"God loved the people of this world so much that he gave his only Son, so that everyone who has faith in him will have eternal life and never die."

The gospel of the Lord.

■ REFLECTION

Do I know how to make the sign of the cross correctly? Do we make the sign of the cross with care? What does it mean to us?

■ CLOSING

adapted from the *Book of Blessings*

Let us remember these intentions:

Let us look at the cross in this room
    and think for a minute
    about how much Jesus loves us.

> stop;
> give everyone a few moments to pray

Lord, your people have raised this cross
    as a sign of redemption.
May the cross be our comfort in trouble,
    our shelter in the face of danger,
    our safeguard on life's journey,
    until you welcome us to our heavenly home.
We ask this through Christ our Lord. **Amen.**

Let us pray with the words that Jesus taught us:

Our Father . . .

> sing
> "alleluia"

Al-le-lu-ia,   al-le-lu-ia,   al-le-lu-ia.

A Blessing of the Cross

Flowers or incense can be placed near the classroom cross or near another cross that has been brought for the occasion. Crosses that are brought from home can be placed on desks and blessed by their owners as the leader blesses the classroom cross.

*Rehearse the response, **"For by your holy cross. . . ."** Practice how you will bow to the cross.*

Begin and end this prayer with a hymn, such as "Lift high the cross" (page 154 in the Hymnal for Catholic Students).

 all make
the sign
of the cross

LEADER
We adore you, O Christ, and we bless you!

ALL
**For by your holy cross
you have redeemed the world.**

READER   Philippians 2:8–11
Listen to the words of the apostle Paul:

Christ was humble.
He obeyed God and even died on a cross.
Then God gave Christ the highest place
and honored his name above all others.
So at the name of Jesus
    everyone will bow down,
those in heaven, on earth,
    and under the earth.
And to the glory of God the Father
everyone will openly agree,
    "Jesus Christ is Lord!"

The word of the Lord.

LEADER   adapted from the *Book of Blessings*
The sign of the cross shall be in the heavens
    when the Lord comes.
Lift up your heads!
Your redemption is near when the Lord comes.

 hold out your hand
toward the cross
in blessing

Loving God,
    in your goodness be near us.
We have raised this cross
    as a sign of our faith.
May we always hold fast
    to the mystery of Christ's suffering
    and enter the joy of his risen life.
He is Lord for ever and ever.

ALL
Amen.

LEADER
We adore you, O Christ, and we bless you!

ALL
**For by your holy cross
    you have redeemed the world.**

 all make
a deep bow
toward the cross

 all make
the sign
of the cross

FRIDAY PRAYER

September 15, 2000

■ INTRODUCTION

Today we continue to celebrate the Holy Cross by remembering Our Lady of Sorrows. This is a title for Mary, the mother of Jesus. She was sorrowful to see Jesus carrying his cross, and she followed him to Mount Calvary *(KAL-vuh-ree)*. She stayed near until he died.

Mary understands the suffering of all her children. She wants us to have compassion for all who are in pain.

Today begins Hispanic Heritage Month in the United States. Hispanic peoples give special honor to Our Lady of Sorrows. They have many titles of respect for Mary.

■ A PSALM FOR SEPTEMBER

 turn to
page 12

■ READING

John 19:25–27

Listen to the words of the holy gospel according to John:

Jesus' mother stood beside his cross with her sister and Mary the wife of Clopas. Mary Magdalene *(MAG-duh-lin)* was standing there too. When Jesus saw his mother and his favorite disciple with her, he said to his mother, "This man is now your son." Then he said to the disciple, "She is now your mother." From then on, that disciple took her into his own home.

The gospel of the Lord.

■ REFLECTION

Does it hurt me when a friend or family member is laughed at or put down? How do we share Christ's suffering? How does Christ share ours?

■ CLOSING

adapted from the *Book of Blessings*

Let us remember these intentions:

Let us look at the cross in this room
  and think for a minute of all those who suffer
  and who do the will of God.

 stop:
give everyone a few moments to pray

Lord, your people have raised this cross
  as a sign of redemption.
May the cross be our comfort in trouble,
  our shelter in the face of danger,
  our safeguard on life's journey,
  until you welcome us to our heavenly home.
We ask this through Christ our Lord. **Amen.**

Let us pray with the words that Jesus taught us:
Our Father . . .

sing
"alleluia"

Al-le-lu - ia,   al - le-lu - ia,   al - le - lu - ia.

WEEKLY PRAYER

With a Reading from the Gospel for Sunday, September 17, 2000

■ INTRODUCTION

We believe that the death of Jesus was a victory, not a disaster. Jesus spent his whole life doing the work that God had given him. He was even willing to die so that we might receive the grace and love of God. He warned his followers that one day he would suffer and die. He knew that it would not be easy for them to stick by him. Today, let us be strong, and stand by Jesus.

September 17 is Catechetical *(KAT-ih-KET-ih-kul)* Sunday. Let us try to greet our religion teachers on that day, and pray for them.

■ A PSALM FOR SEPTEMBER

➤ turn to page 12

■ READING

Mark 8:31, 31–35

Listen to the words of the holy gospel according to Mark:

Jesus began telling his disciples what would happen to him. He said, "[The Son of Man] will be rejected and killed, but three days later he will rise to life." Then Jesus explained clearly what he meant.

Peter took Jesus aside and told him to stop talking like that. But when Jesus turned and saw the disciples, he corrected Peter. He said to him, "Satan, get away from me! You are thinking like everyone else and not like God."

Jesus then told the crowd and the disciples to come closer, and he said, "If any of you want to be my followers, you must forget about yourself.

You must take up your cross and follow me. If you want to save your life, you will destroy it. But if you give up your life for me and for the good news, you will save it."

The gospel of the Lord.

■ REFLECTION

Are we willing to accept the hardships that come with following Jesus? Why is Peter afraid that this message will scare followers away?

■ CLOSING

adapted from the *Book of Blessings*

Let us remember these intentions:

Loving God,
   you give us the cross as a sign of your love
   and a call to our faithfulness.
May the cross be our comfort in trouble,
   our shelter in the face of danger,
   our safeguard on life's journey,
until you welcome us to our heavenly home.
We ask this through Christ our Lord. **Amen.**

Let us pray with the words that Jesus taught us:

Our Father . . .

➤ sing "alleluia"

Al-le-lu-ia,   al-le-lu-ia,   al-le-lu-ia.

September 18, 2000

■ INTRODUCTION

When we are having difficulty, it is a good idea to ask people to pray that God will help us. Even Christians who have died and are with God in glory are happy to pray for those still on earth. We call the bond we have with one another the "communion of saints."

Today we remember Saint Joseph of Cupertino *(koo-per-TEE-no)*. He was so bad at his school-work that he never did get it right, even when he was studying for the priesthood. He is the patron of students who find it hard to learn. This means that he has a special interest in asking God's help for them.

■ A PSALM FOR SEPTEMBER

➤ turn to page 12

■ READING

Mark 4:2–9

Listen to the words of the holy gospel according to Mark:

Jesus used stories to teach [the people] many things, and this is part of what he taught:

"Now listen! A farmer went out to scatter seed in a field. While the farmer was scattering the seed, some of it fell along the road and was eaten by birds. Other seeds fell on thin, rocky ground and quickly started growing because the soil wasn't very deep. But when the sun came up, the plants were scorched and dried up, because they did not have enough roots. Some other seeds fell where thorn bushes grew up and choked out the plants. So they did not produce any grain. But a few seeds did fall on good ground where the plants grew and produced thirty or sixty or even a hundred times as much as was scattered."

Then Jesus said, "If you have ears, pay attention."

The gospel of the Lord.

■ REFLECTION

What do we know about planting seeds and waiting for them to grow? What could the seed stand for in this parable? What could the different kinds of soil stand for? What could the large harvest from the good soil mean?

■ CLOSING

Let us remember these intentions:

Lord, fill our hearts with the seed of your word. Help it to grow in us.
Teach us to receive your word with respect,
    to think it over carefully,
    and to follow it joyfully.
We ask this through Christ our Lord. **Amen.**

Let us pray with the words that Jesus taught us:
Our Father . . .

➤ sing "alleluia"

■ INTRODUCTION

Yesterday we heard Jesus' parable about a farmer who planted seeds. Today we will continue the reading so that we hear the explanation of the parable that Jesus gave.

■ A PSALM FOR SEPTEMBER

turn to
page 12

■ READING

Mark 4:10, 14–20

Listen to the words of the holy gospel according to Mark:

When Jesus was alone with the twelve apostles and some others, they asked him about these stories. Jesus told them, "What the farmer is spreading is really the message about the kingdom. The seeds that fell along the road are the people who hear the message. But Satan soon comes and snatches it away from them. The seeds that fell on rocky ground are the people who gladly hear the message and accept it right away. But they don't have any roots, and they don't last very long. As soon as life gets hard or the message gets them in trouble, they give up.

"The seeds that fell among the thorn bushes are also people who hear the message. But they start worrying about the needs of this life. They are fooled by the desire to get rich and to have all kinds of other things. So the message gets choked out, and they never produce anything. The seeds that fell on good ground are the people who hear and welcome the message. They produce thirty or sixty or even a hundred times as much as was planted."

The gospel of the Lord.

■ REFLECTION

What dangers prevent the seed from growing as it should? What kind of "soil" does my heart offer to the word of God?

■ CLOSING

Let us remember these intentions:

Lord, fill our hearts with the seed of your word.
Help it to grow in us.
Teach us to receive your word with respect,
    to think it over carefully,
    and to follow it joyfully.
We ask this through Christ our Lord. **Amen.**

Let us pray with the words that Jesus taught us:

Our Father . . .

sing
"alleluia"

■ INTRODUCTION

Today we remember Saint Andrew Kim Taegon and many other Koreans who bravely died for their faith between the years 1839 and 1867. Andrew and many others died trying to convince their nation that the Catholic church was not an enemy. Today many people in Korea are faithful Catholics. Let us give God thanks today for the steadfast courage of Andrew and all who have suffered for their faith.

■ A PSALM FOR SEPTEMBER

 turn to page 12

■ READING

Mark 6:35–36, 38–39, 41–43

Listen to the words of the holy gospel according to Mark:

The disciples came to Jesus and said, "This place is like a desert, and it is already late. Let the crowds leave, so they can go to the farms and villages near here and buy something to eat."

Then Jesus said, "How much bread do you have? Go and see!"

They found out and answered, "We have five small loaves of bread and two fish." Jesus told his disciples to have the people sit down on the green grass. Jesus took the five loaves and the two fish. He looked up toward heaven and blessed the food. Then he broke the bread and handed it to his disciples to give to the people. He also divided the two fish, so that everyone could have some.

After everyone had eaten all they wanted, Jesus' disciples picked up twelve large baskets of leftover bread and fish.

The gospel of the Lord.

■ REFLECTION

How do we know that people today are hungry for what Jesus can give? How does Jesus feed us today? How can we help Jesus feed others?

■ CLOSING

Let us remember these intentions:

Loving God,
    we thank you for sending your disciples
    into the whole world
    with your gifts of food and love.
We have been cared for and protected.
We have eaten and been filled.
Show us how to share what we have been given,
    and to be your worthy disciples.
We ask this through Christ our Lord. **Amen.**

Let us pray with the words that Jesus taught us:
Our Father . . .

 sing "alleluia"

THURSDAY PRAYER

September 21, 2000

■ INTRODUCTION

Today is the feast of the apostle Matthew. He was working as a tax collector when he met Jesus. The Jews did not like to give their money to pay the Roman tax, and so many people did not like Matthew. They thought tax collectors were traitors who robbed their own people. They were surprised that Jesus became his friend. Jesus made many friends among those who were rejected, and still does. He was rejected himself.

■ A PSALM FOR SEPTEMBER

turn to
page 12

■ READING

Mark 6:31–34

Listen to the words of the holy gospel according to Mark:

So many people were coming and going that Jesus and the apostles did not even have a chance to eat. Then Jesus said, "Let's go to a place where we can be alone and get some rest." They left in a boat for a place where they could be alone. But many people saw them leave and figured out where they were going. So people from every town ran on ahead and got there first.

When Jesus got out of the boat, he saw the large crowd that was like sheep without a shepherd. He felt sorry for the people and started teaching them many things.

The gospel of the Lord.

■ REFLECTION

Sheep need a shepherd to guard and guide them. How does God act as our shepherd? What would it be like to have no shepherd? Do I sometimes pray to Jesus as the Good Shepherd?

■ CLOSING

Let us remember these intentions:

Jesus, our Good Shepherd,
  you are a sign of God's presence with us.
Accept us as your disciples.
Teach us to be faithful children of a loving God.
And lead us to share in your kingdom,
  where we may be joyful with you,
  now and for ever. **Amen.**

Let us pray with the words that Jesus taught us:

Our Father . . .

sing
"alleluia"

FRIDAY PRAYER

September 22, 2000

■ INTRODUCTION

At exactly 12:28 this afternoon, Central Daylight Time, the exact middle of the earth is turned toward the sun. This is called the autumn equinox *(EE-kwi-nox)*. This means that today will have the same number of hours of daylight as it has of darkness. It is a "day of balance." Buddhists look upon this day as a symbol of peace, equality and harmony.

In today's reading Jesus shows that he is the "balance" between earthly life and heavenly glory. In him all that is human and all that is divine are perfectly connected.

■ A PSALM FOR SEPTEMBER

➤ turn to page 12

■ READING

Mark 9:2–8

Listen to the words of the holy gospel according to Mark:

Jesus took Peter, James, and John with him. They went up on a high mountain, where they could be alone. There in front of the disciples, Jesus was completely changed. And his clothes became much whiter than any bleach on earth could make them. Then Moses and Elijah *(ee-LYE-juh)* were there talking with Jesus.

Peter said to Jesus, "Teacher, it is good for us to be here! Let us make three shelters, one for you, one for Moses, and one for Elijah." But Peter and the others were terribly frightened, and he did not know what he was talking about.

The shadow of a cloud passed over and covered them. From the cloud a voice said, "This is my Son, and I love him. Listen to what he says!" At once the disciples looked around, but they saw only Jesus.

The gospel of the Lord.

■ REFLECTION

What could the symbol of the white clothes mean? What do my clothes tell others about me? What does the voice tell us about Jesus? How do we obey the command to listen?

■ CLOSING

Let us remember these intentions:

Loving God,
  you call us each by name
  and speak to us in the quiet of our hearts.
Speak to us of love for all people.
Speak to us of hope for our world.
Speak to us of your gift of salvation.
Speak to us, for we are listening.
We ask this through Christ our Lord. **Amen.**

Let us pray with the words that Jesus taught us:

Our Father . . .

 sing "alleluia"

WEEKLY PRAYER

With a Reading from the Gospel for Sunday, September 24, 2000

➤ Reminder: Before your next meeting you may want to make copies of October's Psalm, on page 48.

■ INTRODUCTION

In today's reading Jesus promises that when we welcome and care for anyone, we are welcoming God in our midst.

■ A PSALM FOR SEPTEMBER

➤ turn to page 12

■ READING

Mark 9:33–37

Listen to the words of the holy gospel according to Mark:

Jesus and his disciples went to his home in Capernaum *(kuh-PER-nee-um)*. After they were inside the house, Jesus asked them, "What were you arguing about along the way?" They had been arguing about which one of them was the greatest, and so they did not answer.

After Jesus sat down and told the twelve disciples to gather around him, he said, "If you want the place of honor, you must become a slave and serve others!"

Then Jesus had a child stand near him. He put his arm around the child and said, "When you welcome even a child because of me, you welcome me. And when you welcome me, you welcome the one who sent me."

The gospel of the Lord.

■ REFLECTION

Do I ever argue about being first or getting the best place? What is the difference between doing my best and trying to be first? Do I have any little children as friends? What kind of people do little children like to be with?

■ CLOSING

Blessed be God, Creator of days and seasons.
Let us all say: Blessed be God for ever!
Blessed be God for ever!

Let us remember these intentions:

Loving God, you give us this new school year
and new friends with whom to share it.
Bless all who pray and work
and learn together.
And grant a happy year to all the world.
We ask this through Christ our Lord. **Amen.**

Let us pray with the words that Jesus taught us:

Our Father . . .

➤ sing "alleluia"

Al - le - lu - ia, al - le - lu - ia, al - le - lu - ia.

MONDAY PRAYER
September 25, 2000

> Reminder: You may want to make copies of October's Psalm, Meal Prayer and End of the Day Prayer.

■ INTRODUCTION

Today we remember Sergius *(SER-jee-us)*, one of Russia's greatest saints. Sergius was born near Moscow. He and his brother went into the forest to live simply and to pray. Others who heard of their holiness and kindness to the poor joined them and became monks. Sergius was a wise and gifted leader. Many people came to him for his advice.

The monks built a monastery *(MAH-nuh-steh-ree)* there that is now famous. You can visit it if you ever go to Russia.

■ A PSALM FOR SEPTEMBER

> turn to
> page 12

■ READING

Mark 8: 22–25

Listen to the words of the holy gospel according to Mark:

As Jesus and his disciples were going into Beth-saida *(beth-SAY-ih-duh)*, some people brought a blind man to him and begged him to touch the man. Jesus took him by the hand and led him out of the village, where he spit into the man's eyes. He placed his hands on the blind man and asked him if he could see anything. The man looked up and said, "I see people, but they look like trees walking around."

Once again Jesus placed his hands on the man's eyes, and this time the man stared. His eyes were healed, and he saw everything clearly.

The gospel of the Lord.

■ REFLECTION

Do I sometimes act as if I cannot see the needs of others or the beauty of God's world? What is Jesus helping us to see more clearly this year?

■ CLOSING

Let us remember these intentions:

Holy God, you give us the power to see
    so that we can delight in the wonders
        you have made
    and notice the needs of those around us.
You give us the power of movement
    so that we can follow you closely
        and share the journey of your people.
We give you thanks that you have made us
with such loving care.
With Christ we give you glory
    now and for ever. Amen.

Let us pray with the words that Jesus taught us:

Our Father . . .

> sing
> "alleluia"

40

TUESDAY PRAYER

September 26, 2000

■ INTRODUCTION

On this day in 1774, John Chapman was born in a small town in Massachusetts *(mass-uh-CHOO-sits)*. John spent his life traveling with the early pioneers from what is now called Pennsylvania *(pen-sil-VANE-yuh)* to Indiana. Everywhere he went he planted apple orchards. John Chapman praised God for giving him the sun and rain that helped the trees grow. He was a friend to the wild animals, and the Native Americans who knew him respected him as a medicine man. You may know John Chapman by his nickname, Johnny Appleseed.

■ A PSALM FOR SEPTEMBER

▶ turn to
page 12

■ READING

Mark 8:27–29

Listen to the words of the holy gospel according to Mark:

Jesus and his disciples went to the villages near the town of Caesarea Philippi *(sez-uh-REE-uh FILL-uh-pye)*. As they were walking along, he asked them, "What do people say about me?"

The disciples answered, "Some say you are John the Baptist or maybe Elijah *(ee-LYE-juh)*. Others say you are one of the prophets."

Then Jesus asked them, "But who do you say I am?"

"You are the Messiah!" Peter replied.

The gospel of the Lord.

■ REFLECTION

Am I able to put my faith into words, as Peter did? Can I explain to others what it means to call Jesus the Messiah? What other titles do I use for Jesus?

■ CLOSING

Let us remember these intentions:

Gracious God,
    through the gift of your Spirit
    and the teaching of your apostles,
    we can proclaim with all your church
    that Jesus is the Messiah you sent to us.
Strengthen in us this gift of faith.
We ask this through Christ our Lord. **Amen.**

Let us pray with the words that Jesus taught us:
Our Father . . .

▶ sing
"alleluia"

41

WEDNESDAY PRAYER

September 27, 2000

■ INTRODUCTION

Today we remember Saint Vincent de Paul. Vincent was born in France in the year 1581. He moved to Paris when he was a young priest. There he organized groups to help people pray and serve the needs of others.

Vincent loved the poor, especially children. In our own day members of an organization named for him supply food, money and clothing to those in need. There may be a chapter of the Saint Vincent de Paul Society in your parish.

■ A PSALM FOR SEPTEMBER

turn to page 12

■ READING

Mark 8:2, 3–9

Listen to the words of the holy gospel according to Mark:

Jesus said to his disciples, "I feel sorry for these people. If I send them away hungry, they might faint on their way home."

Jesus asked them how much food they had. They replied, "Seven small loaves of bread."

After Jesus told the crowd to sit down, he took the seven loaves and blessed them. He then broke the loaves and handed them to his disciples, who passed them out to the crowd. They also had a few little fish, and after Jesus blessed these, he told the disciples to pass them around.

The crowd of about four thousand people ate all they wanted and the leftovers filled seven large baskets.

The gospel of the Lord.

■ REFLECTION

How does Jesus feed his followers today? Why doesn't Jesus use a miracle to give bread to all the starving people of the world today?

■ CLOSING

Let us remember these intentions:

Loving God,
   we thank you for sending your disciples
      into the whole world
   with your gifts of food and love.
We have been cared for and protected.
We have eaten and been filled.
Show us how to share what we have been given,
   and to be your worthy disciples.
We ask this through Christ our Lord. **Amen.**

Let us pray with the words that Jesus taught us:

Our Father . . .

sing "alleluia"

THURSDAY PRAYER

September 28, 2000

■ INTRODUCTION

Today we remember Wenceslaus *(WEN-sis-lahs)*, who became king of Bohemia *(bo-HEE-mee-uh)* when he was only 18 years old. His country is now part of the Czech *(chek)* Republic, in central Europe. Let us remember all the peoples of central Europe in our prayers today as we honor Wenceslaus, one of their patron saints.

There is a Christmas carol about "good king Wenceslaus." The king was famous for his kindness to people in need and for his wise laws. He was attacked one day by his brother, who wanted his power. As he lay dying, he said, "Brother, may God forgive you."

■ A PSALM FOR SEPTEMBER

▶ turn to
page 12

■ READING

Mark 10:28–30

Listen to the words of the holy gospel according to Mark:

Peter said to Jesus, "Remember, we left everything to be your followers!"

Jesus told him, "You can be sure that anyone who gives up home or brothers or sisters or mother or father or children or land for me and for the good news will be rewarded. In this world they will be given a hundred times as many houses and brothers and sisters and mothers and children and pieces of land, though they will also be mistreated. And in the world to come, they will have eternal life."

The gospel of the Lord.

■ REFLECTION

What have I had to give up to be a good follower of Jesus? Do I treat all the members of my community like brothers and sisters? What kind of mistreatment can followers of Jesus expect?

■ CLOSING

Let us remember these intentions:

Gracious God,
　　through the gift of your Spirit
　　and the teaching of your apostles,
　　we can proclaim with all your church
　　that Jesus is the Messiah you sent to us.
Strengthen in us this gift of faith.
We ask this through Christ our Lord. **Amen.**

Let us pray with the words that Jesus taught us:

Our Father . . .

▶ sing
"alleluia"

43

FRIDAY PRAYER

September 29, 2000

■ INTRODUCTION

Today is the feast of the angels Michael, Gabriel and Raphael. In today's reading, we hear about Raphael, who guides Tobias on a journey.

At sundown the Jewish feast of Rosh Hashana *(ROSH hah-SHAH-nuh)* begins. Jews will welcome the new year with the blowing of a shofar *(SHOW-far),* which is a ram's horn.

■ A PSALM FOR SEPTEMBER

▶ turn to page 12

■ READING

Tobit 5:4–6, 10, 17

Listen to the words of the book of Tobit:

Tobias left to look for someone who knew the way to Media *(MEE-dee-uh).* Suddenly the angel Raphael was standing in front of him, but Tobias did not know that he was one of God's angels. Then Tobias asked, "Do you know the way to Media?" "Yes," he replied, "I have been there many times, and I know all the roads."

Tobias invited the young man, Raphael, to come in and meet his father, Tobit, who immediately greeted him. Then Tobit turned to his son and said, "Get whatever supplies you will need, and then start on the journey with your friend. I pray that God in heaven will watch over you, both going and coming, and that his angel will travel with the two of you and keep you safe."

The word of the Lord.

■ REFLECTION

Do our families pray for safety before a trip? What other times are good for blessings?

■ CLOSING

Let us remember these intentions:

▶ sing this to the melody of "Hymn to Joy," in the *Hymnal for Catholic Students,* page 156.

Michael, image of God's justice,
    angel warrior, God's right arm,
march beside us on our journey;
    ward off evil, fear and harm.
Gabriel, voice of God's salvation,
    messenger with news of grace,
teach us of God's works and wonders
    and the beauty of God's face.

Raphael, star to brighten darkness,
    giving friendship, giving sight,
walk the path that we must travel,
    our companion through the night.
Joined in song by angel guardians,
    let our alleluias ring.
God is with us now and always.
    Glory to our Lord and King!

Let us pray with the words that Jesus taught us:

Our Father . . .

▶ sing "alleluia"

OCTOBER

Sunday, October 1, to Tuesday, October 31

ORDINARY TIME OCTOBER 2000

■ ABOUT THE MONTH

If you live in the North, all at once you will notice that the colors of the trees have become bright. Leaves begin to skip through the air and pile up on the ground. If you live in the South, you may not see these signs during October unless you see them on television. But we all can see

LOOKING AHEAD

certain signs every October, like football and soccer games, scout hikes, orange and green squash in the grocery stores and Indian corn on front doors.

▪ OCTOBER IS A GOOD MONTH TO ENJOY THE OUTDOORS. It is also a good month to think about our earth and what we have done to help or hurt it. We might put new energy into recycling newspapers and aluminum cans or into the other projects we have begun.

This interest in the earth will be carried into our October prayers. Our Psalm this month is the Song of the Three Young Men, from the book of Daniel. An evil king put three of his Hebrew officials into a blazing furnace because they refused to give up the practice of their religion. But they did not die. Instead, they stood up in the fire and called on all creation to sing God's praises. Then even the king joined in their song!

▪ MOST OF THE DAILY READINGS THIS MONTH WILL BE TAKEN FROM THE BOOK OF GENESIS. Genesis is filled with wonderful stories about the beginnings of the earth and of the Hebrew people.

In the book of Genesis there are two stories of God's creation. In October we will read the first one. In that story we find God putting in a full week of work before resting on the Sabbath. We will also read the story of the disobedience of the first man and woman.

Then we will learn more about Abraham and his family. There is much to know about this man who

is called the "father of faith." Each year, we learn a little more.

▪ THE MONTH OF OCTOBER ENDS AND NOVEMBER BEGINS WITH A CELEBRATION THAT MOST STUDENTS REALLY ENJOY—HALLOWEEN! It falls on a Tuesday this year. A blessing for Halloween is on page 80. It can be used as part of your celebration.

Halloween leads into two important days at the very beginning of November, All Saints and All Souls. For ideas about preparing for those days, see November's Looking Ahead, on pages 82 and 83.

■ PREPARATION FOR OCTOBER

If members of the class have copies of *Blessed Be God!* (the prayer book for children), help them find the Psalm for October, the Meal Prayer and the End of the Day Prayer. Otherwise, you may make copies of these prayers for everyone. They are found on pages 48, 49 and 50. Remind everyone to keep these papers in a safe place. They will be needed for the whole month.

The feast of Our Lady of the Rosary is on October 7, which falls on Saturday this year. You might want to say the rosary during October. Instructions are on pages 348 and 349.

▪ THERE ARE THREE BLESSINGS FOR YOU TO USE DURING OCTOBER. The first is a blessing of bulbs for planting on page 53. It can be used on or near the feast of Guardian Angels, October 2. The next is a blessing of pets on page 56 for Saint Francis's Day, October 4. Francis of Assisi became famous for his love of all God's creatures. So his day is a good time to ask God to bless our pets and all the animals on earth. Pets can be brought from home, or drawings and photos of the pets can be used.

The month ends with a blessing for Halloween on page 80. It can be used all by itself or as part of a

party or a parade of costumes. Talk to your teacher about these possibilities.

▪ REMEMBER TO GIVE THE CORRECT RESPONSE AFTER THE READING. If the reading is part of the gospel, the reader says, "The gospel of the Lord." Then we respond, "Praise to you, Lord Jesus Christ." But if the reading is from another book of the Bible, the reader says, "The word of the Lord," and we respond, "Thanks be to God."

▪ THERE ARE PRAYERS IN THIS BOOK TO PRAY WHEN SOMETHING SAD OR TROUBLING HAPPENS. Prayers for Sad Days are on page 346. Prayers for the Sick are on page 347.

▪ SUGGESTED HYMNS: "All creatures of our God and king" (page 100 in the *Hymnal for Catholic Students*) is very similar to the Song of the Three Young Men and is based on Saint Francis of Assisi's "Canticle of the Sun." This is a good song to sing throughout the month of October.

Another good hymn for this month is "For the beauty of the earth" (page 120 in the hymnal).

You may want to sing the petitions each day. This can be done by singing them on a single note. The music on page 40 of the hymnal can be used to sing the petitions and the response, "Lord, have mercy."

▪ THE SCHOOL OF RELIGION

By October you should be familiar with the pattern of Weekly Prayer or with those parts of it that you have been using regularly.

▪ IT IS HARD TO LEARN PRAYERS BY HEART IF YOU USE THEM ONLY ONCE A WEEK. That is why it is a good idea to give every member of the class a copy of the book *Blessed Be God!* It contains all the Psalms, Meal Prayers and End of the Day Prayers used during the year. (The prayers for October are on pages 9 to 11.) Or, students can be given photocopies of these prayers each month. Keep them in your religion book so that you can use them at home as well as during class.

▪ TAKE A FEW MINUTES DURING CLASS TO GO OVER THE METHOD FOR PRAYING THE PSALM. The same method will be used all year long. Members of the class are divided into Side A and Side B. The first group prays with the reader. The other group prays with the leader.

The leader begins with the first statement: "Bless God beyond the stars. Give praise and glory." Then the entire class, led by the reader, gives the answering statement: "Bless God, heaven and earth. Give praise and glory for ever." Each side takes turns reading the Psalm. The leader reads a final statement, and the class ends the Psalm with the "Glory to the Father."

▪ WHEN YOU LEAD PRAYER, BE SURE TO READ EACH WORD CLEARLY. We all need to pray slowly so that we can almost "taste" the words of praise.

The reading for each Weekly Prayer in October is taken from the Sunday liturgy. Instead of using the Weekly Prayers, you may want to substitute the prayers for October's special days. Some of these are: Guardian Angels (October 2), Saint Francis of Assisi (October 4), Saint Luke the evangelist (October 18), and Halloween (October 31). There is a blessing of bulbs for planting on page 53, a blessing of pets on page 56 and a blessing for Halloween on page 80.

A PSALM FOR OCTOBER

▶ all make
the sign
of the cross

Daniel 3:56–57, 62–63, 66, 70, 72–73

LEADER   Bless God beyond the stars.
Give praise and glory.

ALL   **Bless God, heaven and earth.
Give praise and glory for ever.**

SIDE A   Bless God, sun and moon.
Give praise and glory.

SIDE B   Bless God, stars of heaven.
Give praise and glory for ever.

SIDE A   Bless God, fire and heat.
Give praise and glory.

SIDE B   Bless God, frost and sleet.
Give praise and glory for ever.

SIDE A   Bless God, light and darkness.
Give praise and glory.

SIDE B   Bless God, lightning and clouds.
Give praise and glory for ever.

LEADER   Bless God beyond the stars.
Give praise and glory.

ALL   **Bless God, heaven and earth.
Give praise and glory for ever.**

**Glory to the Father, and to the Son,
and to the Holy Spirit:
As it was in the beginning, is now,
and will be for ever. Amen. Alleluia.**

▶ turn back to
Daily Prayer or Weekly Prayer
for today

48

OCTOBER

MEAL PRAYER

LEADER   Let us offer God praise and thanksgiving:

ALL   ▶ all make the sign
of the cross

LEADER   The angel spoke God's message to Mary,
and she conceived of the Holy Spirit.

ALL   **Hail Mary, full of grace,
the Lord is with you!
Blessed are you among women,
and blessed is the fruit
of your womb, Jesus.
Holy Mary, Mother of God,
pray for us sinners,
now and at the hour of our death.
Amen.**

LEADER   "I am the lowly servant of the Lord:
let it be done to me
according to your word."

ALL   **Hail Mary, full of grace . . .**

LEADER   And the Word became flesh and lived among us.

ALL   **Hail Mary, full of grace . . .**

LEADER   Pray for us, holy Mother of God:

ALL   **That we may become worthy
of the promises of Christ.**

LEADER   Let us pray.

Lord, fill our hearts with your grace:
once, through the message of an angel
you revealed to us the incarnation of your Son;
now, through his suffering and death
lead us to the glory of his resurrection.
We ask this through Christ our Lord.

ALL   **Amen.**

▶ all make the sign
of the cross

The Angelus, from *A Book of Prayers*

49

OCTOBER

▶ all make
the sign
of the cross

LEADER   Lord, make me an instrument of your peace:

SIDE A   Where there is hatred, let me sow love;
     where there is injury, pardon;
     where there is doubt, faith.

SIDE B   Where there is despair, hope;
     where there is darkness, light;
     where there is sadness, joy.

SIDE A   O divine Master,
     grant that I may not so much seek
     to be consoled as to console,
     to be understood as to understand,
     to be loved as to love.

SIDE B   For it is in giving that we receive,
     it is in pardoning that we are pardoned,
     it is in dying that we are born to eternal life.

LEADER   ▶ hold out one hand
toward everyone
in blessing, and say:

May the almighty and merciful God
bless and protect us:

ALL   ▶ all make
the sign
of the cross

The Prayer of St. Francis

WEEKLY PRAYER

With a Reading from the Gospel for Sunday, October 1, 2000

➤ Reminders: October's Psalm is on page 9 in *Blessed Be God!* Blessings for the feast of guardian angels and the feast of Saint Francis are on pages 53 and 56. Talk to the teacher about using one of them.

■ INTRODUCTION

As we come to know our faith better, it is good to remember that Jesus came for everyone, not just for those who believe as we believe and worship as we worship.

The reading today, which is taken from the gospel for Sunday, October 1, can remind us of this. It tells about a time when the followers of Jesus tried to stop other people from doing good deeds in his name.

■ A PSALM FOR OCTOBER

➤ turn to page 48

turn to page 48

■ READING

Mark 9:38–41

Listen to the words of the holy gospel according to Mark:

John said to Jesus, "Teacher, we saw a man using your name to force demons out of people. But he wasn't one of us, and we told him to stop."

Jesus said to his disciples, "Don't stop him! No one who works miracles in my name will soon turn and say something bad about me. Anyone who isn't against us is for us. And anyone who gives you a cup of water in my name, just because you belong to me, will surely be rewarded."

The gospel of the Lord.

■ REFLECTION

How does the way we act show people that we are followers of Jesus? Have I ever done something good for another person just because Jesus would have wanted me to do it?

■ CLOSING

Let us remember these intentions:

God of all nations and Creator of all peoples,
　　heal all that divides us.
Teach us to live together in peace.
As our world is one, so our future is one.
Give us one heart and one vision.
Make us one body in Christ Jesus,
　　filled with the joy of your Holy Spirit.
We ask this through Christ our Lord. **Amen.**

Let us pray with the words that Jesus taught us:

Our Father . . .

➤ sing "alleluia"

51

MONDAY PRAYER

October 2, 2000

■ INTRODUCTION

Today, on the feast of guardian angels, we remember that God always guards and protects us. We celebrate the angels in autumn, as the earth grows cold. Some people fear the coming of winter. Almost everyone is afraid of something. The angels bring us comfort whenever we are afraid.

In the Hebrew language, the word "angel" means "messenger." The angels bring God's message of hope.

■ A PSALM FOR OCTOBER

➤ turn to page 48

■ READING

Isaiah 63: 7–9

Listen to the words of the prophet Isaiah:

I will tell about the kind deeds
   the LORD has done.
They deserve praise!
The LORD has shown mercy
to the people of Israel;
he has been kind and good.
The LORD rescued his people, and said,
"They are mine. They won't betray me."
It troubled the LORD to see them in trouble,
and his angel saved them.
The LORD was truly merciful,
so he rescued his people.

The word of the Lord.

■ REFLECTION

When have I acted like someone's guardian angel? Who has protected or guided me like a guardian angel?

■ CLOSING

Let us remember these intentions:

➤ Sing this to the melody of "Hymn to Joy," in the *Hymnal for Catholic Students,* page 156.

Michael, image of God's justice,
   angel warrior, God's right arm,
march beside us on our journey;
   ward off evil, fear and harm.

Gabriel, voice of God's salvation,
   messenger with news of grace,
teach us of God's works and wonders
   and the beauty of God's face.

Raphael, star to brighten darkness,
   giving friendship, giving sight,
walk the path that we must travel,
   our companion through the night.

Joined in song by angel guardians,
   let our alleluias ring.
God is with us now and always.
   Glory to our Lord and King!

Let us pray with the words that Jesus taught us:

Our Father . . .

➤ sing "alleluia"

A Blessing of Flower Bulbs

Bring some bulbs that grow well in your part of the country. Bring a shovel and copies of the song "Michael, image of God's justice," on page 52. The refrain "In the sight of the angels" can be sung as well. See the Hymnal for Catholic Students, page 65.

Gather where you will plant the bulbs. Try to find a sunny spot that is not too wet.

 all make
the sign
of the cross

LEADER
We remember the angels Michael, Gabriel and Raphael, as well as the guardian angels in the autumn when the earth is preparing for its winter sleep. Angels are messengers of God's love and care. They say to us, "Be hopeful. Trust in the Lord." To celebrate our trust in God, we will plant some flower bulbs. One day they will surprise us with their beauty.

READER   Mark 4:26–28
Listen to the words of the holy gospel according to Mark:

Jesus said, "God's kingdom is like what happens when a farmer scatters seed in a field. The farmer sleeps at night and is up and around during the day. Yet the seeds keep sprouting and growing, and he doesn't understand how. It is the ground that makes the seeds sprout and grow into plants that produce grain."

The gospel of the Lord.

LEADER
Let us praise God,
   who has brought us into this autumn season:

ALL
**In the sight of the angels,
   I will sing your praises, Lord.**

LEADER
Let us praise God,
   who will bring us through the winter cold:

ALL
**In the sight of the angels,
   I will sing your praises, Lord.**

LEADER
Let us praise God,
   who will bring us to the beauty of springtime:

ALL
**In the sight of the angels,
   I will sing your praises, Lord.**

LEADER

 hold out one hand
over the bulbs in blessing,
and say:

Creator God,
   we ask your blessing on these bulbs.
May they sleep safely in the winter earth
   and awaken with joy in the warmth of spring.
May they remind us to trust in your promises.
We ask this through Christ our Lord.

ALL
Amen.

 plant the bulbs,
and then sing
"Michael, image of God's justice"

 all make
the sign
of the cross

53

TUESDAY PRAYER

October 3, 2000

▶ Reminder: Tomorrow is the feast of Saint Francis. You may want to use the Blessing of Pets, on page 56. Talk this over with the teacher.

■ INTRODUCTION

Our readings this week tell a story about God creating the world. At the end of each day's work, God looks with pleasure at the newest creatures and says, "That is very good!"

People have always wondered how the world got here, what makes it work, and why it becomes dangerous sometimes. You might take some time today to think about these things. Then you might write a poem or other words of thanksgiving to God.

■ A PSALM FOR OCTOBER

▶ turn to
page 48

■ READING

Genesis 1:1–5

Listen to the words of the book of Genesis:

In the beginning God created the heavens and the earth. The earth was barren, with no form of life; it was under a roaring ocean covered with darkness. But the Spirit of God was moving over the water.

God said, "I command light to shine!" And light started shining. God looked at the light and saw that it was good. He separated light from darkness and named the light "Day" and the darkness "Night." Evening came and then morning—that was the first day.

The word of the Lord.

■ REFLECTION

Even though God created everything, not everything is perfect. Why is that? The writer of this story began with the creation of light. Why is this a good way to begin?

■ CLOSING

Let us all say: All the ends of the earth
    have seen the power of God.
**All the ends of the earth
    have seen the power of God.**

Let us remember these intentions:

Blessed are you, Lord our God,
    Creator of the universe.
You fill the world with your glory,
    and give it to us as a home.
Teach us to recognize its wonders,
    to treasure its variety,
    and to protect its fragile beauty.
We ask this through Christ our Lord. **Amen.**

Let us pray with the words that Jesus taught us:
Our Father . . .

▶ sing
"alleluia"

WEDNESDAY PRAYER

October 4, 2000

Reminder: You can use the Blessing of Pets on page 56 today.

■ INTRODUCTION

Today we honor Saint Francis of Assisi. Francis was rich and happy when he was growing up. But then he became very sick and he was captured in a war. His suffering made him think more about God. He decided to change his life.

So Francis gave away all his money, all his fine clothes and other things. He lived as poor as poor can be, and he became a traveling preacher and a poet.

Wherever Francis went, he asked nothing for himself. He worked for the poor, he tried to bring peace, and he showed great love for all of God's creatures. All over the world people have followed his example.

■ A PSALM FOR OCTOBER

turn to page 48

■ READING

Genesis 1:6–8

Listen to the words of the book of Genesis:

God said, "I command a dome to separate the water above [the earth] from the water below [the earth]." And that's what happened. God made the dome and named it "Sky."

Evening came and then morning—that was the second day.

The word of the Lord.

■ REFLECTION

In what ways do the creatures of the earth depend on water? How does the atmosphere that surrounds the earth protect earth's creatures? What can we do to help protect the water and the air?

■ CLOSING

Let us all say: All the ends of the earth
    have seen the power of God.
**All the ends of the earth
    have seen the power of God.**

Let us remember these intentions:

Blessed are you, Lord our God,
    Creator of the universe.
You fill the world with your glory,
    and give it to us as a home.
Teach us to recognize its wonders,
    to treasure its variety,
    and to protect its fragile beauty.
We ask this through Christ our Lord. **Amen.**

Let us pray with the words that Jesus taught us:

Our Father . . .

sing
"alleluia"

A Blessing of Pets

An image of Saint Francis can be put in a place of honor. If the blessing takes place indoors, and you leave your pets at home, add photos or drawings of them to a bulletin board, prayer center or shrine. If your pets are brought from home, the blessing may take place outdoors. Always be sure to keep your pets' safety in mind.

For this blessing, one leader and two readers are needed. Begin and end with a song such as "All creatures of our God and king" (page 100 in the Hymnal for Catholic Students).

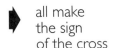
all make
the sign
of the cross

LEADER
Let us bless the Lord,
now and for ever.

ALL
Amen.

LEADER
Animals fill the skies, the earth and the seas. They are God's beloved creatures. Saint Francis remembered this. He called the animals his brothers and sisters.

Today we ask God to bless these animals, our brothers and sisters. We thank God for letting us share the earth with such wonderful and amazing creatures.

FIRST READER   Genesis 1:20–21
Listen to the words of the book of Genesis:

God said, "I command the ocean to be full of living creatures, and I command birds to fly above the earth." So God made the giant sea monsters and all the living creatures that swim in the ocean. He also made every kind of bird. God looked at what he had done, and it was good.

SECOND READER   Genesis 1:24–25
God said, "I command the earth to give life to all kinds of tame animals, wild animals, and reptiles." And that's what happened. God made every one of them. Then he looked at what he had done, and it was good.

The word of the Lord.

LEADER
O God our creator,
 everything that has the breath of life
 gives you praise!

hold out one hand
over the animals
in blessing, and say:

Lord, with love and compassion,
 watch over our pets and all animals.
Keep them in good health.
Guard them against trouble.

May the wisdom of Saint Francis
 and our love for these animals
 deepen our respect for all your creation.
We ask this through Christ our Lord.

ALL
Amen.

all make
the sign
of the cross

THURSDAY PRAYER

October 5, 2000

■ INTRODUCTION

On this day in 1703, Jonathan Edwards was born. He became a great Puritan preacher and spiritual guide. He often spoke of the difference between knowing about God, and feeling God's own presence and goodness. He compared it to the difference between knowing that honey is sweet, and actually tasting its sweetness. He called that difference a "sense of the heart."

All of creation spoke to Jonathan Edwards about God. He wrote, "God's excellency, his wisdom, his purity and love, seemed to appear in every thing: in the sun, moon, and stars; in the clouds and blue sky, in the grass, flowers, trees; in the water, and all nature."

■ A PSALM FOR OCTOBER

➤ turn to page 48

■ READING

Genesis 1:9–13

Listen to the words of the book of Genesis:

God said, "I command the water under the sky to come together in one place, so there will be dry ground." And that's what happened. God named the dry ground "Land," and he named the water "Ocean." God looked at what he had done and saw that it was good.

God said, "I command the earth to produce all kinds of plants, including fruit trees and grain." And that's what happened. The earth produced all kinds of vegetation *(veh-jih-TAY-shun)*. God looked at what he had done, and it was good. Evening came and then morning—that was the third day.

The word of the Lord.

■ REFLECTION

How do we know that God wants us to be creative too? What do I enjoy creating? Do I notice and praise the work of others? What can we do today to celebrate water, plants and trees?

■ CLOSING

Let us all say: All the ends of the earth
    have seen the power of God.
**All the ends of the earth
    have seen the power of God.**

Let us remember these intentions:

Blessed are you, Lord our God,
    Creator of the universe.
You fill the world with your glory,
    and give it to us as a home.
Teach us to recognize its wonders,
    to treasure its variety,
    and to protect its fragile beauty.
We ask this through Christ our Lord. **Amen.**

Let us pray with the words that Jesus taught us:
Our Father . . .

➤ sing "alleluia"

FRIDAY PRAYER

October 6, 2000

■ INTRODUCTION

Today we remember William Tyndale *(TIN-dull),* an English priest. William wanted to translate the Bible into English, but the officials said no.

William did it anyway. He spent his life traveling and hiding so that he could carry on his work. In 1526, he finished the New Testament, and his friends began smuggling copies into England. When he was captured in 1536, his work was almost complete. There are two copies left of that first English-language New Testament. They are real treasures.

William Tyndale loved the word of God. He gave his life so that people could read it for themselves. We can be thankful for William Tyndale when we hear today's reading in our own language.

■ A PSALM FOR OCTOBER

▶ turn to
page 48

■ READING

Genesis 1:14–19

Listen to the words of the book of Genesis:

God said, "I command lights to appear in the sky and to separate day from night and to show the time for seasons, special days, and years. I command them to shine on the earth." And that's what happened. God made two powerful lights, the brighter one to rule the day and the other to rule the night. He also made the stars. Then God put these lights in the sky to shine on the earth, to rule day and night and to separate light from darkness.

God looked at what he had done, and it was good. Evening came and then morning—that was the fourth day.

The word of the Lord.

■ REFLECTION

How much do I know about the solar system and the galaxy? What stories about stars can we share? What do stars teach me about God?

■ CLOSING

Let us all say: All the ends of the earth
   have seen the power of God.
All the ends of the earth
   have seen the power of God.

Let us remember these intentions:

Blessed are you, Lord our God,
   Creator of the universe.
You fill the world with your glory,
   and give it to us as a home.
Teach us to recognize its wonders,
   to treasure its variety,
   and to protect its fragile beauty.
We ask this through Christ our Lord. **Amen.**

Let us pray with the words that Jesus taught us:

Our Father . . .

▶ sing
"alleluia"

WEEKLY PRAYER

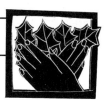

With a reading from the Gospel for Sunday, October 8, 2000

■ INTRODUCTION

Some things are only for adults. Only adults are allowed to drive cars or to run for president. Others things are only for children, such as playing T-ball or taking spelling tests. But most things are for people of all ages.

Belonging to the church is for everyone. It is important to Jesus that people of every age work together and share his love.

In the reading today Jesus tells his followers that children should learn from adults, and adults should learn from children, also.

■ A PSALM FOR OCTOBER

➤ turn to
page 48

■ READING

Mark 10:13–16

Listen to the words of the holy gospel according to Mark:

Some people brought their children to Jesus so that he could bless them by placing his hands on them. But his disciples told the people to stop bothering him.

When Jesus saw this, he became angry and said, "Let the children come to me! Don't try to stop them. People who are like these little children belong to the kingdom of God. I promise you that you cannot get into God's kingdom, unless you accept it the way a child does."

Then Jesus took the children in his arms and blessed them by placing his hands on them.

The gospel of the Lord.

■ REFLECTION

How does it make me feel when someone hugs me? Does anyone bless me? Do I ever bless others? Do adults outgrow the need for hugs and blessings? Is there an adult who needs some hugs from me?

■ CLOSING

Let us remember these intentions:

Jesus, you are kind,
    and you want us close to you.
Accept us as your disciples.
Teach us to be faithful children
    of a loving God.
And lead us to share in your kingdom,
    where we may be joyful with you,
    now and for ever. Amen.

Let us pray with the words that Jesus taught us:

Our Father . . .

➤ sing
"alleluia"

MONDAY PRAYER

October 9, 2000

■ INTRODUCTION

At sundown last night, Yom Kippur *(yahm kee-POOR)* began. It is the Day of Atonement *(uh-TONE-ment)*, the most holy day on the Jewish calendar. The need to ask God for forgiveness is so important that Jews do not work or travel on this day. They pray and fast. They apologize to people they have hurt.

This is Columbus Day in the United States, and a holiday for many families. It is also Thanksgiving Day in Canada. Let us join with people all over the world who today offer prayers of forgiveness and thanksgiving.

■ A PSALM FOR OCTOBER

► turn to
page 48

■ READING

Genesis 1:20–23

Listen to the words the book of Genesis:

God said, "I command the ocean to be full of living creatures, and I command birds to fly above the earth." So God made the giant sea monsters and all the living creatures that swim in the ocean. He also made every kind of bird. God looked at what he had done, and it was good. Then he gave the living creatures his blessing—he told the ocean creatures to live everywhere in the ocean and the birds to live everywhere on earth.

Evening came and then morning—that was the fifth day.

The word of the Lord.

■ REFLECTION

What would our world be like without birds and fish? Can we name the kinds of birds that we have seen in our neighborhood? How is helping the environment a religious duty? How do we help?

■ CLOSING

Let us remember these intentions:

Loving God, you are quick to forgive
   all who ask your forgiveness.
Give life and peace
   to those who keep the Day of Atonement.
Strengthen the Jewish community.
Make them secure in their homes
   around the world.
We ask this through Christ our Lord. **Amen.**

Let us pray with the words that Jesus taught us:

Our Father . . .

► sing
"alleluia"

TUESDAY PRAYER

October 10, 2000

■ INTRODUCTION

Today we remember an English priest who awakened the interest of modern Catholics in the stories of the saints. Alban *(ALL-bun)* Butler was born on this date in 1710. At that time people told many fanciful stories about the saints. People did not know what to believe about them. Alban Butler helped them learn.

After years of study, Father Butler wrote a book with the stories of more than 1600 saints. He tried to show his readers that saints had to struggle against their weaknesses, just as we all do. Yet they all managed to become what God called them to be. Almost 300 years after his death, Butler's *Lives of the Saints* is still being published, to teach and inspire new generations of saints.

■ A PSALM FOR OCTOBER

 turn to
page 48

■ READING

Genesis 1:24–28, 31

Listen to the words of the book of Genesis:

God said, "I command the earth to give life to all kinds of tame animals, wild animals, and reptiles." And that's what happened. God made every one of them. Then he looked at what he had done, and it was good.

God said, "Now we will make humans, and they will be like us. We will let them rule the fish, the birds, and all other living creatures."

So God created humans to be like himself; he made men and women. God gave them his blessing and said, "Have lots of children! Fill the earth with people and bring it under your control. Rule over the fish in the ocean, the birds in the sky, and every animal on the earth."

God looked at what he had done. All of it was very good!

Evening came and then morning—that was the sixth day.

The word of the Lord.

■ REFLECTION

How do humans rule over some parts of nature? Does the Bible say that humans can do anything they want to the world?

■ CLOSING

Let us remember these intentions:

Blessed are you, Lord our God,
    Creator of the universe.
You fill the world with your glory,
    and give it to us as a home.
Teach us to recognize its wonders,
    to treasure its variety,
    and to protect its fragile beauty.
We ask this through Christ our Lord. **Amen.**

Let us pray with the words that Jesus taught us:

Our Father . . .

 sing
"alleluia"

WEDNESDAY PRAYER

October 11, 2000

■ INTRODUCTION

Today we remember Casimir Pulaski *(KAH-zih-meer pull-LASS-key)*. He is a national hero of Poland, where he was born, and of the United States, where he died on this day in 1779. Pulaski believed that the ideals of freedom and citizenship were very important. So he came to help George Washington in the work of creating a new nation based on these ideals.

This is a good day to learn more about some of the people who have shaped our nation.

■ A PSALM FOR OCTOBER

▶ turn to
page 48

■ READING

Genesis 2:1–4

Listen to the words of the book of Genesis:

[During six days] the heavens and the earth and everything else were created. By the seventh day God had finished his work, and so he rested. God blessed the seventh day and made it special because on that day he rested from his work.

That's how God created the heavens and the earth.

The word of the Lord.

■ REFLECTION

Saturday, the seventh day, is kept as a holy day by Jews all over the world. Sunday, the first day,

is kept as the holy day by Christians. What special things can we do this weekend to thank God for creation? Why is a holy day of rest and prayer important?

■ CLOSING

Let us all say: All the ends of the earth
   have seen the power of God.
**All the ends of the earth
   have seen the power of God.**

Let us remember these intentions:

Blessed are you, Lord our God,
   Creator of the universe.
You fill the world with your glory,
   and give it to us as a home.
Teach us to recognize its wonders,
   to treasure its variety,
   and to protect its fragile beauty.
We ask this through Christ our Lord. **Amen.**

Let us pray with the words that Jesus taught us:
Our Father . . .

▶ sing
"alleluia"

THURSDAY PRAYER

October 12, 2000

■ INTRODUCTION

The book of Genesis tells of the beginning of the earth and the beginning of the human race. Today we will hear about the beginning of sin.

This story was written at a time when many people believed that there were good gods and evil gods. They thought that the evil gods had power over human beings and could cause bad things to happen. The Hebrew storyteller wanted to remind us that there is only one God. God is good and does not make evil. Listen to the story and find out where evil comes from.

■ A PSALM FOR OCTOBER

➤ turn to
page 48

■ READING

Genesis 3:1–3, 4–5, 5–7

Listen to the words of the book of Genesis:

The snake was sneakier than any of the other wild animals that the LORD God had made. One day it came to the woman and asked, "Did God tell you not to eat fruit from any tree in the garden?"

The woman answered, "God said we could eat fruit from any tree in the garden, except the one in the middle. He told us not to eat fruit from that tree or even to touch it."

The snake replied, "God understands what will happen on the day you eat fruit from that tree. You will know the difference between right and wrong, just as God does."

The woman stared at the fruit. It looked beautiful and tasty. She wanted the wisdom that it would give her, and she ate some of the fruit. Her husband was there with her, so she gave some to him, and he ate it too. Right away they saw what they had done.

The word of the Lord.

■ REFLECTION

What are some of the things in this world that look "beautiful and tasty" but are forbidden? Do I sometimes want to decide for myself what is right and what is wrong?

■ CLOSING

Let us remember these intentions:

God, our creator,
   you give us your law as a gift
   and not a burden.
It guides us to live in peace with you,
   with each other, and within ourselves.
Help us to keep your law with all our hearts.
We ask this through Christ our Lord. **Amen.**

Let us pray with the words that Jesus taught us:

Our Father . . .

➤ sing
"alleluia"

63

FRIDAY PRAYER

October 13, 2000

■ INTRODUCTION

Today is the first day of the Jewish feast of Sukkot *(soo-COAT)*. Many Jewish people build a booth in their yard or meeting place for this celebration. Each booth is decorated with fruits, vegetables, bright fabrics and drawings. The booths remind us of the harvest shelters people once built in the fields.

■ A PSALM FOR OCTOBER

turn to
page 48

■ READING

Genesis 3:8-9, 11–13, 23

Listen to the words of the book of Genesis:

Late in the afternoon a breeze began to blow, and the man and woman heard the LORD God walking in the garden. They were frightened and hid behind some trees.

The LORD called out to the man and asked, "Did you eat any fruit from that tree in the middle of the garden?"

"It was the woman you put here with me," the man said. "She gave me some of the fruit, and I ate it."

The LORD God then asked the woman, "What have you done?"

"The snake tricked me," she answered. "And I ate some of that fruit."

So the LORD God sent them out of the Garden to a place where they would have to work the ground from which the man had been made.

The word of the Lord.

■ REFLECTION

When we have done something wrong, why do we often try to hide? Why did the man blame the woman? Why did the woman blame the snake? Why do we try to blame something or someone else for what we have done?

■ CLOSING

Let us remember these intentions:

Our God is good and generous,
  giving plants for food and shelter,
  giving flowers for beauty,
  giving sunshine and rain
  for the growth of all living things.
With all who offer songs of thanksgiving
  we join our voices.
O God, give life and peace
  to those who keep the festival of Sukkot.
Strengthen the Jewish community.
Make them secure in their homes
  around the world,
  for ever and ever. **Amen.**

Let us pray with the words that Jesus taught us:

Our Father . . .

sing
"alleluia"

WEEKLY PRAYER

With a Reading from the Gospel for Sunday, October 15, 2000

■ INTRODUCTION

We live in a world that is filled with things: things to wear, things to work with, things to make our life easier.

Sometimes we forget that things are not as important as people. The commandments of God teach us to love and respect other people. The young man in today's reading found that a hard lesson to learn. This reading is taken from the gospel of Sunday, October 15.

■ A PSALM FOR OCTOBER

➤ turn to
  page 48

■ READING

Mark 10:17, 19–22

Listen to the words of the holy gospel according to Mark:

As Jesus was walking down a road, a man ran up to him. He knelt down, and asked, "Good teacher, what can I do to have eternal life?"

Jesus replied, "You know the commandments. 'Do not murder. Be faithful in marriage. Do not steal. Do not tell lies about others. Do not cheat. Respect your father and mother.'"

The man answered, "Teacher, I have obeyed all these commandments since I was a young man."

Jesus looked closely at the man. He liked him and said, "There's one thing you still need to do. Go sell everything you own. Give the money to the poor, and you will have riches in heaven. Then come with me."

When the man heard Jesus say this, he went away gloomy and sad because he was very rich.

The gospel of the Lord.

■ REFLECTION

What do I think Jesus means by this teaching? When have I seen possessions cause problems? When might a person's love of possessions conflict with a person's love for Jesus?

■ CLOSING

Let us remember these intentions:

God our creator,
 you give us your law as a gift
 and not a burden.
It guides us to live in peace with you,
 with each other, and within ourselves.
Help us to keep your law with all our hearts.
We ask this through Christ our Lord. **Amen.**

Let us pray with the words that Jesus taught us:

Our Father . . .

➤ sing
  "alleluia"

65

■ INTRODUCTION

Today's reading will begin the story of Abram and Sarai *(SAIR-eye)*. They made an agreement with God for themselves and their whole family.

God promised to be their God, and to watch over them. God also promised that they would have a great family, and a land where they could make their home. All God asked was that they remain faithful, following the way of life God would teach them. Abram and Sarai put their faith in the love and promises of God.

The agreement between God and Abram and Sarai is called the covenant. They became the first members of the people of the covenant.

■ A PSALM FOR OCTOBER

➤ turn to page 48

■ READING

Genesis 12:1–2, 3, 4, 5, 7

Listen to the words of the book of Genesis:

The LORD said to Abram, "Leave your country, your family, and your relatives and go to the land that I will show you. I will bless you and make your descendants into a great nation. You will become famous and you will be a blessing to others. Everyone on earth will be blessed because of you."

Abram obeyed and left with his wife Sarai *(SAIR-eye),* his nephew Lot, and all their possessions.

When they came to the land of Canaan *(KAY-nun),* the LORD appeared to Abram and promised, "I will give this land to your family forever." Abram then built an altar there for the LORD.

The word of the Lord.

■ REFLECTION

What is the land of Canaan called today? Do I know anyone who left home in order to follow God's call?

■ CLOSING

The Lord is good and listens to our prayers. Let us pray for those who need God's help.

For people who have lost their homes,
    let us pray to the Lord: **Lord, have mercy.**
For people who are far from their families,
    let us pray to the Lord: **Lord, have mercy.**
For all travelers and refugees,
    let us pray to the Lord: **Lord, have mercy.**

Let us also remember these intentions:

Loving God, have mercy on all your people.
Keep us close to your heart.
We ask this through Christ our Lord. **Amen.**

Let us pray with the words that Jesus taught us:

Our Father . . .

➤ sing "alleluia"

TUESDAY PRAYER

October 17, 2000

■ INTRODUCTION

Today we remember Saint Ignatius (*ig-NAY-shus),* who learned about Jesus from the apostles and became a strong Christian. The people of Antioch *(AN-tee-ock)* elected him to be their bishop. When Ignatius was put in prison because of his faith, he wrote letters to strengthen the faith of the people. "I will gladly die for God if only you do not stand in my way," he wrote. He died on this date in about the year 107.

Today we continue the story of Abram and Sarai *(SAIR-eye).* They have settled in Canaan *(KAY-nun)* and have many sheep, tents and workers.

■ A PSALM FOR OCTOBER

► turn to
page 48

■ READING

Genesis 15:1–2, 3–6

Listen to the words of the book of Genesis:

The LORD spoke to Abram in a vision, "Abram, don't be afraid! I will protect you and reward you greatly."

But Abram answered, "LORD All-Powerful, you have given me everything I could ask for, except children. And when I die, this servant of mine will inherit everything."

The LORD replied, "No, he won't! You will have a son of your own and everything you have will be his." Then the LORD took Abram outside and said, "Look at the sky and see if you can count the stars. That's how many descendants you will have." Abram believed the LORD, and the LORD was pleased with him.

The word of the Lord.

■ REFLECTION

Abram believed God's promise. What other promises of God do we know about? Do I believe in God's promises to me?

■ CLOSING

The Lord is good and listens to our prayers. Let us pray for those who need God's help.

For people whose parents abuse them,
    let us pray to the Lord: **Lord, have mercy.**
For people who have trouble with schoolwork,
    let us pray to the Lord: **Lord, have mercy.**
For people who want to have children,
    let us pray to the Lord: **Lord, have mercy.**

Let us also remember these intentions:

Loving God, have mercy on all your people. Keep us close to your heart. We ask this through Christ our Lord. **Amen.**

Let us pray with the words that Jesus taught us:

Our Father . . .

► sing "alleluia"

WEDNESDAY PRAYER

October 18, 2000

■ INTRODUCTION

Today Christians celebrate the feast of Luke the evangelist *(ee-VAN-jel-ist)*. Luke wrote the third gospel and the book called the Acts of the Apostles. He was a doctor, and some people think he also was an artist. Luke became a Christian after Jesus had ascended to his Father, so Luke had to learn about Jesus from other Christians. Luke became a missionary. He traveled with Saint Paul and brought the good news of Jesus to many nations.

   To honor Saint Luke today we will read the introduction to his gospel.

■ A PSALM FOR OCTOBER

turn to
page 48

■ READING

Luke 1:1–4

Listen to the words of the holy gospel according to Luke:

Many people have tried to give an orderly account of the events that happened among us. They have written down just what was told to them by the people who actually saw these events. Information also came from those who serve God by bringing the word to others.

   I have carefully studied everything that happened, from the very first. I have decided to write an orderly account for you, Theophilus *(thee-AH-fill-us)*. Then you will see that what you have been taught is true.

The gospel of the Lord.

■ REFLECTION

What are the events that Luke is going to put in order? What would have happened to the stories of Jesus if the evangelists had not written them down? Do we treat the gospels with respect? Do I ever read them on my own?

■ CLOSING

Let us remember these intentions:

Divine Wisdom,
   you led Saint Luke
   and other men and women
   to put into the holy Bible
   words that would bring us closer to you.
Help us understand the Bible
   better and better each day.
Let your word, like good seed,
   take root in our hearts
   and bear fruit in our lives.
We ask this through Christ our Lord. **Amen.**

Let us pray with the words that Jesus taught us:

Our Father . . .

sing
"alleluia"

THURSDAY PRAYER

October 19, 2000

■ INTRODUCTION

Today we remember eight French missionaries who came to North America about 350 years ago. They were killed for preaching the gospel. Two of them were Isaac *(EYE-zik)* Jogues and John de Brébeuf *(bray-BUFF)*.

Even now, Christians often risk danger to preach the gospel. Let us pray for missionaries around the world today.

■ A PSALM FOR OCTOBER

turn to page 48

■ READING

Genesis 18:1, 1–5, 6, 8, 10

Listen to the words of the book of Genesis:

One hot summer afternoon Abraham was sitting by the entrance to his tent, when the LORD appeared to him. Abraham looked up and saw three men standing nearby. He quickly ran to meet them, bowed with his face to the ground, and said, "Please come to my home where I can serve you. I'll have some water brought, so you can wash your feet, then you can rest under the tree. Let me get you some food to give you strength before you leave."

Abraham quickly went to his tent and said to Sarah, "Hurry! Get a large sack of flour and make some bread." He then served his guests some yogurt and milk together with the meat.

One of the guests was the LORD, and he said, "I'll come back about this time next year, and when I do, Sarah will already have a son."

The word of the Lord.

■ REFLECTION

Abraham and Sarah gave hospitality to the travelers, and God blessed them. What other Bible stories tell about sharing food? How do people I know show hospitality?

■ CLOSING

The Lord is good and listens to our prayers. Let us pray for those who need God's help.

For people who are hungry,
    let us pray to the Lord: **Lord, have mercy.**
For people who share with others,
    let us pray to the Lord: **Lord, have mercy.**
For people who bring good news,
    let us pray to the Lord: **Lord, have mercy.**

Let us also remember these intentions:

Loving God, have mercy on all your people. Keep us close to your heart. We ask this through Christ our Lord. **Amen.**

Let us pray with the words that Jesus taught us: **Our Father . . .**

sing "alleluia"

69

FRIDAY PRAYER

October 20, 2000

■ INTRODUCTION

Today we remember Saint Bertilla Boscardin. Bertilla's father was an alcoholic *(al-kuh-HAW-lick),* and he was often violent. Her family was poor, so Bertilla did not go to school much. But she did not let these problems keep her from what she wanted to do with her life. She became a sister and spent many years caring for sick children in a hospital. She died on this day in the year 1922.

■ A PSALM FOR OCTOBER

➤ turn to page 48

■ READING

Genesis 21:1–4, 6

Listen to the words of the book of Genesis:

The LORD was good to Sarah and kept his promise. Although Abraham was very old, Sarah had a son exactly at the time God had said. Abraham named his son Isaac *(EYE-zik),* and when the boy was eight days old, Abraham circumcised *(SIR-kum-sized)* him, just as the LORD had commanded.

Sarah said, "God has made me laugh. Now everyone will laugh with me."

The word of the Lord.

■ REFLECTION

Sarah laughed with joy over her son. Do we ever make our parents laugh with joy? The name "Isaac" means "laughter." Does my name have a meaning? Why did my parents choose it?

■ CLOSING

The Lord is good and listens to our prayers. Let us pray for those who need God's help.

For families that have new babies,
   let us pray to the Lord: **Lord, have mercy.**
For families where there is much laughter,
   let us pray to the Lord: **Lord, have mercy.**
For families where there is much sadness,
   let us pray to the Lord: **Lord, have mercy.**

Let us also remember these intentions:

Loving God, have mercy on all your people.
Keep us close to your heart.
We ask this through Christ our Lord. **Amen.**

Let us pray with the words that Jesus taught us:
Our Father . . .

➤ sing "alleluia"

WEEKLY PRAYER

With a Reading from the Gospel for Sunday, October 22, 2000

◼ INTRODUCTION

On most Sundays during the past year we have listened to readings from the gospel of Mark. In Mark's gospel Jesus never stops teaching about the rule of God.

God does not rule the way kings and queens rule. God's kingdom has no army. It has no police force. Its only power is love. God shows us love and respect, and in return we trust and respect God. Because of that we let God have authority in our hearts. That is where God wants to rule.

Today's reading tells us more about the rule of God.

◼ A PSALM FOR OCTOBER

▶ turn to
page 48

◼ READING

Mark 10:35–37, 39, 40–42, 43

Listen to the words of the holy gospel according to Mark:

James and John, the sons of Zebedee *(ZEH-beh-dee),* came up to Jesus and asked, "Teacher, will you do us a favor?" Jesus asked them what they wanted, and they answered, "When you come into your glory, please let one of us sit at your right side and the other at your left."

Then Jesus replied, "It isn't for me to say who will sit at my right side and at my left. That is for God to decide."

When the ten other disciples heard this, they were angry with James and John. But Jesus called the disciples together and said, "You know that those who call themselves kings like to order their people around. But don't act like them. If you want to be great, you must be the servant of all the others."

The gospel of the Lord.

◼ REFLECTION

Why do most people like to be first? Do I get angry at people who try to take the first place? Why? What would happen at school if everyone helped others and no one tried to be the first?

◼ CLOSING

Let us remember these intentions:

God of grace and wisdom,
   you continually raise up good people
   who show with their lives
   that they follow a holy and loving God.
Let our lives be as true as our faith.
We ask this through Christ our Lord. **Amen.**

Let us pray with the words that Jesus taught us:

Our Father . . .

▶ sing
"alleluia"

MONDAY PRAYER

October 23, 2000

◼ INTRODUCTION

In the days of Abraham and Sarah it was a father's duty to find a good wife for his son. When Isaac *(EYE-zik)* grew up, Abraham sent a trusted servant to his hometown to choose a bride from among his relatives. The servant looked for someone kind and generous.

◼ A PSALM FOR OCTOBER

 turn to
page 48

◼ READING

Genesis 24:11, 12–14, 15, 17–18, 19, 21

Listen to the words of the book of Genesis:

When the servant got there, he let the camels rest near the well outside the city. The servant prayed, "You, LORD, are the God my master Abraham worships. Please keep your promise to him and let me find a wife for Isaac today. The young women of the city will soon come to this well for water, and I'll ask one of them for a drink. If she gives me a drink and then offers to get some water for my camels, I'll know she is the one you have chosen."

While he was still praying, a beautiful unmarried young woman came by with a water jar on her shoulder. She was Rebekah *(ruh-BEK-uh)*. Abraham's servant ran to her and said, "Please let me have a drink of water."

"I'll be glad to," she answered. After he had finished, she said, "Now I'll give your camels all the water they want."

Abraham's servant did not say a word, but he watched everything Rebekah did, because he wanted to know for certain if this was the woman the LORD had chosen.

The word of the Lord.

◼ REFLECTION

What did it show when Rebekah gave water to the camels? What qualities will I look for in the person I marry?

◼ CLOSING

The Lord is good and listens to our prayers. Let us pray for those who need God's help.

For people who seek good husbands or wives,
    let us pray to the Lord: **Lord, have mercy.**
For people who trust in the word of God,
    let us pray to the Lord: **Lord, have mercy.**
For people who give water to the thirsty,
    let us pray to the Lord: **Lord, have mercy.**

Let us also remember these intentions:

Loving God, have mercy on all your people.
Keep us close to your heart.
We ask this through Christ our Lord. **Amen.**

Let us pray with the words that Jesus taught us:

Our Father . . .

 sing
"alleluia"

■ INTRODUCTION

Today we remember Saint Anthony Claret *(CLAIR-et)*. He was born in Spain in 1807. For six years Anthony was bishop of Cuba. His great love for others taught many people to be better Christians. But his concern for the slaves in Cuba turned the slave owners against him. Fifteen attempts were made on his life, and finally the slave owners had Anthony sent back to Spain. Anthony was a fine writer. He is a patron saint of writers and of the nation of Cuba.

■ A PSALM FOR OCTOBER

turn to page 48

■ READING

Genesis 25:19–20, 21–22, 24–26, 27–28

Listen to the words of the book of Genesis:

Isaac *(EYE-zik)* was the son of Abraham, and he was forty years old when he married Rebekah *(ruh-BEK-uh)*. Isaac asked the LORD to let her have a child, and the LORD answered his prayer.

Before Rebekah gave birth, she knew she was going to have twins, because she could feel them inside her, fighting each other. When Rebekah gave birth, the first baby was covered with red hair, so he was named Esau *(EE-saw)*. The second baby grabbed on to his brother's heel, so they named him Jacob.

As Jacob and Esau grew older, Esau liked the outdoors and became a good hunter, while Jacob settled down and became a shepherd.

Esau would take the meat of wild animals to his father Isaac, and so Isaac loved him more, but Jacob was his mother's favorite son.

The word of the Lord.

■ REFLECTION

What do I think about the way Isaac and Rebekah loved one child more than another? How do we try to love all of our family members?

■ CLOSING

The Lord is good and listens to our prayers.
Let us pray for those who need God's help

For people who love their families,
    let us pray to the Lord: **Lord have mercy.**
For people who are good at outdoor activities,
    let us pray to the Lord: **Lord, have mercy.**
For people who are quiet and shy,
    let us pray to the Lord: **Lord, have mercy.**

Let us remember these intentions:

Loving God, have mercy on all your people.
Keep us close to your heart.
We ask this through Christ our Lord. **Amen.**

Let us pray with the words that Jesus taught us:
Our Father . . .

sing "alleluia"

WEDNESDAY PRAYER

■ INTRODUCTION

Today's reading is a famous story about Jacob. In a dream Jacob sees angel messengers going up and down a ladder to heaven. In the story we hear God repeat the promise that was made to Abraham and Sarah.

In each generation, God renews the covenant. All those who are children of Abraham and Sarah through birth or faith are part of the covenant. The covenant is a bond of love and trust that has shaped the people of God from that day until now.

■ A PSALM FOR OCTOBER

turn to
page 48

■ READING

Genesis 28:11–13, 14–16, 17

Listen to the words of the book of Genesis:

At sunset Jacob stopped for the night and went to sleep, resting his head on a large rock. In a dream he saw a ladder that reached from earth to heaven, and God's angels were going up and down on it.

The LORD was standing beside the ladder and said, "I am the LORD God who was worshiped by Abraham and Isaac *(EYE-zik)*. Your descendants will spread over the earth in all directions and will become as numerous as the specks of dust. Your family will be a blessing to all people. Wherever you go, I will watch over you, and later I will bring you back to this land. I won't leave you—I will do all I have promised."

Jacob woke up suddenly and thought, "The LORD is in this place, and I didn't even know it. It must be the house of God and the ladder to heaven."

The word of the Lord.

■ REFLECTION

Where have I felt God close to me? What might Jacob's dream mean?

■ CLOSING

The Lord is good and listens to our prayers. Let us pray for those who need God's help.

For people who do not know of God's closeness,
    let us pray to the Lord: **Lord, have mercy.**
For people who speak to God in prayer,
    let us pray to the Lord: **Lord, have mercy.**
For all the descendants of Abraham, Isaac
    and Jacob,
    let us pray to the Lord: **Lord, have mercy.**

Let us also remember these intentions:

Loving God, have mercy on all your people. Keep us close to your heart. We ask this through Christ our Lord. **Amen.**

Let us pray with the words that Jesus taught us:

Our Father . . .

 sing "alleluia"

 Reminder: You may want to make copies of November's Psalm, Meal Prayer and End of the Day Prayer, page 84 to 86.

■ INTRODUCTION

In today's reading we find that the twins Jacob and Esau *(EE-saw)* are enemies. It began when Jacob cheated his brother. Esau tried to kill Jacob, but Jacob escaped. After many years, Jacob decided to make peace with his brother.

■ A PSALM FOR OCTOBER

 turn to page 48

■ READING

Genesis 32:3, 4, 5–6, 9, 11; 33:1, 4, 10

Listen to the words of the book of Genesis:

Jacob sent messengers to say to Esau *(EE-saw),* "Master, I have lived with Laban *(LAY-bun)* all this time, and now I own cattle, donkeys, and sheep. Master, I am sending these messengers in the hope that you will be kind to me."

When the messengers returned, they told Jacob, "We went to your brother Esau, and now he is heading this way with four hundred men."

Then Jacob prayed: "You, LORD, are the God who was worshiped by my grandfather Abraham and by my father Isaac *(EYE-zik).* Please rescue me from my brother. I am afraid he will come and attack not only me, but my wives and children as well."

Later that day Jacob met Esau coming with his four hundred men. But Esau ran toward Jacob and hugged and kissed him. Then the two brothers started crying.

Jacob said, "When you welcomed me and I saw your face, it was like seeing the face of God."

The word of the Lord.

■ REFLECTION

Am I as forgiving as Esau? How is a person who forgives like God? How do I ask forgiveness?

■ CLOSING

The Lord is good and listens to our prayers.
Let us pray for those who need God's help.

For people who forgive others from their hearts,
    let us pray to the Lord: **Lord,** have mercy.
For people who need to ask forgiveness,
    let us pray to the Lord: **Lord, have mercy.**
For people who are peacemakers,
    let us pray to the Lord: **Lord, have mercy.**

Let us also remember these intentions:

Loving God, have mercy on all your people.
Keep us close to your heart.
We ask this through Christ our Lord. **Amen.**

Let us pray with the words that Jesus taught us:
Our Father . . .

 sing "alleluia"

75

■ INTRODUCTION

On this day in 1466, Desiderius Erasmus *(day-sih-DAY-ree-us ee-RAZ-muss)* was born in Holland. He became a priest and traveled to many countries studying, preaching and writing.

Erasmus used his learning and his sense of humor to wake up people who were false or lazy Christians. He tried to make peace between people who wanted to reform the church and others who wanted the reformers punished. Erasmus urged all to be calm, open and loving when they discussed the faith of the church. It broke his heart to see the church divided when Jesus had prayed that all might be one.

■ A PSALM FOR OCTOBER

→ turn to
page 48

■ READING

Romans 4:16, 18, 20

Listen to the words of the apostle Paul:

Everything depends on having faith in God, so that God's promise is assured by his great kindness. This promise isn't only for Abraham's descendants who have the Law. It is for all who are Abraham's descendants because they have faith, just as he did. Abraham is the ancestor of us all.

God promised Abraham a lot of descendants. And when it all seemed hopeless, Abraham still had faith in God and became the ancestor of many nations. Abraham never doubted or ques-tioned God's promise. His faith made him strong, and he gave all the credit to God.

The word of the Lord.

■ REFLECTION

Is my faith in God strong? What do I believe about God? Abraham is the father of Jews, Christians and Muslims. How then should Jews, Christians and Muslims treat each other?

■ CLOSING

Let us remember these intentions:

God of the covenant,
  you promised Abraham
  that he would be the father of many nations.
Grant to Jewish, Christian and Muslim
  believers around the world
  faith in your mercy,
  hope in your promises,
  and unity in their love for you.
We ask this through Christ our Lord. **Amen.**

Let us pray with the words that Jesus taught us:

Our Father . . .

→ sing
"alleluia"

WEEKLY PRAYER

With a Reading from the Gospel of Sunday, October 29, 2000

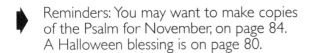

Reminders: You may want to make copies of the Psalm for November, on page 84. A Halloween blessing is on page 80.

■ INTRODUCTION

In today's reading we hear the story of a blind man who lived by begging. When Jesus came, the blind man was not afraid to ask him for what he needed. We too need things that only God can give us. God is near to us when we pray, so let us ask God for the things we need.

■ A PSALM FOR OCTOBER

turn to page 48

■ READING

Mark 10:46–52

Listen to the words of the holy gospel according to Mark:

A blind beggar by the name of Bartimaeus *(bar-tih-MAY-us)* was sitting beside the road. When he heard that Jesus was walking by, he shouted, "Jesus, Son of David, have pity on me!" Many people told the man to stop, but he shouted even louder, "Son of David, have pity on me!"

Jesus stopped and said, "Call him over!"

They called out to the blind man and said, "Don't be afraid! Come on! He is calling for you." The man threw off his coat as he jumped up and ran to Jesus.

Jesus asked him, "What do you want me to do for you?"

The blind man answered, "Master, I want to see!" Jesus told him, "You may go. Your eyes are healed because of your faith." Right away the man could see, and he went down the road with Jesus.

The gospel of the Lord.

■ REFLECTION

Even if our eyes work well, sometimes we are blind in other ways. How? What kind of sight shall I pray for? When he could see, Bartimaeus "went down the road with Jesus." How are we able to walk with Jesus?

■ CLOSING

Let us remember these intentions:

Holy God, you give us the power to see
   so we can delight in the world you have made
   and notice the needs of those around us.
You give us the power of movement
   so we can follow you closely
   and share in the journey of your holy people.
We give you thanks that you have made us
   with such loving care.
With Christ we give you glory
   now and for ever. **Amen.**

Let us pray with the words that Jesus taught us:

Our Father . . .

sing "alleluia"

MONDAY PRAYER

October 30, 2000

> Reminders: Wednesday is All Saints' Day; Thursday is All Souls' Day. Ways of preparing for the feasts are on page 83. Talk this over with the teacher.

◼ INTRODUCTION

On Wednesday we will celebrate the feast of All Saints. Let us prepare by remembering what it means to be a saint. Sometimes we think only of the saints who have their pictures and statues in the church. But Saint Paul wrote that all members of the community who are trying to be faithful to God are saints. Sometimes we forget that when we were baptized, we were invited to become holy people who follow a holy God.

This is a day to think about the qualities that we look for in saints. Are these the qualities we look for in our friends? Are these the qualities that make people popular in our school?

◼ A PSALM FOR OCTOBER

> turn to page 48

◼ READING

I John 3:18–19, 23–24

Listen to the words of the first letter of John:

Children, you show love for others by truly helping them, and not merely talking about it. When we love others, we know that we belong to the truth, and we feel at ease in the presence of God.

God wants us to have faith in his Son Jesus Christ and to love each other. This is also what Jesus taught us to do. If we obey God's commandments, we will stay one in our hearts with him, and he will stay one with us. The Spirit that he has given us is proof that we are one with him.

The word of the Lord.

◼ REFLECTION

Which commandments do I have trouble keeping? Which commandments are most important for people our age? Do I bring God with me wherever I go?

◼ CLOSING

Let us remember these intentions:

God of grace and wisdom,
  you continually raise up good people
  who show with their lives
  that they follow a holy and loving God.
Let our lives be as true as our faith.
We ask this through Christ our Lord. **Amen.**

Let us pray with the words that Jesus taught us:

Our Father . . .

> sing "alleluia"

78

TUESDAY PRAYER

October 31, 2000

▶ Reminder: If you are planning a Halloween celebration, you might use the blessing on page 80.

■ INTRODUCTION

Tonight is Halloween! The word "hallow" is another word for a saint, a holy person.

Tonight, some of the rules of life change a bit. Instead of ordinary clothes, we wear costumes. We can play the part of saints or heroes or people with special talents. We can play funny tricks and ask neighbors for treats. We also change the rules of fear. We laugh at things that scare us—spooks, skeletons and slimy things that go "boo!" They cannot separate us from Jesus and the joy of his resurrection.

■ A PSALM FOR OCTOBER

▶ turn to page 48

■ READING

I John 3:1–3

Listen to the words of the first letter of John:

Think how much the Father loves us. He loves us so much that he lets us be called his children, as we truly are. But since the people of this world did not know who Christ is, they don't know who we are.

My dear friends, we are already God's children, though what we will be hasn't yet been seen. But we do know that when Christ returns, we will be like him, because we will see him as he truly is. This hope makes us keep ourselves holy, just as Christ is holy.

The word of the Lord.

■ REFLECTION

Do I have a "family resemblance" with Jesus? Do I feel as comfortable with God as I do with my mother and father? Do I try to be holy as Jesus is holy?

■ CLOSING

Let us remember these intentions:

God of all harvests and all happiness,
we thank you for the festival of All Saints,
    for saints to befriend us
    and teach us the way of the gospel,
      for apples and raisins and Halloween candy,
      for stories and costumes and celebrations,
      for families who love us and keep us safe.
Keep our hearts always open
    to those who need us.
We ask this through Christ our Lord. **Amen.**

Let us pray with the words that Jesus taught us:

Our Father . . .

▶ sing "alleluia"

A Blessing for Halloween

This is an appropriate beginning for a Halloween or All Saints' Day party, or for a parade of costumes. During the procession, sing "When the saints go marchin' in" or "Sing with all the saints in glory" (Hymnal for Catholic Students, page 184). Music for "Great is the Lord" is in the hymnal on page 61.

 all make
the sign
of the cross

LEADER
Great is the Lord, worthy of praise!

ALL
**Tell all the nations "God is King";
spread the news of God's love.**

LEADER   Psalm 96: 1–3
A new song for the Lord!
Sing it and bless God's name,
everyone, everywhere!
Tell the whole world
God's triumph day to day,
God's glory, God's wonder.
Great is the Lord, worthy of praise!

ALL
**Tell all the nations "God is King";
spread the news of God's love.**

READER   Revelation 7:13–14, 17
Listen to the words of the book of Revelation:

One of the elders asked me, "Do you know who these people are that are dressed in white robes? Do you know where they come from?"
  "Sir," I answered, "you must know."
  Then he told me:

"These are the ones
who have gone through the great suffering.
They have washed their robes
in the blood of the Lamb
and have made them white.
The Lamb in the center of the throne
will be their shepherd.
He will lead them to streams
of life-giving water,
and God will wipe all tears
from their eyes."

The word of the Lord.

LEADER

 hold out one hand
toward everyone
in blessing, and say:

May God be ever before us,
  leading the procession of saints.
May God be at our side
  as a companion on our journey.
May God be at the center,
  the source of our joy and celebration.
We ask this through Christ our Lord.

ALL
Amen.

LEADER
Great is the Lord, worthy of praise!

ALL
**Tell all the nations, "God is King";
spread the news of God's love.**

 all make
the sign
of the cross

80

NOVEMBER

Wednesday, November 1, to Friday, December 1

ORDINARY TIME
NOVEMBER 2000

■ ABOUT THE MONTH

In most parts of the country, November is the month when the earth closes itself up for the winter. Grass turns brown. Trees give up their last leaves and hold dark, empty branches up to the sky. There are many bright, crisp days, but nature gradually

LOOKING AHEAD

turns down the heat. By the end of the month, many of us will definitely need our cold-weather clothes.

Long ago, families had to gather and store enough food to last through the winter. Some people still have to do this. This is hard on people who live where the crops have not been good and who live in climates where winter is long and harsh. The food they store might not be enough. They might run out of firewood, or a blizzard might kill the farm animals. It is easy to see why in November people's thoughts turn to death.

▪ NOVEMBER BEGINS WITH A DOUBLE FEAST IN REMEMBRANCE OF THOSE WHO HAVE DIED. The saints, people whom God has "harvested" into heaven, are remembered on November 1, All Saints' Day. Many members of our own families have died. They also are part of God's "harvest." We pray for them on November 2, All Souls' Day. During these days, we pray that one day all people will share the glory of the saints.

All through the month, we offer prayers to remember the dead and to thank God for the harvest. We also ask God to provide enough for the poor of the world. We offer prayers of intercession for those who suffer most: the poor, the hungry, the homeless, the jobless.

▪ AT DAILY PRAYER, MOST OF OUR READINGS ARE TAKEN FROM THE BOOK OF EXODUS. This book tells the story of Moses, the greatest prophet, hero and leader of Israel. God chose Moses to gain freedom for the Hebrew people. Moses then led them during their many years in the desert, where they made a covenant with God. The events of the passover and exodus formed the people of Israel into a nation.

Toward the end of November, we hear the story of Ruth and her mother-in-law, Naomi. The story takes place at harvest time. It is a love story. While Ruth is gathering grain, she meets her future husband, Boaz.

Finally, both Hebrew and Christian writers urge us to share the gifts that God gives us. These readings prepare us all for Thanksgiving.

■ PREPARATION FOR NOVEMBER

If you do not use *Blessed Be God!* you may want to make copies of the Psalm for November and the Meal and End of the Day Prayers. They are found on pages 84, 85 and 86.

▪ ALL SAINTS' DAY AND ALL SOULS' DAY FALL ON THE FIRST TWO DAYS OF THE MONTH. If the school celebrates the eucharist on either of these days you may want to skip Daily Prayer or shorten it. On page 90 there is a special prayer for your family members and friends who have died. You can use it on any day during November. The same prayer is on page 47 in *Blessed Be God!*

▪ MANY PEOPLE ARRANGE A SHRINE TO HONOR PEOPLE WHO HAVE DIED. In Japan, people burn incense on these shrines. In Mexico, where All Souls' Day is called "The Day of the Dead" *(El Dia de los Muertos),* shrines are often elaborately decorated with symbols of death and resurrection. Some symbols are beans, corn, pumpkins, gourds, bread, the crucifix, the paschal candle, candy skulls, skeletons in bright party clothes, the tree of life made of wood or papier-maché, miniature scenes from daily life, and lots of real or paper flowers.

A shrine can be as simple as a candle and a list of people you want to remember. Or you can bring

pictures, memorial cards or drawings of people you want to pray for, along with harvest symbols (such as jack-o'-lanterns).

- DURING NOVEMBER MANY PEOPLE COLLECT CLOTHING, FOOD OR MONEY FOR THE POOR. If your school or parish does this, you may want to place the things you collect near your prayer center. These gifts really help other people. At the same time, they also represent the way we should care all year long about the poor, the hungry and the homeless people of the world.

If you bring together gifts for others, you may want to bless them before sending them out for Thanksgiving. A Blessing of Gifts is on page 350. There is also a Thanksgiving prayer on page 108. You can combine the Prayer for Thanksgiving with the Blessing of Gifts or the Blessing of Food for Sharing (page 351).

- ARE YOU KEEPING A FEW MINUTES OF SILENCE AFTER THE READING EACH DAY? It takes time for the words of the Bible to sink deeply into our hearts and to take root there. Without roots, a tree can be blown down by even a little breeze. If God's word is well-rooted in our hearts, it can grow strong.

- SUGGESTED HYMNS: "Sing with all the saints in glory" (page 184 in the *Hymnal for Catholic Students*) uses the melody for Beethoven's "Hymn to joy." Other great songs to sing from Halloween until Thanksgiving include "Come, ye thankful people, come" (page 116 in the hymnal) and "Now thank we all our God" (page 158 in the hymnal).

"What wondrous love is this" (page 208 in the hymnal) can be sung to help us remember the dead. This song was begun long ago by the people of the Appalachian Mountains. People taught it by heart to their children. When these children grew up, they taught it to their children too. This is a good song for November, which is American Music Month.

■ THE SCHOOL OF RELIGION

Readings for Weekly Prayer are from the Sunday gospel. During November the readings reflect the church's focus on the "last things," that is, death and judgment. We are reminded to put first things first with the proclamation of the two most important commandments on November 5, and the story of the generous widow on November 12. On November 19 we are urged to be always ready for the coming of our Lord. The church year ends with the feast of Christ the King on November 26.

You may want to celebrate the special days of November by using Daily Prayer on those days instead of Weekly Prayer: November 1 and 2 are All Saints' Day and All Souls' Day. The prayers for November 20, 21, and 22, as well as the prayer on page 108, focus on Thanksgiving.

- YOU MIGHT BE ABLE TO MAKE A SHRINE TO REMEMBER RELATIVES WHO HAVE DIED. In doing this, you might join the day-school students who also use your classroom. Your teachers can talk this over and see what kinds of symbols you can bring.

A PSALM FOR NOVEMBER

all make
the sign
of the cross

Psalm 65:2, 5, 10–12

LEADER   Blessed be the name of the Lord:
ALL   **Now and for ever.**

LEADER   Praise is yours, God in Zion.
ALL   **Fill us with the plenty of your house.**

SIDE A   You tend and water the land.
How wonderful the harvest!

SIDE B   You fill your springs,
ready the seeds, prepare the grain.

SIDE A   With softening rain
you bless the land with growth.

SIDE B   You crown the year with riches.
All you touch comes alive.

LEADER   Praise is yours, God in Zion.
ALL   **Fill us with the plenty of your house.**

**Glory to the Father, and to the Son,
    and to the Holy Spirit:
As it was in the beginning, is now,
    and will be for ever. Amen. Alleluia.**

turn back to
Daily Prayer or Weekly Prayer
for today

NOVEMBER

MEAL PRAYER

LEADER Let us offer God praise and thanksgiving:

ALL ▶ all make
the sign
of the cross

LEADER Blessed be the name of the Lord:

ALL **Now and for ever.**

LEADER Loving God,
all that we have
comes from your goodness
and the work of those who love us.
Bless us and the food we share.
Watch over those who care for us.
Open our eyes to the needs of the poor
during this time of harvest
and thanksgiving.
We make our prayer in the name of Jesus,
who is Lord for ever and ever.

ALL **Amen.**

▶ the melody for this song
is found in many hymnals:

**Now thank we all our God
with hearts and hands and voices,
Who wondrous things has done,
in whom this world rejoices;
Who, from our mother's arms,
has blessed us on our way
With countless gifts of love,
and still is ours today. Amen.**

▶ all make
the sign
of the cross

NOVEMBER

> all make
> the sign
> of the cross

LEADER Blessed be the name of the Lord:
ALL **Now and for ever.**

LEADER May all the saints look after us
>   and lead us safely home.
> May they guide our steps in goodness,
>   befriend us in loneliness,
>   refresh us in weariness,
>   and strengthen us in danger.
> We ask this in the name of Jesus,
>   who is our Way, our Truth and our Life,
>   now and for ever.

ALL **Amen.**

LEADER > hold out one hand
> toward everyone
> in blessing, and say:

May the almighty and merciful God
bless and protect us:

ALL > all make
> the sign
> of the cross

END OF THE DAY PRAYER

WEDNESDAY PRAYER

November 1, 2000

➤ Reminder: The Closing is the Litany of the Saints, on page 89. November's Psalm, Meal Prayer and End of the Day Prayer are on pages 12 to 14 of *Blessed Be God!*

■ INTRODUCTION

Today is All Saints' Day, the first of a two-day celebration of the saints and all who have died. November is a time of harvest and the beginning of the earth's winter sleep. This time of year sometimes turns people's thoughts to those who have fallen asleep in death. And so today we celebrate the communion of saints—the union of prayer and love between saints on earth (perhaps you and me) and the saints in heaven.

Some saints are famous. Their names are in prayer books and their pictures are in the newspaper or on the walls and windows of churches. Their stories teach us that there are many ways to follow Christ.

Today all the saints, both living and dead, join hands and sing one song of praise to God.

■ A PSALM FOR NOVEMBER

➤ turn to page 84

■ READING

Revelation 7:9 10, 13 14

Listen to the words of the book of Revelation:

I saw a large crowd with more people than could be counted. They were from every race, tribe, nation, and language, and they stood before the throne and before the Lamb. They wore white robes and held palm branches in their hands, as they shouted,

"Our God, who sits upon the throne,
has the power to save his people,
and so does the Lamb."

One of the elders asked me, "Do you know who these people are that are dressed in white robes? Do you know where they come from?"

"Sir," I answered, "you must know."

Then he told me, "These are the ones who have gone through the great suffering. They have washed their robes in the blood of the Lamb and have made them white."

The word of the Lord.

■ REFLECTION

What might the saints' robes represent? When do people wear special clothing? Which saints do I really admire and follow as an example? Which saints does my family honor?

■ CLOSING

Let us now keep silence,
while we let the word of God
sink down into our hearts.

➤ be quiet for half a minute or more; then begin the Litany of the Saints, found on page 89

THURSDAY PRAYER

November 2, 2000

Reminders: The Closing is the Litany of the Saints, on page 89. A prayer for relatives and friends who have died is on page 90 of this book and on page 47 of *Blessed Be God!* This can be used today or any day during November. Talk this over with the teacher.

■ INTRODUCTION

Today is All Souls' Day, the second day of our remembrance of saints. Today we remember our relatives and friends who have died.

Many of them are not famous. Their statues are not in the church, but their pictures are in our homes. And their stories may be alive in our families. We know of their goodness and their struggles. We know that they were not perfect, but that they tried to do their best. We pray for them, and we remember them with love.

■ A PSALM FOR NOVEMBER

turn to
page 84

■ READING

John 11: 17, 20–27

Listen to the words of the holy gospel according to John:

When Jesus got to Bethany, he found that Lazarus had already been in the tomb four days. When Martha heard that Jesus had arrived, she went out to meet him. Martha said to Jesus, "Lord, if you had been here, my brother would not have died. Yet even now I know that God will do anything you ask."

Jesus told her, "Your brother will live again!" Martha answered, "I know that he will be raised to life on the last day, when all the dead are raised."

Jesus then said, "I am the one who raises the dead to life! Everyone who has faith in me will live, even if they die. And everyone who lives because of faith in me will never die. Do you believe this?"

"Yes, Lord!" she replied. "I believe that you are Christ, the Son of God. You are the one we hoped would come into the world."

The gospel of the Lord.

■ REFLECTION

Martha's faith is a model for every Christian. How does my family keep alive the memory of its dead members? What are the sad things about death? What are the happy things about death and about remembering the dead?

■ CLOSING

Let us now keep silence,
while we let the word of God
sink down into our hearts.

be quiet for half a minute or more; then begin the Litany of the Saints, on page 89

Litany of the Saints

the leader's part is in the left-hand column; the responses are in the right-hand column.

Lord, have mercy.	**Lord, have mercy.**
Christ, have mercy.	**Christ, have mercy.**
Lord, have mercy.	**Lord, have mercy.**

Holy Mary, Mother of God,	**pray for us.**
Saint Michael,	**pray for us.**
Holy angels of God,	**pray for us.**
Saint Abraham and Saint Sarah,	**pray for us.**
Saint Isaac and Saint Rebekah,	**pray for us.**
Saint John the Baptist,	**pray for us.**
Saint Joseph,	**pray for us.**
Saint Peter and Saint Paul,	**pray for us.**
Saint Mary Magdalene,	**pray for us.**
Saint Stephen,	**pray for us.**
Saint Agnes,	**pray for us.**
Saint Martin,	**pray for us.**
Saint Margaret,	**pray for us.**
Saint Catherine,	**pray for us.**
Saint Benedict,	**pray for us.**
Saint Francis,	**pray for us.**
Saint Clare,	**pray for us.**
Saint Dominic,	**pray for us.**
Saint Theresa,	**pray for us.**
Saint Elizabeth Ann Seton,	**pray for us.**

other names of saints may be added

the Litany of the Saints concludes with this prayer:

Let us pray.

We praise you, O God,
and we honor all your holy ones.

We ask the help of those men and women
who struggled against evil and stood firm,
who loved one another,
who worked for justice and peace,
who healed the sick and fed the hungry.

We on earth and they in heaven
sing one song of praise.
We in grace and they in glory
form one communion in Christ, your Son.

Make us and all those we love
worthy to be called your saints.
We ask this through Christ our Lord.
Amen.

Let us pray with the words that Jesus taught us:

Our Father . . .

sing "alleluia"

Al-le-lu-ia,   al-le-lu-ia,   al-le-lu-ia.

All holy men and women,	**pray for us.**

A Prayer for the Dead

This is an order of prayer for friends and relatives who have died. It is also on page 47 in Blessed Be God! *This prayer can be used at any time, especially during the month of November.*

There is information on pages 82 and 83 about making a November shrine with pictures, names and symbols of people you wish to remember. If you have a shrine, gather around it.

Open and close with a song, such as "What wondrous love is this" (page 208 in the Hymnal for Catholic Students).

 all make
the sign
of the cross

LEADER
Blessed be God,
    who raised Jesus Christ from the dead.
Let us all say: Blessed be God for ever.

ALL
Blessed be God for ever.

LEADER
In silence, let us take a few moments now
to remember the dead.

 stop; allow a minute or so of silence,
and then say:

Lord God, whose days are without end
    and whose mercies beyond counting,
    keep us mindful that life is short
    and the hour of death unknown.

Let your Spirit guide our days on earth
    in the ways of holiness and justice,
    that we may serve you
        in union with the whole church,
            sure in faith, strong in hope,
        perfected in love.
And when our earthly journey is ended,
    lead us rejoicing into your kingdom,
    where you live for ever and ever.

ALL
Amen.

LEADER
Eternal rest grant unto them, O Lord.

ALL
And let perpetual light shine upon them.

LEADER
May they rest in peace.

ALL
Amen.

LEADER
May their souls
    and the souls of all the faithful departed,
    through the mercy of God, rest in peace.

ALL
Amen.

 all make
the sign
of the cross

adapted from *Catholic Household Blessings and Prayers*

FRIDAY PRAYER

November 3, 2000

■ INTRODUCTION

Today we remember Saint Martin de Porres *(dee POUR-rez)*. His father was Spanish and his mother was African. When he was twelve, Martin began to care for the sick, and this is what he did even after he joined a monastery. He gave special love to those who were poor and alone. Because of his good works, he is a patron of social action. Because he loved people of all races, he is a patron of race relations. His kindness made him famous, but he didn't want to be famous. He just wanted to love God and other people. He died in 1639 in Peru.

In honor of Martin our reading today is about the love of God.

■ A PSALM FOR NOVEMBER

  turn to
page 84

■ READING

I John 4:16, 19–21

Listen to the words of the first letter of John:

God is love. If we keep on loving others, we will stay one in our hearts with God, and he will stay one with us.

We love because God loved us first. But if we say we love God and don't love each other, we are liars. We cannot see God. So how can we love God, if we don't love the people we can see? The commandment that God has given us is: "Love God and love each other!"

The word of the Lord.

■ REFLECTION

Who are the "others" this reading tells us to love? Am I as good to the members of my family as I am to my friends? Are we friendly to all the other people at our school?

■ CLOSING

Blessed be God
    who raised Jesus Christ from the dead.
Let us all say: Blessed be God for ever!
Blessed be God for ever!
Let us remember our relatives and friends
    who have died.

  allow a minute or two
of silence

Eternal rest grant unto them, O Lord,
    and let perpetual light shine upon them.
May they rest in peace. **Amen.**

May their souls
    and the souls of all the faithful departed,
    through the mercy of God, rest in peace.
Amen.

Let us also remember these intentions:

Let us pray with the words that Jesus taught us:
Our Father . . .

  sing
"alleluia"

91

WEEKLY PRAYER

With a Reading from the Gospel for Sunday, November 5, 2000

> Reminders: November's Psalm is on page 12 of *Blessed Be God!* The Closing today is the Litany of the Saints on page 89.
>
> A prayer on page 90, for relatives and friends who have died, can be used today or any day during November.

■ INTRODUCTION

During the month of November, we remember those who have died. The lives of our relatives and friends can teach us about Christian love and Christian life. Today's reading is the heart of the gospel of Jesus. It is like a bright light that shows Jesus' followers what it means to be a Christian.

People sometimes think that these two laws of love were presented by Jesus as a new teaching. But he was quoting scriptures that his listeners knew very well. The first law comes from the book of Deuteronomy *(doo-ter-AH-nuh-mee)*. Jews still say it in prayer every day. The second law comes from the book of Leviticus *(luh-VIT-uh-kus)*. Jesus showed his listeners the meaning of the scripture.

■ A PSALM FOR NOVEMBER

> turn to
> page 84

■ READING

Mark 12:28–31

Listen to the words of the holy gospel according to Mark:

One of the teachers of the Law of Moses asked Jesus, "What is the most important commandment?"

Jesus answered, "The most important one says: 'People of Israel, you have only one Lord and God. You must love him with all your heart, soul, mind, and strength.' The second most important commandment says: 'Love others as much as you love yourself.' No other commandment is more important than these."

The gospel of the Lord.

■ REFLECTION

Do we know this teaching by heart? How do people our age keep these commandments? How does the church help us to follow these commandments in our lives?

■ CLOSING

Let us now keep silence,
while we let the word of God sink
down into our hearts.

> be quiet for half a minute or more; then begin the Litany of the Saints, found on page 89

MONDAY PRAYER

November 6, 2000

■ INTRODUCTION

During November we remember the saints and heroes of our people. One of the greatest of these was Moses. He led the Israelites to freedom. They were slaves in Egypt and were not allowed to worship God in their own way. God wanted them to be free, so God called Moses to lead them.

During the next two weeks we will read this story from the second book of the Bible.

■ A PSALM FOR NOVEMBER

 turn to
page 84

■ READING

Exodus 3:1, 2–6

Listen to the words of the book of Exodus:

One day, Moses was taking care of the sheep and goats of his father-in-law. An angel of the LORD appeared to him from a burning bush. Moses saw that the bush was on fire, but it was not burning up. "This is strange!" he said to himself. "I'll go and see why the bush isn't burning up."

When the LORD saw Moses coming near the bush, he called him by name, and Moses answered, "Here I am."

God replied, "Don't come any closer. Take off your sandals—the ground where you are standing is holy. I am the God who was worshiped by your ancestors Abraham, Isaac *(EYE-zik),* and Jacob." Moses was afraid to look at God, and so he hid his face.

The word of the Lord.

■ REFLECTION

Muslims take off their shoes when they pray. What signs of respect for God do we use when we pray?

■ CLOSING

Blessed be God
    who raised Jesus Christ from the dead.
Let us all say: Blessed be God for ever!
Blessed be God for ever!
Let us remember our relatives and friends
    who have died.

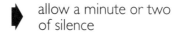 allow a minute or two
of silence

Eternal rest grant unto them, O Lord,
    and let perpetual light shine upon them.
May they rest in peace. **Amen.**
May their souls
    and the souls of all the faithful departed,
    through the mercy of God, rest in peace.
Amen.

Let us also remember these intentions:

Let us pray with the words that Jesus taught us:
Our Father . . .

 sing
"alleluia"

93

TUESDAY PRAYER
November 7, 2000

■ INTRODUCTION

When we are asked to do a difficult thing we usually ask questions. "Why me?" "Who is going to help me?" But the most important question is, "Who is asking me to do this?"

When God asked Moses to do something difficult, Moses asked, "Who are you?" God's answer gave Moses courage. This was the God who had cared for Abraham and Sarah and their descendants. This was a trustworthy God!

■ A PSALM FOR NOVEMBER

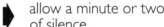
turn to page 84

■ READING

Exodus 3:9–12, 13–15

Listen to the words of the book of Exodus: The LORD said to Moses, "My people have begged for my help, and I have seen how cruel the Egyptians are to them. Now go to the king! I am sending you to lead my people out of his country." But Moses said, "Who am I to go to the king and lead your people out of Egypt?" God replied, "I will be with you."

Moses answered, "I will tell the people of Israel that the God their ancestors worshiped has sent me to them. But what should I say, if they ask me your name?"

God said to Moses, "I am the eternal God. So tell them that the LORD, whose name is 'I Am,' has sent you."

The word of the Lord.

■ REFLECTION

What could the name "I AM" mean? What other names do we use for God? What name do I use when I pray alone?

■ CLOSING

Blessed be God
    who raised Jesus Christ from the dead.
Let us all say: Blessed be God for ever!
Blessed be God for ever!
Let us remember our relatives and friends
    who have died.

allow a minute or two
of silence

Eternal rest grant unto them, O Lord,
    and let perpetual light shine upon them.
May they rest in peace. **Amen.**
May their souls
    and the souls of all the faithful departed,
    through the mercy of God, rest in peace.
Amen.

Let us also remember these intentions:

Let us pray with the words that Jesus taught us:
Our Father . . .

sing
"alleluia"

94

WEDNESDAY PRAYER

November 8, 2000

■ INTRODUCTION

The Passover showed the Israelites that God was powerful to save them.

This memory has held the Jewish people together for more than 3,000 years. When they celebrate Passover each year they remember that they are beloved children of God.

■ A PSALM FOR NOVEMBER

 turn to page 84

■ READING

Exodus 12:3, 7–8, 11–13, 14

Listen to the words of the book of Exodus:

The LORD said to Moses, "Tell the people of Israel that the head of each family must choose a lamb or young goat for his family to eat. Some of the blood must be put on the two doorposts and above the door of each house where the animals are to be eaten. That night the animals are to be roasted and eaten, together with bitter herbs and thin bread made without yeast.

"When you eat the meal, be dressed and ready to travel. Have your sandals on, carry your walking stick in your hand, and eat quickly. That same night I will pass through Egypt and kill the first-born son in every family and the first-born male of all animals. The blood on the houses will show me where you live, and when I see the blood, I will pass over you. Remember this day and celebrate it each year as a festival in my honor."

The word of the Lord.

■ REFLECTION

When do Jews celebrate Passover? Why is this Jewish celebration important to Christians?

■ CLOSING

Blessed be God
who raised Jesus Christ from the dead.
Let us all say: Blessed be God for ever!
Blessed be God for ever!
Let us remember our relatives and friends
who have died.

 allow a minute or two of silence

Eternal rest grant unto them, O Lord,
and let perpetual light shine upon them.
May they rest in peace. **Amen.**
May their souls
and the souls of all the faithful departed,
through the mercy of God, rest in peace.
Amen.

Let us also remember these intentions:

Let us pray with the words that Jesus taught us:
Our Father . . .

 sing "alleluia"

THURSDAY PRAYER

November 9, 2000

■ INTRODUCTION

Today we honor the church of Saint John Lateran in Rome. It is one of the oldest Christian churches there is. It was dedicated in the year 324. It is the cathedral *(kuh-THEE-drul)* of Rome's bishop, who is also the pope. That means that Saint John Lateran is the home church for Catholics all over the world.

People usually have good feelings about their church. We might visit our parish church this week and learn something new about it.

■ A PSALM FOR NOVEMBER

turn to
page 84

■ READING

I Corinthians 3:9–11, 16–17

Listen to the words of the apostle Paul:

You are God's garden and God's building.

God was kind and let me become an expert builder. I laid a foundation on which others have built. But we must each be careful how we build, because Christ is the only foundation.

All of you surely know that you are God's temple and that his Spirit lives in you. Together you are God's holy temple, and God will destroy anyone who destroys his temple.

The word of the Lord.

■ REFLECTION

How are we like God's building? How is Jesus like the foundation of my life?

■ CLOSING

music for the response "How lovely..." is on page 61 of the *Hymnal for Catholic Students*

Let us all say (sing):
How lovely is your dwelling place,
    O Lord of hosts!
How lovely is your dwelling place,
    O Lord of hosts!

Let us remember these intentions:

Loving God,
    you created the world
        and filled it with wonders
    and made it your dwelling.
You have built your people
    into a house of saints
    and made them your dwelling also.
You call us and make us strong.
You build us on a solid foundation.
And so we say (sing):
How lovely is your dwelling place,
    O Lord of hosts!
How lovely is your dwelling place,
    O Lord of hosts!

Let us pray with the words that Jesus taught us:
Our Father . . .

 sing "alleluia"

FRIDAY PRAYER

November 10, 2000

■ INTRODUCTION

Today we remember Saint Leo, who was pope during the fifth century. When Leo was pastor of the church, a fierce warrior named Attila *(uh-TILL-uh)* led an army over the Alps, across northern Italy, and south toward Rome. In the city, the emperor was afraid. The generals were afraid. Everyone was afraid. Alone and unarmed, Leo rode out to speak to the enemy. His courage and faith convinced Attila to turn his army away from Rome.

Leo was like Moses. As we shall see from today's reading, Moses also led people who were sometimes afraid.

■ A PSALM FOR NOVEMBER

turn to
page 84

■ READING

Exodus 14:10–13

Listen to the words of the book of Exodus:

When the Israelites *(IS-ree-uh-lites)* saw the king coming with his army, they were frightened and begged the LORD for help. They also complained to Moses, "Wasn't there enough room in Egypt to bury us? Is that why you brought us out here to die in the desert? Why did you bring us out of Egypt anyway? While we were there, didn't we tell you to leave us alone? We would rather be slaves in Egypt than die in this desert!"

But Moses answered, "Don't be afraid! Be brave, and you will see the LORD save you today."

The word of the Lord.

■ REFLECTION

Do I know anyone who complains when they should be grateful? Do I become crabby when I am tired or afraid, or when I don't get my way? Do I remember to turn to the Lord at those times, as Moses did?

■ CLOSING

Blessed be God
    who raised Jesus Christ from the dead.
Let us all say: Blessed be God for ever!
Blessed be God for ever!
Let us remember our relatives and friends
    who have died.

allow a minute or two
of silence

Eternal rest grant unto them, O Lord,
    and let perpetual light shine upon them.
May they rest in peace. **Amen.**
May their souls
    and the souls of all the faithful departed,
    through the mercy of God, rest in peace.
Amen.

Let us also remember these intentions:

Let us pray with the words that Jesus taught us:
Our Father . . .

sing
"alleluia"

With a Reading from the Gospel for Sunday, November 12, 2000

■ INTRODUCTION

The church year will soon end. At this time the church reminds us of some important things. On Sunday, November 12, the gospel tells the story of a widow who was generous, even though she did not have much to share. November is a good time to think about sharing because it is harvest time, and time to begin preparing for winter. In many parishes there will be collections of food near Thanksgiving. The story of the generous widow reminds us that we, too, must share what we have, even if we have very little.

■ A PSALM FOR NOVEMBER

➤ turn to
   page 84

■ READING

Mark 12:41–44

Listen to the words of the holy gospel according to Mark:

Jesus was sitting in the temple near the offering box and watching people put in their gifts. He noticed that many rich people were giving a lot of money. Finally, a poor widow came up and put in two coins that were worth only a few pennies. Jesus told his disciples to gather around him. Then he said, "I tell you that this poor widow has put in more than all the others. Everyone else gave what they didn't need. But she is very poor and gave everything she had. Now she doesn't have a cent to live on."

The gospel of the Lord.

■ REFLECTION

How do people in our parish help care for people who are poor? How do members of this school help? Do I share what I have generously?

■ CLOSING

Let us remember these intentions:

Loving God,
   we thank you for sending your followers
      into the whole world
   with your gifts of food and love.
We have been cared for and protected.
We have eaten and been filled.
Show us how to share what we have been given,
   and to be your worthy followers.
We ask this through Christ our Lord. **Amen.**

Let us pray with the words that Jesus taught us:

Our Father . . .

➤ sing
   "alleluia"

MONDAY PRAYER

November 13, 2000

■ INTRODUCTION

Today we remember Saint Frances Cabrini (*kuh-BREE-nee*), the first American citizen to be named a saint. Mother Cabrini came from Italy in 1899 to work with Italian immigrants who had moved to America for a better life.

Mother Cabrini began an order of sisters who opened hospitals and helped people make their way in their new country. The sisters continue this work today.

■ A PSALM FOR NOVEMBER

➤ turn to
page 84

■ READING

Exodus 14:21–23, 26–27, 28, 30

Listen to the words of the book of Exodus:

Moses stretched his arm over the sea, and the LORD sent a strong east wind that blew all night until there was dry land where the water had been. The sea opened up, and the Israelites *(IS-ree-uh-lites)* walked through on dry land with a wall of water on each side.

The Egyptian chariots and cavalry went after them. The LORD told Moses, "Stretch your arm toward the sea—the water will cover the Egyptians and their cavalry and chariots." Moses stretched out his arm, and at daybreak the water rushed toward the Egyptians. The water came and covered the chariots, the cavalry, and the whole Egyptian army.

On that day, the Israelites knew that the LORD had saved them.

The word of the Lord.

■ REFLECTION

Water is important in many Bible stories. What stories do I know that mention water? How is water used in church?

■ CLOSING

Let us remember these intentions:

God of our ancestors,
    you freed the children of Israel
        from slavery and from fear.
You were with them by day and by night.
Be with us on our journey.
Guide and protect us,
    and bring us to the joy of your kingdom.
We ask this through Christ our Lord. **Amen.**

Let us pray with the words that Jesus taught us:

Our Father . . .

➤ sing
"alleluia"

TUESDAY PRAYER

November 14, 2000

■ INTRODUCTION

Our daily readings have been following Moses and the Israelites on their journey. God helped them escape from Egypt. Now God offers to make a covenant with them. A covenant is an agreement. The Israelites would be God's specially loved people—God promised this. The Israelites would live according to God's law—the people promised this.

■ A PSALM FOR NOVEMBER

➤ turn to page 84

■ READING

Exodus 19:1–6, 7–8

Listen to the words of the book of Exodus:

Two months after leaving Egypt, the Israelites *(IS-ree-uh-lites)* arrived at the desert near Mount Sinai *(SYE-nye),* where they set up camp at the foot of the mountain.

Moses went up the mountain to meet with the LORD God, who told him to say to the people, "You saw what I did in Egypt, and you know how I brought you here to me, just as a mighty eagle carries its young. Now if you will faithfully obey me, you will be my very own people. The whole world is mine, but you will be my holy nation and serve me as priests."

After Moses went back, he reported to the leaders what the LORD had said, and they promised, "We will do everything the LORD has commanded."

The word of the Lord.

■ REFLECTION

When I am older, what will my choice be? Am I willing to say, "I will do everything the Lord has commanded"? Am I trying to do what the Lord asks of me now?

■ CLOSING

Let us remember these intentions:

God of our ancestors,
    you freed the children of Israel
        from slavery and from fear.
You were with them by day and by night.
Be with us on our journey.
Guide and protect us,
    and bring us to the joy of your kingdom.
We ask this through Christ our Lord. **Amen.**

Let us pray with the words that Jesus taught us:

Our Father . . .

 sing "alleluia"

■ INTRODUCTION

Today we remember Saint Roque *(rock)* Gonzalez, a Jesuit priest who brought the word of God to the native peoples of Paraguay *(PAHR-uh-gway)* in South America. He and his companions often drew attention by playing musical instruments. Then they would tell about God's love.

Father Gonzalez helped people to build farms and communities in the wilderness. The communities attracted thousands because they were not like other European settlements. In them the native peoples governed themselves, and they were safe from slave traders and other dangers. Father Gonzalez died for his faith in 1628.

■ A PSALM FOR NOVEMBER

turn to
page 84

■ READING

Exodus 19:16–19

Listen to the words of the book of Exodus:

On the morning of the third day there was thunder and lightning. A thick cloud covered the mountain, a loud trumpet blast was heard, and everyone in camp trembled with fear. Moses led them out of the camp to meet God, and they stood at the foot of the mountain.

Mount Sinai was covered with smoke because the LORD had come down in a flaming fire. Smoke poured out of the mountain just like a furnace, and the whole mountain shook.

The word of the Lord.

■ REFLECTION

Many people compare the coming of God at Mount Sinai to the coming of the Holy Spirit at Pentecost. In what ways are these stories alike? Would I pay more attention to the presence of God at the Sunday eucharist if there were fire and smoke?

■ CLOSING

Let us remember these intentions:

God of our ancestors,
　　you freed the children of Israel
　　　　from slavery and from fear.
You were with them by day and by night.
Be with us on our journey.
Guide and protect us,
　　and bring us to the joy of your kingdom.
We ask this through Christ our Lord. **Amen.**

Let us pray with the words that Jesus taught us:

Our Father. . .

sing
"alleluia"

THURSDAY PRAYER

November 16, 2000

■ INTRODUCTION

We have been reading about Moses and his people. They are often called "children of Israel" or "Israelites." Israel was the name given to Jacob, the grandson of Abraham. It is to Israel that the twelve tribes trace their beginnings. So they are all called by his name.

The family had first settled in the land of Canaan *(KAY-nun)*. So that is where the Israelites wanted to return when they left Egypt. In time, that land was also named Israel.

■ A PSALM FOR NOVEMBER

➤ turn to
page 84

■ READING

Exodus 20:1–4, 5, 7, 8, 12–17

Listen to the words of the book of Exodus:

God said to the people of Israel:
"I am the LORD your God
the one who brought you out of Egypt,
    where you were slaves.
Do not worship any god except me.
Do not make idols.
Do not bow down and worship idols.
Do not misuse my name.
Remember that the Sabbath Day
    belongs to me.
Respect your father and your mother,
    and you will live a long time
    in the land that I am giving you.
Do not murder.
Be faithful in marriage.
Do not steal.
Do not tell lies about others.
Do not want anything
    that belongs to someone else."

The word of the Lord.

■ REFLECTION

Do we know these commandments by heart? Which ones do I find most difficult to keep?

■ CLOSING

Let us remember these intentions:

God of the Exodus,
    you give us your law as a gift
        and not a burden.
It guides us to live in peace with you,
    with each other and within ourselves.
Help us to keep your law with all our hearts.
We ask this through Christ our Lord. **Amen.**

Let us pray with the words that Jesus taught us:
Our Father . . .

 sing
"alleluia"

FRIDAY PRAYER

November 17, 2000

■ INTRODUCTION

Today we remember Saint Elizabeth, queen of Hungary, who died in 1231. Elizabeth gave large sums of money to help the sick and the homeless. She was very prayerful, and welcomed Saint Francis of Assisi when he visited her country. When Elizabeth's husband died, his brother expelled her from the castle. Elizabeth had to live in poverty but she never lost her joy in life, her sense of humor, and her love for the poor.

■ A PSALM FOR NOVEMBER

▶ turn to
page 84

turn to
page 84

■ READING

Exodus 24:4–8

Listen to the words of the book of Exodus:

Moses got up early. He built an altar at the foot of the mountain and set up a large stone for each of the twelve tribes of Israel. He also sent some young men to burn offerings and to sacrifice bulls as special offerings to the LORD. Moses put half of the blood from the animals into bowls and sprinkled the rest on the altar. Then he read aloud the LORD's commands and promises, and the people shouted, "We will obey the LORD and do everything he has commanded!"

Moses took the blood from the bowls and sprinkled it on the people. Next, he told them, "With this blood the LORD makes his agreement with you."

The word of the Lord.

■ REFLECTION

God and the people made a solemn agreement. How will God keep this promise? How will the people keep this promise? What have I promised to God?

■ CLOSING

Let us remember these intentions:

God of the covenant,
    you give us your law as a gift
        and not a burden.
It guides us to live in peace with you,
    with each other and within ourselves.
Help us to keep your law with all our hearts.
We ask this through Christ our Lord. **Amen.**

Let us pray with the words that Jesus taught us:

Our Father . . .

▶ sing
"alleluia"

WEEKLY PRAYER

With a Reading from the Gospel for Sunday, November 19, 2000

■ INTRODUCTION

As the church's year comes to a close, we turn our minds to the coming of God's rule to our world. Some people wanted Jesus to bring about God's rule through a great war or revolution *(re-voh-LU-shun)*. But Jesus knew that the revolution has to take place first in people's hearts. Jesus told his followers that there will be great changes in the world when God's coming is near. He tells us to "watch out and be ready."

■ A PSALM FOR NOVEMBER

▶ turn to
page 84

■ READING

Mark 13:24–29, 33

Listen to the words of the holy gospel according to Mark:

Jesus said, "In those days, right after that time of suffering, the sun will become dark, and the moon will no longer shine. The stars will fall, and the powers in the sky will be shaken.

"Then the Son of Man will be seen coming in the clouds with great power and glory. He will send his angels to gather his chosen ones from all over the earth.

"Learn a lesson from a fig tree. When its branches sprout and start putting out leaves, you know summer is near. So when you see all these things happening, you will know that the time has almost come. So watch out and be ready! You don't know when the time will come."

The word of the Lord.

■ REFLECTION

If Jesus were coming to see me tomorrow, is there something I would change? How would I get ready? Are there things that we can change now to prepare for his coming?

■ CLOSING

Let us remember these intentions:

Lord of justice and mercy,
   show us your face
      when we look at the people around us.
Open our eyes to the needs of others.
Fill us with your grace,
   so that our works and our words
   may be signs of your coming.
We ask this through Christ our Lord. **Amen.**

Let us pray with the words that Jesus taught us:

Our Father . . .

 sing
"alleluia"

 Reminder: You may want to use the Thanksgiving Prayer on page 108 this week.

■ INTRODUCTION

Thursday is Thanksgiving. We can prepare for it by discussing the blessings that we enjoy.

We also might read the account of the first Thanksgiving. It was a celebration of a good harvest after two years of struggle and starvation. And it was a dinner of peace and respect between Pilgrims and Native Americans.

■ A PSALM FOR NOVEMBER

turn to
page 84

■ READING

1 Timothy 6: 7–10, 17–18

Listen to the words of the apostle Paul:

We didn't bring anything into this world, and we won't take anything with us when we leave. So we should be satisfied just to have food and clothes. People who want to be rich fall into all sorts of temptations and traps. They are caught by foolish and harmful desires that drag them down and destroy them. The love of money causes all kinds of trouble.

Warn the rich people of this world not to be proud or to trust in wealth that is easily lost. Tell them to have faith in God, who is rich and blesses us with everything we need to enjoy life. Instruct them to do as many good deeds as they can and to help everyone. Remind the rich to be generous and share what they have.

The word of the Lord.

■ REFLECTION

How does the love of money "cause all kinds of trouble"? In what ways am I rich? How do I share my riches with others? How will I help my family give thanks to God on Thanksgiving?

■ CLOSING

The Lord is good and listens to our prayers. During this season of harvest,
    let us pray for those who need God's help.

For those who need food,
    let us pray to the Lord: **Lord, have mercy.**

For those who see that others are fed,
    let us pray to the Lord: **Lord, have mercy.**

For those who are made holy
      in the sharing of food,
    let us pray to the Lord: **Lord, have mercy.**

Let us also remember these intentions:

Merciful Lord, teach us to be grateful
    for what we have and for those who love us.
We ask this through Christ our Lord. **Amen.**

Let us pray with the words that Jesus taught us:
Our Father . . .

 sing
"alleluia"

TUESDAY PRAYER

November 21, 2000

■ INTRODUCTION

Today we remember the Presentation of Mary in the Temple. This feast recalls a legend that Mary's parents dedicated her to God at the Temple when she was three years old.

Today's reading tells how Mary and Joseph took Jesus to the Temple when he was a boy.

■ A PSALM FOR NOVEMBER

turn to
page 84

■ READING

Luke 2:41–43, 46–48, 49

Listen to the words of the holy gospel according to Luke:

Every year Jesus' parents went to Jerusalem *(juh-ROO-suh-lem)* for Passover. And when Jesus was twelve years old, they all went there as usual for the celebration. After Passover his parents left, but they did not know that Jesus had stayed on in the city.

Three days later they found Jesus sitting in the temple, listening to the teachers and asking them questions. Everyone who heard him was surprised at how much he knew and at the answers he gave.

His mother said, "Son, why have you done this to us? Your father and I have been very worried, and we have been searching for you!" Jesus answered, "Why did you have to look for me? Didn't you know that I would be in my father's house?"

The gospel of the Lord.

■ REFLECTION

What could Jesus' statement mean to us? Do we take opportunities to learn more about our religion, and to discuss it with others? Am I ever confused about where to find Jesus?

■ CLOSING

The Lord is good and listens to our prayers.
During this season of harvest,
    let us pray for those who need God's help.

For lost children and worried parents,
    let us pray to the Lord: **Lord, have mercy.**

For good teachers and wise students,
    let us pray to the Lord: **Lord, have mercy.**

For all those who search for God
    and try to do God's will,
    let us pray to the Lord: **Lord, have mercy.**

Let us also remember these intentions:

Merciful Lord, teach us to be grateful
    for what we have and for those who love us.
We ask this through Christ our Lord. **Amen.**

Let us pray with the words that Jesus taught us:

Our Father . . .

 sing
"alleluia"

WEDNESDAY PRAYER

November 22, 2000

 Reminder: If you celebrate the eucharist today, you may skip or shorten this prayer.

■ INTRODUCTION

Today is the day before Thanksgiving. Let us call to mind all that we have, all that we are and all whom we love. All this comes from God.

The earth offers its gifts to everyone, but there are seasons when food is scarce. In some nations, food is always scarce. God does not hand each person a plate of food, but leaves the gathering, the cooking and the serving to us. God leaves it to us to be fair with the gifts of the land.

■ A PSALM FOR NOVEMBER

 turn to
page 84

■ READING

2 Corinthians 9:7, 7, 8, 10–11

Listen to the words of the apostle Paul:

Each of you must make up your own mind about how much to give. God loves people who love to give. God can bless you with everything you need, and you will always have more than enough to do all kinds of good things for others.

God gives seed to farmers and provides everyone with food. He will increase what you have, so that you can give even more to those in need. You will be blessed in every way, and you will be able to keep on being generous. Then many people will thank God when we deliver your gift.

The word of the Lord.

■ REFLECTION

God does not give anything without asking us to share that gift with others. What is our nation asked to share? What is our class asked to share? How can I do my part?

■ CLOSING

The Lord is good and listens to our prayers.
During this season of harvest,
    let us pray for those who need God's help.

For those who produce food for the world.
    let us pray to the Lord: **Lord, have mercy.**

For those who share their food with others,
    let us pray to the Lord: **Lord, have mercy.**

For those who are starving today,
    let us pray to the Lord: **Lord, have mercy.**

Let us also remember these intentions:

Merciful Lord, teach us to be grateful
    for what we have and for those who love us.
We ask this through Christ our Lord. **Amen.**

Let us pray with the words that Jesus taught us:
Our Father . . .

 sing
"alleluia"

A Prayer for Thanksgiving

Students should prepare four or five petitions for the needs of others. Decorate the room with banners or posters that represent the people, relationships, talents and events for which we are thankful.

The service might continue with the Blessing of Gifts (on page 350) or the Blessing of Food for Sharing (on page 351).

Begin and end with song, such as "Now thank we all our God" (page 158 in the Hymnal for Catholic Students), *or "All creatures of our God and king" (page 100).*

Introduction

In celebration of Thanksgiving, we gather to praise the Lord. We pray for the needs of others, and we hope that all God's wonderful gifts will be shared fairly in our world.

We begin by praying the Psalm for November.

A Psalm for November

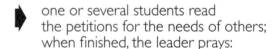

turn to
page 84

Reading

Matthew 15:33-37

Listen to the words of the holy gospel according to Matthew:

The disciples of Jesus said, "This place is like a desert. Where can we find enough food to feed such a crowd?" Jesus asked them how much food they had. They replied, "Seven small loaves of bread and a few little fish."

After Jesus had told the people to sit down, he took the seven loaves of bread and the fish, and gave thanks. He then broke them and handed them to his disciples, who passed them around to the crowds.

Everyone ate all they wanted, and the leftovers filled seven large baskets.

The gospel of the Lord.

Petitions for Those in Need

Jesus, you heal us and you feed us.
Hear the prayers we offer you today.

> one or several students read
> the petitions for the needs of others;
> when finished, the leader prays:

Continue to watch over your people, Lord.
Feed, comfort and protect them,
 now and for ever. **Amen.**

Let us pray with the words that Jesus taught us:

Our Father . . .

Blessing

> turn to page 350 or 351,
> or hold out one hand toward
> everyone in blessing and say:

At this time of Thanksgiving,
 may our gracious God,
  the giver of the harvest,
 bless and protect us:

> all make
> the sign
> of the cross

> all sing
> a closing song

WEEKLY PRAYER

With a Reading from the Gospel for Sunday, November 26, 2000

Reminders: A Prayer for Thanksgiving is on page 108. A Blessing of Gifts is on page 350. Before your next meeting, you may want to make an Advent wreath and make copies of the Psalm on page 118.

■ INTRODUCTION

On Sunday, November 26, we celebrate the festival of Christ the King. We must get ready for the kingdom that Jesus promised. It is a kingdom of the heart and a kingdom of truth.

Calling Jesus our king also reminds us that we are called to be loyal to God above all. Christians love their country. They are loyal to their government, but they do not give country or government the same kind of love and loyalty that they give to God.

■ A PSALM FOR NOVEMBER

turn to page 84

■ READING

John 18:33, 36–37

Listen to the words of the holy gospel according to John:

Pilate called Jesus over and asked, "Are you the king of the Jews?"

Jesus answered, "My kingdom doesn't belong to this world. If it did, my followers would have fought to keep me from being handed over to our leaders. No, my kingdom doesn't belong to this world."

"So you are a king," Pilate replied.

"You are saying that I am a king," Jesus told him. "I was born into this world to tell about the truth. And everyone who belongs to the truth knows my voice."

The gospel of the Lord.

■ REFLECTION

Why is truth important? Why do Christians who love the truth try to listen to the voice of Jesus? What would living in a "kingdom of truth" be like?

■ CLOSING

Let us remember these intentions:

King of justice and compassion,
   show us your face when we look at
      the people around us.
Open our eyes to the needs of others.
Fill us with your grace,
   so that our works and our words
      may be signs of your coming.
We ask this through Christ our Lord. **Amen.**

Let us pray with the words that Jesus taught us:

Our Father . . .

sing "alleluia"

MONDAY PRAYER

November 27, 2000

■ INTRODUCTION

As the new moon is sighted tonight, the Muslim month of prayer, Ramadan *(RAH-muh-don)*, begins. All over the world, Muslims will fast between sunrise and sunset. Their late evening meal is then a festive gathering of family and friends. Let us remember the Muslim people in our prayers in the coming weeks.

Today's reading tells one way the Jewish people cared for the poor. People with farms and orchards were told to leave something behind after the harvest. Poor people could pick up what was left. Later this week we will read about two women who needed such help.

■ A PSALM FOR NOVEMBER

▶ turn to page 84

■ READING

Deuteronomy 24:19–21

Listen to the words of the book of Deuteronomy *(doo-ter-AH-nuh-mee):*

Moses said to Israel, "If you forget to bring in a stack of harvested grain, don't go back in the field to get it. Leave it for the poor, including for-eigners *(FOR-in-erz),* orphans, and widows, and the LORD will make you successful in everything you do.

"When you harvest your olives, don't try to get them all for yourself, but leave some for the poor. And when you pick your grapes, go over the vines only once, then let the poor have what is left. You lived in poverty as slaves in Egypt until the LORD your God rescued you. That's why I am giving you these laws."

The word of the Lord.

■ REFLECTION

God asks us to share our gifts with others. What have we been given? How do we share those gifts with others in need?

■ CLOSING

The Lord is good and listens to our prayers.
During this season of harvest,
    let us pray for those who need God's help.

For those who need food,
    let us pray to the Lord: **Lord, have mercy.**

For those who see that others are fed,
    let us pray to the Lord: **Lord, have mercy.**

For those who bring food to the table,
    let us pray to the Lord: **Lord, have mercy.**

Let us also remember these intentions:

Merciful Lord, teach us to be grateful
    for what we have and for those who love us.
We ask this through Christ our Lord. **Amen.**

Let us pray with the words that Jesus taught us:

Our Father . . .

 sing "alleluia"

TUESDAY PRAYER

November 28, 2000

■ INTRODUCTION

In today's reading we hear about Naomi *(nay-OH-mee)*. First her husband died, and then her two sons died. Naomi and her two daughters-in-law had to find new homes, because in those days women could not live by themselves. They were very sad, because first they had lost their husbands and sons, and now they would probably lose each other, too.

■ A PSALM FOR NOVEMBER

turn to
page 84

■ READING

Ruth 1:8–9, 14, 16, 18

Listen to the words of the book of Ruth:

Naomi *(nay-OH-mee)* said to her two daughters-in-law, "Don't you want to go back home to your own mothers? You were kind to my husband and sons, and you have always been kind to me. I pray that the LORD will be just as kind to you. May he give each of you another husband and a home of your own."

They cried again. Orpah kissed her mother-in-law good-by, but Ruth held on to her. Ruth answered, "Please don't tell me to leave you and return home! I will go where you go. I will live where you live; your people will be my people, your God will be my God." When Naomi saw that Ruth had made up her mind to go with her, she stopped urging her to go back.

The word of the Lord.

■ REFLECTION

What difficulties do widows and single women face today? What difficulties do children of divorced or single parents have? How can we make things easier for them?

■ CLOSING

The Lord is good and listens to our prayers.
During this season of harvest,
    let us pray for those who need God's help.

For families where there is divorce,
    let us pray to the Lord: **Lord, have mercy.**

For families where there is death,
    let us pray to the Lord: **Lord, have mercy.**

For families who stand by one another,
    let us pray to the Lord: **Lord, have mercy.**

Let us also remember these intentions:

Loving Lord, have mercy on your people,
    and strengthen families around the world.
We ask this through Christ our Lord. **Amen.**

Let us pray with the words that Jesus taught us:

Our Father . . .

sing
"alleluia"

WEDNESDAY PRAYER

November 29, 2000

■ INTRODUCTION

On this day, 20 years ago, Dorothy Day died. She led a wild life as a young woman, but later she joined the Catholic church and dedicated her life to service. Dorothy began the Catholic Worker movement and published its newspaper.

■ A PSALM FOR NOVEMBER

 turn to page 84

■ READING

Ruth 1:22; 2:3, 5–6, 8, 9–11, 12

Listen to the words of the book of Ruth:

The barley harvest was just beginning when Naomi *(nay-OH-mee)* and Ruth, her daughter-in-law, arrived in Bethlehem *(BETH-luh-hem).* So right away, Ruth went out to pick up grain in a field owned by Boaz *(BO-az).* Boaz asked the man in charge of the harvest workers, "Who is that young woman?" The man answered, "She is the one who came back from Moab *(MO-ab)* with Naomi."

Boaz went over to Ruth and said, "I have warned the men not to bother you, and whenever you are thirsty, you can drink from the water jars they have filled." Ruth bowed down to the ground and said, "You know I come from another country. Why are you so good to me?"

Boaz answered, "I've heard how you've helped your mother-in-law ever since your husband died. I pray that the LORD God of Israel will reward you for what you have done."

The word of the Lord.

■ REFLECTION

How do family members take care of each other today? What examples have I seen in my own family? How do I help cousins, grandparents or other relatives?

■ CLOSING

The Lord is good and listens to our prayers.
During this season of harvest,
    let us pray for those who need God's help.

For people who have to eat what is left behind,
    let us pray to the Lord: **Lord, have mercy.**

For people who are refugees in a foreign land,
    let us pray to the Lord: **Lord, have mercy.**

For people who provide for the poor,
    let us pray to the Lord: **Lord, have mercy.**

Let us also remember these intentions:

Loving God, have mercy on your people.
Open our eyes to one another's needs.
We ask this through Christ our Lord. **Amen.**

Let us pray with the words that Jesus taught us:
Our Father . . .

 sing "alleluia"

THURSDAY PRAYER

November 30, 2000

■ INTRODUCTION

Today is the feast of Saint Andrew. He and his brother Peter were fishermen. When they met Jesus they knew that he was the savior John the Baptist had told them about, so they became disciples of Jesus.

We have been reading about Naomi and Ruth. When Boaz *(BO-az)* saw Ruth gathering leftover grain, he asked his workers to drop some on purpose, so that she would have enough.

■ A PSALM FOR NOVEMBER

 turn to page 84

■ READING

Ruth 2:17, 18, 19–20, 23

Listen to the words of the book of Ruth:

Ruth worked in the field until evening. She took the grain to town and showed Naomi *(nay-OH-mee)* how much she had picked up.

Naomi said, "Where did you work today? Whose field was it? God bless the man who treated you so well!" Then Ruth told her that she had worked in the field of a man named Boaz *(BO-az)*.

"The LORD bless Boaz!" Naomi replied. "He has shown that he is still loyal to the living and to the dead. Boaz is a close relative, one of those who is supposed to look after us."

Ruth worked in the fields until the barley and wheat were harvested. And all this time she lived with Naomi.

The word of the Lord.

■ REFLECTION

Would I be embarrassed to pick up the grain that the harvesters dropped? How do the poor of our country find food? What does our parish do to help?

■ CLOSING

The Lord is good and listens to our prayers.
During this season of harvest,
    let us pray for those who need God's help.

For those who need food,
    let us pray to the Lord: **Lord, have mercy.**

For those who see that others are fed,
    let us pray to the Lord: **Lord, have mercy.**

For those who are made holy
    in the sharing of food,
    let us pray to the Lord: **Lord, have mercy.**

Let us also remember these intentions:

Merciful Lord, teach us to be grateful
    for what we have and for those who love us.
We ask this through Christ our Lord. **Amen.**

Let us pray with the words that Jesus taught us:
Our Father . . .

 sing "alleluia"

113

FRIDAY PRAYER

December 1, 2000

■ INTRODUCTION

On this day in 1955, a woman named Rosa Parks got on a bus in Montgomery, Alabama. She was tired, but the only empty seats were in the section where African Americans were not allowed to sit. Rosa Parks decided to sit down anyway. She challenged an unjust law and the conscience *(KON-shens)* of all Americans who heard her story.

In today's reading we hear the end of the story of Ruth, the poor woman from Moab. She became the mother of a great family.

■ A PSALM FOR NOVEMBER

turn to
page 84

■ READING

Ruth 4:13–14, 15–17

Listen to the words of the book of Ruth:

Boaz married Ruth, and the LORD blessed her with a son. After his birth, the women said to Naomi, "Praise the LORD! Today he has given you a grandson. He will make you happy and take care of you in your old age, because he is the son of your daughter-in-law. And she loves you more than seven sons of your own would love you."

Naomi loved the boy and took good care of him. The neighborhood women named him Obed, but they called him "Naomi's Boy."

When Obed grew up he had a son named Jesse, who later became the father of King David.

The word of the Lord.

■ REFLECTION

Our parish is like a family of faith. What obligations do we have to members of our parish? What do we owe other members of our school?

■ CLOSING

The Lord is good and listens to our prayers.
During this season of harvest,
    let us pray for those who need God's help.

For people who work to bring in the harvest,
    let us pray to the Lord: **Lord, have mercy.**

For those who see that others are fed,
    let us pray to the Lord: **Lord, have mercy.**

For those who are made holy
    in the sharing of food,
    let us pray to the Lord: **Lord, have mercy.**

Let us also remember these intentions:

Merciful Lord, teach us to be grateful
    for what we have and for those who love us.
We ask this through Christ our Lord. **Amen.**

Let us pray with the words that Jesus taught us:

Our Father . . .

sing
"alleluia"

114

ADVENT

Sunday, December 3, to Sunday, December 24

ADVENT 2000

■ ABOUT THE SEASON

On Sunday, December 3, Advent begins. Advent is a period of simple living and extra prayer. It is a time to prepare for a new coming of Jesus our Savior.

The first coming of Jesus, at Bethlehem, will not happen again. At Christmas we will remember that coming, but now we prepare for a new coming. Every time Jesus comes, it surprises us. It is never exactly the way we expect it to happen.

LOOKING AHEAD

Some people want the Savior to come with great power to reward them and wipe out their enemies. But Jesus is a loving and peaceful Savior. He calls his followers to make the whole world loving and peaceful. During Advent, we try to prepare our homes and our lives for Jesus, the King of glory and the Prince of peace.

■ MANY PEOPLE DO NOT UNDERSTAND ADVENT. They use the time to celebrate Christmas early. Maybe we cannot do anything about the decorations in the shopping malls that get put up so early, but we can do something in our classroom. We can wait for Christmas decorations and gifts and parties. We can wait as the world waited long ago for the coming of Jesus and as we wait now for Jesus' coming in glory.

We also can help our families keep the peace of Advent by not worrying about what we are going to get for Christmas. This is very hard because it is so exciting to get presents! It will be easier if we spend time thinking about the good things we can give to the people we love. We can start early and make things to give. We can help make some of the decorations we use at home. This way we have the joy of making as well as the joy of giving. Parents especially love things their children make.

■ WE KNOW THAT CHRISTMAS IS MORE THAN JUST GIFTS. We also know that Christmas is more than just one day. December 25 is the first day of Christmastime, a season that lasts until January 8, the feast of the Baptism of the Lord.

During Advent, we can talk about what the Christmas season means to us. We can help with the preparations. Once we start doing these things, it may become easier to keep a peaceful Advent.

■ THE READINGS FOR DAILY PRAYER DURING THE EARLY PART OF ADVENT COME FROM THE BOOK OF ISAIAH. The words of this book come from several prophets who tried to comfort the people during their years of exile and suffering. They are words of hope. They tell about future days, when God will bring peace to those who remain patient and faithful. During the last week of Advent, our readings will come from the gospel of Luke. These readings tell how God prepared those people who would be the family of Jesus. They would be the first to welcome Jesus and to make a home for him.

■ PREPARATION FOR ADVENT

The Advent Psalm, Meal Prayer and End of the Day Prayer are on pages 15, 16 and 17 of *Blessed Be God!* If students do not have that booklet, you may want to make copies of those prayers for the whole class. They are found on pages 118, 119 and 120 of this book.

■ CLASSROOM DECORATIONS: For Advent, you can use purple, silver or dark blue stars to celebrate the long nights. Or you can use paper snowflakes, pine cones or other things that are signs of winter in your part of the country. You may want to put out an empty stable as a sign that the Savior will soon come. You can set up an Advent calendar and open up one window each day.

■ THE MOST IMPORTANT THING TO HAVE IS AN ADVENT WREATH. An Advent wreath is a circle of

evergreen branches with four candles placed in or around it. The circular wreath is a sign of God's loving care, which has no ending. There are four candles for the four Sundays of this season.

Usually, three of the candles are purple and one is rose-colored. (The rose candle is first lighted during the third week of Advent.) Or, all four of the candles can be white, red or purple. Some people hang the wreath from the ceiling with four wide ribbons.

Before you use your Advent wreath for the first time, bless it. A Blessing of the Advent Wreath is on page 121.

▪ DURING THE LAST FEW DAYS BEFORE CHRISTMAS BREAK, you may want to decorate the classroom (but not the prayer center) for Christmas. That way the Christmas decorations will be there to greet you when you return in January. You still will have several days of Christmastime to enjoy when you return to school after Christmas break.

On page 140 is the Blessing before Christmas Break. Remind the teacher about this blessing.

On page 147 is the Blessing of the Stable, which is to be used at the first class meeting after the Christmas break. You may want to look it over and make some preparations for it before the break so that you are ready on the day you return to class.

Remember the Farewell Blessing on page 345. It can be used for a student or teacher who leaves before the school year is over.

▪ SUGGESTED HYMNS: "O come, O come, Emmanuel" (page 166 in the *Hymnal for Catholic Students)* is a famous Advent song that comes from France. The Hebrew word "Emmanuel" means "God is with us." Emmanuel is one name we use for Jesus. This song has a special verse for each day of the final week of Advent. It is used every day of Advent in Daily and Weekly Prayer.

The Psalm for Advent is the Canticle of Zechariah. (Zechariah was the father of John the Baptist.) If you wish to sing Zechariah's song instead of reciting it, use the music on page 8 in the hymnal.

"Soon and very soon" (page 190 in the hymnal) is an Advent gospel song. "Prepare the way of the Lord" (page 174 in the hymnal) is a round that can be sung over and over.

In honor of the Immaculate Conception, celebrated on December 8, and Our Lady of Guadalupe, December 12, sing Mary's own song, the Magnificat (page 16 or 158 in the hymnal), or you can sing "Immaculate Mary" (page 140 in the hymnal).

▪ THE SCHOOL OF RELIGION

Will it be difficult to make an Advent wreath or to store it between meetings? This may take some extra thought. Perhaps the entire school of religion will come together for opening prayer around a single large wreath and then go to their classrooms. If this is done, all the students should make an extra effort to come on time and to move smoothly to their classrooms when prayer is over. This way, the Advent prayers will be pleasant and peaceful.

If you want an Advent wreath for your individual space, you might work with the students who use your classroom on weekdays and make just one wreath for all of you. Perhaps one group of students could bring the candles and the others could bring the evergreen branches.

▪ THERE ARE MANY WONDERFUL DAYS DURING DECEMBER. On any day of Advent you can use the day's Daily Prayer or the week's Weekly Prayer with equal ease.

A PSALM FOR ADVENT

> all make
> the sign
> of the cross

The Canticle of Zechariah, Luke 1:68–71, 78–79

> light the correct number of candles
>   of the Advent wreath:
> December 3 to 9: one (purple) candle
> December 10 to 16: two (purple) candles
> December 17 to 23: three candles
>   (one rose and two purple)
> December 24: all four candles

LEADER Praise the Lord, the God of Israel,
who shepherds the people and sets them free.

ALL **God raises from David's house
a child with power to save.**

SIDE A Through the holy prophets,
God promised in ages past
to save us from enemy hands,
from the grip of all who hate us.

SIDE B Out of God's deepest mercy
a dawn will come from on high,
light for those shadowed by death,
a guide for our feet on the way to peace.

LEADER Praise the Lord, the God of Israel,
who shepherds the people and sets them free.

ALL **God raises from David's house
a child with power to save.**

**Glory to the Father, and to the Son,
and to the Holy Spirit:
as it was in the beginning, is now,
and will be for ever. Amen. Alleluia.**

> turn back to
> Daily Prayer or Weekly Prayer
> for today

118

ADVENT

LEADER Let us offer God praise and thanksgiving:

ALL ▶ all make
the sign
of the cross

LEADER Come, Lord Jesus!
ALL **Come quickly!**

LEADER Blessed are you, Lord, God of all creation:
in the darkness and in the light.
Blessed are you
in this food and in our sharing.
Blessed are you as we wait in joyful hope
for the coming of our Savior,
Jesus Christ.
For the kingdom, the power
and the glory are yours,
now and for ever.

ALL **Amen.**

▶ all make
the sign
of the cross

ADVENT

END OF THE DAY PRAYER

> all make
> the sign
> of the cross

LEADER   In the quiet waiting of Advent,
             let us pray to the Lord.

> stop; allow a minute or so of silence,
> and then say:

God of the promise, listen to our prayers.
Be with us through this evening
    and through the night.
Be close to us in our fears
    and in our hopes,
      and bring us to the brightness of morning.
We ask this in the name of Jesus the Lord.

ALL   **Amen.**

> the following words can be sung to the
> melody for "Creator of the stars of night" or
> "Praise God from whom all blessings flow":

All praise, eternal Son, to thee
Whose advent sets thy people free;
Whom with the Father we adore
And Holy Spirit ever more.

LEADER   Come, Lord Jesus!
ALL   **Come quickly!**

> all make
> the sign
> of the cross

120

A Blessing of the Advent Wreath

This blessing can be used at any time after the wreath is prepared but before the first candle is lighted. A bowl of burning incense can be placed near or in the middle of the wreath.

 all make
the sign
of the cross

LEADER
Our help is in the name of the Lord:

ALL
Who made heaven and earth.

LEADER
Come, Lord Jesus!

ALL
Come quickly!

LEADER
It is wintertime. Days are short and nights are long. We need the light of Christ. We need Christ's warmth, love and joy. And so we gather around this wreath in hope.

The circle of this wreath will remind us
    of the coming of Christ,
        whose love for us has no end.

The light of these candles will remind us
    of the coming of Christ,
        who is the light of the world.

The green color of these branches will remind us
    of the coming of Christ,
        who brings us eternal life.

My friends, let us bless the Lord.

 stop; allow a minute or so of silence,
and then say:

By day and by night,
    and through every season,
        you watch over us, Lord.

We praise you for this Advent wreath.
It is the evergreen crown of your royal people,
    and it shines with the promise of victory.

By the light of this wreath
    we shall wait in patience for your Son,
        our Lord Jesus Christ.

He will comfort our fears
    and bring hope to our waiting world.
All glory be yours,
    now and for ever.

ALL
Amen.

 all make
the sign
of the cross

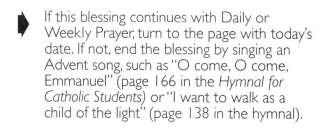 If this blessing continues with Daily or Weekly Prayer, turn to the page with today's date. If not, end the blessing by singing an Advent song, such as "O come, O come, Emmanuel" (page 166 in the *Hymnal for Catholic Students*) or "I want to walk as a child of the light" (page 138 in the hymnal).

WEEKLY PRAYER

With a Reading from the Gospel for Sunday, December 3, 2000

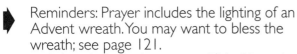 Reminders: Prayer includes the lighting of an Advent wreath. You may want to bless the wreath; see page 121.
Advent's Psalm is on page 15 in *Blessed Be God!*

■ INTRODUCTION

On Sunday, December 3, we begin the important and happy season of Advent. This is an important time because we turn our thoughts to the coming of Jesus who is the savior of the world. Jesus is the Son of God, present among the people God loves. That is good news, and it makes us happy to remember that Jesus will come again in glory. During Advent we think about the many ways God comes to be with us.

■ A PSALM FOR ADVENT

turn to page 118

■ READING

Luke 21:25–28

Listen to the words of the holy gospel according to Luke:

Jesus said, "Strange things will happen to the sun, moon, and stars. The nations on earth will be afraid of the roaring sea and tides, and they won't know what to do. People will be so frightened that they will faint because of what is happening to the world. Every power in the sky will be shaken. Then the Son of Man will be seen, coming in a cloud with great power and glory. When all of this starts happening, stand up straight and be brave. You will soon be set free."

The gospel of the Lord.

■ REFLECTION

What changes do you think God will make in the way nations and people act? Why does the idea of God's coming frighten some people? How can God's coming set us free?

■ CLOSING

Let us remember these intentions:

Let us pray with the words that Jesus taught us:

Our Father . . .

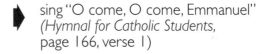 sing "O come, O come, Emmanuel" *(Hymnal for Catholic Students, page 166, verse 1)*

Lord our God, you bring light and joy
to the darkness of this world.
Let us carry your light in our hearts this day.
Come, Lord Jesus!
Come quickly!

put out the candle of the Advent wreath

MONDAY PRAYER

December 4, 2000

> Reminders: Prayer includes lighting the Advent wreath. You can bless it before you begin prayer today; see page 121.

■ INTRODUCTION

Today we remember Saint Barbara. Her name means "foreigner" *(FOR-in-er)*. It reminds us that we are really foreigners—no matter where we live—because our true home is heaven. Some people put a small branch from a flowering tree in water on this day. It may blossom by Christmas. These "Barbara branches" remind us of Jesus, who is called a branch on King David's family tree.

In today's reading, Isaiah *(eye-ZAY-uh)* comforts the people whose country is invaded by a strong army. The people are seeing their farms, towns and homes being destroyed. Isaiah told them to think of the joy that God will one day bring them.

■ A PSALM FOR ADVENT

 turn to
page 118

■ READING

Isaiah 2:3–5

Listen to the words of the prophet Isaiah:

In the future, many people will come and say,

"Let's go to the mountain of the LORD God of Jacob and worship in his temple."

The LORD will teach us his Law from Jerusalem, and we will obey him.

He will settle arguments between nations.

They will pound their swords and their spears into rakes and shovels; they will never make war or attack one another.

People of Israel, let's live by the light of the LORD.

The word of the Lord.

■ REFLECTION

What would a world without any guns or wars be like? What will it be like when no one is dangerous to anyone else? How can we make our classroom into a place like that?

■ CLOSING

Let us remember these intentions:

Let us pray with the words that Jesus taught us:

Our Father . . .

> sing "O come, O come, Emmanuel"
> *(Hymnal for Catholic Students,*
> page 166, verse 1)

Lord our God, you bring light and joy
  to the darkness of this world.
Let us carry your light in our hearts this day.
Come, Lord Jesus!
Come quickly!

 put out the candle
of the Advent wreath

123

TUESDAY PRAYER

December 5, 2000

■ INTRODUCTION

The four weeks of Advent are well begun! The word "advent" means "coming." During this season we prepare ourselves to welcome Jesus when he comes.

Of course, Jesus does not come just once a year. He comes when we are in trouble, when we rejoice, when we pray, when we celebrate, when we love one another in his name. We take this time every year to practice being ready—so we can receive Jesus every day of our lives!

■ A PSALM FOR ADVENT

turn to
page 118

■ READING

Isaiah 1:1–4, 5

Listen to the words of the prophet Isaiah:

Like a branch that sprouts from a stump,
    someone from David's family
        will someday be king.
The Spirit of the LORD will be with him
    to give him understanding, wisdom,
        and insight.
He will be powerful,
    and he will know and honor the LORD.
His greatest joy will be to obey the LORD.
This king won't judge by appearances
    or listen to rumors.
The poor and the needy will be treated
    with fairness and with justice.
Honesty and fairness will be his royal robes.

The word of the Lord.

■ REFLECTION

How is Jesus like a branch sprouting from David's family tree? How are we like branches on the family tree of Jesus? How does the family of Jesus treat poor and needy people "with fairness and justice"?

■ CLOSING

Let us remember these intentions:

Let us pray with the words that Jesus taught us:

Our Father . . .

sing "O come, O come, Emmanuel"
(Hymnal for Catholic Students,
page 166, verse 1)

Lord our God, you bring light and joy
    to the darkness of this world.
Let us carry your light in our hearts this day.
Come, Lord Jesus!
Come quickly!

put out the candle
of the Advent wreath

124

WEDNESDAY PRAYER

December 6, 2000

■ INTRODUCTION

Can you guess the name of the saint we remember today? He was a bishop of the early church. He is the patron of sailors and sea travelers. He is the protector of children. He is admired by people all over the world, and many stories have been made up about him. In one story, he gave poor girls dowry *(DOW-ree)* money so they could marry.

Dutch settlers who came to this country called this saint and bishop Sinter Klaas. That is why we sometimes call him by a name that sounds very much like that, Santa Claus. Do you know his real name? It is Saint Nicholas!

■ A PSALM FOR ADVENT

► turn to
page 118

■ READING

Isaiah 25:6, 8–10

Listen to the words of the prophet Isaiah:

On this mountain the LORD All-Powerful
    will prepare for all nations
        a feast of the finest foods.
Choice wines and the best meats will be served.
The LORD All-Powerful will destroy
    the power of death
        and wipe away all tears.
No longer will his people be insulted
    everywhere.
The LORD has spoken!
At that time, people will say,
    "The LORD has saved us!

Let's celebrate. We waited and hoped—
    now our God is here."
The powerful arm of the LORD will protect
    this mountain.

The word of the Lord.

■ REFLECTION

In what ways can I wipe away other people's tears? How can I help people who are insulted? What are other ways I can give comfort?

■ CLOSING

Let us remember these intentions:

Let us pray with the words that Jesus taught us:

Our Father . . .

 sing "O come, O come, Emmanuel"
(Hymnal for Catholic Students,
page 166, verse 1)

Lord our God, you bring light and joy
    to the darkness of this world.
Let us carry your light in our hearts this day.
Come, Lord Jesus!
Come quickly!

 put out the candle
of the Advent wreath

125

THURSDAY PRAYER

December 7, 2000

■ INTRODUCTION

Today we remember Saint Ambrose, a great teacher of the fourth century. He was also a lawyer, well-known for giving speeches. When he tried to stop an argument within the church at Milan in Italy, a child called out, "Ambrose for bishop!" Everyone thought this was a good idea, so they elected Ambrose to be the bishop of Milan. He was not even baptized at that time, but this was soon done, and Ambrose became an excellent bishop.

Tomorrow is an important day. It is the feast of the Immaculate Conception. This is a title for Mary, the Mother of God, who is a patron of the United States. Catholics are asked to go to Mass on that day. Please remind your family about this.

■ A PSALM FOR ADVENT

turn to
page 118

■ READING

Isaiah 26:1–4

Listen to the words of the prophet Isaiah:

The time is coming when the people of Judah
    will sing this song:
"Our city is protected. The LORD is our fortress,
    and he gives us victory.
Open the city gates for a law-abiding nation
    that is faithful to God.
The LORD gives perfect peace
    to those whose faith is firm.

So always trust in the LORD
    because he is forever our mighty rock."
The word of the Lord.

■ REFLECTION

How is God like a fortress for me? Isaiah says that God gives peace to those whose faith is firm. What does it mean to have firm faith? Do I trust God like a mighty rock? What other images of trustworthiness can we think of?

■ CLOSING

Let us remember these intentions:

Let us pray with the words that Jesus taught us:
Our Father . . .

sing "O come, O come, Emmanuel"
(Hymnal for Catholic Students,
page 166, verse 1)

Lord our God, you bring light and joy
    to the darkness of this world.
Let us carry your light in our hearts this day.
Come, Lord Jesus!
Come quickly!

put out the candle
of the Advent wreath

FRIDAY PRAYER

December 8, 2000

 Reminder: Today please use October's Meal Prayer, the Angelus, on page 49, and the End of the Day Prayer on page 25.
    If you will celebrate the eucharist today, you may wish to skip or shorten Friday Prayer. Talk these things over with the teacher.

■ INTRODUCTION

Today we remember the Immaculate Conception *(ee-MAC-you-lit con-SEP-shun)* of Mary. We celebrate our belief that Mary was filled with God's grace from the first moment of her life, even in her mother's womb.

God gave Mary this honor because she would be invited to be the mother of the Savior.

■ A PSALM FOR ADVENT

 turn to
page 118

■ READING

Revelation 12:1, 5–6

Listen to the words of the book of Revelation:

Something important appeared in the sky. It was a woman whose clothes were the sun. The moon was under her feet, and a crown made of twelve stars was on her head.

The woman gave birth to a son, who would rule all nations with an iron rod. The boy was snatched away. He was taken to God and placed on his throne. The woman ran into the desert to a place that God had prepared for her.

The word of the Lord.

■ REFLECTION

Where in my home and parish are there images of Mary? Do any of these images have the moon and stars mentioned in this reading? What is Mary's importance in God's plan? What is her importance to me?

■ CLOSING

Let us remember these intentions:

Let us pray with the words that Jesus taught us:

Our Father . . .

 sing "O come, O come, Emmanuel" *(Hymnal for Catholic Students, page 166, verse 1)*

Lord our God, you bring light and joy
  to the darkness of this world.
Let us carry your light in our hearts this day.
Come, Lord Jesus!
Come quickly!

 put out the candle
of the Advent wreath

127

WEEKLY PRAYER

With a Reading from the Gospel for Sunday, December 10, 2000

■ INTRODUCTION

During Advent we remember two great prophets, Isaiah *(eye-ZAY-uh)*, and John the Baptist. They were prophets who boldly preached the word of God. Isaiah told the people of Israel to stop sinning and to be ready for God's coming. Many hundreds of years later, John the Baptist came with the same message. "Turn away from your sins. Turn to God and be forgiven," he said. We try during Advent to listen carefully to this message. We try to prepare our hearts for the coming of our Savior.

Today's reading is taken from the gospel for December 10, the second Sunday of Advent.

■ A PSALM FOR ADVENT

▶ turn to
page 118

■ READING

Luke 3:2–6

Listen to the words of the holy gospel according to Luke:

God spoke to Zechariah's *(zek-uh-RYE-uhz)* son John, who was living in the desert. So John went along the Jordan Valley, telling the people, "Turn back to God and be baptized, then your sins will be forgiven." Isaiah the prophet wrote about John when he said,

"In the desert someone is shouting,
'Get the road ready for the Lord!
Make a straight path for him.
Fill up every valley
    and level every mountain and hill.

Straighten the crooked paths
    and smooth out the rough roads.
Then everyone will see
    the saving power of God.'"

The gospel of the Lord.

■ REFLECTION

Isaiah says that the road between us and God is full of rocks and potholes. We cannot see God down that road, and God cannot get to us. What are the rocks and potholes between me and God?

■ CLOSING

Let us remember these intentions:

Let us pray with the words that Jesus taught us:

Our Father . . .

▶ sing "O come, O come, Emmanuel"
(Hymnal for Catholic Students,
page 166, verse 1)

Lord our God, you bring light and joy
    to the darkness of this world.
Let us carry your light in our hearts this day.
Come, Lord Jesus!
Come quickly!

▶ put out the candles
of the Advent wreath

MONDAY PRAYER

December 11, 2000

■ INTRODUCTION

Today we remember Saint Damasus *(DAM-uh-sus)*, who died in the year 384. Damasus grew up in Rome, Italy, where his father was a priest, and he became a deacon in his father's parish. When he was 60, Damasus was elected pope. He set about repairing the catacombs *(KAT-uh-combs)* and other tombs of the martyrs *(MAR-terz)*, which were crumbling. And he protected the early records of the church's life.

Damasus is honored most, however, for asking his secretary, Saint Jerome, to translate the Bible into Latin so that everyone could read and study it.

■ A PSALM FOR ADVENT

▶ turn to
page 118

■ READING

Isaiah 29:18–19, 23–24

Listen to the words of the prophet Isaiah:

The LORD says this:
"In the future the deaf will be able to hear
    whatever is read to them;
the blind will be freed from a life of darkness.
The poor and the needy
    will celebrate and shout
because of the LORD, the holy God of Israel.
When they see how great
    I have made their nation,
they will praise and honor me,
    the holy God of Israel.

Everyone who is confused will understand,
    and all who have complained
        will obey my teaching."

The word of the Lord.

■ REFLECTION

Isaiah says that deafness and blindness do not exist in God's kingdom. There are no misunderstandings and no complaints. Does this sound like a kingdom worth living in? How can we live in this kingdom?

■ CLOSING

Let us remember these intentions:

Let us pray with the words that Jesus taught us:
Our Father . . .

 sing "O come, O come, Emmanuel"
(Hymnal for Catholic Students,
page 166, verse 1)

Lord our God, you bring light and joy
    to the darkness of this world.
Let us carry your light in our hearts this day.
Come, Lord Jesus!
Come quickly!

▶ put out the candles
of the Advent wreath

TUESDAY PRAYER

December 12, 2000

Reminder: Today please use October's Meal Prayer, the Angelus, on page 49, and the End of the Day Prayer on page 25.

■ INTRODUCTION

Today we celebrate the feast of Our Lady of Guadalupe *(gwah-da-LOO-pay)*. In the year 1531, Mary appeared to an Aztec Indian named Juan Diego *(hwan dee-AY-go)*. Juan saw the Mother of God dressed as an Aztec woman. She promised to help all who called on her.

The vision and Mary's message brought faith and comfort to the Aztec people, who had been treated with great cruelty by the Spanish explorers. Our Lady of Guadalupe is the patron of Mexico, and she is honored throughout the Americas.

■ A PSALM FOR ADVENT

turn to
page 118

■ READING

Zechariah 2:8, 10–13

Listen to the words of the prophet Zechariah *(zek-uh-RYE-uh)*:

The glorious LORD All-Powerful ordered me to say this to the nations:

"City of Zion, sing and celebrate! The LORD has promised to come and live with you. When he does, many nations will turn to him and become his people. At that time you will know that I am a prophet of the LORD All-Powerful.

Then Judah will be his part of the holy land, and Jerusalem will again be his chosen city.

"Everyone be silent! The LORD is present and moving about in his holy place."

The word of the Lord.

■ REFLECTION

The prophet delivers God's promise to come and live among all people. In Jesus, God has kept this promise. What difference does God's presence make in my life? How does a school community that knows God is present live together?

■ CLOSING

Let us remember these intentions:

Let us pray with the words that Jesus taught us:
Our Father . . .

sing "O come, O come, Emmanuel" *(Hymnal for Catholic Students, page 166, verse 1)*

Lord our God, you bring light and joy
    to the darkness of this world.
Let us carry your light in our hearts this day.
Come, Lord Jesus!
Come quickly!

put out the candles of the Advent wreath

■ INTRODUCTION

Today we remember Saint Lucy. In Latin and Italian her name is Santa Lucia *(loo-CHEE-uh),* which means "holy light." Her feast is in Advent when we think about light and darkness and remember that Jesus, our light, is coming.

Lucy was killed for her faith about 20 years before it became legal to be Christian. She may have been about 12 years old. In some countries on this day, one girl in each family is the "Lucy Queen." With a wreath of candles in her hair, she wakes the rest of the family in the morning and serves them breakfast.

■ A PSALM FOR ADVENT

turn to
page 118

■ READING

Isaiah 35: 1–2, 2–4, 4

Listen to the words of the prophet Isaiah:

Thirsty deserts will be glad;
   barren lands will celebrate
   and blossom with flowers.
Deserts will bloom everywhere
   and sing joyful songs.
Everyone will see the wonderful splendor
   of the LORD our God.
Here is a message for all who are weak,
   trembling, and worried:
"Cheer up! Don't be afraid.
   Your God is coming to rescue you."

The word of the Lord.

■ REFLECTION

Isaiah lived in a hot, dry, rocky country. When he dreamed of God's kingdom, he saw a garden filled with flowers. What is my dream of God's kingdom? What pictures and words do we use for it?

■ CLOSING

Let us remember these intentions:

Let us pray with the words that Jesus taught us:
Our Father . . .

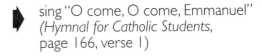

   sing "O come, O come, Emmanuel"
   (Hymnal for Catholic Students,
   page 166, verse 1)

Lord our God, you bring light and joy
   to the darkness of this world.
Let us carry your light in our hearts this day.
Come, Lord Jesus!
Come quickly!

   put out the candles
   of the Advent wreath

December 14, 2000

■ INTRODUCTION

One job of a prophet *(PRAH-fit)* is to show the meaning of God's words in daily life. Today we remember a Christian prophet whose name is Saint John of the Cross.

John was a member of the Carmelite *(KAR-muh-lite)* order who was put in prison by some other priests of his order. Instead of becoming bitter and angry, John prayed and wrote about the spiritual life. John said, "Where there is no love, it is for you to bring love." Even in prison, John of the Cross was a prophet of God's love.

The whole people of God are called to be prophets, as the reading today tells us.

■ A PSALM FOR ADVENT

 turn to
page 118

■ READING

Isaiah 40:3–5

Listen to the words of the prophet Isaiah:

Someone is shouting:
"Clear a path in the desert!
   Make a straight road for the LORD our God.
Fill in the valleys;
   flatten every hill and mountain.
Level the rough and rugged ground.
Then the glory of the LORD
   will appear for all to see.
The LORD has promised this!"

The word of the Lord.

■ REFLECTION

What are some "hills and mountains" that prevent us from seeing the glory of God? How can we "make a straight road" for the Lord during the remaining days of Advent?

■ CLOSING

Let us remember these intentions:

Let us pray with the words that Jesus taught us:
Our Father . . .

 sing "O come, O come, Emmanuel"
(Hymnal for Catholic Students,
page 166, verse 1)

Lord our God, you bring light and joy
   to the darkness of this world.
Let us carry your light in our hearts this day.
Come, Lord Jesus!
Come quickly!

put out the candles
of the Advent wreath

FRIDAY PRAYER

December 15, 2000

■ INTRODUCTION

Today we will listen again to the teaching of Isaiah the prophet. Life was very difficult for the people of Isaiah's day. Enemies were destroying their cities, stealing their goods, and capturing their leaders. Isaiah reminded them that God would give them powerful help when the time was right. But Isaiah also told them to act with justice. They were not to imitate the violence they saw around them but remain faithful to their God.

■ A PSALM FOR ADVENT

➤ turn to
  page 118

■ READING

Isaiah 45:6–8, 21–22

Listen to the words of the prophet Isaiah:

The LORD said:
"Everyone from east to west
    will learn that I am the LORD.
  No other gods are real.
I create light and darkness,
    happiness and sorrow.
  I, the LORD, do all of this.
Tell the heavens to send down justice
    like showers of rain.
Prepare the earth for my saving power
    to sprout and produce justice
  that I, the LORD, create.
I am the only God! There are no others.
  I bring about justice,
    and have the power to save.

I invite the whole world to turn to me
    and be saved.
  I alone am God! No others are real."

The word of the Lord.

■ REFLECTION

Do I act justly, even when people around me act with injustice or violence? How does knowing that there is only one God help us to make good decisions? What good decisions have I made during this Advent?

■ CLOSING

Let us remember these intentions:

Let us pray with the words that Jesus taught us:

Our Father . . .

sing "O come, O come, Emmanuel"
(Hymnal for Catholic Students,
page 166, verse 1)

Lord our God, you bring light and joy
    to the darkness of this world.
Let us carry your light in our hearts this day.
Come, Lord Jesus!
Come quickly!

put out the candles
of the Advent wreath

WEEKLY PRAYER

With a Reading from the Gospel for Sunday, December 17, 2000

■ INTRODUCTION

Today's reading tells us more about the preaching of John the Baptist. John knew that people were eager for the coming of the Messiah. They wanted the joy of knowing that God was near to them and ready to help them.

But John did not want people to sit back and wait. They needed to change the way they lived. John helped them understand what it means to be holy and to live as children of God.

■ A PSALM FOR ADVENT

turn to
page 118

■ READING

Luke 3:10–16

Listen to the words of the holy gospel according to Luke:

The crowds asked John [the Baptist], "What should we do?" John told them, "If you have two coats, give one to someone who doesn't have any. If you have food, share it with someone else."

When tax collectors came to be baptized, they asked John, "Teacher, what should we do?" John told them, "Don't make people pay more than they owe."

Some soldiers asked him, "And what about us? What do we have to do?" John told them, "Don't force people to pay money to make you leave them alone. Be satisfied with your pay."

Everyone became excited and wondered, "Could John be the Messiah?"

John said, "I am just baptizing with water. But someone more powerful is going to come, and I am not good enough even to untie his sandals. He will baptize you with the Holy Spirit and with fire."

The gospel of the Lord.

■ REFLECTION

If we students asked John what we should do, what might he answer? What might he tell teachers? parents? brothers and sisters? What am I doing during Advent to follow Jesus more faithfully?

■ CLOSING

Let us remember these intentions:

Let us pray with the words that Jesus taught us:
Our Father . . .

sing "O come, O come, Emmanuel"
(Hymnal for Catholic Students,
page 166, verse 1)

Lord our God, you bring light and joy
  to the darkness of this world.
Let us carry your light in our hearts this day.
Come, Lord Jesus!
Come quickly!

put out the candles
of the Advent wreath

MONDAY PRAYER

December 18, 2000

■ INTRODUCTION

Each day of the week before Christmas has a special prayer called an "O Antiphon" *(AN-tih-fon)*. The verses of the song "O come, O come, Emmanuel" are based on these prayers. Our closing prayers will include the "O Antiphon" each day.

In today's closing prayer we call Jesus "O Sacred Lord."

■ A PSALM FOR ADVENT

turn to
page 118

■ READING

Luke 1:6–7, 8, 11–15

Listen to the words of the holy gospel according to Luke:

Zechariah *(zek-uh-RYE-uh)* and Elizabeth were good people and pleased the Lord God by obeying all that he had commanded. But they did not have children.

One day Zechariah's group of priests were on duty, and he was serving God as a priest. All at once an angel from the Lord appeared to Zechariah at the right side of the altar. Zechariah was confused and afraid when he saw the angel. But the angel told him, "Don't be afraid, Zechariah! God has heard your prayers. Your wife Elizabeth will have a son, and you must name him John. His birth will make you very happy, and many people will be glad. Your son will be a great servant of the Lord."

The gospel of the Lord.

■ REFLECTION

Today we heard the announcement of the birth of John the Baptist. All birth, all life is precious to the Lord. How can we thank God for the gift of life itself?

■ CLOSING

Let us remember these intentions:

O sacred Lord of ancient Israel,
who showed yourself to Moses
in the burning bush,
who gave him the holy law
on Sinai mountain:
Come, stretch out your mighty hand
to set us free.

Let us pray with the words that Jesus taught us:

Our Father . . .

sing "O come, O come, Emmanuel"
*(Hymnal for Catholic Students,
page 166, verse 3)*

Lord our God, you bring light and joy
to the darkness of this world.
Let us carry your light in our hearts this day.
Come, Lord Jesus!
Come quickly!

put out the candles
of the Advent wreath

135

TUESDAY PRAYER

December 19, 2000

▶ Reminder: You may want to make copies of Christmastime's Prayers, pages 144 to 146.

■ INTRODUCTION

In today's prayer we call Jesus the "Flower of Jesse." Jesse, grandson of Ruth and Boaz, was the father of King David. People believed that the next great king would come from David's family.

■ A PSALM FOR ADVENT

▶ turn to page 118

■ READING

Luke 1:39–42, 45–48

Listen to the words of the holy gospel according to Luke:

Mary hurried to a town in the hill country of Judea *(joo-DEE-uh)*. She went into Zechariah's *(zek-uh-RYE-uhz)* home, where she greeted Elizabeth. When Elizabeth heard Mary's greeting, her baby moved within her.

The Holy Spirit came upon Elizabeth. Then in a loud voice she said to Mary, "God has blessed you more than any other woman! He has also blessed the child you will have. The Lord has blessed you because you believed that he will keep his promise."

Mary said, "With all my heart I praise the Lord, and I am glad because of God my Savior. He cares for me, his humble servant. From now on, all people will say God has blessed me."

The gospel of the Lord.

■ REFLECTION

All people who keep God's word are like Mary. They carry Christ within themselves. Do I recognize people who carry Christ?

■ CLOSING

Let us remember these intentions:

O Flower of Jesse's stem,
    you have been raised up
        as a sign for all peoples;
rulers stand silent in your presence;
    the nations bow down in worship before you.
Come, let nothing keep you from coming
    to our aid.

Let us pray with the words that Jesus taught us:

Our Father . . .

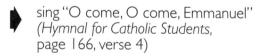

▶ sing "O come, O come, Emmanuel" *(Hymnal for Catholic Students,* page 166, verse 4)

Lord our God, you bring light and joy
    to the darkness of this world.
Let us carry your light in our hearts this day.
Come, Lord Jesus!
Come quickly!

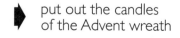

▶ put out the candles
of the Advent wreath

WEDNESDAY PRAYER

December 20, 2000

■ INTRODUCTION

In today's reading we hear the words of Mary's humble joy that God had blessed her by making her the mother of the Savior. We call Mary's prayer the "Magnificat" *(mahg-NEE-fee-caht)*.

In today's "O Antiphon" *(AN-tih-fon)*, we call Jesus the "Key of David." People with keys are often people with authority. Jesus is the key that opens the gate of heaven for us.

■ A PSALM FOR ADVENT

 turn to
page 118

■ READING

Luke 1:46–49, 53–55

Listen to the words of the holy gospel according to Luke:

Mary spoke these words:
"With all my heart I praise the Lord,
    and I am glad because of God my Savior.
God cares for me, his humble servant.
From now on, all people will say
        God has blessed me.
God All-Powerful has done great things for me,
    and his name is holy.
God gives the hungry good things to eat,
    and sends the rich away with nothing.
God helps his servant Israel
    and is always merciful to his people.
The Lord made this promise to our ancestors,
    to Abraham and his family forever!"

The gospel of the Lord.

■ REFLECTION

Do I, like Mary, praise God with "all my heart"? How is Mary's child the fulfillment of God's promise to Abraham's family?

■ CLOSING

Let us remember these intentions:

O Key of David, O royal power of Israel,
    controlling at your will the gate of heaven:
Come, unlock the prison walls of death
    for those who dwell in darkness
        and the shadow of death,
    and lead your captive people into freedom.

Let us pray with the words that Jesus taught us:
Our Father . . .

 sing "O come, O come, Emmanuel"
(Hymnal for Catholic Students,
page 166, verse 5)

Lord our God, you bring light and joy
    to the darkness of this world.
Let us carry your light in our hearts this day.
Come, Lord Jesus!
Come quickly!

 put out the candles
of the Advent wreath

137

THURSDAY PRAYER

December 21, 2000

■ INTRODUCTION

Today is the winter solstice, the shortest day of the year. So we call upon God to be light to us. In the "O Antiphon" *(AN-tih-fon)* we name Jesus the "dawn." He is our "sun of justice" and the "light of the world."

The Jewish festival of Hanukkah begins tonight. It will last for eight days. According to a legend, one day's supply of oil kept the lamp of the temple burning for eight days. It was a gentle light shining to give the Jewish people hope. They will never forget this miracle.

■ A PSALM FOR ADVENT

▶ turn to
page 118

■ READING

Luke 1:57–64

Listen to the words of the holy gospel according to Luke:

When Elizabeth's son was born, her neighbors and relatives heard how kind the Lord had been to her, and they too were glad.

Eight days later they did for the child what the Law of Moses commands. They were going to name him Zechariah, after his father. But Elizabeth said, "No! His name is John."

The people argued, "No one in your family has ever been named John." So they motioned to Zechariah to find out what he wanted to name his son.

Zechariah asked for a writing tablet. Then he wrote, "His name is John." Everyone was amazed. Right away Zechariah started speaking and praising God.

The gospel of the Lord.

■ REFLECTION

How do our families show their joy at the birth of a baby? How was my name chosen?

■ CLOSING

Let us remember these intentions:

O Radiant Dawn,
    splendor of eternal light, sun of justice:
Come, shine on those who dwell in darkness
    and the shadow of death.

Let us pray with the words that Jesus taught us:

Our Father . . .

▶ sing "O come, O come, Emmanuel"
(Hymnal for Catholic Students,
page 166, verse 6)

Lord our God, you bring light and joy
    to the darkness of this world.
Let us carry your light in our hearts this day.
Come, Lord Jesus!
Come quickly!

▶ put out the candles
of the Advent wreath

■ INTRODUCTION

In today's "O Antiphon" we call Jesus our king and our keystone. The keystone is the stone in the middle of an arch. It holds the other stones in place so that the arch does not fall.

■ A PSALM FOR ADVENT

 turn to
page 118

■ READING

Luke 1:67–71, 74–79

Listen to the words of the holy gospel according to Luke:

The Holy Spirit came upon Zechariah, and he began to speak: "Praise the Lord, the God of Israel! He has come to save his people. Our God has given us a mighty Savior from the family of David his servant. Long ago the Lord promised by the words of his holy prophets to save us from our enemies and from everyone who hates us. Then we could serve him without fear, by being holy and good as long as we live.

"You, my son, will be called a prophet of God in heaven above. You will go ahead of the Lord to get everything ready for him. You will tell his people that they can be saved when their sins are forgiven. God's love and kindness will shine upon us like the sun that rises in the sky. On us who live in the dark shadow of death this light will shine to guide us into a life of peace."

The gospel of the Lord.

■ REFLECTION

There are places where people cannot serve God "without fear." Do we remember those people in our prayers?

■ CLOSING

Let us remember these intentions:

O King of all the nations,
   the only joy of every human heart;
O Keystone of the mighty arch of humankind,
   come and save the creature
   you fashioned from the dust.

Let us pray with the words that Jesus taught us:

Our Father . . .

 sing "O come, O come, Emmanuel"
(Hymnal for Catholic Students,
page 166, verse 7)

Lord our God, you bring light and joy
   to the darkness of this world.
Let us carry your light in our hearts this day.
Come, Lord Jesus!
Come quickly!

put out the candles
of the Advent wreath

A Blessing before Christmas Break

Shortly before dismissal, the students gather so that the teacher will be able to bless each one.

▶ all make
the sign
of the cross

TEACHER
May the Lord's face shine on us,
    and may the Lord guide our feet
        into the way of peace.
Blessed be the name of the Lord,
    now and forever.

ALL
Amen.

TEACHER
Let us put ourselves into the hands of the Lord
    and pray that God will bless us
        and our families
    during the coming holy days.
May each of us help to make our home
    a place of joy, love, peace and safety.

May we be generous and considerate,
    not thinking only about ourselves
    but helping others enjoy the blessings
        of Christmas.

Please respond "Amen" as I bless each of you.

▶ the teacher goes to each student in turn,
places a hand on the student's head
or shoulder, and says:

N., go with God.

ALL
Amen.

▶ when these individual blessings
are completed,
prayer continues:

TEACHER
My dear friends and students,
    may almighty God give you light and joy.
And, until we gather here again,
    may God bless all of us:

ALL

▶ all make
the sign
of the cross

▶ end with a hymn such as "The King of glory"
(Hymnal for Catholic Students, page 193)
or "Shalom chaverim" (page 177)

CHRISTMASTIME

Monday, December 25, to Monday, January 8

CHRISTMASTIME 2000–2001

■ ABOUT THE SEASON

It is hard for Christians, whether they are adults or children, to remember that it is not gifts under the tree that make Christmas so important. If the presents were the only things we looked forward to, then when the presents were opened, Christmas would be over for us.

LOOKING AHEAD

But Christmastime is not just one day. It is a season of almost three weeks after December 25. Many good days come during Christmastime. There is Holy Family Day, Saint John's Day and the feast of the Holy Innocents, too. On January 1 we celebrate the solemnity of Mary, the Mother of God. The feast of the Epiphany on January 6 also marks the end of the Great Jubilee celebration. The Christmas season draws to a close with the feast of the Baptism of the Lord.

Most of these days are spent at home during the school break. But when we come back, there is still a week of Christmastime left to celebrate at school with our friends. We can talk to one another about the events of the vacation. We can celebrate the beginning of the twenty-first century. We can keep the season from ending too soon. We can balance the prayers of preparation that we shared during Advent with the prayers of celebration we will share during this joyful time.

▪ CHRISTMASTIME IS A CELEBRATION OF PROMISES KEPT AND PROPHECIES FULFILLED. During Advent, we heard Isaiah's prophecy of a savior who would be sent from God. During Christmastime, at home and at church, we hear the good news of the birth of that savior, Jesus of Nazareth.

We take this week of Christmastime to hear the words of the gospel of John. They tell us of the preaching of John the Baptist. He recognized Jesus as the one the people had been waiting for, and so he told his own disciples to follow Jesus. In this way, the work of Jesus began.

▪ SUNDAY, JANUARY 7, IS THE EPIPHANY OF THE LORD. This is one of the greatest feasts of the church. In many parts of the world, Epiphany is the merriest day of Christmastime. We do what we can to make it one of the happiest days of the year.

The word "epiphany" means "showing." We rejoice that the glory of God is shown through Jesus our Savior. That glory is shown to the Magi who came from far away and followed the star to Bethlehem. The wise men are the first of many people who would seek Jesus and find him.

The Magi are not the only ones who discover the glory of God. Jesus showed God's glory in many ways to many people. The followers of John saw the heavens opened on the day Jesus was baptized in the Jordan. The voice of God was heard, and this voice invited all those who saw Jesus to listen to his message.

The feast of the Baptism of the Lord is Monday, January 8. It closes the Christmas season and prepares us to follow the teachings of Jesus during the coming year.

▪ JANUARY IS THE FIRST MONTH OF THE NEW YEAR. It is also the beginning of the new century and the new millennium. The word January comes from the Latin word *janua*. It means "doorway." It is an old custom to bless doorways at epiphany, and this custom is a part of the Blessing of the Classroom, found on page 148. January is the year's doorway, an entrance into a bright new beginning!

Jesus is always beginning again the work of salvation in us and among us. It is true that sin is not finished. Hatred and greed are not destroyed. Even winter is not over. Yet we have begun a new year. The hours of darkness are shrinking before the strengthening sun. We see the Savior and our hopes are made new.

Like Magi, we bring the gold, frankincense and myrrh of our own talents and gifts to the kingdom. We look at each other with new understanding,

new generosity and new energy. That is a big task. We cannot do it alone.

■ PREPARATION FOR CHRISTMASTIME

The Psalm, Meal Prayer and End of the Day Prayer for Christmastime are found on pages 18, 19 and 20 of *Blessed Be God!* If the students do not use *Blessed Be God!* prayers may be photocopied from pages 144, 145 and 146 of this book. Use these prayers for the final week of Christmastime.

You will use a new set of prayers beginning on January 9, when Ordinary Time begins. You might copy both sets of prayers at the same time. The next set, for the rest of January, is found on pages 158 to 160 in this book.

▪ IT IS A VERY OLD TRADITION TO BLESS OUR HOMES AND CLASSROOMS AT EPIPHANY. As part of this blessing, doorways are marked with chalk. You can hold the blessing ritual for your classroom, or you might involve the whole school. Instructions and prayers for the blessing are on page 148 of this book.

▪ PUT A CANDLE IN THE PRAYER CENTER. You will light it for Daily and Weekly Prayer, and also for Prayer at the End of the Day.

You may want to add Christmas decorations to your prayer center. A fresh wreath, evergreens, and bright red and gold ribbons can be used. Of course, the stable will now have all its statues added. Don't forget the Blessing of the Stable on page 147.

Be sure to wait until after Christmastime to take down any decorations. See if you can keep the classroom looking cheerful all through the winter. The end of the Christmas season should not be sad. In fact, some people leave their Christmas stable up until February 2, the feast of the Presentation of the Lord, or Candlemas, as it is also called.

▪ SUGGESTED HYMNS: The Closing of prayer includes the singing of "Joy to the world" (page 146 in the *Hymnal for Catholic Students)*. Isaac Watts based this hymn on Psalm 98. This is our Psalm for Christmastime. Another hymn based on that psalm is "Sing a new song" (page 179 in the hymnal).

There are many beautiful Christmas hymns and carols that we can sing during the season. "O come, all ye faithful" (page 164 in the hymnal) is a hymn for Christmas. "Songs of thankfulness and praise" (page 188) is a hymn for Epiphany. "Go tell it on the mountain" (page 128) and "The canticle of Zachary" (page 8) are good hymns for the beginning of the new century. "Gloria" (page 128) and "Jubilate Deo" *(you-bee-LAH-tay DAY-oh,* page 147) are lively songs, especially when they are sung as rounds.

■ THE SCHOOL OF RELIGION

If you kept the spirit of Advent and did not have a party before Christmas, you might want to use your first gathering after Christmas break for a celebration. Enjoy some holiday food. Invite some musicians to help you sing Christmas carols. You can begin this celebration with the Blessing of the Stable (page 147).

Some places have a visit from the three wise men. Sometimes the wise men lead the blessing of the room for the new year. You can find prayers and instructions for this blessing on page 148.

A PSALM FOR CHRISTMASTIME

Psalm 98:1–3

▶ all make
the sign
of the cross

LEADER Rise up in splendor, Jerusalem!
ALL **The glory of the Lord shines upon you.**

▶ light a candle,
and then say:

LEADER God's holy day has dawned for us at last.
ALL **Come, all you peoples, and adore the Lord.**

SIDE A Sing to the Lord a new song,
the Lord of wonderful deeds.
Right hand and holy arm
brought victory to God.

SIDE B God made that victory known,
revealed justice to nations,
remembered a merciful love
loyal to the house of Israel.

ALL **The ends of the earth have seen
the victory of our God.**

LEADER God's holy day has dawned for us at last.
ALL **Come, all you peoples, and adore the Lord.**

**Glory to the Father, and to the Son,
and to the Holy Spirit:
as it was in the beginning, is now,
and will be for ever. Amen. Alleluia.**

▶ turn back to
Daily Prayer or Weekly Prayer
for today

144

CHRISTMASTIME

LEADER   Let us offer God praise and thanksgiving:

ALL ▶ all make
      the sign
      of the cross

LEADER   Rise up in splendor, Jerusalem!
ALL   **The glory of the Lord shines upon you.**
LEADER   God's holy day has dawned for us at last.
ALL   **Come, all you peoples, and adore the Lord.**

**Bless us, O Lord, and these your gifts
which we are about to receive
from your bounty.
Through Christ our Lord. Amen.**

▶ all make
   the sign
   of the cross

CHRISTMASTIME

END OF THE DAY PRAYER

> all make
> the sign
> of the cross

LEADER Rise up in splendor, Jerusalem!
  ALL **The glory of the Lord shines upon you.**

> light a candle,
> and then say:

LEADER The angels rejoiced at the coming of Jesus.
We, too, rejoice. And we sing:

> use music from the liturgy
> or the refrain from a Christmas carol
> to sing this response:

  ALL **Glory to God in the highest,
and peace to God's people on earth.**

LEADER The shepherds came to worship Jesus.
We, too, worship Jesus. And we sing:

  ALL **Glory to God . . .**

LEADER The Magi offered good gifts to Jesus.
We, too, bring gifts to Jesus. And we sing:

  ALL **Glory to God . . .**

LEADER ▶ hold out one hand
toward everyone
in blessing, and say:

May the light of Christ shine through us
for others:

  ALL ▶ all make
the sign
of the cross

> put out
> the candle

A Blessing of the Stable

This is a blessing for the first class meeting after Christmas Day. The stable is set up with only the figures of Mary and Joseph, the animals and the manger. The students are ready to put the figures of Jesus, the angels and the shepherds in place. Begin with silence, but end with carols.

LEADER
Come, Lord Jesus!

ALL
Come quickly!

LEADER
My friends, let us be silent for a moment to prepare ourselves to hear the good news.

   allow a minute or two of silence, then light a candle

READER   Luke 2:5–14
Listen to the words of the holy gospel according to Luke:

Mary was engaged to Joseph and traveled with him to Bethlehem *(BETH-luh-hem).* She was soon going to have a baby, and while they were there, she gave birth to her first-born son. She dressed him in baby clothes and laid him in a manger, because there was no room for them in the inn.

   place the figure of Jesus in the manger, then continue the reading:

That night in the fields near Bethlehem some shepherds were guarding their sheep. All at once an angel came down to them from the Lord, and the brightness of the Lord's glory flashed around them. The shepherds were frightened. But the angel said, "Don't be afraid! I have good news for you, which will make everyone happy. This very day in King David's hometown a Savior was born for you. He is Christ the Lord. You will know who he is, because you will find him dressed in baby clothes and lying in a manger."

Suddenly many other angels came down from heaven and joined in praising God. They said: "Praise God in heaven!

Peace on earth to everyone who pleases God."

The gospel of the Lord.

   place the shepherds and angels near the stable

LEADER
My friends,
let us hold a hand out in blessing.

   all hold out a hand
   toward the stable

We praise and thank you, O God,
    for the coming of Jesus.
Bless these images that tell us
    how Mary gave birth to Jesus
    and how angels sang the good news
        to the shepherds.
May we always give you thanks
    through Christ our Lord.

ALL
Amen.

   sing Christmas
   carols

A Blessing of the Classroom

Blessing the home is an Epiphany custom. In that spirit we can bless our classroom. Gather chalk, a chair or ladder to stand on, a bowl of water and a small evergreen branch to sprinkle the water with. (The letters C, M, B stand for the traditional names of the wise men: Caspar, Melchior and Balthasar). Begin and end with a Christmas song.

▶ all make
the sign
of the cross

LEADER

It is the time of Epiphany. We honor the wise men who followed a star. God still leads those who want to find the savior. God's glory will be shown to all of them.

READER   Matthew 2:1–2, 4–5, 8–11

Listen to the words of the holy gospel according to Matthew:

Some wise men from the east came to Jerusalem *(juh-ROO-suh-lem)* and said, "Where is the child born to be king of the Jews? We saw his star in the east and have come to worship him."

King Herod brought together all the chief priests and the teachers of the Law of Moses and asked them, "Where will the Messiah be born?"

They told him, "He will be born in Bethlehem" *(BETH-luh-hem).*

Herod told the wise men, "Go to Bethlehem and search carefully for the child. As soon as you find him, let me know. I want to go and worship him too."

The wise men listened to what the king said and then left. And the star they had seen in the east went on ahead of them until it stopped over the place where the child was. They were thrilled and excited to see the star.

When the men went into the house and saw the child with Mary, his mother, they knelt down and worshiped him. They took out their gifts of gold, frankincense *(FRANK-in-sens)*, and myrrh *(mer)* and gave them to him.

The gospel of the Lord.

▶ figures of the Magi
may be added to the stable

LEADER

▶ mark above the door with chalk:
20 + C + M + B + 01

Lord God,
    fill this room with kindness for one another
        and with respect for guests.
Fill us with the wisdom to seek Jesus always,
    now and for ever.

ALL
Amen.

▶ move to each corner of the room;
sprinkle each corner with water,
then say the following words:

LEADER

Lord God, fill every corner of our world
    with safety, peace and love.
Guide us to the glory of Jesus our Savior.
We ask this through Christ our Lord.

ALL
Amen.

TUESDAY PRAYER

January 2, 2001

Reminder: Use the Blessing of the Stable, on page 147, and the Blessing of the Classroom, on page 148, this week.

■ INTRODUCTION

Happy Christmastime and a happy new year. And a happy new century and new millennium as well! All this week we will continue to celebrate the Christmas season.

Today we remember Abel, the son of Adam and Eve. When Abel gave an offering to God, the Lord honored him. His brother Cain became jealous and finally killed Abel. Let us pray that God will turn all hearts away from jealousy and violence.

■ A PSALM FOR CHRISTMASTIME

turn to
page 144

■ READING

John 1:19, 23, 25–27

Listen to the words of the holy gospel according to John:

The leaders asked John [the Baptist] who he was. John answered in the words of the prophet Isaiah, "I am only someone shouting in the desert, 'Get the road ready for the Lord!'"

They asked him, "Why are you baptizing people, if you are not the Messiah or Elijah or the Prophet?" John told them, "I use water to baptize people. But here with you is someone you don't know. Even though I came first, I am not good enough to untie his sandals."

The gospel of the Lord.

■ REFLECTION

Why do people sometimes think a religious leader is the Messiah? What does baptism mean to me?

■ CLOSING

Blessed be God, Creator of days and seasons. Let us all say: Blessed be God for ever!
Blessed be God for ever!

Let us remember these intentions:

Loving God, you give us this new year
 and good friends with whom to share it.
Bless all who pray and work
 and learn together.
And grant a happy year to all the world.
We ask this through Christ our Lord. **Amen.**

Let us pray with the words that Jesus taught us:
Our Father . . .

sing "Joy to the world"
(Hymnal for Catholic Students,
page 146)

May the light of Christ
shine through us for others,
now and for ever. Amen.

put out
the candle

149

WEDNESDAY PRAYER

January 3, 2001

■ INTRODUCTION

On this day in Christmastime we remember Saint Genevieve *(JEN-uh-veev)*, who is honored by French-speaking people around the world. She was a strong leader who saved her city from war and starvation.

Today's reading tells us how John the Baptist knew that Jesus was the Messiah and how John helped others to know this, too.

■ A PSALM FOR CHRISTMASTIME

➤ turn to
page 144

■ READING

John 1:29–30, 32–34

Listen to the words of the holy gospel according to John:

John [the Baptist] saw Jesus coming toward him and said, "Here is the Lamb of God who takes away the sin of the world! He is the one I told you about when I said, 'Someone else will come. He is greater than I am, because he was alive before I was born.'

"I was there and saw the Spirit come down on him like a dove from heaven. And the Spirit stayed on him. Before this I didn't know who he was. But the one who sent me to baptize with water had told me. 'You will see the Spirit come down and stay on someone. Then you will know that he is the one who will baptize with the Holy Spirit.' I saw this happen, and I tell you that he is the Son of God."

The gospel of the Lord.

■ REFLECTION

Would I know about Jesus if someone had not told me about him? Do we tell others what we know of Jesus? How can we show our faith?

■ CLOSING

Blessed be God, Creator of days and seasons.
Let us all say: Blessed be God for ever!
Blessed be God for ever!

Let us remember these intentions:

Loving God, you give us this new year
  and good friends with whom to share it.
Bless all who pray and work
  and learn together.
And grant a happy year to all the world.
We ask this through Christ our Lord. **Amen.**

Let us pray with the words that Jesus taught us:

Our Father . . .

sing "Joy to the world"
(Hymnal for Catholic Students,
page 146)

May the light of Christ
  shine through us for others,
  now and for ever. **Amen.**

put out
the candle

150

THURSDAY PRAYER

January 4, 2001

■ INTRODUCTION

We remember Elizabeth Ann Seton today. She was the first person born in the United States to be declared a saint.

Elizabeth Seton grew up in New York, married, and had five children. After her husband died, she became a Catholic. Then she began the first community of religious sisters started in this country. They are the Sisters of Charity of Saint Joseph. Mother Seton died on January 4, 1821.

■ A PSALM FOR CHRISTMASTIME

 turn to page 144

■ READING

John 1:35–37, 40–41, 42

Listen to the words of the holy gospel according to John:

John was at the Jordan River, and two of his followers were with him. When he saw Jesus walking by, he said, "Here is the Lamb of God!" John's two followers heard him, and they went with Jesus.

One of the two men who had heard John and had gone with Jesus was Andrew, the brother of Simon Peter. The first thing Andrew did was to find his brother and tell him, "We have found the Messiah!" The Hebrew word "Messiah" means the same as the Greek word "Christ."

Andrew brought his brother to Jesus. And when Jesus saw him, he said, "Simon son of John, you will be called Cephas *(SEE-fuhs)*." This name can be translated as "Peter."

The gospel of the Lord.

■ REFLECTION

What do the titles "Lamb of God" and "Messiah" mean? How can Jesus speak to us in person? Am I willing to become his disciple?

■ CLOSING

Blessed be God, Creator of days and seasons. Let us all say: Blessed be God for ever! **Blessed be God for ever!**

Let us remember these intentions:

Loving God, you give us this new year
   and good friends with whom to share it.
Bless all who pray and work
   and learn together.
And grant a happy year to all the world.
We ask this through Christ our Lord. **Amen.**

Let us pray with the words that Jesus taught us:

Our Father . . .

 sing "Joy to the world" (Hymnal for Catholic Students, page 146)

May the light of Christ
shine through us for others,
now and for ever. Amen.

put out the candle

FRIDAY PRAYER
January 5, 2001

■ INTRODUCTION

Today we remember Saint John Neumann *(NEW-mun)*. In 1836, John came to America with only the clothes he wore and a suitcase of books. He wanted very much to become a priest. John did become a priest, and a bishop. He did God's work with great energy and learning.

During Christmastime we are reading about how the public work of Jesus began. Jesus was baptized by his cousin John. John told his followers that Jesus was the Messiah that Israel had been waiting for.

■ A PSALM FOR CHRISTMASTIME

▶ turn to
page 144

■ READING

John 1:43–45, 47, 48–49

Listen to the words of the holy gospel according to John:

Jesus met Philip, who was from the hometown of Andrew and Peter. Jesus said to Philip, "Come with me." Philip then found Nathanael *(nuh-THAN-yull)* and said, "We have found the one that Moses and the Prophets wrote about. He is Jesus, the son of Joseph from Nazareth."

When Jesus saw Nathanael coming toward him, he said, "Here is a true descendant of our ancestor Israel." "How do you know me?" Nathanael asked. Jesus answered, "Before Philip called you, I saw you under the fig tree." Nathanael said, "Rabbi, you are the Son of God and the King of Israel!"

The gospel of the Lord.

■ REFLECTION

Jesus knows Nathanael well. Jesus knows each of us well. Does this make me more comfortable with Jesus? How can this help us to pray?

■ CLOSING

Blessed be God, Creator of days and seasons. Let us all say: Blessed be God for ever!
Blessed be God for ever!

Let us remember these intentions:

Loving God, you give us this new year
    and good friends with whom to share it.
Bless all who pray and work
    and learn together.
And grant a happy year to all the world.
We ask this through Christ our Lord. **Amen.**

Let us pray with the words that Jesus taught us:
Our Father . . .

▶ sing "Joy to the world"
    (Hymnal for Catholic Students,
    page 146)

May the light of Christ
    shine through us for others,
    now and for ever. **Amen.**

▶ put out
    the candle

152

WEEKLY PRAYER

With a Reading from the Gospel for Sunday, January 7, 2001

■ INTRODUCTION

Sunday, January 7, is the feast of Epiphany *(eh-PIF-uh-nee)*, when we rejoice that the Savior is revealed to all those who truly seek him.

■ A PSALM FOR CHRISTMASTIME

turn to
page 144

■ READING

Matthew 2:1–2, 8–9, 11–12

Listen to the words of the holy gospel according to Matthew:

Some wise men from the east came to Jerusalem *(juh-ROO-suh-lem)* and said, "Where is the child born to be king of the Jews? We saw his star in the east and have come to worship him."

Herod told them, "Go to Bethlehem *(BETH-luh-hem)* and search carefully for the child. As soon as you find him, let me know. I want to go and worship him too."

The wise men listened to what the king said and then left. And the star they had seen in the east went on ahead of them until it stopped over the place where the child was.

When the men went into the house and saw the child with Mary, his mother, they knelt down and worshiped him. They took out their gifts of gold, frankincense *(FRANK-in-sens)*, and myrrh *(mer)*, and gave them to him.

Later they were warned in a dream not to return to Herod, and they went back home by another road.

The gospel of the Lord.

■ REFLECTION

Where have we found Jesus our Savior this year? Who has been like a bright star leading me to Jesus?

■ CLOSING

Let us remember these intentions:

Loving God, you give us this new year
   and good friends with whom to share it.
Bless all who pray and work
   and learn together.
And grant a happy year to all the world.
We ask this through Christ our Lord. **Amen.**

Let us pray with the words that Jesus taught us:

Our Father . . .

sing "Joy to the world"
(Hymnal for Catholic Students,
page 146)

May the light of Christ
   shine through us for others,
   now and for ever. Amen.

put out
the candle

MONDAY PRAYER

January 8, 2001

■ INTRODUCTION

Today is the feast of the Baptism of the Lord. We will hear the story of his baptism from the gospel of Luke.

For many years Jesus lived in Nazareth *(NAZ-uh-reth),* the town where he was raised. But after his baptism he traveled to many towns, teaching others the good news of God's love.

■ A PSALM FOR CHRISTMASTIME

 turn to page 144

■ READING

Luke 3:15–16, 21–23

Listen to the words of the holy gospel according to Luke:

Everyone became excited and wondered, "Could John be the Messiah?" John said, "I am just baptizing with water. But someone more powerful is going to come, and I am not good enough even to untie his sandals. He will baptize you with the Holy Spirit and with fire."

While everyone else was being baptized, Jesus himself was baptized. Then as he prayed, the sky opened up, and the Holy Spirit came down upon him in the form of a dove. A voice from heaven said, "You are my own dear Son, and I am pleased with you."

When Jesus began to preach, he was about thirty years old.

The gospel of the Lord.

■ REFLECTION

What did it mean when John baptized people? What does baptism seem to mean to people in our parish? Have I asked my family why they brought me to be baptized?

■ CLOSING

Let us remember these intentions:

Loving God, you give us this new year
    and good friends with whom to share it.
Bless all who pray and work
    and learn together.
And grant a happy year to all the world.
We ask this through Christ our Lord. **Amen.**

Let us pray with the words that Jesus taught us:

Our Father . . .

 sing "Joy to the world" *(Hymnal for Catholic Students,* page 146)

May the light of Christ
    shine through us for others,
    now and for ever. **Amen.**

put out
the candle

JANUARY

Tuesday, January 9, to Wednesday, January 31

ORDINARY TIME
JANUARY 2001

■ ABOUT THE MONTH

Christmastime is over. Now things get back to normal. In the language of prayer, this normal time is called Ordinary Time. This means that the church is between seasons.

But "ordinary" is not the same as "unimportant."

LOOKING AHEAD
We do not disappear between holidays. We do not stop eating or studying or growing. We do not stop praying or caring about one another. And we do not stop being God's dearest children.

So, during Ordinary Time we still try to do ordinary things well. We will try to pray well, and we will try to do our schoolwork well. We will also have a chance to enjoy the feasts and festivals that occur in January and February.

▪ WE WANT TO PRAY EACH TIME WE GATHER. Perhaps we could improve our prayer in some way for this new year of 2001. Should we sing more? Are we taking turns? Can we hear the readers? Do the leaders need to prepare a little better? Are we in too much of a hurry when we pray? Does anyone have good ideas for improvement?

▪ DURING JANUARY, NATURE CAN BE HARSH. Cold winds blow. Layers of extra clothing begin to be annoying. For us the winter can seem too long. For many people, however, winter is not just long. It is the hardest time of the year. We want to remember that hungry and homeless people need our help. Our help may be a matter of life and death to them. People need the most help after Christmastime, especially if the weather turns bad for a long time. Perhaps we can learn how our parish helps people in trouble.

▪ OUR READINGS FOR DAILY PRAYER WILL TRACE THE INFLUENCE OF THE PROPHET SAMUEL ON THE SCATTERED TRIBES OF ISRAEL. The miraculous birth and calling of Samuel tell us that he was chosen by God for a special role. He grew up to become a judge of Israel.

Judges were women or men of religious or military power who governed one or more tribes. The tribes lived independently in those days, about 3,000 years ago. But they often acted together to fight other people who also wanted the land.

Samuel was a powerful leader. When he grew old, people wanted him to pass his authority to someone young and strong. Against his better judgment Samuel agreed to name a king. First came King Saul, a mighty warrior but an unreliable ruler. Then came King David. He brought the people peace. Ever since David was king, people have looked back to his time as if it were the best of times.

■ PREPARATION FOR JANUARY

The Psalm, Meal Prayer and End of the Day Prayers for Ordinary Time in January are on pages 21, 22 and 23 in the student booklet *Blessed Be God!* If students do not use *Blessed Be God!* the Psalm and Prayers for January may be photocopied. These Prayers are found in this book on pages 158, 159 and 160.

▪ MARTIN LUTHER KING DAY IS CELEBRATED ON MONDAY, JANUARY 15. We may want to prepare something special for that holiday.

▪ THE WEEK OF PRAYER FOR CHRISTIAN UNITY LASTS FROM JANUARY 18 TO JANUARY 25. As a class we can pray for the unity of all Christian churches. A prayer for Christian unity is found on page 170.

▪ CATHOLIC SCHOOLS WEEK IS JANUARY 28 TO FEBRUARY 3. No doubt there are special events and celebrations planned for that week. January is dedicated to peace. Perhaps we can share pictures and

stories of famous peacemakers. There may be peacemakers in our families who help others get along and calm people down when things get tense. We can tell their stories too.

We will find the themes of religious unity and racial harmony in the prayers each day. There may be additional opportunities during the month for activities or discussions about peace and cooperation among people.

- THE PRAYER CENTER CAN BE MADE NEW WITH A CLOTH OR A NEW RELIGIOUS PICTURE. If you put up some signs of winter during Advent, such as pine cones or paper snowflakes, they can remain, or new signs can be added.

- SUGGESTED HYMNS: "Sing a new song" (page 179 in the *Hymnal for Catholic Students)* is a hymn of gladness that can help chase away the winter blues.

Learn a new melody for the "alleluia." A good one that you might choose is the "Celtic alleluia" (page 75 in the hymnal).

During the Week of Christian Unity, we can sing "In Christ there is no east or west" (page 141 in the hymnal). The melody of this song is a spiritual that Martin Luther King sang many times. Another famous spiritual is "We shall overcome" (page 203 in the hymnal).

On the last days of January and the first days of February, the Closing of prayer each day includes the first verse of Psalm 27, "The Lord is my light and my salvation; of whom should I be afraid?" These words can be even more powerful if they are sung. Music can be found on page 59 of the hymnal. Someone with a good voice can sing the words first, and then everyone can repeat them. You can even repeat the verse twice.

It is good to sing all the verses of a hymn if that is possible. Why? Because the words of most hymns are poems. When we skip verses, the poem isn't complete. The ideas or attitudes that the poem

expresses aren't complete. Also, when songs are short, we sometimes don't have enough time to pick up their spirit.

■ THE SCHOOL OF RELIGION

In winter, many students are absent from classes. We get colds and flu. It is dark out and cold. It might be easier to keep up our enthusiasm if we make a fresh start on the routines of our class sessions.

Perhaps more responsibility for the preparation and leadership of prayer can be shared among students. Perhaps we can tell about favorite religious rituals kept in our families. Special attention might be paid to the saints and heroes of this month.

- THE READINGS FOR WEEKLY PRAYER ARE TAKEN FROM THE SUNDAY GOSPELS. In Ordinary Time in 2001, the church reads through Luke's gospel Sunday by Sunday, with occasional readings from the gospel of John.

Through the eyes of Luke and John we see Jesus revealed to those around him. First we see him at Cana, where his actions reveal his mission of renewal. Next, his words in Nazareth reveal his role as Messiah.

- THE BLESSING OF CANDLES (ON PAGE 191) CAN TAKE PLACE ANY TIME DURING THE WEEK THAT ENDS JANUARY AND BEGINS FEBRUARY, even though the feast of Candlemas, or the Presentation of the Lord, as it is also called, falls on Friday, February 2.

A PSALM FOR JANUARY

▶ all make
the sign
of the cross

Psalm 8:2, 4–10

LEADER   Lord our God, the whole world tells
the greatness of your name.

ALL   **Your glory reaches beyond the farthest star.**

SIDE A   I see your handiwork
in the heavens:
the moon and the stars
you set in place.

SIDE B   What is humankind
that you remember them,
the human race
that you care for them?

SIDE A   You treat them like gods,
dressing them in glory and splendor.
You give them charge of the earth,
laying all at their feet:

SIDE B   Cattle and sheep,
wild beasts,
birds of the sky,
fish of the sea.

LEADER   Lord our God, the whole world tells
the greatness of your name.

ALL   **Your glory reaches beyond the farthest star.**

**Glory to the Father, and to the Son,
and to the Holy Spirit:
as it was in the beginning, is now,
and will be for ever. Amen. Alleluia.**

▶ turn back to
Daily Prayer or Weekly Prayer
for today

158

JANUARY

LEADER   Let us offer God praise and thanksgiving:

ALL   ▶ all make
           the sign
           of the cross

LEADER   We thank you, God, for the gift of life.
           And we thank you for all that helps us grow.

           Lord, we hunger for bread,
             and we hunger for justice.

ALL   **Lord, have mercy.**

LEADER   Christ, we hunger for freedom,
             and we hunger for peace.

ALL   **Christ, have mercy.**

LEADER   Lord, we hunger for your love,
             and we hunger for your kingdom.

ALL   **Lord, have mercy.**

       Bless us, O Lord, and these your gifts
          which we are about to receive from your bounty.
       Through Christ our Lord. Amen.

    ▶ all make
         the sign
         of the cross

JANUARY

> all make
> the sign
> of the cross

LEADER   For the circles of your universe
        we bless you,
Maker of suns and seasons.

While winter brings rest and renewal
    to the land,
    open our eyes every day to marvel
      at what is lovely in these weeks,
    to see also those who need
      shelter and warmth
    and swiftly to help them.
In the beauty and the fierceness of winter
    be praised, our Lord, for ever and ever.

ALL   **Amen.**

LEADER
> hold out one hand
> toward everyone
> in blessing, and say:

May the Lord bless us,
    protect us from all evil,
    and bring us to everlasting life:

ALL
> all make
> the sign
> of the cross

**END OF THE DAY
PRAYER**

TUESDAY PRAYER

January 9, 2001

Reminder: The Psalm, Meal and End of Day Prayers are in *Blessed Be God!* pages 21 to 23.

INTRODUCTION

During the next few weeks our readings will tell about Samuel, one of Israel's great prophets.

In those days, about 3,000 years ago, men could have more than one wife. Therefore, some families were large and it was often difficult for everyone to get along. People who live in stepfamilies and blended families can understand some of the problems in Samuel's family.

A PSALM FOR JANUARY

turn to page 158

READING

I Samuel 1:2, 6–9, 10–11

Listen to the words of the first book of Samuel:

A man named Elkanah *(el-KAN-uh)* had two wives, Hannah and Peninnah *(pen-NEE-nuh)*. Although Peninnah had children, Hannah did not have any. Peninnah liked to make Hannah feel miserable about not having any children, especially when the family went to the house of the LORD each year.

One day, Elkanah was there offering a sacrifice, when Hannah began crying and refused to eat. So Elkanah asked, "Hannah, why are you crying? Why won't you eat? Why do you feel so bad? Don't I mean more to you than ten sons?"

When the sacrifice had been offered, and they had eaten the meal, Hannah got up and went to pray. Hannah was brokenhearted and was crying as she prayed, "LORD All-Powerful, I am your servant, but I am so miserable! Please let me have a son. I will give him to you for as long as he lives."

The word of the Lord.

REFLECTION

Hannah was mocked for something that was not her fault. Am I ever blamed for things that are not my fault? Can I put my troubles in God's hands, as Hannah did?

CLOSING

Let us remember these intentions:

Lord God,
you have given us this day
as a gift of great value.
Let it be for us a day of rejoicing.
In the quiet of our hearts
and the work of this day,
be with us, Lord, now and for ever. **Amen.**

Let us pray with the words that Jesus taught us:

Our Father . . .

sing "alleluia"

WEDNESDAY PRAYER

January 10, 2001

■ INTRODUCTION

Today we learn more about how sad Hannah was because she did not have any children. But you may have noticed that she prayed for a son. In those days, boys grew up to take over their father's business and his household. Then, if the father died, sons would support their mother. Daughters, however, could not do that. It is not a surprise that every woman wanted at least one son back then.

■ A PSALM FOR JANUARY

▶ turn to page 158

■ READING

I Samuel 1:19–23, 24, 26–28

Listen to the words of the first book of Samuel:

The LORD blessed Elkanah (el-KAN-uh) and Hannah with a son. She named him Samuel because she had asked the LORD for him. The next time Elkanah and his family went to offer their yearly sacrifice, he took along a gift that he had promised to give to the LORD. But Hannah stayed home, because she had told Elkanah, "Samuel and I won't go until he's old enough for me to stop nursing him. Then I'll give him to the LORD, and he can stay there at Shiloh (SHY-low) for the rest of his life."

"You know what is best," Elkanah said.

When it was the time of the year to go to Shiloh again, Hannah and Elkanah took Samuel to the LORD's house. "Sir," said Hannah [to the priest], "a few years ago I stood here beside you and asked the LORD to give me a child. Here he is! The LORD gave me just what I asked for. Now I am giving him to the LORD, and he will be the LORD's servant for as long as he lives."

The word of the Lord.

■ REFLECTION

Not everyone is as thankful for the birth of a child as Hannah was. Do we pray for children who have no one to welcome them? Did my parents bring me to church when I was small to dedicate me to God?

■ CLOSING

Let us remember these intentions:

Lord God,
  you have given us this day
  as a gift of great value.
Let it be for us a day of rejoicing.
In the quiet of our hearts
    and the work of this day,
  be with us, Lord, now and for ever. **Amen.**

Let us pray with the words that Jesus taught us:

Our Father . . .

▶ sing "alleluia"

162

THURSDAY PRAYER

January 11, 2001

■ INTRODUCTION

The church calls the weeks between Christmas and Lent "Ordinary Time." But even ordinary days can still be filled with life and joy.

Today's reading continues the story of Samuel. The boy is studying at the temple in Shiloh *(SHY-low)*, with the priest, Eli *(EE-lie)*.

■ A PSALM FOR JANUARY

➤ turn to page 158

■ READING

I Samuel 3:2, 3–6, 8–10

Listen to the words of the first book of Samuel:

One night, Eli *(EE-lie)* was asleep in his room, and Samuel was sleeping in the LORD's house. They had not been asleep very long when the LORD called out Samuel's name.

"Here I am!" Samuel answered. Then he ran to Eli and said, "Here I am. What do you want?" "I didn't call you, " Eli answered. "Go back to bed." Samuel went back.

Again the LORD called out Samuel's name. Samuel got up and went to Eli. "Here I am," he said. "What do you want?" Eli told him, "Son, I didn't call you. Go back to sleep."

When the LORD called out his name for the third time, Samuel went to Eli again and said, "Here I am. What do you want?" Eli finally realized that it was the LORD who was speaking to Samuel. So he said, "Go back and lie down! If someone speaks to you again, answer, 'I'm listening, LORD. What do you want me to do?'"

Once again Samuel went back and lay down. The LORD then stood beside Samuel and called out as he had done before, "Samuel! Samuel!"

"I'm listening," Samuel answered. "What do you want me to do?"

The word of the Lord.

■ REFLECTION

Will I recognize the voice of God when it comes to me? God sometimes speaks through dreams. How else does God speak to us?

■ CLOSING

Let us remember these intentions:

Loving God,
   you call us each by name
      and speak to us in the quiet of our hearts.
Speak to us of love for all people.
Speak to us of hope for our world.
Speak to us of your gift of salvation.
Speak to us, for we are listening.
We ask this through Christ our Lord. **Amen.**

Let us pray with the words that Jesus taught us:
Our Father . . .

➤ sing "alleluia"

163

FRIDAY PRAYER

January 12, 2001

Reminder: Monday is Martin Luther King Day. Thursday begins the Week of Christian Unity. A Prayer is on page 170.

■ INTRODUCTION

During January many communities of Native Americans hold sacred ceremonies. The Iroquois *(EAR-uh-kwoy),* who live in the Northeast, hold a six-day ritual of healing and renewal. Masked figures called "false faces" visit houses.

In the Southwest, the Hopi *(HOPE-ee)* people perform sacred kiva *(KEE-vuh)* and buffalo dances. The kiva is a round room like a chapel. Smoke from a fire in the center of the room rises through a hole in ceiling. This symbolizes the prayers and hopes of the people, rising up to the Great Spirit.

■ A PSALM FOR JANUARY

turn to page 158

■ READING

I Samuel 3:19—4:1, 7:15—17

Listen to the words of the first book of Samuel:

As Samuel grew up, the LORD helped him and made everything Samuel said come true. From the town of Dan in the north to the town of Beersheba in the south, everyone in the country knew that Samuel was truly the LORD's prophet. The LORD often appeared to Samuel at Shiloh *(SHY-low)* and told him what to say. Then Samuel would speak to the whole nation of Israel.

Samuel was a leader in Israel all his life. Every year he would go around to the towns of Bethel *(beth-EL),* Gilgal, and Mizpah *(MITTS-puh)* where he served as judge for the people. Then he would go back to his home in Ramah *(rah-MAH)* and do the same thing there. He also had an altar built for the LORD at Ramah.

The word of the Lord.

■ REFLECTION

Samuel was both a prophet and a ruler. How did his faith help him to govern justly? How do I learn the values of my school? my town? my country?

■ CLOSING

Let us remember these intentions:

Loving God,
 you call us each by name
  and speak to us in the quiet of our hearts.
Speak to us of love for all people.
Speak to us of hope for our world.
Speak to us of your gift of salvation.
Speak to us, for we are listening.
We ask this through Christ our Lord. **Amen.**

Let us pray with the words that Jesus taught us:

Our Father . . .

sing "alleluia"

164

WEEKLY PRAYER

With a Reading from Sunday, January 14, 2001

 Reminder: The Psalm for Ordinary Time in January is on page 21 of *Blessed Be God!*

■ INTRODUCTION

Three gospel stories are connected to the feast of Epiphany *(eh-PIF-uh-nee)*. In the first story Jesus is revealed to the wise men. In the second Jesus is revealed at his baptism. Today we will read the third story. In it Jesus reveals himself when he changes water into wine at a wedding.

■ A PSALM FOR JANUARY

 turn to page 158

■ READING

John 2:1–11

Listen to the words of the holy gospel according to John:

Mary, the mother of Jesus, was at a wedding feast in the village of Cana in Galilee. Jesus and his disciples had also been invited and were there. When the wine was all gone, Mary said to Jesus, "They don't have any more wine." Jesus replied. "Mother, my time has not yet come! You must not tell me what to do."

Mary then said to the servants. "Do whatever Jesus tells you to do." At the feast there were six stone water jars. Jesus told the servants to fill them to the top with water. Then he said, "Now take some water and give it to the man in charge of the feast."

The man in charge drank some of the water that had now turned into wine. He called the bridegroom over and said, "The best wine is always served first. But you have kept the best until last!"

This was Jesus' first miracle, and he did it in the village of Cana in Galilee. There Jesus showed his glory, and his disciples put their faith in him.

The gospel of the Lord.

■ REFLECTION

Why did Mary tell Jesus about the wine? What can I do when I see that someone does not have what they need? Why is this a good reading to begin the year?

■ CLOSING

Let us remember these intentions:

God of all nations and Creator of all peoples,
   heal all that divides us.
Teach us to live together in peace.
As our world is one, so our future is one.
Give us one heart and one vision.
Make us one body in Christ Jesus,
filled with the joy of your Holy Spirit.
We ask this through Christ our Lord. **Amen.**

Let us pray with the words that Jesus taught us:

Our Father . . .

 sing "alleluia"

MONDAY PRAYER

January 15, 2001

▶ Reminder: The Week of Prayer for Christian Unity begins on Thursday. You may want to use the prayer on page 170. Talk this over with the teacher.

■ INTRODUCTION

Today we observe the birthday of Martin Luther King, Jr. He led African Americans in their struggle for civil rights. He preached Christian love and unity, and he tried to win justice without using violence.

Dr. King was a Baptist minister and a powerful speaker. He used his great talents in the work of building Christian love and unity. Today let us pray for justice and cooperation among people of all races.

Today's reading is taken from the prayer of Jesus for unity among his followers.

■ A PSALM FOR JANUARY

▶ turn to page 158

■ READING

John 17:1, 20–22

Listen to the words of the holy gospel according to John:

Jesus looked up toward heaven and prayed, "Father, I am not praying just for these followers. I am also praying for everyone else who will have faith because of what my followers will say about me. I want all of them to be one with each other, just as I am one with you and you are one with me. I also want them to be one with us.

Then the people of this world will believe that you sent me.

"I have honored my followers in the same way that you honored me, in order that they may be one with each other, just as we are one."

The gospel of the Lord.

■ REFLECTION

Do I have friends who belong to different Christian churches? Do we discuss ideas about God? What have I done to promote good feelings and understanding between my group and another group?

■ CLOSING

Let us remember these intentions:

God of all nations and Creator of all peoples,
    heal all that divides us.
Teach us to live together in peace.
As our world is one, so our future is one.
Give us one heart and one vision.
Make us one body in Christ Jesus,
    filled with the joy of your Holy Spirit.
We ask this through Christ our Lord. **Amen.**

Let us pray with the words that Jesus taught us:

Our Father . . .

▶ sing "alleluia"

166

TUESDAY PRAYER

January 16, 2001

■ INTRODUCTION

Today we continue reading the story of Samuel. He was the last of the judges. These were people who ruled the tribes of Israel when they were settling down and building cities. Now the people have asked Samuel to find them a king.

The people wanted a strong government. They wanted a king who could lead an army against their enemies. Samuel will seek God's help in finding the right person.

■ A PSALM FOR JANUARY

turn to
page 158

■ READING

I Samuel 8:4, 5, 10, 11, 14–15, 19–22

Listen to the words of the first book of Samuel:

One day the nation's leaders came to Samuel at Ramah *(rah-MAH)* and said, "We want a king to be our leader, just like all the other nations. Choose one for us!"

Samuel told the people: "If you have a king, this is how he will treat you. He will force your sons to join his army. The king will take your best fields, as well as your vineyards, and olive orchards and give them to his own officials. He will also take a tenth of your grain and grapes and give it to his officers and officials.

The people would not listen to Samuel. "No!" they said. "We want to be like other nations. We want a king to rule us and lead us in battle."

Samuel listened to them and then told the LORD exactly what they had said. "Do what they want," the LORD answered. "Give them a king."

The word of the Lord.

■ REFLECTION

Does God care whether we have good or bad government? Who have we allowed to become leaders among our friends? Have I ever chosen something that I knew might turn out badly?

■ CLOSING

Let us remember these intentions:

God of all nations and Creator of all peoples,
  heal all that divides us.
Teach us to live together in peace.
As our world is one, so our future is one.
Give us one heart and one vision.
Make us one body in Christ Jesus,
  filled with the joy of your Holy Spirit.
We ask this through Christ our Lord. **Amen.**

Let us pray with the words that Jesus taught us:

Our Father . . .

sing
"alleluia"

167

WEDNESDAY PRAYER

January 17, 2001

■ INTRODUCTION

Today we remember Saint Anthony of Egypt. He gave away everything he owned. Then he went alone into the wilderness so that he could pray without interruptions. But many people came to learn from him. Anthony taught them how to keep silence and how to live a simple life. Anthony was able to see what was important.

■ A PSALM FOR JANUARY

 turn to page 158

■ READING

1 Samuel 9:3–6, 10, 14, 17, 20, 26; 10:1

Listen to the words of the first book of Samuel:

Kish owned some donkeys, but they had run off. So he told [his son] Saul, "Take one of the servants and go look for the donkeys." Saul and the servant went through the hill country, but they could not find the donkeys.

Saul told his servant, "If we don't go back soon, my father will stop worrying about the donkeys and start worrying about us!"

"Wait!" the servant answered, "There's a man of God who lives in a town near here. Maybe he can tell us where to look."

Saul and his servant went to the town where the prophet lived. Just as they were going through the gate, Samuel was coming out on his way to the place of worship. Samuel looked at Saul, and the LORD told Samuel, "This is the man I told you about. He's the one who will rule Israel."

[Samuel said], "Don't worry about your donkeys that ran off three days ago. They've already been found."

About sunrise the next morning, Samuel took a small jar of olive oil and poured it on Saul's head. Then he kissed Saul and told him, "The LORD has chosen you to be the leader and ruler of his people."

The word of the Lord.

■ REFLECTION

Saul went to the prophet Samuel for help. To whom do I go when I need help?

■ CLOSING

Let us remember these intentions:

God of all nations and Creator of all peoples,
    heal all that divides us.
Teach us to live together in peace.
As our world is one, so our future is one.
Give us one heart and one vision.
Make us one body in Christ Jesus,
    filled with the joy of your Holy Spirit.
We ask this through Christ our Lord. **Amen.**

Let us pray with the words that Jesus taught us:

Our Father . . .

 sing "alleluia"

THURSDAY PRAYER

January 18, 2001

■ INTRODUCTION

Today begins the Week of Prayer for Christian Unity. This is a time to pray that all Christian churches will someday be united. People of all races, of all countries and of all religions really can love one another and work together. Let us do our part to make this happen.

To honor the Week of Prayer for Christian Unity, today's reading is taken from the prayer of Jesus for unity among his followers.

■ A PSALM FOR JANUARY

turn to
page 158

■ REFLECTION

Do I have friends who belong to a different faith? Do I discuss ideas about God with them? What activities does our parish share with other churches in our neighborhood?

■ CLOSING

Let us remember these intentions:

■ READING

John 10:3–5, 14–16

Listen to the words of the holy gospel according to John:

Jesus said:
"The sheep know their shepherd's voice. He calls each of them by name and leads them out. When he has led out all of his sheep, he walks in front of them, and they follow, because they know his voice. The sheep will not follow strangers. They don't recognize a stranger's voice, and they run away.

"I am the good shepherd. I know my sheep, and they know me. Just as the Father knows me, I know the Father, and I give up my life for my sheep. I have other sheep that are not in this sheep pen. I must bring them together too, when they hear my voice. Then there will be one flock of sheep and one shepherd."

The gospel of the Lord.

God of all nations and Creator of all peoples,
    heal all that divides us.
Teach us to live together in peace.
As our world is one, so our future is one.
Give us one heart and one vision.
Make us one body in Christ Jesus,
    and fill us with the joy of your Holy Spirit.
We ask this through Christ our Lord. **Amen.**

Let us pray with the words that Jesus taught us:
Our Father . . .

sing
"alleluia"

A Prayer for Christian Unity

Gather near the baptismal font or around a bowl of water from the font. Bring a pine branch for sprinkling and copies of January's Psalm. Begin and end with a song, such as "In Christ there is no east or west" or "Lord, you give the great commission."

Introduction

All who are baptized in Jesus Christ form one body, one church. Although we now see many churches, all who live in Christ are called to unity through the Holy Spirit.

We begin by praying the Psalm for January.

A Psalm for January

▶ turn to page 158

Reading

Ephesians 4:3–5

Listen to the words of the apostle Paul:

Try your best to let God's Spirit keep your hearts united. Do this by living at peace. All of you are part of the same body. There is only one Spirit of God, just as you were given one hope when you were chosen to be God's people. We have only one Lord, one faith, and one baptism.

The word of the Lord.

Blessing with Baptismal Water

Let us bless the Lord with all the saints
  who show us what it is
  to live as followers of Christ.
Let us all say: Thanks be to God.
Thanks be to God.

For Martin Luther, Teresa of Avila
and all who speak out for reform
  in the churches,
  let us bless the Lord:
Thanks be to God.

For Martin Luther King, Oscar Romero
and all who suffer for the sake of justice,
  let us bless the Lord:
Thanks be to God.

For Mother Teresa, Dorothy Day
and all who serve the poor and homeless,
  let us bless the Lord:
Thanks be to God.

For Harriet Tubman, John Wesley and all
who preach and sing to the glory of God,
  let us bless the Lord:
Thanks be to God.

▶ the leader holds out one hand
  toward the baptismal water and says:

Jesus, our Lord and Messiah,
  we praise you for giving us new birth
    in the waters of baptism.
Deepen the faith and strengthen the unity
    of our churches,
  until we meet around one table
  to proclaim your kingdom now and for ever.
Amen.

▶ sprinkle the community with baptismal
  water; all sing "alleluia" during the sprinkling

Let us pray with the words that Jesus taught us:
Our Father . . .

▶ all sing
  a closing song

170

FRIDAY PRAYER

January 19, 2001

■ INTRODUCTION

Today our reading continues the story of Samuel and Saul. King Saul has gathered an army from the tribes of Israel. Now that the tribes are working together, they are strong enough to defeat their enemies. Whenever people unite, they become stronger.

■ A PSALM FOR JANUARY

turn to page 158

■ READING   I Samuel 14:48; 15:1, 3, 7, 9, 10, 12, 14, 15, 22, 24, 25

Listen to the words of the book of Samuel:

King Saul was a brave commander and always won his battles. One day, Samuel told Saul, "Now listen to this message from the LORD: 'Go and attack the Amalekites *(uh-MAL-uh-kites)!* Destroy them and all their possessions.'"

Saul attacked the Amalekites from Havilah *(hah-vee-LAH)* to Shur. Saul and his army let King Agag *(AY-gag)* live, and they also spared the best sheep and cattle.

The LORD told Samuel, "Saul has stopped obeying me, and I'm sorry that I made him king." Early the next morning Samuel went to talk with Saul. "Why," Samuel asked, "do I hear sheep and cattle?" "The army took them from the Amalekites," Saul explained, "so they could sacrifice them to the LORD your God." "Tell me," Samuel said, "Does the LORD really want sacrifices and offerings? No! He doesn't want your sacrifices. He wants you to obey him."

"I have sinned," Saul admitted. "I disobeyed both you and the LORD. Please forgive me and come back with me so I can worship the LORD."

The word of the Lord.

■ REFLECTION

Do I admit my sins and ask forgiveness, as Saul did? How do we turn to God when we are sorry? Do I talk to anyone about these things the way Saul and Samuel talked?

■ CLOSING

Let us remember these intentions:

God of all nations and Creator of all peoples,
    heal all that divides us.
Teach us to live together in peace.
As our world is one, so our future is one.
Give us one heart and one vision.
Make us one body in Christ Jesus,
    filled with the joy of your Holy Spirit.
We ask this through Christ our Lord. **Amen.**

Let us pray with the words that Jesus taught us:
Our Father . . .

sing
"alleluia"

171

WEEKLY PRAYER

With a Reading from the Gospel for Sunday, January 21, 2001

▶ Reminder: The Week of Prayer for Christian Unity lasts from January 18 to 25. You may want to use the prayer on page 170.

■ INTRODUCTION

When Jews gather on the Sabbath, they pray, listen to readings from the Bible, and hear a commentary on the reading by a rabbi. In this way they continue to learn what the word of God means for their lives. This form of worship is familiar to us, because we follow it as well.

Today's reading tells of a time when Jesus led the liturgy of the word at his meeting place.

■ A PSALM FOR JANUARY

▶ turn to page 158

■ READING

Luke 4:16–21

Listen to the words of the holy gospel according to Luke:

Jesus went to the meeting place on the Sabbath. When he stood up to read from the Scriptures, he was given the book of Isaiah the prophet. He opened it and read,

"The Lord's Spirit has come to me,
because he has chosen me
to tell the good news to the poor.
The Lord has sent me
to announce freedom for prisoners,
to give sight to the blind,
to free everyone who suffers,
and to say, 'This is the year the Lord
has chosen.'"

Jesus closed the book, then handed it back to the man in charge and sat down. Everyone in the meeting place looked straight at Jesus.

Then Jesus said to them, "What you have just heard me read has come true today."

The gospel of the Lord.

■ REFLECTION

If he had continued, what might Jesus have said? How are the words of Isaiah true in my life? How is this a "year the Lord has chosen?"

■ CLOSING

Let us remember these intentions:

God of all nations and Creator of all peoples,
    heal all that divides us.
Teach us to live together in peace.
As our world is one, so our future is one.
Give us one heart and one vision.
Make us one body in Christ Jesus,
    filled with the joy of your Holy Spirit.
We ask this through Christ our Lord. **Amen.**

Let us pray with the words that Jesus taught us:

Our Father . . .

▶ sing "alleluia"

MONDAY PRAYER

January 22, 2001

■ INTRODUCTION

Today we remember Saint Vincent Pallotti. His teacher once said that he was a nice boy, "but a bit thick-headed." Vincent did not let the opinion of one person discourage him. He became a priest and a famous educator in Rome.

■ A PSALM FOR JANUARY

► turn to page 158

■ READING

I Samuel 16:1, 4, 6–7, 10–13

Listen to the words of the first book of Samuel:

The LORD said to Samuel, "Put some olive oil in a small jar and go visit a man named Jesse *(JESS-ee),* who lives in Bethlehem. I've chosen one of his sons to be my king."

Samuel did what the LORD told him and went to Bethlehem. The town leaders went to meet him. When Jesse and his sons arrived, Samuel noticed Jesse's oldest son. "He has to be the one the LORD has chosen," Samuel said to himself.

But the LORD told him, "Samuel, don't think [he] is the one just because he's tall and handsome. He isn't the one I've chosen. People judge others by what they look like, but I judge people by what is in their hearts."

Jesse had all seven of his sons go over to Samuel. Finally Samuel said, "Jesse, the LORD hasn't chosen any of these young men. Do you have any more sons?"

"Yes," Jesse answered. "My youngest son David is out taking care of the sheep." "Send for him!" Samuel said. As soon as David came, the LORD told Samuel, "He's the one!"

Samuel poured the oil on David's head. At that moment, the Spirit of the LORD took control of David and stayed with him from then on.

The word of the Lord.

■ REFLECTION

God said, "People judge others by what they look like, but I judge people by what is in their hearts." What does this mean? What does God see in my heart?

■ CLOSING

Let us remember these intentions:

God of all nations and Creator of all peoples,
  heal all that divides us.
Teach us to live together in peace.
As our world is one, so our future is one.
Give us one heart and one vision.
Make us one body in Christ Jesus,
  filled with the joy of your Holy Spirit.
We ask this through Christ our Lord. **Amen.**

Let us pray with the words that Jesus taught us:
Our Father . . .

► sing "alleluia"

173

■ INTRODUCTION

We have been reading this week about the first kings of Israel. King Saul was chosen and anointed by the prophet Samuel. He was a fine general. He organized the army and led them successfully against their enemies. But Saul did not remain faithful to religious laws. So Samuel looked for a successor.

God led Samuel to David, a young man still living at home and tending sheep. Samuel anointed David, but many years would pass before David became Israel's king.

■ A PSALM FOR JANUARY

▶ turn to
page 158

■ READING

I Samuel 16:14–16, 18, 19, 21, 23

Listen to the words of the first book of Samuel:

The Spirit of the LORD had left Saul, and an evil spirit from the LORD was terrifying him. Saul's officials told him, "Your Majesty, let us go and look for someone who is good at playing the harp. He can play for you whenever the evil spirit from God bothers you, and you'll feel better."

"A man named Jesse who lives in Bethlehem has a son who can play the harp," one official said. Saul sent a message to Jesse, "Tell your son David to leave your sheep and come here to me." David went to Saul and started working for him. Saul liked him so much that he put David in charge of carrying his weapons.

Whenever the evil spirit from God bothered Saul, David would play his harp. Saul would relax and feel better, and the evil spirit would go away.

The word of the Lord.

■ REFLECTION

Do we know people who have an illness like Saul's? Is there a certain kind of music that can calm me when I am anxious or upset? Am I able, like David, to bring peace to others?

■ CLOSING

Let us remember these intentions:

God of all nations and Creator of all peoples,
    heal all that divides us.
Teach us to live together in peace.
As our world is one, so our future is one.
Give us one heart and one vision.
Make us one body in Christ Jesus,
    filled with the joy of your Holy Spirit.
We ask this through Christ our Lord. **Amen.**

Let us pray with the words that Jesus taught us:

Our Father . . .

 sing
"alleluia"

WEDNESDAY PRAYER

January 24, 2001

■ INTRODUCTION

Today we remember a holy bishop, Saint Francis de Sales. He lived at a time when Christians were fighting over the meaning of their faith. Francis brought many people back to the peace and love that Jesus taught.

Today the Chinese New Year begins. This is called the Year of the Snake. In China, snakes are a sign of wisdom and humor.

■ A PSALM FOR JANUARY

turn to
page 158

■ READING

I Samuel 17:2–4, 8–9, 24, 32–35, 37

Listen to the words of the first book of Samuel:

King Saul and the Israelite army got ready to fight the Philistine *(FILL-iss-teen)* army. The Philistine army had a hero named Goliath *(guh-LYE-eth)* who was over nine feet tall. Goliath went out and shouted to the army of Israel, "I'm the best soldier in our army. Choose your best soldier to come out and fight me! If he can kill me, our people will be your slaves. But if I kill him, your people will be our slaves." When the Israelite soldiers saw Goliath, they were scared and ran off.

"Your Majesty," David said, "this Philistine shouldn't turn us into cowards. I'll go out and fight him myself!"

"You don't have a chance against him," Saul replied. "You're only a boy, and he's been a soldier all his life." But David told him, "Your Majesty, I take care of my father's sheep. And

when one of them is dragged off by a lion or a bear, I go after it and beat the wild animal until it lets the sheep go. The LORD has rescued me from the claws of lions and bears, and he will keep me safe from the hands of this Philistine."

"All right," Saul answered, "go ahead and fight him. And I hope the LORD will help you."

The word of the Lord.

■ REFLECTION

What kind of person was David? Have I ever been told that I was too young to do something important? Do I trust God to help me?

■ CLOSING

Let us remember these intentions:

God of all nations and Creator of all peoples,
    heal all that divides us.
Teach us to live together in peace.
As our world is one, so our future is one.
Give us one heart and one vision.
Make us one body in Christ Jesus,
    filled with the joy of your Holy Spirit.
We ask this through Christ our Lord. **Amen.**

Let us pray with the words that Jesus taught us:

Our Father . . .

sing
"alleluia"

THURSDAY PRAYER

January 25, 2001

■ INTRODUCTION

Today we celebrate the Conversion of Saint Paul. Paul was an important missionary of the early church. His feast day ends our Week of Prayer for Christian Unity.

Amazingly, in the years before Paul helped the church, he attacked it. Our reading today tells about Paul's conversion. In the Hebrew language, Paul's name was Saul.

■ A PSALM FOR JANUARY

➤ turn to
page 158

■ READING

Acts 22:4, 6–8

Listen to the words of the book of the Acts of the Apostles:

Paul said, "I made trouble for everyone who followed the Lord's Way, and I even had some of them killed. I had others arrested and put in jail. I didn't care if they were men or women.

"One day about noon I was getting close to Damascus *(duh-MASS-kus)*, when a bright light from heaven suddenly flashed around me. I fell to the ground and heard a voice asking, 'Saul, Saul, why are you so cruel to me?'

"'Who are you?'" I answered.

"The Lord replied, 'I am Jesus from Nazareth! I am the one you are so cruel to.'"

The word of the Lord.

■ REFLECTION

What did Paul discover about Jesus on the road to Damascus? Does thinking about the unity of Christ with his followers help me to treat other people with kindness?

■ CLOSING

Let us remember these intentions:

God of all nations and Creator of all peoples,
    heal all that divides us.
Teach us to live together in peace.
As our world is one, so our future is one.
Give us one heart and one vision.
Make us one body in Christ Jesus,
    and fill us with the joy of your Holy Spirit.
We ask this through Christ our Lord. **Amen.**

Let us pray with the words that Jesus taught us:

Our Father . . .

 sing
"alleluia"

FRIDAY PRAYER

January 26, 2001

■ INTRODUCTION

Today we remember two bishops of the early church: Timothy and Titus. In the Bible there are two letters from Saint Paul to Timothy and one letter to Titus. The letters show Paul's great respect for his two friends and for the important part bishops play in the life of the church.

Today's reading tells of young David's fight with the giant Goliath *(guh-LYE-eth)*.

■ A PSALM FOR JANUARY

turn to page 158

■ READING

I Samuel 17:38–40, 42, 44, 45, 47–50

Listen to the words of the first book of Samuel:

Saul had his own military clothes and armor put on David. David strapped on a sword and tried to walk around, but he was not used to wearing those things. "I can't move with all this stuff on," David said. David took off the armor and picked up his shepherd's stick. He went out to a stream and picked up five smooth rocks and put them in his leather bag. Then with his sling in his hand, he went straight toward Goliath.

When Goliath saw that David was just a boy, he made fun of him. "Come on! When I'm finished with you, I'll feed you to the birds and wild animals!"

David answered, "The LORD always wins his battles, and he will help us defeat you."

When Goliath started forward, David ran toward him. He put a rock in his sling and swung the sling around by its straps. When he let go of one strap, the rock flew out and hit Goliath on the forehead. It cracked his skull, and he fell face down on the ground. David defeated Goliath with a sling and a rock. He killed him without even using a sword.

The word of the Lord.

■ REFLECTION

The adults urged David to wear armor but it weighed him down. When do I feel like David? How can we know when to take other people's advice and when to follow our own ideas?

■ CLOSING

Let us remember these intentions:

Loving God,
 you call us your children
 and save us through your own suffering.
Defend us against evil.
Make us brave and faithful,
 and strengthen us in times of trouble.
We ask this through Christ our Lord. **Amen.**

Let us pray with the words that Jesus taught us:

Our Father . . .

sing "alleluia"

177

WEEKLY PRAYER

With a Reading from the Gospel for Sunday, January 28, 2001

➤ Reminder: You may want to make copies of February's Psalm on page 186. Next week you may want to use the Blessing of Candles, on page 191. Talk this over with your teacher.

■ INTRODUCTION

Jesus grew up in the town of Nazareth. Then he moved away and became a famous preacher and healer. This was hard for the people of Nazareth to understand. They could not believe that he was not as ordinary as they always thought. When Jesus visited Nazareth, he was asked to proclaim the reading and give the homily. Today we will hear what happened next.

■ A PSALM FOR JANUARY

➤ turn to page 158

■ READING

Luke 4:22–24, 28–30

Listen to the words of the holy gospel according to Luke:

All the people in the meeting place started talking about Jesus and were amazed at the wonderful things he said. They kept on asking, "Isn't he Joseph's son?"

Jesus answered, "You will tell me to do the same things here in my own hometown that you heard I did in Capernaum *(kuh-PER-nee-um)*. But you can be sure that no prophets are liked by the people of their own hometown."

When the people in the meeting place heard Jesus say this, they became so angry that they got up and threw him out of town. They dragged him to the edge of the cliff on which the town was built, because they wanted to throw him down from there. But Jesus slipped through the crowd and got away.

The gospel of the Lord.

■ REFLECTION

Do people ever surprise me with their talents or good ideas? Have I ever been jealous of someone when they did something well and got praise for it?

■ CLOSING

Let us remember these intentions:

Loving God,
    you call us your children
    and save us through your own suffering.
Defend us against evil.
Make us brave and faithful,
    and strengthen us in times of trouble.
We ask this through Christ our Lord. **Amen.**

Let us pray with the words that Jesus taught us:

Our Father . . .

➤ sing "alleluia"

178

MONDAY PRAYER

January 29, 2001

■ INTRODUCTION

Catholic Schools Week began yesterday. There probably will be interesting events planned for us and our families during the coming days. We can use this opportunity to make our school a place of welcome, joy and peace.

In today's reading, we hear how David beame king of Israel. David's reign was long and eventful, but he kept up with his music. Some say he wrote almost half of the Psalms!

■ A PSALM FOR JANUARY

 turn to
page 158

■ READING

2 Samuel 5:1–4

Listen to the words of the second book of Samuel:

After King Saul died, Israel's leaders met with David at Hebron *(HEE-brun)* and said, "We are your relatives. Even when Saul was king, you led our nation in battle. And the LORD promised that someday you would rule Israel and take care of us like a shepherd."

During the meeting, David made an agreement with the leaders and asked the LORD to be their witness. Then the leaders poured olive oil on David's head to show that he was now the king of Israel.

David was thirty years old when he became king, and he ruled for forty years.

The word of the Lord.

■ REFLECTION

How was David's life as a shepherd like his life as a king? Do our rulers today act like good shepherds of the people? Are there any people who act like good shepherds in my life?

■ CLOSING

Psalm 27:1

Let us all repeat:
The Lord is my light and my salvation;
   of whom shall I be afraid?
The Lord is my light and my salvation;
   of whom shall I be afraid?

Let us remember these intentions:

Be a light to your people, Lord,
   and lead them when the road is dark.
We ask this through Christ our Lord. **Amen.**

Let us pray with the words that Jesus taught us:
Our Father . . .

 sing
"alleluia"

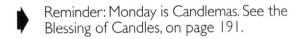

Reminder: Monday is Candlemas. See the Blessing of Candles, on page 191.

■ INTRODUCTION

On this Tuesday of Catholic Schools Week, we learn more about King David. He ruled the southern tribes for seven years. He led the army against many enemies. Then the leaders of the northern tribes asked him to be their king, too. So David united them into one nation. He moved his capital to Jerusalem *(juh-ROO-suh-lem)*.

■ A PSALM FOR JANUARY

turn to page 158

■ READING

2 Samuel 7:8–10, 16, 18–20, 28

Listen to the words of the second book of Samuel:

The LORD said to David, "I brought you in from the fields where you took care of sheep, and I made you the leader of my people. Wherever you went, I helped you and destroyed your enemies. I have made you one of the most famous people in the world. I have given my people Israel a land of their own where they can live in peace, and they won't have to tremble with fear any more. I will make sure that one of your descendants will always be king."

David prayed, "LORD All-Powerful, my family and I don't deserve what you have already done for us, and yet you have promised to do even more. I am your servant, and you know my thoughts, so there is nothing more that I need to say. LORD All-Powerful, you are greater than all others. No one is like you, and you alone are God."

The word of the Lord.

■ REFLECTION

Do I ever thank and praise God without asking for anything? What blessings has my family received that I can thank God for today?

■ CLOSING

Psalm 27:1

Let us all repeat:
The Lord is my light and my salvation;
  of whom shall I be afraid?
**The Lord is my light and my salvation;
  of whom shall I be afraid?**

Let us remember these intentions:

Be a light to your people, Lord,
  and lead them when the road is dark.
We ask this through Christ our Lord. **Amen.**

Let us pray with the words that Jesus taught us:
Our Father . . .

sing "alleluia"

WEDNESDAY PRAYER

January 31, 2001

■ INTRODUCTION

On this Wednesday of Catholic Schools Week, we remember Saint John Bosco, who died in 1888. John spent his life helping teens in the poor neighborhoods of Turin, Italy. He even did acrobatic tricks to get their attention so that he could tell them about Jesus. He was a great teacher and a holy priest.

■ A PSALM FOR JANUARY

turn to
page 158

■ READING

I Kings 2:1–4, 10–11

Listen to the words of the first book of Kings:

Not long before David died, he told Solomon, "My son, I will soon die, as everyone must. But I want you to be strong and brave. Do what the LORD your God commands and follow his teachings. Obey everything written in the Law of Moses. Then you will be a success, no matter what you do or where you go. You and your descendants must always faithfully obey the LORD. If you do, he will keep the solemn promise he made to me that someone from our family will always be king of Israel."

David was king of Israel forty years. He ruled seven years from Hebron *(HEE-brun)* and thirty-three years from Jerusalem *(juh-ROO-suh-lem)*. Then he died and was buried in Jerusalem. His son Solomon became king and took control of David's kingdom.

The word of the Lord.

■ REFLECTION

What advice did David give his son? What advice do my parents give me? Why are the lives of children so important to their parents?

■ CLOSING

Psalm 27:1

Let us all repeat:
The Lord is my light and my salvation;
  of whom shall I be afraid?
The Lord is my light and my salvation;
  of whom shall I be afraid?

Let us remember these intentions:

Be a light to your people, Lord,
  and lead them when the road is dark.
We ask this through Christ our Lord. **Amen.**

Let us pray with the words that Jesus taught us:
Our Father . . .

sing
"alleluia"

FEBRUARY

Thursday, February 1, to Tuesday, February 27

ORDINARY TIME
FEBRUARY 2001

■ ABOUT THE MONTH

No matter what corner of the country you live in, February just does not have as much personality as some of the other months. It is a month of flu bugs and "winter blahs."

The beginning of something is almost always

LOOKING AHEAD

exciting. We pay more attention to things that are new. But now our school year is about half over. We are in the middle.

Middles can be more difficult than beginnings or endings. School work is not more difficult. Being respectful to each other is not more difficult. It's just that we sometimes don't find these things as interesting as we once did. Our most important job now is to stay alert, to stay interested—and at least to stay awake!

There are some festivities in February that can brighten the winter. On Friday, February 2, we celebrate the Presentation of the Lord. The feast of Saint Blase on February 3, falls on Saturday this year. Wednesday, February 14, is Valentine's Day. A Blessing for Saint Valentine's Day is on page 202. The following Monday, February 19, is Presidents' Day. On Tuesday, February 27, it's time to celebrate Mardi Gras, the festival of food and fun that helps us to get ready for Lent which begins the next day, Ash Wednesday, February 28.

■ FEBRUARY IS AFRICAN AMERICAN HISTORY MONTH. Since 1926, Americans have taken some time during this month to remember the contributions that African Americans have made to this country. This time of the year was chosen because it is the month of the birthdays of Abraham Lincoln and Frederick Douglass. Do you know why these two people are important in American history?

■ DURING FEBRUARY MOST OF OUR READINGS WILL BE FROM THE GOSPEL OF LUKE. The readings used for Weekly Prayer will be taken from the Sunday gospels. Those used for Daily Prayer will match their spirit. They will fill out Luke's picture of the work of Jesus.

During the first week of February we hear about Jesus working great signs. He heals sick people and calms storms. Jesus is able to command creation. During the following week we follow Jesus as he teaches and as he sends out disciples.

During the last week of February we learn about being a disciple of Jesus. We begin with the parable of the sower. Then we read about the women who followed Jesus. Then, on February 23, we read the most important passage: the proclamation of faith by Peter.

The last week of February begins with two days to enjoy a carnival spirit, and then we enter the season of Lent.

■ PREPARATION FOR FEBRUARY

If it is your custom, remember to make copies of the Psalm for February, the Meal Prayer and the End of the Day Prayer (see pages 186, 187 and 188). If you are using *Blessed Be God!* these prayers are found on pages 24 to 26.

■ ON FEBRUARY 2 WE CELEBRATE THE FEAST OF THE PRESENTATION OF THE LORD, WHICH IS ALSO CALLED "CANDLEMAS." Forty days after Jesus was born, Joseph and Mary brought him to Jerusalem. They met two prophets there, Simeon and Anna, who understood that Jesus was the Messiah.

Simeon called Jesus the "light of revelation." So some people bring their "lights," candles, to Mass on Candlemas for a blessing. There is a prayer on page 191 to use if you wish to bless candles for the classroom and candles brought from home. This can be done on any day close to the feast.

Some people leave their Bethlehem scene up until February 2. On Candlemas they tuck a few flowers into its straw as promises of spring. Then, at the end of the day, the stable is packed away.

You might know February 2 as "Groundhog Day." According to legend, on Candlemas even animals hope for spring! That's why the groundhog peeks out of its burrow to check the weather.

- THE DAYS BEFORE ASH WEDNESDAY ARE THE TIME OF CARNIVAL, A TIME FOR FUN BEFORE LENT BEGINS. We can bring the Carnival spirit into the classroom. Some crepe-paper streamers can do a lot to change the room and make us feel festive.

At Carnival we should have something good to eat too. The Carnival feast says, "Spring is coming!" In the old days during Lent, adults gave up eating meat. The word "carnival" means "good-bye to eating meat."

The last day of Carnival, February 27, is Mardi Gras *(MAR-dee grah)*. These are the French words for "Fat Tuesday," a day when many people eat pancakes and doughnuts. Perhaps we can share some in the classroom. On the next day, Ash Wednesday, the season of Lent begins.

We can end Carnival with a ritual of saying farewell to the alleluia. We will not sing that happy song again until we rejoice at Easter. The ritual is on page 214.

- SUGGESTED HYMNS: A beautiful Irish melody is used in the song "Lord of all hopefulness" (page 155 in the *Hymnal for Catholic Students).*

On Candlemas we can sing Christmas carols one last time. Because of this feast, in early February our prayers often mention light. We can sing "This little light of mine" (page 196 in the hymnal), an African American spiritual. "All creatures of our God and king" (page 100 in the hymnal) and "Jubilate Deo" *(you-bee-LAH-tay DAY-oh,* page 147 in the hymnal) are good songs for Carnival because they have many alleluias.

At Daily Prayer during the first days of the month we can sing the words "The Lord is my light . . ." (from Psalm 27). Music is on page 59 of the hymnal.

Someone with a good voice can sing the words first, and then everyone can repeat them.

■ THE SCHOOL OF RELIGION

The middle of winter can be difficult. The weather may be harsh, and there are often many absences because of illness. This is a good time for spirit-building events, such as Candlemas and Mardi Gras.

Perhaps students can take the roles of reader and leader if they are not doing that already. A choir might be formed to give a lift to the music.

At your meeting closest to February 2, you may want to bless candles using the blessing on page 191. The week of February 14 almost always brings special celebrations. The Blessing for Saint Valentine's Day on page 202 can be a part of the fun.

Be sure to bring the spirit of Carnival to your last meeting before Lent. That certainly will bring a boost to the spirit! Tuesday Prayer for February 27, might be used at this meeting even if you do not meet on a Tuesday. The Farewell to the Alleluia (on page 214) can be the final moment of the festivities.

A PSALM FOR FEBRUARY

> all make
> the sign
> of the cross

Psalm 146:1–2, 5–9

LEADER Praise the Lord, my heart!
My whole life, give praise.

ALL **Let me sing to God as long as I live.**

SIDE A They are wise who depend on God,
who look to Jacob's Lord,

SIDE B creator of heaven and earth,
maker of the teeming sea.

SIDE A The Lord keeps faith for ever,
giving food to the hungry,

SIDE B justice to the poor,
freedom to captives.

SIDE A The Lord opens blind eyes
and straightens the bent,

SIDE B comforting widows and orphans,
protecting the stranger.

LEADER Praise the Lord, my heart!
My whole life, give praise.

ALL **Let me sing to God as long as I live.**

**Glory to the Father, and to the Son,
and to the Holy Spirit:
as it was in the beginning, is now,
and will be for ever. Amen. Alleluia.**

> turn back to
> Daily Prayer or Weekly Prayer
> for today

186

FEBRUARY

MEAL PRAYER

LEADER   Let us offer God praise and thanksgiving:

ALL   ▶ all make
        the sign
        of the cross

LEADER   Praise the Lord, my heart!
        My whole life, give praise.

ALL   **Let me sing to God as long as I live.**

LEADER   Blessed are you, Lord:
        You have fed us from our earliest days.
        You give food to every living creature.
        Fill our hearts with joy and delight.
        Let us always have enough
            and something to spare
                for works of mercy
                in honor of Christ Jesus, our Lord.
        Through Christ
            may glory, honor and power be yours
            for ever and ever.

ALL   **Amen.**

        ▶ all make
        the sign
        of the cross

FEBRUARY

END OF THE DAY PRAYER

> all make
> the sign
> of the cross

LEADER God, come to my assistance.
ALL **Lord, make haste to help me.**
LEADER Our help is in the name of the Lord:
ALL **Who made heaven and earth.**
LEADER May God, ever wakeful,
keep you from stumbling;
the guardian of Israel
neither rests nor sleeps.

God shelters you from evil,
securing your life.
God watches over you near and far,
now and always.

> hold out one hand
> toward everyone
> in blessing, and say:

May the Lord bless us,
    protect us from all evil,
    and bring us to everlasting life:

ALL
> all make
> the sign
> of the cross

Psalm 121:2–4, 7–8

THURSDAY PRAYER

February 1, 2001

Reminders: February's Psalm, Meal Prayer and End of the Day Prayer are on pages 24 to 26 in *Blessed Be God!* Tomorrow is Candlemas. A blessing for this day is on page 191. Talk this over with the teacher.

■ INTRODUCTION

In our reading today Isaiah announces that the savior to come will bring light and hope to all. This helps us look to tomorrow's feast of the Presentation of the Lord in the Temple. There, Jesus was recognized as the light of the world. On this Thursday in Catholic Schools Week, let us try to be light to one another.

■ A PSALM FOR FEBRUARY

turn to
page 186

■ READING

Isaiah 42:1, 4, 6–7

Listen to the words of the prophet Isaiah:

The LORD says this:
"Here is my servant!
   I have made him strong.
He is my chosen one;
   I am pleased with him.
I have given him my Spirit,
   and he will bring justice to the nations.
He won't quit or give up
   until he brings justice everywhere on earth.
I chose you to bring justice,
   and I am here at your side.
I selected and sent you to bring light
   and my promise of hope to the nations.

You will give sight to the blind.
   You will set prisoners free
      from dark dungeons."

The word of the Lord.

■ REFLECTION

God's servant will bring light and hope to all nations. What kind of light do nations need today? How can I be a light?

■ CLOSING

Psalm 27:1

Let us all repeat:
The Lord is my light and my salvation;
   of whom should I be afraid?
**The Lord is my light and my salvation;
   of whom should I be afraid?**

Let us remember these intentions:

Be a light to your people, Lord,
   and lead them when the road is dark.
We ask this through Christ our Lord. **Amen.**

Let us pray with the words that Jesus taught us:

Our Father . . .

 sing "alleluia"

FRIDAY PRAYER

February 2, 2001

Reminder: You can use the prayer on page 191 to bless candles today.

■ INTRODUCTION

Today we celebrate the Presentation of the Lord. Mary and Joseph brought Jesus to the Temple 40 days after he was born. Jesus was greeted there by the prophet Simeon and Anna. They knew that he was the Messiah, the light of the world.

Today is also called "Candlemas" because candles are blessed on this day. Saturday is the feast of Saint Blase. It is a tradition to pray for health with a blessing of throats on that day.

■ A PSALM FOR FEBRUARY

turn to
page 186

■ READING

Luke 2:25–27, 27–32

Listen to the words of the holy gospel according to Luke:

Simeon was a good man. He loved God and was waiting for God to save the people of Israel. God's Spirit came to him and told him that he would not die until he had seen Christ the Lord.

When Mary and Joseph brought Jesus to the temple, the Spirit told Simeon to go into the temple. Simeon took the baby Jesus in his arms and praised God,

"Lord, I am your servant,
    and now I can die in peace,
because you have kept your promise to me.

With my own eyes I have seen
    what you have done to save your people,
    and foreign nations will also see this.
Your mighty power is a light for all nations,
    and it will bring honor
    to your people Israel."

The gospel of the Lord.

■ REFLECTION

Why are some people who have had a glimpse of God not afraid of dying? Where can I see glimpses of God?

■ CLOSING

Psalm 27:1

Let us all repeat:
The Lord is my light and my salvation,
    of whom should I be afraid?
**The Lord is my light and my salvation;
    of whom should I be afraid?**

Let us remember these intentions:

Be a light to your people, Lord,
    and lead them when the road is dark.
We ask this through Christ our Lord. **Amen.**

Let us pray with the words that Jesus taught us:
Our Father . . .

sing
"alleluia"

A Blessing of Candles

This blessing can be used at any time, but especially on Candlemas, February 2, the feast of the Presentation of the Lord.

Candles used in the prayer center may be blessed along with any candles students bring from home. All the candles are gathered in one place, such as on a table or desk covered with a beautiful cloth. At least one candle should be lighted before the blessing begins. Older students might hold lighted candles.

It is an old custom on Candlemas to put a few spring flowers near the statue of the Christ child from the nativity set.

You can sing the words "The Lord is my light . . ." from Psalm 27. The music is found on page 59 in the Hymnal for Catholic Students. *Begin and end this blessing by singing a Christmas carol, such as "Joy to the world."*

all make
the sign
of the cross

LEADER
Jesus Christ is the light of the world,
a light no darkness can overpower!

Let us all repeat:
The Lord is my light and my salvation;
  of whom should I be afraid?

ALL
**The Lord is my light and my salvation;
of whom should I be afraid?**

LEADER
On the day of baptism, we were given a lighted candle with these words: "Walk always as children of the light, and keep the flame of faith alive in your hearts."

Let us now renew that faith and ask God to bless these candles. They are a sign of Christ, who is light and life to us.

hold out one hand
over the candles in blessing,
and say:

God our Creator and Redeemer,
  bless these candles
as signs of your presence
  and signs of our faith.
In the beauty of your holy light,
  keep us in quiet and in peace.
Keep us safe and turn our hearts to you
  that we may be light for our world.
All praise be yours through Christ,
  the light of nations, the glory of Israel,
    now and forever.

ALL
Amen.

all make
the sign
of the cross

WEEKLY PRAYER

With a Reading from the Gospel for Sunday, February 4, 2001

■ INTRODUCTION

In today's reading, Simon Peter and his partners listen to the teaching of Jesus, and see his wonderful works. In this way they learn about Jesus.

Something like that can happen to us. We notice God's care for us. We hear the voice of God in our hearts and in the Bible. And we see the courage of others who follow him. Then, when Jesus asks us to follow, we are ready.

■ A PSALM FOR FEBRUARY

▶ turn to page 186

■ READING

Luke 5:1, 1–6, 8, 10–11

Listen to the words of the holy gospel according to Luke:

Jesus was standing on the shore, teaching the people as they crowded around him to hear God's message. Near the shore he saw two boats left there by some fishermen who had gone to wash their nets. Jesus got into the boat that belonged to Simon and asked him to row it out a little way from the shore. Then Jesus sat down in the boat to teach the crowd.

When Jesus had finished speaking, he told Simon, "Row the boat out into the deep water and let your nets down to catch some fish."

"Master," Simon answered, "we have worked hard all night long and have not caught a thing. But if you tell me to, I will let the nets down." They did it and caught so many fish that their nets began ripping apart.

When Simon Peter saw this happen, he knelt down in front of Jesus and said, "Lord, don't come near me! I am a sinner."

Jesus told Simon, "Don't be afraid! From now on you will bring in people instead of fish." The men pulled their boats up on the shore. Then they left everything and went with Jesus.

The gospel of the Lord.

■ REFLECTION

Simon was a fisherman, so Jesus used fishing as a symbol of the work Simon would do for God. How could Jesus describe the way students and teachers work for Jesus?

■ CLOSING

Let us remember these intentions:

Gracious God,
   through the gift of your Spirit
   and the teaching of your apostles,
we can proclaim with all your church
   that Jesus is the Messiah you sent to us.
Strengthen and deepen this gift of faith.
We ask this through Christ our Lord. **Amen.**

Let us pray with the words that Jesus taught us:

Our Father . . .

▶ sing "alleluia"

MONDAY PRAYER

February 5, 2001

■ INTRODUCTION

Today we remember Saint Agatha *(AG-uh-thuh)*. She died for her faith on the island of Sicily *(SIS-uh-lee)* in the year 251. It is reported that she said to those who arrested her, "To be a servant of Christ is to be truly free."

The people of Sicily turn to Agatha in prayer when their volcano looks like it will erupt. Agatha was an important witness in the early church. She is named in the prayers of the Mass.

■ A PSALM FOR FEBRUARY

 turn to
page 186

■ READING

Luke 5:12–16

Listen to the words of the holy gospel according to Luke:

Jesus came to a town where there was a man who had leprosy *(LEP-ruh-see)*. When the man saw Jesus, he knelt down to the ground in front of Jesus and begged, "Lord, you have the power to make me well, if only you wanted to."

Jesus put his hand on him and said, "I want to! Now you are well." At once the man's leprosy disappeared. Jesus told him, "Don't tell anyone about this, but go and show yourself to the priest, just as Moses commanded, and everyone will know that you have been healed."

News about Jesus kept spreading. Large crowds came to listen to him teach and to be healed of their diseases. But Jesus would often go to some place where he could be alone and pray.

The gospel of the Lord.

■ REFLECTION

Writers around the time the gospels were set down often used leprosy as a symbol for sin. How can knowing that give new meanings to the story? How can we help Jesus heal the sick? Do I find quiet times to pray, as Jesus did?

■ CLOSING

Psalm 27:1

Let us all repeat:
The Lord is my light and my salvation; of whom should I be afraid?
The Lord is my light and my salvation; of whom should I be afraid?

Let us remember these intentions:

Be a light to your people, Lord, and lead them when the road is dark.
We ask this through Christ our Lord. **Amen.**

Let us pray with the words that Jesus taught us:
Our Father . . .

 sing "alleluia"

193

TUESDAY PRAYER

February 6, 2001

■ INTRODUCTION

Today we remember Saint Paul Miki and his companions. Christian missionaries brought the gospel to Japan in the sixteenth century. Many people began to believe in Jesus. Paul Miki became a priest and worked among the people. Later the emperor turned against the Christians. In 1597, Paul and his friends were arrested and put on crosses to die like Jesus.

■ A PSALM FOR FEBRUARY

turn to
page 186

■ READING

Luke 5:18–25

Listen to the words of the holy gospel according to Luke:

Some people came to the house where Jesus was staying, carrying a crippled man on a mat. They tried to take him inside the house and put him in front of Jesus. But because of the crowd, they could not get him to Jesus. So they went up on the roof, where they removed some tiles and let the mat down in the middle of the room.

When Jesus saw how much faith they had, he said to the crippled man. "My friend, your sins are forgiven." Some people began arguing. "Jesus must think he is God! Only God can forgive sins." Jesus said, "Is it easier for me to tell this crippled man that his sins are forgiven or to tell him to get up and walk? But now you will see that the Son of Man has the right to forgive sins here on earth." Jesus then said to the man. "Get up! Pick up your mat and walk home."

At once the man stood up in front of everyone. He picked up his mat and went home, giving thanks to God.

The gospel of the Lord.

■ REFLECTION

Where does Jesus' power over sin and forgiveness come from? How can sin paralyze us and keep us from making the right moves?

■ CLOSING

Psalm 27:1

Let us all repeat:
The Lord is my light and my salvation;
   of whom should I be afraid?
**The Lord is my light and my salvation;
   of whom should I be afraid?**

Let us remember these intentions:

Be a light to your people, Lord,
   and lead them when the road is dark.
We ask this through Christ our Lord. **Amen.**

Let us pray with the words that Jesus taught us:
Our Father . . .

sing
"alleluia"

WEDNESDAY PRAYER

■ INTRODUCTION

During the weeks of February nature looks cold and dead in many parts of the country. This is "ordinary time" on the church calendar, and it is easy to think that nothing special is happening these days.

But we know that the earth is only sleeping before it wakes up again in spring. And we know that God is here with us, giving peace and warmth. And that makes each of our days much more than "ordinary" time.

■ A PSALM FOR FEBRUARY

turn to
page 186

■ READING

Luke 7:1–4, 6–10

Listen to the words of the holy gospel according to Luke:

In the town of Capernaum *(kuh-PER-nee-um)* an army officer's servant was sick and about to die. The officer liked this servant very much. And when he heard about Jesus, he sent some Jewish leaders to ask him to come and heal the servant. The leaders went to Jesus and begged him to do something. So Jesus went with them.

When Jesus was not far from the house, the officer sent some friends to tell him, "Lord, don't go to any trouble for me! I am not good enough for you to come into my house. Just say the word, and my servant will get well. I have officers who give orders to me, and I have soldiers who take orders from me. I can say to one

of them, 'Go!' and he goes. I can say to another, 'Come!' and he comes."

When Jesus heard this, he was so surprised that he turned and said to the crowd following him, "In all of Israel I've never found anyone with this much faith!"

The officer's friends returned and found the servant well.

The gospel of the Lord.

■ REFLECTION

Do I believe that Jesus can cure sickness and death? Why doesn't Jesus cure everyone?

■ CLOSING

Psalm 27:1

Let us all repeat:
The Lord is my light and my salvation;
   of whom should I be afraid?
**The Lord is my light and my salvation;
   of whom should I be afraid?**

Let us remember these intentions:

Be a light to your people, Lord,
   and lead them when the road is dark.
We ask this through Christ our Lord. **Amen.**

Let us pray with the words that Jesus taught us:
Our Father . . .

sing
"alleluia"

■ INTRODUCTION

Today we remember Jerome Emiliani *(aye-mee-lee-AH-nee),* an Italian priest. In Jerome's time, a terrible disease was killing people. When their parents died, children had no place to go. So Jerome took them into his home. He began many homes for children without parents.

Let us join our prayers today to those of Saint Jerome. Let us remember all children who have lost a parent, who are abused or neglected, or who have no place to live.

■ A PSALM FOR FEBRUARY

➤ turn to
page 186

■ READING

Luke 7:11–16

Listen to the words of the holy gospel according to Luke:

Jesus and his disciples were on their way to the town of Nain *(NAY-in),* and a big crowd was going along with them. As they came near the gate of the town, they saw people carrying out the body of a widow's only son. Many people from the town were walking along with her.

When the Lord saw the woman, he felt sorry for her and said, "Don't cry!" Jesus went over and touched the stretcher on which the people were carrying the dead boy. They stopped, and Jesus said, "Young man, get up!" The boy sat up and began to speak. Jesus then gave him back to his mother.

Everyone was frightened and praised God. They said, "A great prophet is here with us! God has come to his people."

The gospel of the Lord.

■ REFLECTION

What do I say or do to comfort people who have a death in their family? In those days, women could not live alone, but had to live in a man's house. Jesus restored the widow's way of life when he gave life to her son. How does the church help the homeless and lonely today?

■ CLOSING

Let us remember these intentions:

Loving God, you send women and men
   to bring your love and healing touch
    to all your suffering people.
Bless, protect, and guide them.
Make us truly grateful for constant care,
   and show us the choices that lead to
    eternal life.
We ask this through Christ our Lord. **Amen.**

Let us pray with the words that Jesus taught us:

Our Father . . .

➤ sing
"alleluia"

FRIDAY PRAYER

February 9, 2001

■ INTRODUCTION

In today's reading Jesus forgives a sinful woman. The gospels sometimes say that sinfulness is like an illness. In today's gospel, we learn that sinfulness is also like owing someone a lot of money.

■ A PSALM FOR FEBRUARY

turn to
page 186

■ READING

Luke 7:36–39, 41–44, 47

Listen to the words of the holy gospel according to Luke:

A Pharisee *(FAIR-ih-see)* invited Jesus to have dinner with him. When a sinful woman in that town found out that Jesus was there, she came and stood behind Jesus. She cried and started washing his feet with her tears and drying them with her hair.

The Pharisee said to himself, "If this man really were a prophet, he would know what kind of woman is touching him!" Jesus told him, "Two people were in debt to a moneylender. One of them owed him 500 silver coins, and the other owed him 50. The moneylender said that they didn't have to pay him anything. Which one of them will like him more?" The Pharisee answered, "I suppose it would be the one who had owed more and didn't have to pay it back."

"You are right," Jesus said. He turned toward the woman and said to the Pharisee, "Have you noticed this woman? I tell you that all her sins are forgiven, and that is why she has shown great love."

The gospel of the Lord.

■ REFLECTION

How is sinfulness like owing a lot of money? How do we show that we are sorry for our sins? How do we show that we are grateful to be forgiven? When have I experienced God's forgiveness and peace?

■ CLOSING

Let us remember these intentions:

Holy God,
   you welcome all your children
      when they turn to you for help.
Teach us how to repent,
   teach us how to forgive,
and teach us not to place burdens
   on one another.
We ask this through Christ our Lord. **Amen.**

Let us pray with the words that Jesus taught us.

Our Father . . .

sing
"alleluia"

197

WEEKLY PRAYER

With a Reading from the Gospel for Sunday, February 11, 2001

■ INTRODUCTION

In today's reading Jesus says that it is a blessing to be poor, hungry, sad and oppressed. This reading has been a favorite of Christians in every age because it is such a mystery. How can things that seem bad be a blessing? Think about this mystery today.

■ A PSALM FOR FEBRUARY

➤ turn to
page 186

■ READING

Luke 6:17, 18, 20–23

Listen to the words of the holy gospel according to Luke:

Jesus and his apostles went down from the mountain and came to some flat, level ground. Many other disciples were there to meet him. These people had come to listen to Jesus and to be healed of their diseases.

Jesus looked at his disciples and said,
"God will bless you people who are poor.
His kingdom belongs to you!
God will bless you hungry people.
You will have plenty to eat!
God will bless you people who are crying.
You will laugh!
God will bless you when others hate you
and won't have anything to do with you.
God will bless you when people insult you
and say cruel things about you,
all because you are a follower of the
Son of Man.

When this happens to you, be happy and
jump for joy.
You will have a great reward in heaven."

The gospel of the Lord.

■ REFLECTION

Have I ever been really hungry? What kinds of things make me cry? Am I ever excluded because I do the right thing? Do I ever mock people because they are "goody-goodys"?

■ CLOSING

Let us remember these intentions:

Wise and loving God,
   fill our minds with your word
so that we may know what is true and right,
so that we may know what is holy,
so that we may know your peace.
We ask this through Christ our Lord. **Amen.**

Let us pray with the words that Jesus taught us:

Our Father . . .

➤ sing
"alleluia"

MONDAY PRAYER

February 12, 2001

▶ Reminder: A blessing for Saint Valentine's Day is on page 202. You may want to use it some time on Wednesday.

■ INTRODUCTION

On this day in 1809, two important people were born. One was Abraham Lincoln, the president who helped end slavery in the United States. The other was Charles Darwin, an English biologist. He studied the way living things keep changing. Both men shaped the way we think about life on this planet. Let us pray for even greater knowledge and justice in our world.

■ A PSALM FOR FEBRUARY

▶ turn to page 186

■ READING

Luke 8:22–25

Listen to the words of the holy gospel according to Luke:

One day, Jesus and his disciples got into a boat, and he said, "Let's cross the lake." They started out, and while they were sailing across, he went to sleep.

Suddenly a windstorm struck the lake, and the boat started sinking. They were in danger. So they went to Jesus and woke him up. "Master, Master! We are about to drown!"

Jesus got up and ordered the wind and waves to stop. They obeyed, and everything was calm. Then Jesus asked the disciples, "Don't you have any faith?"

But they were frightened and amazed. They said to each other, "Who is this? He can give orders to the wind and the waves, and they obey him!"

The gospel of the Lord.

■ REFLECTION

Are there dangerous storms in my life and in the lives of people I know? Do we firmly believe that Jesus can help us through life's storms? How do I pray in times of sadness or trouble?

■ CLOSING

Let us remember these intentions:

Loving God,
we seek you in the wind,
    and find you in the storm.
We call to you in faith,
    and trust you in danger.
Be with us always
    when we pass through troubled waters.
We ask this through Christ our Lord. **Amen.**

Let us pray with the words that Jesus taught us:

Our Father . . .

▶ sing "alleluia"

199

TUESDAY PRAYER

■ INTRODUCTION

Today we remember Absalom Jones. He was born into slavery but worked hard to buy his wife's freedom and then his own. He taught himself to read, and became a preacher at his church in Philadelphia *(fill-uh-DELL-fee-uh)*. One day he and the other African Americans were told that they could not sit with the white members of the church, so they left that church and formed a new one. Saint Thomas African Episcopal *(ee-PIS-kuh-pull)* Church was the first in the United States to be organized and led by African Americans.

It is good to remember Absalom Jones during Black History Month.

■ A PSALM FOR FEBRUARY

turn to page 186

■ READING

Luke 10:38–42

Listen to the words of the holy gospel according to Luke:

The Lord and his disciples were traveling along and came to a village. When they got there, a woman named Martha welcomed him into her home. She had a sister named Mary, who sat down in front of the Lord and was listening to what he said. Martha was worried about all that had to be done. Finally, she went to Jesus and said, "Lord, doesn't it bother you that my sister has left me to do all the work by myself? Tell her to come and help me!"

The Lord answered, "Martha, Martha! You are worried and upset about so many things, but only one thing is necessary. Mary has chosen what is best, and it will not be taken away from her."

The gospel of the Lord.

■ REFLECTION

Was Jesus being fair to Martha? Why was Mary's choice better? Do I ever become so busy with my work that I am rude to the people around me?

■ CLOSING

Let us remember these intentions:

Loving God,
you have words to speak to us
    because we are your children
        and you love us.
Keep us close to you always
    so that we can listen to your words.
We ask this through Christ our Lord. **Amen.**

Let us pray with the words that Jesus taught us:

Our Father . . .

 sing "alleluia"

February 14, 2001

> Reminder: A Blessing for Saint Valentine's Day is on the next page. You may want to use it sometime today.

■ INTRODUCTION

Saint Valentine was a bishop who died bravely for his faith, long ago in Rome. The name Valentine means "valiant" and "brave." An old legend says that birds pick their mates on February 14. That is a sign of spring. Secret notes of love and friendship sent on this day are called Saint Valentine's notes, or valentines.

Let us be sure to give cards, kisses or hugs to the people whose love makes our lives better. Today's reading tells about true love.

■ A PSALM FOR FEBRUARY

> turn to
> page 186

■ READING

I Corinthians 13:4–8, 13

Listen to the words of the apostle Paul:

Love is kind and patient,
    never jealous, boastful, proud, or rude.
Love isn't selfish or quick tempered.
It doesn't keep a record of wrongs
    that others do.
Love rejoices in the truth, but not in evil.
Love is always supportive,
    loyal, hopeful, and trusting.
Love never fails!

For now there are faith, hope and love.
But of these three, the greatest is love.

The word of the Lord.

■ REFLECTION

Valentines are messages of love and friendship from one person to another. How can we be God's valentines?

■ CLOSING

Let us remember these intentions:

Wise and loving God,
    fill us with your grace
so that we may love you
    with all our heart,
    with all our soul,
    and with all our might.
And strengthen us
    in the power of your Holy Spirit
so that we may love one another
    as you love us.
We ask this through Christ our Lord. **Amen.**

Let us pray with the words that Jesus taught us:

Our Father . . .

> sing
> "alleluia"

201

A Blessing for Saint Valentine's Day

Valentines, heart-shaped decorations, posters for the classroom or a plate of Saint Valentine's Day cookies could be blessed.

Students stand or sit in a circle. If valentines are brought, they can be held or placed on the floor in front of their owners. Any containers of food should be in the center.

Begin with a song, such as "This little light of mine" (page 196 in the Hymnal for Catholic Students) or "Blessed feasts of blessed martyrs" (page 110).

 all make
the sign
of the cross

LEADER
The love of Christ has gathered us together.
Let us all say:
Let us rejoice and be glad.

ALL
Let us rejoice and be glad.

READER   1 John 4:11–12, 16
Listen to the words of the first letter of John:

Dear friends, since God loved us this much, we must love each other.

No one has ever seen God. But if we love each other, God lives in us, and his love is truly in our hearts.

God is love. If we keep on loving others, we will stay one in our hearts with God, and he will stay one with us.

The word of the Lord.

LEADER   adapted from A Book of Family Prayer
We are children of a loving God.
We carry God's own love in our hearts.
Let us never be afraid to show friendship, appreciation and love.

 hold out one hand in blessing
over the valentines or food,
and say:

God our Creator,
    bless the love that brings people together
    and grows ever stronger in our hearts.
May all the messages that carry the name
    of your holy Bishop Valentine
    be sent in joy
    and received in delight.
We ask this through Christ our Lord.

ALL
Amen.

 all make
the sign
of the cross

 sing the same song
you sang at the beginning

THURSDAY PRAYER

February 15, 2001

■ INTRODUCTION

Today we remember Ben Salmon, who spent two years in prison for refusing to serve in the military. In 1918, he became the first Roman Catholic to register as a "conscientious objector" *(kon-she-EN-shus ob-JEK-tor)* because of his religion. Most people, even Catholic priests, called Ben Salmon a traitor and a coward. Salmon wrote a book showing that the teachings of Jesus and of the Catholic church urge non-violence.

■ A PSALM FOR FEBRUARY

turn to page 186

■ READING

Luke 10:1–9

Listen to the words of the holy gospel according to Luke:

The Lord chose 72 followers and sent them out two by two to every town and village where he was about to go. He said to them, "A large crop is in the fields, but there are only a few workers. Ask the Lord in charge of the harvest to send out workers to bring it in.

"Now go, but remember, I am sending you like lambs into a pack of wolves. Don't take along a moneybag or a traveling bag or sandals. As soon as you enter a home, say, 'God bless this home with peace.' If the people living there are peace-loving, your prayer for peace will return to you. Stay with the same family, eating and drinking whatever they give you, because workers are worth what they earn.

"If the people of a town welcome you, eat whatever they offer. Heal their sick and say, 'God's kingdom will soon be here!'"

The gospel of the Lord.

■ REFLECTION

What harvest is Jesus talking about? How do we know when people are peace-loving? What makes me feel that "God's kingdom" will be here soon? What makes me think that it is very far away?

■ CLOSING

Let us remember these intentions:

Lord God, we thank you
  for sending apostles to the whole world.
We welcome those who bring your good news.
We pray for them and listen to their teaching.
Call on us, onc day, to become apostles, too.
We ask this through Christ our Lord. **Amen.**

Let us pray with the words that Jesus taught us:

Our Father . . .

sing "alleluia"

FRIDAY PRAYER

February 16, 2001

▶ Reminder: Today's reading includes the Lord's Prayer, but the words are different from the ones we know by heart. The reader will have to take extra care when reading. Practice will help.

■ INTRODUCTION

One of the treasures that Jesus gave his church is the prayer we call the Our Father. It is probably the first part of the Bible that you learned by heart, and a prayer that you say often at home and at church. The whole parish joins in saying it each time they gather for the eucharist.

Christians have great love for this prayer. Jesus himself taught it to us. It reminds us of God's care. It shows us how to praise God, how to ask for the things we need each day, and how to ask for God's help in avoiding sin and forgiving those who hurt us. It teaches us to look beyond the problems of today, and hope for the final coming of God's kingdom.

■ A PSALM FOR FEBRUARY

▶ turn to page 186

■ READING

Luke 11:1–4

Listen to the words of the holy gospel according to Luke:

When Jesus had finished praying, one of his disciples said to him, "Lord, teach us to pray, just as John taught his followers to pray."

So Jesus told them, "Pray in this way:
'Father, help us to honor your name.

Come and set up your kingdom.
Give us each day the food we need.
Forgive our sins,
 as we forgive everyone
  who has done wrong to us.
And keep us from being tempted.'"

The gospel of the Lord.

■ REFLECTION

This reading is another version of the "Our Father," the prayer we call "The Lord's Prayer." What are the five petitions in the Lord's Prayer? How are they important in our life as followers of Jesus?

■ CLOSING

Let us remember these intentions:

Loving God,
 you have words to speak to us
because we are your children
 and you love us.
Keep us close to you always
so that we can listen to your words.
We ask this through Christ our Lord. Amen.

Let us pray with the words that Jesus taught us:

Our Father . . .

 ▶ sing "alleluia"

WEEKLY PRAYER

With a Reading from the Gospel for Sunday, February 18, 2001

■ INTRODUCTION

In today's reading Jesus calls us to be people of love. Does that mean we should love our friends? Yes! Does it mean that we should love the people in our families? Yes! But it means more than that. Jesus wants us to love everyone, even people who don't love us back.

This message of love will be the gospel at Mass on Sunday, February 18. It is a good message for the Sunday following Valentine's Day.

■ A PSALM FOR FEBRUARY

turn to page 186

■ READING

Luke 6:27–28, 31–33, 35

Listen to the words of the holy gospel according to Luke:

Jesus told everyone who would listen, "Love your enemies, and be good to everyone who hates you. Ask God to bless anyone who curses you, and pray for everyone who is cruel to you. Treat others just as you want to be treated.

"If you love only someone who loves you, will God praise you for that? Even sinners love people who love them. If you are kind only to someone who is kind to you, will God be pleased with you for that? Even sinners are kind to people who are kind to them.

"But love your enemies and be good to them. Then you will get a great reward, and you will be the true children of God in heaven."

The gospel of the Lord.

■ REFLECTION

Jesus knows that it is not easy to be good to people who are not good to us. What would it be like if everyone was really good to everyone else? What feelings and thoughts keep me from treating some people with kindness?

■ CLOSING

Let us remember these intentions:

Loving God,
    you forgive us with all your heart
    for the wrong we do.
Help us to forgive those who wrong us.
Help us to make peace in our families,
    our schools and our neighborhoods.
We ask this through Christ our Lord. **Amen.**

Let us pray with the words that Jesus taught us:
Our Father . . .

sing "alleluia"

■ INTRODUCTION

Today is Presidents' Day, a national holiday. This is a good day to read more about George Washington and Abraham Lincoln, memorize a list of presidents, or make a big banner. Perhaps we can give speeches or write poems or just think about the things that Washington and Lincoln thought were important.

It is the duty of each citizen to be sure that the country is a place where the seeds of goodness and respect are encouraged to grow, and where everyone is made safe. We are not too young to be concerned about those things.

■ A PSALM FOR FEBRUARY

➤ turn to
   page 186

■ READING

Luke 8:4–8

Listen to the words of the holy gospel according to Luke:

When a large crowd from several towns had gathered around Jesus, he told them this story:

"A farmer went out to scatter seed in a field. While the farmer was doing it, some of the seeds fell along the road and were stepped on or eaten by birds. Other seeds fell on rocky ground and started growing. But the plants did not have enough water and soon dried up. Some other seeds fell where thornbushes grew up and choked the plants. The rest of the seeds fell on good ground where they grew and produced a hundred times as many seeds."

When Jesus had finished speaking, he said, "If you have ears, pay attention!"

The gospel of the Lord.

■ REFLECTION

What could this parable mean? What could the seeds be? Jesus spoke of a "harvest" and "workers" when he sent the 72 disciples out to preach. What connection might there be between that harvest and these seeds?

■ CLOSING

Let us remember these intentions:

Lord, fill our hearts
   with the seed of your word.
Help it to grow in us.
Teach us to receive your word with respect,
   to think it over carefully,
      and to follow it joyfully.
We ask this through Christ our Lord. **Amen.**

Let us pray with the words that Jesus taught us:

Our Father . . .

 sing
"alleluia"

TUESDAY PRAYER

February 20, 2001

■ INTRODUCTION

Jesus often used parables—stories with hidden meanings. Today we hear the parable we heard yesterday and Jesus' explanation of it.

■ A PSALM FOR FEBRUARY

turn to
page 186

■ READING

Luke 8:4–15

Listen to the words of the holy gospel according to Luke:

Jesus told this story:

"A farmer went out to scatter seed in a field. While the farmer was doing it, some of the seeds fell along the road and were stepped on or eaten by birds. Other seeds fell on rocky ground and started growing. But the plants did not have enough water and soon dried up. Some other seeds fell where thornbushes grew up and choked the plants. The rest of the seeds fell on good ground where they grew and produced a hundred times as many seeds."

Jesus' disciples asked him what the story meant. So he answered: "The seed is God's message, and the seeds that fell along the road are the people who hear the message. But the devil comes and snatches the message out of their hearts, so that they will not believe and be saved. The seeds that fell on rocky ground are the people who gladly hear the message and accept it. But they don't have deep roots, and they believe only for a little while. As soon as life gets hard, they give up.

"The seeds that fell among the thornbushes are also people who hear the message. But they are so eager for riches and pleasures that they never produce anything. Those seeds that fell on good ground are the people who listen to the message and keep it in good and honest hearts. They last and produce a harvest."

The gospel of the Lord.

■ REFLECTION

What prevents the seed from growing as it should? What kind of "soil" is my heart?

■ CLOSING

Let us remember these intentions:

Lord, fill our hearts
    with the seed of your word.
Help it to grow in us.
Teach us to receive your word with respect,
    to think it over carefully,
        and to follow it joyfully.
We ask this through Christ our Lord. **Amen.**

Let us pray with the words that Jesus taught us:

Our Father . . .

sing
"alleluia"

207

WEDNESDAY PRAYER

February 21, 2001

▶ Reminder: Next Monday and Tuesday are days of festivity as we get ready for Lent. Plan something enjoyable for those days. A ceremony for saying "farewell to the alleluia" is on page 214. Talk this over with the teacher.

■ INTRODUCTION

As we begin to look ahead to the holy season of Lent, we think of the coming of spring. There may not be any signs of it yet in our part of the country. We may even be coming to school through piles of snow. But we know that the days are getting longer and the sun's rays are getting stronger. The dullness and darkness of late winter will pass away.

Until it does, we can be patient. We can enjoy the cold weather. And we can share hot chocolate and tell stories around our dinner tables.

■ A PSALM FOR FEBRUARY

▶ turn to page 186

■ READING

Luke 6:37–38

Listen to the words of the holy gospel according to Luke:

Jesus said to his disciples, "Don't judge others, and God won't judge you. Don't be hard on others, and God won't be hard on you. Forgive others, and God will forgive you.

"If you give to others, you will be given a full amount in return. It will be packed down, shaken together, and spilling over into your lap. The way you treat others is the way you will be treated."

The gospel of the Lord.

■ REFLECTION

What has God given me "packed down, shaken together, and spilling over"? Am I generous with my time? my encouragement? What would our school be like if everyone stopped blaming and judging others?

■ CLOSING

Let us remember these intentions:

God of all nations and Creator of all peoples,
    heal all that divides us.
Teach us to live together in peace.
As our world is one, so our future is one.
Give us one heart and one vision.
Make us one body in Christ Jesus,
    filled with the joy of your Holy Spirit.
We ask this through Christ our Lord. **Amen.**

Let us pray with the words that Jesus taught us:
Our Father . . .

 sing "alleluia"

THURSDAY PRAYER

February 22, 2001

■ INTRODUCTION

Today's feast has an interesting name. It is called the Chair of Peter. Why does the church have a feast for furniture? At one time there was only one chair at official meetings. It was the bench of the judge, the throne of a queen, or the cathedra *(KATH-eh-druh)* of a bishop. Whoever guided the meeting sat in this important chair. Perhaps you have been the chairperson of a meeting.

This feast is about the unity of the church. We are all gathered around the chair of Saint Peter, who became the bishop of Rome and the leader among the bishops of the early church. The person who is the bishop of Rome now is Pope John Paul II. Let us pray for him today.

■ A PSALM FOR FEBRUARY

turn to
page 186

■ READING

Luke 8:1–3

Listen to the words of the holy gospel according to Luke:

Jesus was going through towns and villages, telling the good news about God's kingdom. His twelve apostles were with him, and so were some women who had been healed of evil spirits and all sorts of diseases. One of the women was Mary Magdalene *(MAG-duh-lin),* who once had seven demons in her.

Joanna, Susanna, and many others had also used what they owned to help Jesus and his disciples. Joanna's husband was one of Herod's officials.

The gospel of the Lord.

■ REFLECTION

Do we know women who are helping to spread the word of God? Where does the money come from to support missionaries today? Do I give part of my spending money to the church?

■ CLOSING

Let us remember these intentions:

Lord God, we thank you
    for sending apostles to the whole world.
We welcome those who bring your good news.
We pray for them and listen to their teaching.
Call on us, one day, to become apostles, too.
We ask this through Christ our Lord. **Amen.**

Let us pray with the words that Jesus taught us:
Our Father . . .

sing
"alleluia"

FRIDAY PRAYER

February 23, 2001

▶ Reminder: You may want to make copies of the Psalm, Meal Prayer and End of the Day Prayers for Early Lent, on pages 218 to 220.

■ INTRODUCTION

Today we remember Saint Polycarp, a bishop who was taught about Jesus by the apostle John. When Bishop Polycarp was arrested for being a Christian, he was 80 years old. He prayed, "Lord God, I bless you for thinking me worthy to join the martyrs. I will drink the cup of your Anointed One. That is how I will be raised to eternal life through your Holy Spirit." Polycarp was very sure in his faith.

Saint Peter was also sure in his faith. In today's reading we hear him state the most basic belief of every Christian. One day he would die for that faith, as Polycarp did.

■ A PSALM FOR FEBRUARY

▶ turn to page 186

■ READING

Luke 9:18–20

Listen to the words of the holy gospel according to Luke:

One day when Jesus was alone praying, his disciples came to him, and he asked them, "What do people say about me?"

They answered, "Some say that you are John the Baptist or Elijah *(ee-LYE-juh)* or a prophet from long ago who has come back to life."

Jesus then asked them, "But who do you say I am?"

Peter answered, "You are the Messiah sent from God."

The gospel of the Lord.

■ REFLECTION

How does the church tell about its faith in Jesus? Why do people who believe in Jesus think it is so important to tell other people? How do I express my faith? What difference does this faith make in my life?

■ CLOSING

Let us remember these intentions:

Gracious God,
   through the gift of your Spirit
   and the teaching of your apostles,
we can proclaim with all your church
   that Jesus is the Messiah you sent to us.
Strengthen and deepen this gift of faith.
We ask this through Christ our Lord. **Amen.**

Let us pray with the words that Jesus taught us:

Our Father . . .

▶ sing "alleluia"

WEEKLY PRAYER

With a Reading from the Gospel for Sunday, February 25, 2001

Reminder: If you meet on February 26, 27 or 28, you may want to use the day's Daily Prayer, on page 212, 213, or 222.

■ INTRODUCTION

The week before Lent begins is a time of Carnival. It's a Carnival tradition to eat rich, tasty foods, such as pancakes. Carnival ends on Mardi Gras *(MAR-dee grah),* "Fat Tuesday." Then on Ash Wednesday, Lent begins.

The church asks that we take more time to pray during Lent. This gives us a chance to examine the way we live and to see how we can become better followers of Jesus. We ask, "What does Jesus tell us about holiness and goodness? How do we follow Jesus? How can we follow Jesus even better?" This is called "examining our conscience" *(KON-shens).*

The reading today helps us begin Lent with the right attitude. It tells us to correct our own problems before we try to correct other people.

■ A PSALM FOR FEBRUARY

turn to page 186

■ READING

Luke 6:39, 41–42

Listen to the words of the holy gospel according to Luke:

Jesus used some sayings as he spoke to the people.

He said, "You can see the speck in your friend's eye. But you don't notice the log in your own eye. How can you say, 'My friend, let me take the speck out of your eye,' when you don't see the log in your own eye? You showoffs! First get the log out of your own eye. Then you can see how to take the speck out of your friend's eye."

The gospel of the Lord.

■ REFLECTION

What could the speck and the log mean? Why do we need to see clearly before we help others see clearly? What "logs" block my sight?

■ CLOSING

Let us remember these intentions:

Loving God, you call us each by name.
You speak to us in the quiet of our hearts.
Speak to us of love for all people.
Speak to us of hope for our world.
Speak to us of your gift of salvation.
Speak to us, for we are listening.
We ask this through Christ our Lord. **Amen.**

Let us pray with the words that Jesus taught us:

Our Father . . .

sing
"alleluia"

211

▶ Reminder: Today or tomorrow you may want to use the ritual for saying farewell to the alleluia (page 214) or for preparing ashes for Ash Wednesday (page 221).

■ INTRODUCTION

Lent begins on Wednesday. At one time, people did not eat any meat at all during Lent. So they ate all the meat before Lent began. It was a great feast called Carnival, a word that means "good-bye to meat." Today's reading tells us that even in King David's time people celebrated God's goodness by enjoying good things to eat.

■ A PSALM FOR FEBRUARY

▶ turn to page 186

■ READING
1 Chronicles 16: 2–3, 7, 31–33

Listen to the words of the first book of Chronicles (KRON-ih-kulls):

King David blessed the people in the name of the LORD and gave every person in the crowd a small loaf of bread, some meat, and a handful of raisins.

That same day, David taught Asaph (ah-SAF) and his relatives for the first time to sing these praises to the LORD:

Tell the heavens and the earth
    to be glad and celebrate!
And announce to the nations,
    "The LORD is King!"

Command the ocean to roar
    with all of its creatures
and the fields to rejoice with all of their crops.
Then every tree in the forest
    will sing joyful songs to the LORD.

The word of the Lord.

■ REFLECTION

Why is food a sign of happiness? What do I have that I should thank God for today?

■ CLOSING

Let us remember these intentions:

Loving God,
we thank you for the promise
    that springtime will follow
        these last days of winter.
We thank you for the promise
    that Easter will follow
        the hard work of Lent.
We thank you for this Carnival time
    and the chance to rejoice together.
We thank you through Christ our Lord. **Amen.**

Let us pray with the words that Jesus taught us.

Our Father . . .

▶ sing "alleluia"

TUESDAY PRAYER

February 27, 2001

■ INTRODUCTION

Happy Mardi Gras *(MAR-dee grah)*! That's French for "Fat Tuesday," the day before Ash Wednesday. Today, to prepare for Lent's fasting, some people cook all the meat they have and use the fat for delicious gravy. They use their butter and other oils for pancakes, doughnuts and other sweet things.

As you can see, Mardi Gras is a day to enjoy! In today's reading, the prophet encourages the people with visions of feasts and festivals.

■ A PSALM FOR FEBRUARY

turn to page 186

■ READING

Isaiah 25: 6–9

Listen to the words of the prophet Isaiah:

On this mountain the LORD All-Powerful
   will prepare for all nations a feast
     of the finest foods.
Choice wines and the best meats will be served.
Here the LORD will strip away
   the burial clothes that cover the nations.
The LORD All-Powerful
   will destroy the power of death
     and wipe away all tears.
At that time, people will say,
   "The LORD has saved us!
Let's celebrate."

The word of the Lord.

■ REFLECTION

In what ways is a picnic on a mountain like the reign of God? What kinds of foods are served at our favorite celebrations? How will we help our families celebrate Mardi Gras and get ready for the season of Lent?

■ CLOSING

Let us remember these intentions:

Loving God,
we thank you for the promise
   that springtime will follow
     these last days of winter.
We thank you for the promise
   that Easter will follow
     the hard work of Lent.
We thank you for Mardi Gras
   and the chance to rejoice together.
We thank you through Christ our Lord. **Amen.**

Let us pray with the words that Jesus taught us.

Our Father . . .

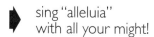

sing "alleluia"
with all your might!

Farewell to the Alleluia

Before Lent, we say good-bye to the alleluia. This word means "praise God" in the Hebrew language. We will not sing this song of joy during Lent, but we will sing alleluia over and over once Lent is finished and Easter comes.

Make a beautiful banner or scroll with the word "alleluia" on it. Find a box to fit it and a dry place to bury it or lock it away. Gather bells, noisemakers, horns and other instruments.

Learn the song "Jubilate Deo" (page 147 in the Hymnal for Catholic Students), *and sing it in rounds. Or sing the "Celtic alleluia" (page 75 in the hymnal).*

When you are ready to begin, form a procession. Carry the bells and other instruments, the shovel or lock and key, the box and the banner.

LEADER
Let us go forth in peace
   to bury our song of joy.
Let us go forth in peace
   with strong voices and happy hearts.

Everyone should go in procession to the place of burial, singing "Jubilate Deo" or "Alleluia" and waving the alleluia banner.

At the place, keep singing while you open the cupboard or dig a hole. Raise the alleluia banner so all can see it. End the song. Ring the bells and noisemakers, or play the instruments for a minute. Then the leader gives a signal for silence. (Someone should collect all the noisemakers to keep them quiet.)

In silence, put the banner in the box. Bury it or lock it up. When this is done, the leader says the following prayer:

LEADER
Lord God of joyful noise
   and of solemn silence,
      give us a good and holy Lent.
In peace,
   bring us back to this place in forty days,
      when Lent is finished,
   to claim our right to Easter joy.
We ask this through Christ our Lord.

ALL
Amen.

 in perfect silence
return to the classroom

EARLY LENT

Ash Wednesday, February 28, to Friday, March 23

EARLY LENT 2001

■ ABOUT THE SEASON

In some ways, Lent is the most famous of all the church's seasons. People seem to know the most about Lent. Its seven weeks will take us from the end of winter clear through to the beginning of spring.

Lent has many traditions. For example, during **LOOKING AHEAD** Lent we put away the lively song of "alleluia." We will not sing it again until Easter, when we rejoice in the resurrection of Jesus. (On page 214 there is a ritual to help us say farewell to the alleluia.)

During Lent, we also try to put away parties and dances and entertainment. In many Catholic parishes, decorations and flowers—and even baptisms and weddings—are put away, too. Everything is made simple so that we can prepare for Easter.

■ LENT IS NOT AN UNHAPPY TIME, BUT IT IS A SERIOUS TIME. With our families, we take this time to think about how much the gospel means to us and how well we are living up to God's law of love. We watch and pray with Christ. We all do our part.

■ LENT IS CELEBRATED BY CATHOLICS OF ALL AGES. And it is celebrated at home as well as at church and school. Our parents and grandparents can probably tell us how they kept Lent when they were young.

Let us help our families make good plans for Lent. We can choose actions that everyone can cooperate with. And those actions can help us to become more prayerful, to make our lives more simple and to share what we have with those who are in need. That is the purpose of Lenten sacrifices.

■ THE READINGS FOR DAILY PRAYER ARE USUALLY TAKEN FROM THE WRITINGS OF THE PROHPETS. The readings tell us about our loving and forgiving God. We hear God's command to forgive others. We also are told not to judge others. Instead, we should look at our own lives. Are we living up to God's commands?

We end the first half of Lent with the story about the Samaritan woman who met Jesus at Jacob's well. Jesus was thirsty for water. The woman was thirsty for truth. At Easter, people are baptized into the church. They too are thirsty for truth.

■ PREPARATION FOR EARLY LENT

Decorations and clutter should be cleared away. One of the reasons for putting things away is that it is easier to clean the room. You've heard of spring cleaning? Lent is the church's spring!

■ AFTER WE HAVE CLEANED UP, WE CAN PUT SOMETHING IN THE PRAYER CENTER TO REMIND US OF LENT. It can be a cross made of twigs or the classroom crucifix put in a special place of honor. It can be a bowl of ashes to remind us of Ash Wednesday, the beginning of Lent. It can be an empty, dry bowl to remind us that we are waiting for the water of baptism at Easter. It can be a bowl of flower bulbs or seeds or a pot of bare branches that will remind us that Lent is a time of growth and a preparation for the flowering of Easter joy.

■ IT'S AN IMPORTANT PART OF OUR TRADITION TO COLLECT ALMS DURING LENT. The word "alms" means "compassion." We give part of our allowance or baby-sitting money to help the poor. We bring in canned goods or clothes. We promise our time to do something good, like shoveling a sidewalk for someone who can't do it, raking a lawn or helping out with the spring cleaning at home.

A container for these alms and for our promises to do good might be put in the prayer center.

■ ON PAGE 218 THERE IS A PSALM FOR EARLY LENT. The Meal Prayer and the End of the Day Prayer are on pages 219 and 220. These are for the first half of Lent, from February 28, Ash Wednesday, until Friday, March 23. These prayers are also on pages 27 to 29 in *Blessed Be God!*

- ON PAGE 221 IS A RITUAL FOR BURNING PALMS TO MAKE ASHES FOR ASH WEDNESDAY. The afternoon before Ash Wednesday is a good time for this ceremony. Put the ashes in a beautiful box or crock. If this outdoor ritual takes place on Ash Wednesday, you might follow it indoors with the blessing and distribution of ashes. You will need holy water, a sacramentary or the *Book of Blessings,* and song books or other participation materials. Ordinarily a deacon or priest blesses the ashes, but anyone can distribute them.

- MONDAY, MARCH 19 IS SAINT JOSEPH'S DAY. It is a day to take a break from Lent and to celebrate with something festive, such as a special food.

- PRAYERS OF SORROW FOR SIN ARE TRADITIONAL DURING LENT. The class or the whole school may hold a penance service. It may include an opportunity for older students to celebrate the sacrament of reconciliation. This will take thoughtful and prayerful preparation. Another traditional prayer used during Lent is known as the "Stations of the Cross."

- SUGGESTED HYMNS: There are many good choices. "O Sun of justice" (page 172 in the *Hymnal for Catholic Students),* "Again we keep this solemn fast"(page 99 in the hymnal) and "Lord, who throughout these forty days" (page 156 in the hymnal) are classics. Every Catholic deserves to learn this part of our heritage.

"Amazing grace" (page 108 in the hymnal) is easy to sing as a round. "Somebody's knockin' at your door" (page 186 in the hymnal) is also good for Lent. A soloist can sing some parts of this song, and then everyone can respond.

The End of the Day Prayer for Early Lent is the Canticle of Mary, a song Mary sang when she visited her cousin Elizabeth. This is the church's favorite prayer for the evening. You can sing Mary's song. An English version is on page 16 in the hymnal. A Latin version, called the "Magnificat" after the first word in Latin, is on page 158 in the hymnal.

■ THE SCHOOL OF RELIGION

The readings for Weekly Prayer follow the gospels for the Sundays of Lent. They are taken from Year C, the lectionary year that is shaped around the gospel of Luke. On the first Sunday we see Jesus spend time in the desert before he begins his public ministry. On the following Sunday we read about his transfiguration, and finally we hear Jesus' parable of the fig tree.

Many parishes use the Mass readings of Year A, not Year C, on the third, fourth and fifth Sundays of Lent. These readings have significance for those preparing for the Easter sacraments of baptism, confirmation and first eucharist. In parishes where this is the case, the Year A gospels can be used for Weekly Prayer. Substitute John 4:6–15 for the reading on page 237, John 9:1–7 for the reading on page 249, and John 11:1–4, 17–27, 38–45 for the reading on page 255.

- MANY FAMILIES TRY TO PRAY TOGETHER DURING LENT. Many would be glad to have a copy of the Psalm, the Meal Prayer and the End of the Day Prayer. Families can pray the Psalm in the morning and pray the End of the Day Prayer at bedtime.

Some members of your families might be able to come to the farewell to the alleluia, the preparation of ashes or to other times of prayer during Lent. Talk this over with the teacher. Try to keep your families informed about your religion classes and the things you are learning about the prayer of the church.

A PSALM FOR EARLY LENT

Psalm 18:2–4, 7, 47

▶ all make
the sign
of the cross

LEADER Behold! Now is the acceptable time!
ALL **Now is the day of salvation!**

LEADER I love you, God my strength,
ALL **my rock, my shelter, my stronghold.**

SIDE A My God, I lean on you,
my shield, my rock,
my champion, my defense.

SIDE B When I call for help,
I am safe from my enemies.

SIDE A From the depths I cried out,
my plea reached the heavens.
God heard me.

SIDE B The Lord lives!
blessed be my rock,
the God who saves me.

LEADER I love you, God my strength,
ALL **my rock, my shelter, my stronghold.**

**Glory to the Father, and to the Son,
and to the Holy Spirit:
as it was in the beginning, is now,
and will be for ever. Amen.**

▶ turn back to
Daily Prayer or Weekly Prayer
for today

EARLY LENT

LEADER   Let us offer God praise and thanksgiving:

ALL   ▶ all make
the sign
of the cross

LEADER   Behold! Now is the acceptable time!

ALL   **Now is the day of salvation!**

LEADER   I was hungry:

ALL   **And you gave me food.**

LEADER   I was thirsty:

ALL   **And you gave me drink.**

LEADER   I was a stranger:

ALL   **And you welcomed me.**

LEADER   I was naked:

ALL   **And you clothed me.**

LEADER   I was ill:

ALL   **And you cared for me.**

LEADER   I was in jail:

ALL   **And you visited me.**

LEADER   Lord Jesus Christ,
    be with all those who are in need.
Bless us,
    and bless the food we eat today.
Help our families, our school and our parish
    keep a good and holy Lent.
And bring us quickly to the glory of Easter.
We ask this through Christ our Lord.

ALL   **Amen.**

  all make
the sign
of the cross

Matthew 25:35–36

EARLY LENT

END OF THE DAY PRAYER

> all make
> the sign
> of the cross

LEADER   I acclaim the greatness of the Lord.
ALL   **I delight in God my savior.**

SIDE A   Truly from this day on
all ages will call me blest.
For God, wonderful in power,
has used that strength for me.

SIDE B   Holy the name of the Lord!
whose mercy embraces the faithful,
one generation to the next.

SIDE A   The Lord fills the starving
and lets the rich go hungry.

SIDE B   God rescues lowly Israel,
recalling the promise of mercy,
the promise made to our ancestors,
to Abraham's heirs for ever.

LEADER   I acclaim the greatness of the Lord.
ALL   **I delight in God my savior.**

LEADER   ▶ hold out one hand
toward everyone
in blessing, and say:

May the almighty and merciful God
bless and protect us:

ALL   ▶ all make
the sign
of the cross

The Canticle of Mary, Luke 1:46–50, 53–54

220

The Preparation of Ashes

Bring palms to an outdoor place away from the wind. Place foil in the bottom of a barbecue grill. Bring a lighter, a poker to stir the fire, a kitchen strainer, a big spoon and a box or crock large enough to hold the ashes. If the blessing and giving of ashes will take place after this preparation, see the suggestions on page 217.

 all make
the sign
of the cross

LEADER
Praised be the God of grace, mercy and peace.
Let us all say: Blessed be God for ever!

ALL
Blessed be God for ever!

LEADER
A year ago we held these palms and sang "Hosanna" to Jesus our Messiah. We marched in procession to show that we would follow him. Today we burn these palms and renew our promise to follow Christ our Lord.

READER   Joel 2:12, 13, 15, 16, 17
Listen to the words of the prophet Joel:

The LORD said, "It isn't too late.
You can still return to me with all your heart.
Turn back to me with broken hearts.
I am merciful, kind, and caring.

"Sound the trumpet on Zion!
Call the people together.
Bring adults, children, babies,
and even bring newlyweds from their festivities.

Offer this prayer near the altar:
'Save your people, LORD God!'"

The word of the Lord.

 light the fire;
wait in silence until the fire burns out

LEADER   adapted from *Catholic Household Blessings and Prayers*
Merciful God,
   you called us forth from the dust of the earth.
You claimed us for Christ
   in the waters of baptism.
Look upon us as we enter these Forty Days
   bearing the mark of ashes.
Bless our journey through the desert of Lent
   to the font of rebirth.
May our fasting be a hunger for justice;
   our alms, a making of peace;
   our prayer, the chant of humble
      and grateful hearts.
All that we do and pray is in the name of Jesus,
   for in his cross you proclaim your love
      now and for ever.

ALL
Amen.

 all make
the sign
of the cross

To gather the ashes, pour them from the foil into the strainer. Hold the strainer over the box. Stir the ashes through the strainer with a spoon. Cover the box or crock so the ashes will not spill.

WEDNESDAY PRAYER

February 28, 2001

> Reminder: The Psalm, Meal Prayer, and End of the Day Prayer for Early Lent are found on pages 27 to 29 in *Blessed Be God!*

■ INTRODUCTION

Today, Ash Wednesday, many Christians receive a cross of ashes on their foreheads. This powerful sign has been used by God's people for hundreds of years. The cross of ashes tells friends and neighbors that we know we are not perfect.

We sometimes break the law of God. We hurt other people. We act selfishly. Today we tell God and each other that we are sorry. With the help of Jesus, we will try during Lent to become better. The cross of ashes means all of these things.

■ A PSALM FOR EARLY LENT

turn to
page 218

■ READING

Daniel 9:3-5, 9

Listen to the words of the prophet Daniel:

To show my sorrow, I went without eating and dressed in sackcloth and sat in ashes. I confessed my sins and earnestly prayed to the LORD my God:

"Our LORD, you are a great and fearsome God, and you faithfully keep your agreement with those who love and obey you. But we have sinned terribly by rebelling against you and rejecting your laws and teachings. LORD God, you are merciful and forgiving."

The word of the Lord.

■ REFLECTION

What do ashes remind us of? Why are ashes put on our heads in the sign of the cross? When I wear ashes today, people will know that I am a Christian. How does that make me feel?

■ CLOSING

adapted from *Catholic Household Blessings and Prayers*

Let us remember these intentions:

Merciful God,
    you called us forth from the dust of the earth.
You claimed us for Christ
    in the waters of baptism.
Look upon us as we enter these Forty Days
    bearing the mark of ashes,
Bless our journey through the desert of Lent
    to the font of rebirth.
May our fasting be hunger for justice;
    our alms, a making of peace;
    our prayer, the chant of humble
      and grateful hearts.
All that we do and pray is in the name of Jesus,
    for in his cross you proclaim your love
      now and for ever. **Amen.**

Let us pray with the words that Jesus taught us:

Our Father . . .

THURSDAY PRAYER

March 1, 2001

■ INTRODUCTION

This week we can bring to the classroom things that are symbols of Lent. We can place them on a table near the Bible or the crucifix.

A bowl of seeds or bulbs can remind us of our need to grow. Bare branches from a tree are also good symbols. We are like bare branches waiting for God's Easter grace to bring us to life. If we put the branches in water, they might grow leaves. This will help us count the days until it is Easter.

■ A PSALM FOR EARLY LENT

 turn to
page 218

■ READING

2 Corinthians 5:19, 20—6:2

Listen to the words of the apostle Paul:

God was in Christ, offering peace and forgiveness to the people of this world. We speak for Christ and sincerely ask you to make peace with God. Christ never sinned! But God treated him as a sinner, so that Christ could make us acceptable to God.

We work together with God, and we beg you to make good use of God's kindness to you. In the Scriptures God says, "When the time came, I listened to you, and when you needed help, I came to save you."

That time has come. This is the day for you to be saved.

The word of the Lord.

■ REFLECTION

How do I feel when I have done something wrong? Do I ever wish that someone else could take my place when it is time to face the consequences? What does it mean "to make good use of God's kindness"?

■ CLOSING

adapted from the Byzantine rite

Receive Lent with gladness, O people!
Let us all say:
Be strong, and turn your life toward God.
Be strong, and turn your life toward God.

Let us remember these intentions:

Merciful God,
    as your loving children,
    we are eager to do what is right.
Send your Holy Spirit to live with us
    and to fill us with your light.
We ask this through Christ our Lord. **Amen.**

Let us pray with the words that Jesus taught us:
Our Father . . .

FRIDAY PRAYER

March 2, 2001

■ INTRODUCTION

Today is the World Day of Prayer. All over the world many Christians will put aside their concerns for their own lives and families. We let our spirits move from one country to another, around the whole earth. With God's eyes we look out and try to see the people in need because of wars and earthquakes, floods and famines, crimes and diseases and loneliness.

Let us offer our prayers today for all the people of the earth: those who suffer and those who share, those who seek and those who serve.

■ A PSALM FOR EARLY LENT

▶ turn to
page 218

■ READING

Isaiah 58:5, 6—8

Listen to the words of the prophet Isaiah:

The prophet said to the people of Israel:
Do you think the LORD wants you
    to give up eating
Or to dress in sackcloth and sit in ashes?
I'll tell you what it really means
    to worship the LORD.
Remove the chains of prisoners who are
    chained unjustly.
Free those who are abused!
Share your food with everyone who is hungry;
    share your home with the poor and homeless.
Give clothes to those in need;
    don't turn away your relatives.

Then your light will shine like the dawning sun,
    and you will quickly be healed.

The word of the Lord.

■ REFLECTION

How will I share in the spirit of sacrifice? How will my family keep Lent together? What can we do during Lent to make our school more kind and loving?

■ CLOSING

adapted from the Byzantine rite

Receive Lent with gladness, O people!
Let us all say:
Be strong, and turn your life toward God.
Be strong, and turn your life toward God.

Let us remember these intentions:

Merciful God,
    as your loving children,
    we are eager to do what is right.
Send your Holy Spirit to live with us
    and to fill us with your light.
We ask this through Christ our Lord. **Amen.**

Let us pray with the words that Jesus taught us:
Our Father . . .

WEEKLY PRAYER

With a Reading from the Gospel for Sunday, March 4, 2001

■ INTRODUCTION

This is a time of change for the church. We turn from carnival joy to ashes and repentance, as we enter into the spirit of the season of Lent. For the next 40 days Christians will try to become better followers of Jesus.

Let us make plans to pray and read the Bible more often during Lent. We also want to become more generous and thoughtful, and make our homes more peaceful. During Lent we should all try to live less wastefully.

■ A PSALM FOR EARLY LENT

➤ turn to page 218

■ READING

Luke 4:1–2, 3–6, 7–12

Listen to the words of the holy gospel according to Luke:

The Holy Spirit led Jesus into the desert. For 40 days Jesus was tested by the devil, and during that time he went without eating. The devil said to Jesus, "If you are God's Son, tell this stone to turn into bread." Jesus answered, "The Scriptures say, 'No one can live only on food.'"

Then the devil led Jesus up to a high place and quickly showed him all the nations on earth. The devil said, "Just worship me, and you can have it all." Jesus answered, "The Scriptures say, 'Worship the Lord your God and serve only him!'"

Finally, the devil took Jesus to Jerusalem *(juh-ROO-suh-lem)* and had him stand on top of the temple. The devil said, "If you are God's Son, jump off. The Scriptures say, 'God will tell his angels to take care of you. They will catch you in their arms.'"

Jesus answered, "The Scriptures also say, 'Don't try to test the Lord your God!'"

The gospel of the Lord.

■ REFLECTION

How are we sometimes tempted to do evil for bread? for glory and power? What can the third temptation mean?

■ CLOSING

adapted from the Byzantine rite

Receive Lent with gladness, O people!
Let us all say:
Be strong, and turn your life toward God.
Be strong, and turn your life toward God.

Let us remember these intentions:

Merciful God,
   as your loving children,
     we are eager to do what is right.
Send your Holy Spirit to live with us
   and to fill us with your light.
We ask this through Christ our Lord. **Amen.**

Let us pray with the words that Jesus taught us:
Our Father . . .

MONDAY PRAYER

March 5, 2001

■ INTRODUCTION

Have we and our families made special plans for Lent? During Lent the church asks adults to pray, fast and give alms. Alms are gifts to the poor. Fasting means eating less than usual. When we turn 14 years old, we are asked not to eat meat on the Fridays of Lent.

Young people can share the Lenten spirit by giving up something they enjoy, such as candy or television. And they can do good works, such as reading extra books or helping other people.

■ A PSALM FOR EARLY LENT

➤ turn to
page 218

■ READING

Ezekiel 18:21–23, 30, 32

Listen to the words of the prophet Ezekiel *(ee-ZEE-kee-ul):*

The LORD says this:

"Suppose wicked people stop sinning and start obeying my laws and doing right. All their sins will be forgiven, and they will live because they did right. I, the LORD God, don't like to see wicked people die. I enjoy seeing them turn from their sins and live.

"I will judge each of you for what you've done. So stop sinning, or else you will certainly be punished. I, the LORD God, don't want to see that happen to anyone. So stop sinning and live!"

The word of the Lord.

■ REFLECTION

All during Lent we hear the same message over and over: No matter what you have done, God will forgive you! No matter how mean or foolish you feel, God wants you to start again! Do I really believe this in my heart? Do we forgive others this way?

■ CLOSING

adapted from the Byzantine rite

Receive Lent with gladness, O people!
Let us all say:
Be strong, and turn your life toward God.
Be strong, and turn your life toward God.

Let us remember these intentions:

Merciful God,
    as your loving children,
    we are eager to do what is right.
Send your Holy Spirit to live with us
    and to fill us with your light.
We ask this through Christ our Lord. **Amen.**

Let us pray with the words that Jesus taught us:
Our Father . . .

TUESDAY PRAYER

March 6, 2001

■ INTRODUCTION

Lent invites us to spend some time looking at ourselves in our mental mirror. In that mirror we can see the ways we are sometimes mean or selfish. We can see the ways we sometimes avoid the truth. We can also see how much we have tried to be agreeable and to act with kindness toward others. Mirrors show us both the good and the bad.

Another name for our mental mirror is "conscience" *(KON-shens)*.

■ A PSALM FOR EARLY LENT

turn to
page 218

■ READING   Ezekiel 36:24–28, 37, 38

Listen to the words of the prophet Ezekiel *(ee-ZEE-kee-ul)*:

The LORD says this:

"I will gather you from the foreign *(FOR-in)* nations and bring you home. I will sprinkle you with clean water, and you will be clean and acceptable to me.

"I will take away your stubborn heart and give you a new heart and a desire to be faithful. You will have only pure thoughts, because I will put my Spirit in you and make you eager to obey my laws and teachings. You will be my people, and I will be your God.

"I will once again answer your prayers, and I will let your nation grow until you are like a large flock of sheep. Then you will know that I am the LORD."

The word of the Lord.

■ REFLECTION

What can it mean to have a "stubborn heart" and a "new heart"? What other parts of the Bible speak of God's people as a "flock of sheep"? When I am discouraged, do I remember to pray to God's Spirit within me?

■ CLOSING   adapted from the Byzantine rite

Receive Lent with gladness, O people!
Let us all say:
Be strong, and turn your life toward God.
Be strong, and turn your life toward God.

Let us remember these intentions:

Merciful God,
    as your loving children,
    we are eager to do what is right.
Send your Holy Spirit to live with us
    and to fill us with your light.
We ask this through Christ our Lord. **Amen.**

Let us pray with the words that Jesus taught us:
Our Father . . .

WEDNESDAY PRAYER

March 7, 2001

■ INTRODUCTION

Today the church remembers Perpetua *(per-PET-choo-uh)* and Felicity *(fuh-LISS-ih-tee)*, two brave African women. In the year 203 they were arrested along with other members of their families for being Christians.

Felicity had a baby girl while she was in prison. The women were taken into a sports arena and killed. The bravery of the women amazed everyone, and their story was written down. It is one of the oldest stories of our early saints. The story ends: "O brave and blessed martyrs, truly called and chosen to glorify our Lord Jesus Christ!"

■ A PSALM FOR EARLY LENT

➤ turn to page 218

■ READING

Deuteronomy 26:16–19

Listen to the words of the book of Deuteronomy *(doo-ter-AH-nuh-mee):*

Moses said to Israel:

"Today the LORD your God has commanded you to obey these laws and teachings with all your heart and soul.

"In response, you have agreed that the LORD will be your God, that you will obey all his laws and teachings, and that you will listen when he speaks to you.

"Since you have agreed to obey the LORD, he has agreed that you will be his people and that you will belong to him, just as he promised. You will belong only to the LORD your God, just as he promised."

The word of the Lord.

■ REFLECTION

What are some of the "laws and teachings" that God has made known to us through the church? When did God adopt us as his special people? Can I find a way, during Lent, to renew my agreement to listen to God and obey God's teachings?

■ CLOSING

adapted from the Byzantine rite

Receive Lent with gladness, O people!
Let us all say:
Be strong, and turn your life toward God.
Be strong, and turn your life toward God.

Let us remember these intentions:

Merciful God,
    as your loving children,
    we are eager to do what is right.
Send your Holy Spirit to live with us
    and to fill us with your light.
We ask this through Christ our Lord. **Amen.**

Let us pray with the words that Jesus taught us:
Our Father . . .

228

THURSDAY PRAYER

March 8, 2001

■ INTRODUCTION

At sundown today the Jewish feast of Purim *(poo-REEM)* begins. This feast honors Queen Esther, who saved the Jewish people from being killed by a wicked official.

Esther wanted to tell her husband, the king of Persia, of this plot. But anyone who went to the king without being invited could be put to death. Esther knew that she had to go anyway. Today's reading tells us how Esther prepared to speak to the king.

■ A PSALM FOR EARLY LENT

 turn to
page 218

■ READING

Esther 14:1–4, 12–14

Listen to the words of the book of Esther:

Queen Esther was worried and upset, and she realized that only the Lord could save her people from being killed. So Esther took off her beautiful royal robes and put on clothes that showed this was a time of suffering and death. She put ashes and dirt all over her head rather than using any of her expensive lotions. And instead of doing everything she could to look beautiful and dignified, Esther just let her long hair hang down in tangles. Then she prayed to the Lord God of Israel:

"You, Lord, are the only king we have. No one but you can help me now, because I am all alone."

The word of the Lord.

■ REFLECTION

Do you pray for courage when you need to act boldly? Do we take a chance and speak up for others? How are Queen Esther's preparations like our ways of keeping Lent?

■ CLOSING

Let us remember these intentions:

Blessed are you, Lord God,
   filled with love and mercy.
When your people are in danger,
   you save them.
When your people are suffering,
   you strengthen them.
When your people are joyful,
   you bless them.
O God, strengthen the Jewish community
   as they keep the day of Purim.
Make them secure in their homes
   around the world,
   now and forever. **Amen.**

Let us pray with the words that Jesus taught us:

Our Father . . .

229

FRIDAY PRAYER

March 9, 2001

■ INTRODUCTION

Today we remember Saint Frances of Rome. She was blessed with a good husband and three children. When two of her children died, Frances was very sad. But she found strength by offering her sorrow to God in prayer.

Frances cared for the poor in the worst areas of the city of Rome by bringing them food and firewood. Other women joined her. Some became sisters. They were some of the first sisters who went into the homes of the poor and sick. Frances died in the year 1440.

■ A PSALM FOR EARLY LENT

turn to page 218

■ READING

Isaiah 41:13, 14, 17–20

Listen to the words of the prophet Isaiah:

The LORD says this:
"I am the LORD your God.
I am holding your hand,
    so don't be afraid. I am here to help you.
I am the holy God of Israel,
    who saves and protects you.
When the poor and needy are dying of thirst
    and cannot find water,
I, the LORD God of Israel, will come
    to their rescue.
I won't forget them.
I will make rivers flow on mountain peaks.
I will send streams to fill the valleys.

Dry and barren land will flow with springs
    and become a lake.
I will fill the desert with all kinds of trees.
Everyone will see this and know that I,
    the holy LORD God of Israel, created it all."

The word of the Lord.

■ REFLECTION

In what ways am I "poor and needy" this Lent? What help do I seek for myself? What help do we seek for the world? What do the symbols of desert and water mean?

■ CLOSING

adapted from the Byzantine rite

Receive Lent with gladness, O people!
Let us all say:
Be strong, and turn your life toward God.
Be strong, and turn your life toward God.

Let us remember these intentions:

Merciful God,
    as your loving children,
    we are eager to do what is right.
Send your Holy Spirit to live with us
    and to fill us with your light.
We ask this through Christ our Lord. **Amen.**

Let us pray with the words that Jesus taught us:
Our Father . . .

WEEKLY PRAYER

With a Reading from the Gospel for Sunday, March 11, 2001

■ INTRODUCTION

All during Lent the church prepares for Easter. On that day many parishes welcome new members. They will be baptized and confirmed. They will celebrate their first communion.

Baptism, confirmation and eucharist *(YOU-kuh-rist)* are called sacraments of initiation *(ih-nish-ee-AY-shun)*. This means that they begin a person's life in the church. Is someone preparing to join our community at Easter? We can send them a card or letter of welcome.

■ A PSALM FOR EARLY LENT

▶ turn to
page 218

■ READING

Luke 9:28–31, 33–36

Listen to the words of the holy gospel according to Luke:

Jesus took Peter, John, and James with him and went up on a mountain to pray. While he was praying, his face changed, and his clothes became shining white. Suddenly Moses and Elijah *(ee-LYE-juh)* were there speaking with him. They appeared in heavenly glory and talked about all that Jesus' death in Jerusalem *(juh-ROO-suh-lem)* would mean.

Peter said to Jesus, "Master, it is good for us to be here! Let us make three shelters, one for you, one for Moses, and one for Elijah." While Peter was still speaking, a shadow from a cloud passed over them, and they were frightened as the cloud covered them. From the cloud a voice spoke, "This is my chosen Son. Listen to what he says!"

After the voice had spoken, Peter, John, and James saw only Jesus.

The gospel of the Lord.

■ REFLECTION

This vision reminds us of the glory of Jesus' resurrection. Why does the church remind us of Easter at the beginning of Lent? How are apostles (Peter, John, James) and prophets (Moses and Elijah) important to us?

■ CLOSING

adapted from the Byzantine rite

Receive Lent with gladness, O people!
Let us all say:
Be strong, and turn your life toward God.
Be strong, and turn your life toward God.

Let us remember these intentions:

Merciful God,
   as your loving children,
   we are eager to do what is right.
Send your Holy Spirit to live with us
   and to fill us with your light.
We ask this through Christ our Lord. **Amen.**

Let us pray with the words that Jesus taught us:
Our Father . . .

231

MONDAY PRAYER
March 12, 2001

■ INTRODUCTION

Long before the coming of Jesus, the Hebrew people kept seasons of repentance and renewal, just as we are keeping Lent. This week we have been listening as Hebrew prophets and writers tell us how to become more faithful children of God. "Listen to God's word," they say, "and obey it."

Today we listen to the words of the book of Leviticus *(luh-VIT-uh-kus),* as Jesus listened to them long ago. We take these words into our hearts, just as he did.

■ A PSALM FOR EARLY LENT

▶ turn to page 218

▶ turn to
page 218

■ READING

Leviticus 19:1–4, 9–10

Listen to the words of the book of Leviticus:

The LORD told Moses to say to the community of Israel:

"I am the LORD your God. I am holy, and you must be holy too! Respect your father and your mother, honor the Sabbath, and don't make idols or images. I am the LORD your God.

"When you harvest your grain, always leave some of it standing along the edges of your fields and don't pick up what falls on the ground. Don't strip your grapevines clean or gather the grapes that fall off the vines. Leave them for the poor and for those foreigners *(FOR-in-erz)* who live among you. I am the LORD your God."

The word of the Lord.

■ REFLECTION

Do I find some of these teachings easier to keep than others? Will I become holy just by avoiding evil? Is anyone in our school ever embarrassed because they do not have as much money as other students?

■ CLOSING

adapted from the Byzantine rite

Receive Lent with gladness, O people!
Let us all say:
Be strong, and turn your life toward God.
Be strong, and turn your life toward God.

Let us remember these intentions:

Merciful God,
    as your loving children,
      we are eager to do what is right.
Send your Holy Spirit to live with us
    and to fill us with your light.
We ask this through Christ our Lord. **Amen.**

Let us pray with the words that Jesus taught us:
Our Father . . .

TUESDAY PRAYER

March 13, 2001

■ INTRODUCTION

Yesterday we read from the book of Leviticus *(luh-VIT-uh-kus),* the third book of the Bible. That book contains many laws of the Hebrew people. These laws help us to know how to live as the holy people of a holy God.

The heart of Jewish law is the "decalogue" *(DEK-uh-log),* or Ten Commandments. They appear many times in the Bible. But they are not always written exactly the same way every time. That is because the people never stop learning more about what each commandment means.

Today we continue the book of Leviticus.

■ A PSALM FOR EARLY LENT

turn to
page 218

■ READING

Leviticus 19:11–17

Listen to the words of the book of Leviticus:

The LORD says this:

"Do not steal or tell lies or cheat others. Do not misuse my name by making promises you don't intend to keep. I am the LORD your God.

"Do not steal anything or cheat anyone, and don't fail to pay your workers at the end of each day. I am the LORD your God, and I command you not to make fun of the deaf or to cause a blind person to stumble. Be fair, no matter who is on trial—don't favor either the poor or the rich. Don't be a gossip, but never hesitate to speak up in court, especially if your testimony can save someone's life. Don't hold grudges. On the other hand, it's wrong not to correct someone who needs correcting. Stop being angry and don't try to take revenge. I am the LORD, and I command you to love others as much as you love yourself."

The word of the Lord.

■ REFLECTION

How does the last commandment in this list include all the others? Are there any commandments listed here that I can pay particular attention to during this Lent? Which of these laws do we keep very well?

■ CLOSING

adapted from the Byzantine rite

Receive Lent with gladness, O people!
Let us all say:
Be strong, and turn your life toward God.
Be strong, and turn your life toward God.

Let us remember these intentions:

Merciful God,
    as your loving children,
    we are eager to do what is right.
Send your Holy Spirit to live with us
    and to fill us with your light.
We ask this through Christ our Lord. **Amen.**

Let us pray with the words that Jesus taught us:
Our Father . . .

WEDNESDAY PRAYER

March 14, 2001

Reminder: Monday is Saint Joseph's Day. You may want to plan something special.

■ INTRODUCTION

Today is Wednesday of the second week of Lent. During Lent we turn our hearts to God in penance and to our neighbors in charity.

During this season we listen to the prophets *(PRAH-fits)*. They tell us to turn from everything that keeps us from loving God.

■ A PSALM FOR EARLY LENT

turn to
page 218

■ READING

Isaiah 1:2, 4, 15 – 18, 27

Listen to the words of the prophet Isaiah:

The LORD has said, "Listen, heaven and earth! You have turned from the LORD, the holy God of Israel. No matter how much you pray, I won't listen. You are too violent.

"Wash yourselves clean! Stop doing wrong and learn to live right. See that justice is done. Defend widows and orphans and help those in need.

"I, the LORD, invite you to come and talk it over. Your sins are scarlet red, but they will be whiter than snow or wool.

"Jerusalem, you will be saved by showing justice; Zion's people who turn to me will be saved by doing right."

The word of the Lord.

■ REFLECTION

How does violence in our world affect us? How can people our age make our world more just? What sins do I need to talk over with God?

■ CLOSING

My brothers and sisters,
    during this season of Lent
  let us admit that we are sinners,
      express our sorrow,
  and ask God to forgive us.

Our responses to the three petitions are "Lord, have mercy," then "Christ, have mercy," and then "Lord, have mercy."

Lord, we ask your forgiveness for all our sins.
    Lord, have mercy.
Christ, we turn our hearts toward you.
    Christ, have mercy.
Lord, we ask your blessing on us during Lent.
    Lord, have mercy.

Let us remember these intentions:

Let us pray with the words that Jesus taught us:
Our Father . . .

THURSDAY PRAYER

March 15, 2001

■ INTRODUCTION

Today we remember Saint Louise de Marillac *(loo-EEZ duh MAH-ree-ack)*. After her husband died, Louise worked with Saint Vincent de Paul to care for the poor people living in Paris. Together they founded an order of sisters called the Daughters of Charity. Louise told them to "love the poor, honor them, as you would honor Christ himself." She died in 1660.

■ A PSALM FOR EARLY LENT

▶ turn to
page 218

■ READING

Isaiah 12:1–2, 4–6

Listen to the words of the prophet Isaiah:

At that time you will say, "I thank you, LORD! You were angry with me, but you stopped being angry and gave me comfort. I trust you to save me, LORD God, and I won't be afraid. My power and my strength come from you, and you have saved me."

At that time you will say, "Our LORD, we are thankful, and we worship only you. We will tell the nations how glorious you are and what you have done. Because of your wonderful deeds we will sing your praises everywhere on earth."

Sing, people of Zion! Celebrate the greatness of the holy LORD of Israel. God is here to help you.

The word of the Lord.

■ REFLECTION

Does thinking about God give me comfort and strength? Does it make me fearless and joyful? Or does God seem to be more interested in sins than in happiness? Do my ideas about God make it difficult to see God's love in my life?

■ CLOSING

My brothers and sisters,
    during this season of Lent
    let us admit that we are sinners,
        express our sorrow,
    and ask God to forgive us.

Our responses to the three petitions are "Lord, have mercy," then "Christ, have mercy," and then "Lord, have mercy."

Lord, we ask your forgiveness for all our sins.
    Lord, have mercy.
Christ, we turn our hearts toward you.
    Christ, have mercy.
Lord, we ask your blessing on us during Lent.
    Lord, have mercy.

Let us remember these intentions:

Let us pray with the words that Jesus taught us:
Our Father . . .

FRIDAY PRAYER

■ INTRODUCTION

The prophets of Israel told the people to repent. "Remember God, and turn from your evil ways," they said. But they brought a message of hope as well. "No matter how bad things seem to be, God has not forgotten you," they said. "God will be your savior."

When their country was at war and there was not enough to eat, the people remembered these promises. They prayed and waited for the Savior. During Lent we listen again to these messages of repentance and of hope.

■ A PSALM FOR EARLY LENT

▶ turn to page 218

■ READING

Jeremiah 1:4–10

Listen to the words of the prophet Jeremiah:

The LORD said, "Jeremiah, I am your Creator, and before you were born, I chose you to speak for me to the nations."

I replied, "I'm not a good speaker, LORD, and I'm too young." "Don't say you're too young," the LORD answered. "If I tell you to go and speak to someone, then go! And when I tell you what to say, don't leave out a word! I promise to be with you and keep you safe, so don't be afraid."

The LORD reached out his hand, and then he touched my mouth and said, "I am giving you the words to say, and I am sending you with authority to speak to the nations for me."

The word of the Lord.

■ REFLECTION

Jeremiah did not think he was able to do what God called him to do. Am I being called to do something I think is too much for me? Is there someone who can help me do it?

■ CLOSING

My brothers and sisters,
        during this season of Lent
    let us admit that we are sinners,
        express our sorrow,
    and ask God to forgive us.

Our responses to the three petitions are "Lord, have mercy," then "Christ, have mercy," and then "Lord, have mercy."

Lord, we ask your forgiveness for all our sins.
    Lord, have mercy.
Christ, we turn our hearts toward you.
    Christ, have mercy.
Lord, we ask your blessing on us during Lent.
    Lord, have mercy.

Let us remember these intentions:

Let us pray with the words that Jesus taught us:
Our Father . . .

WEEKLY PRAYER

With a Reading from the Gospel for Sunday, March 18, 2001

Reminder: You may wish to make copies of the Psalm for Late Lent, on page 246.

■ INTRODUCTION

Most of the Sunday readings each year come from one of the gospels. This year we have been listening to the gospel of Luke. The three middle Sundays of Lent, however, have a choice of readings: either Luke or John.

The readings from John's gospel are often used in parishes that will welcome new members at Easter. Those readings will be used for Daily Prayer in weeks ahead.

■ A PSALM FOR EARLY LENT

turn to page 218

■ READING

Luke 13:6–9

Listen to the words of the holy gospel according to Luke:

Jesus told this story:
A man had a fig tree growing in his vineyard *(VIN-yerd)*. One day he went out to pick some figs, but he didn't find any. So he said to the gardener, "For three years I have come looking for figs on this tree, and I haven't found any yet. Chop it down! Why should it take up space?"

The gardener answered, "Master, leave it for another year. I'll dig around it and put some manure on it to make it grow. Maybe it will have figs on it next year. If it doesn't, you can have it cut down."

The gospel of the Lord.

■ REFLECTION

Gardeners and farmers use manure for fertilizer. If God is the gardener of the story, what could the fig tree represent? How is the year of delay like Lent? Have my friends and I ever needed time to "bear fruit"?

■ CLOSING

My brothers and sisters,
　　during this season of Lent
　　let us admit that we are sinners,
　　express our sorrow,
　　and ask God to forgive us.

Our responses to the three petitions are "Lord, have mercy," then "Christ, have mercy," and then "Lord, have mercy."

Lord, we ask your forgiveness for all our sins.
　　Lord, have mercy.
Christ, we turn our hearts toward you.
　　Christ, have mercy.
Lord, we ask your blessing on us during Lent.
　　Lord, have mercy.

Let us remember these intentions:

Let us pray with the words that Jesus taught us:
Our Father . . .

March 19, 2001

■ INTRODUCTION

Today we remember Saint Joseph, the husband of Mary and the foster father of Jesus. Joseph was a descendant of the royal family of King David, but he was not rich. He worked as a carpenter in the town of Nazareth *(NAZ-uh-reth)*.

Many people celebrate this feast with great joy. Some parishes and even some families prepare a "Saint Joseph's Table," which is often a potluck supper. Everyone brings something to give to the poor.

■ A PSALM FOR EARLY LENT

▶ turn to
page 218

■ READING

Matthew 1:18–21, 24

Listen to the words of the holy gospel according to Matthew:

A young woman named Mary was engaged to Joseph from King David's family. But before they were married, she learned that she was going to have a baby by God's Holy Spirit. Joseph was a good man and did not want to embarrass Mary in front of everyone. So he decided to quietly call off the wedding.

While Joseph was thinking about this, an angel from the Lord came to him in a dream. The angel said, "Joseph, the baby that Mary will have is from the Holy Spirit. Go ahead and marry her. Then after her baby is born, name him Jesus, because he will save his people from their sins."

After Joseph woke up, he and Mary were soon married, just as the Lord's angel had told him to do.

The gospel of the Lord.

■ REFLECTION

Saint Joseph is the patron of working parents, adoptive parents, foster parents and stepparents. Do you know any parents who ought to get a big hug and a "thank you" today in honor of today's saint?

■ CLOSING

Let us remember these intentions:

Loving God,
    you put your Son, Jesus, in the care of Joseph.
Put us also in Joseph's care.
Let him watch over the whole church.
Let this celebration of his day
    remind us to share what we have
        with the poor.
We ask this through Christ our Lord. **Amen.**

Let us pray with the words that Jesus taught us:

Our Father . . .

TUESDAY PRAYER

March 20, 2001

▶ Reminder: Next week we begin using the Prayers for Late Lent, on pages 246 to 248.

■ INTRODUCTION

Today the sun passes directly across the middle of the earth. This is known as the equinox *(EE-kwi-nox)*. Today spring begins in the Northern Hemisphere. All over the world, there is a balance of light and darkness. The day and the night are both twelve hours long. From now until September, our days will be longer than our nights. Surely Easter cannot be far away!

Today's reading is about two other things that are also in perfect balance. They are the two great commandments of Jesus.

■ A PSALM FOR EARLY LENT

▶ turn to page 218

■ READING

Luke 10:25–28

Listen to the words of the holy gospel according to Luke:

An expert in the Law of Moses stood up and asked Jesus a question to see what he would say. "Teacher," he asked, "What must I do to have eternal life?" Jesus answered, "What is written in the Scriptures? How do you understand them?"

The man replied, "The Scriptures say, 'Love the Lord your God with all your heart, soul, strength, and mind.' They also say, 'Love your neighbors as much as you love yourself.'"

Jesus said, "You have given the right answer. If you do this, you will have eternal life."

The gospel of the Lord.

■ REFLECTION

Some people say that everything Jesus taught is summed up in this story. What would the world be like if everyone lived by these words? How have we tried to strengthen our love of God since Lent began? How have we strengthened our love of neighbor?

■ CLOSING

My brothers and sisters,
    during this season of Lent
  let us admit that we are sinners,
      express our sorrow,
  and ask God to forgive us.

Lord, we ask your forgiveness for all our sins.
  Lord, have mercy.
Christ, we turn our hearts toward you.
  Christ, have mercy.
Lord, we ask your blessing on us during Lent.
  Lord, have mercy.

Let us remember these intentions:

Let us pray with the words that Jesus taught us:
Our Father . . .

WEDNESDAY PRAYER

March 21, 2001

■ INTRODUCTION

Today we begin a long story from the gospel of John. It is often used on the third Sunday of Lent to prepare people for Easter baptism.

It is a story about a Samaritan *(suh-MAIR-ih-tun)* woman who meets Jesus. At that time, Jews did not speak to Samaritans. Also, men were not allowed to speak to women they did not know.

■ A PSALM FOR EARLY LENT

▶ turn to
page 218

■ READING

John 4:7–11, 13–14

Listen to the words of the holy gospel according to John:

A Samaritan *(suh-MAIR-ih-tun)* woman came to draw water from the well. Jesus asked her, "Would you please give me a drink of water?"

"You are a Jew," she replied, "and I am a Samaritan woman. How can you ask me for a drink of water when Jews and Samaritans won't have anything to do with each other?"

Jesus answered, "You don't know what God wants to give you, and you don't know who is asking you for a drink. If you did, you would ask me for the water that gives life."

"Sir," the woman said, "you don't even have a bucket, and the well is deep. Where are you going to get this life-giving water?"

Jesus answered, "Everyone who drinks this water will get thirsty again. But no one who drinks the water I give will ever be thirsty again. The water I give is like a flowing fountain that gives eternal life."

The gospel of the Lord.

■ REFLECTION

How did Jesus deal with the hateful feelings between Jews and Samaritans? How can this be a model for us? What can Jesus mean by "life-giving water"?

■ CLOSING

My brothers and sisters,
　　during this season of Lent
　　let us admit that we are sinners,
　　　　express our sorrow,
　　and ask God to forgive us.

Lord, we ask your forgiveness for all our sins.
　　Lord, have mercy.
Christ, we turn our hearts toward you.
　　Christ, have mercy.
Lord, we ask your blessing on us during Lent.
　　Lord, have mercy.

Let us remember these intentions:

Let us pray with the words that Jesus taught us:
Our Father . . .

240

THURSDAY PRAYER

March 22, 2001

■ INTRODUCTION

As the year goes by, we celebrate many saints and heroes of our people. Each time we remember them, we learn again about their courage or their wisdom or their love of justice. We pick up a bit of their strength or their love of the poor or their prayerfulness to carry with us on our own journey.

Let us thank God for the saints. And during Lent, let us ask them to help us turn our hearts to God in penance and to our neighbors in charity.

■ A PSALM FOR EARLY LENT

turn to
page 218

■ READING

John 4:19–21, 23, 24

Listen to the words of the holy gospel according to John:

The Samaritan *(suh-MAIR-ih-tun)* woman said to Jesus, "Sir, I can see that you are a prophet, [so explain this to me]. My ancestors worshiped on this mountain, but you Jews say Jerusalem is the only place to worship."

Jesus said to her, "Believe me, the time is coming when you won't worship the Father either on this mountain or in Jerusalem. Even now the true worshipers are being led by the Spirit to worship the Father according to the truth. God is Spirit, and those who worship God must be led by the Spirit to worship him according to the truth."

The gospel of the Lord.

■ REFLECTION

Have we learned to pray well in the classroom? Do I find it better or easier to worship in one place rather than another? What might it mean to worship God "in truth"?

■ CLOSING

My brothers and sisters,
   during this season of Lent
   let us admit that we are sinners,
   express our sorrow,
   and ask God to forgive us.

Lord, we ask your forgiveness for all our sins.
   Lord, have mercy.
Christ, we turn our hearts toward you.
   Christ, have mercy.
Lord, we ask your blessing on us during Lent.
   Lord, have mercy.

Let us remember these intentions:

Let us pray with the words that Jesus taught us:
Our Father . . .

FRIDAY PRAYER

March 23, 2001

■ INTRODUCTION

Today we remember Saint Turibius *(ter-REE-bee-us)*. In Spain he was elected bishop even though he was not yet a priest. Then, in 1581, he was sent to Peru in South America. There was evil in the church and in the government of Peru at that time. Bishop Turibius tried to reform the church. He became a model of Christian life for his people. Two children who were confirmed by Bishop Turibius became saints. They are Martin de Porres *(duh POUR-ez)* and Rose of Lima.

Today we read more of the story of Jesus and the woman at the well.

■ A PSALM FOR EARLY LENT

turn to page 218

■ READING

John 4:25–26, 28–30, 39, 41–42

Listen to the words of the holy gospel according to John:

The Samaritan *(suh-MAIR-ih-tun)* woman said, "I know that the Messiah will come. He is the one we call Christ. When he comes, he will explain everything to us."

"I am that one," Jesus told her. The woman left her water jar and ran back into town. She said to the people, "Come and see a man who told me everything I have ever done! Could he be the Messiah?" Everyone in town went out to see Jesus. A lot of Samaritans in that town put their faith in Jesus because [of what] the woman had said. Many more Samaritans put their faith in Jesus because of what they heard him say. They told the woman, "We no longer have faith in Jesus just because of what you told us. We have heard him ourselves, and we are certain that he is the Savior of the world!"

The gospel of the Lord.

■ REFLECTION

The woman brought others to Jesus. Who has brought me to believe in Jesus? How do we hear Jesus "for ourselves"?

■ CLOSING

My brothers and sisters,
during this season of Lent
let us admit that we are sinners,
express our sorrow,
and ask God to forgive us.

Lord, we ask your forgiveness for all our sins.
Lord, have mercy.
Christ, we turn our hearts toward you.
Christ, have mercy.
Lord, we ask your blessing on us during Lent.
Lord, have mercy.

Let us remember these intentions:

Let us pray with the words that Jesus taught us:
Our Father . . .

242

LATE LENT

Sunday, March 25 to Thursday, April 12

LATE LENT 2001

■ ABOUT THE SEASON

We are still in the season of Lent. Has it begun to seem long? Lent is 40 days long. We count the 40 days from the First Sunday of Lent through Holy Thursday. The four days from Ash Wednesday to the First Sunday of Lent are a kind of "invitation" to keep the season.

LOOKING AHEAD

We are now halfway through Lent, and that is good news! That means we are halfway to Easter. Have we forgotten some of the things we were going to do during Lent? Now is the time to renew plans and refresh our energy.

▪ THE NUMBER "40" APPEARS IN THE BIBLE MANY TIMES. The most important "40" is the 40 years that the Hebrew people lived in the desert after they left their lives as slaves in Egypt and before they moved into the promised land. That certainly was a long time, but when they thought about it later, they decided that God had kept them in the desert as long as it took to make them ready to hear God's word and to live as that word commanded.

Do you remember the story about Noah and his ark? In that story, the rain fell for 40 days and nights. Maybe the author meant that God kept Noah and his family away from their "promised land" until they were ready to hear the word and live by it.

Jesus spent 40 days and nights in the desert before he began his preaching. Maybe God was giving him a chance to become strong before his work began. Has God been making us strong during Lent? Our 40 days are not over yet, so it is not too late to make a fresh start.

▪ REMEMBER: LENT IS NOT JUST ABOUT DOING SPECIAL THINGS AND SAYING SPECIAL PRAYERS. The things we do and the prayers we say can help us understand God's word more clearly and live according to that word more generously. If they do not do that, then they are not useful.

Another good thing to remember is that Christians should be joyful. Joy isn't always loud and full of smiles. Sometimes joy is quiet and thoughtful. During Lent, we are full of quiet joy. Many people are listening to God. Many people are turning away from sin. Many are preparing to be baptized at Easter. Many are helping each other, working for peace and carrying the good news of Jesus to every corner of the world.

▪ IN LATE LENT THE READINGS FOR DAILY AND WEEKLY PRAYER ARE TAKEN FROM THE GOSPELS OF LUKE AND JOHN. The story of the man cured of blindness, and the story of the raising of Lazarus are told during the fourth and fifth weeks of Lent. These gospels are usually read on the fourth and fifth Sundays if people are preparing for baptism. These stories of conversion and new life form a link between Lent and Easter.

Readings for the last week of Lent describe the events that led up to the suffering, death and resurrection of Jesus. They prepare us, step by step, for the celebration of the Easter Triduum.

■ PREPARATION FOR LATE LENT

There is a new Psalm, a new Meal Prayer and a new End of the Day Prayer for the rest of Lent. They are on pages 246, 247 and 248. These same prayers are found on pages 30, 31 and 32 of the student booklet *Blessed Be God!*

▪ THE FEAST OF THE ANNUNCIATION OF THE LORD IS CELEBRATED ON MONDAY, MARCH 26, THIS YEAR. You will want to make plans for that day during the previous week.

▪ AFTER PALM SUNDAY, ADD PALMS AND OTHER SPRING BRANCHES TO YOUR PRAYER CORNER. They are signs of resurrection and eternal life. At home, many people tuck palms behind a crucifix or

behind a holy picture. During the final days of Lent, some people use red or purple cloth to give special honor to the cross. You might want to do that in the classroom.

It's a good idea to clean the classroom before Easter. Put away Lenten decorations before you leave for Easter break. Then the room will be ready for the colorful decorations of Eastertime.

▪ LENT ENDS ON HOLY THURSDAY, APRIL 12. On page 266 is a blessing that the teacher can use before the Easter holidays. You may want to remind the teacher of this.

▪ WE LEAVE SCHOOL IN TIME TO KEEP THE THREE HOLIEST DAYS OF THE YEAR WITH OUR FAMILIES. These days are counted from sundown on Holy Thursday to sundown on Easter Sunday. We call these days the Paschal Triduum.

"Triduum" is a Latin word meaning "three days." And the word "paschal" means "Passover." These three days are the Christian Passover feast.

▪ SUGGESTED HYMNS: A beautiful song for Late Lent is "What wondrous love is this" (page 208 in the *Hymnal for Catholic Students*). According to the first verse of this hymn, the "dreadful curse" that Jesus bears for us is the curse of death. Jesus died to put death itself to death. The words of the final verse express our hope in the resurrection: "when from death we're free, we'll sing and joyful be."

Other songs for Late Lent are "Were you there" (page 204 in the hymnal) and *"Ubi caritas et amor, Deus ibi est"* (page 197 in the hymnal). These Latin words mean "Where charity and love are found, God is there."

During these weeks you can also use the other songs suggested for Lent on page 217 of this book. You might take some time to learn the music you will sing in church during the Paschal Triduum. The services in church are very beautiful. Maybe you can have someone talk about them with the class.

■ THE SCHOOL OF RELIGION

If you have been using the Psalm for Early Lent since Ash Wednesday, you are probably just getting comfortable with it now. And your families might be saying the prayers from copies that you brought home. If this is true, it might be a good idea to stick with those prayers and not use the new Psalm, Meal Prayer and End of the Day Prayer for Late Lent.

The Psalm for Early Lent and the Psalm for Late Lent are both beautiful, and they both deepen in us the spirit of Lent. Look them over and decide as a class whether you want to continue using the Psalm for Early Lent (on page 218) or the Psalm for Late Lent (on page 246). But keep in mind that the directions on the Weekly Prayer pages will send you to page 246, the Psalm for Late Lent.

▪ IF YOU WILL HAVE AN EASTER BREAK from religion meetings, remind the teacher to use the blessing on page 266.

A PSALM FOR LATE LENT

▶ all make
the sign
of the cross

Psalm 130:1–7

LEADER Behold! Now is the acceptable time!
ALL **Now is the day of salvation!**

LEADER From the depths I call to you,
Lord, hear my cry.
ALL **Catch the sound of my voice
raised up, pleading.**

SIDE B If you record our sins,
Lord, who could survive?
But because you forgive
we stand in awe.

SIDE A I trust in God's word,
I trust in the Lord.
More than sentries for dawn
I watch for the Lord.

SIDE B More than sentries for dawn
let Israel watch.
The Lord will bring mercy
and grant full pardon.

LEADER From the depths I call to you,
Lord, hear my cry.
ALL **Catch the sound of my voice
raised up, pleading.**

**Glory to the Father, and to the Son,
and to the Holy Spirit:**
**as it was in the beginning, is now,
and will be for ever. Amen.**

▶ turn back to
Daily Prayer or Weekly Prayer
for today

246

LATE LENT

LEADER Let us offer God praise and thanksgiving:

ALL ▶ all make
the sign
of the cross

LEADER Behold! Now is the acceptable time!
ALL **Now is the day of salvation!**

LEADER Blessed are you, Lord, God of all creation:
ALL **You make us hunger and thirst for holiness.**

LEADER Blessed are you, Lord, God of all creation:
ALL **You call us to true fasting:**
to set free the oppressed,
to share our bread with the hungry,
and to shelter the homeless.

LEADER May your gifts refresh us, O Lord,
and your grace give us strength.

ALL ▶ all make
the sign
of the cross

LATE LENT

END OF THE DAY PRAYER

> all make
> the sign
> of the cross

LEADER Let us look back over our day
and ask forgiveness
for anything we did
that was harmful or wrong.

> stop; allow a minute or so of silence,
> and then say:

LEADER To you, O Lord, I lift up my soul.
ALL **In you, my God, I put my trust.**

**I confess to almighty God,
and to you, my brothers and sisters,
that I have sinned through my own fault
In my thoughts and in my words,
in what I have done,
and in what I have failed to do;
and I ask blessed Mary, ever virgin,
all the angels and saints,
and you, my brothers and sisters,
to pray for me to the Lord our God.**

LEADER ▶ hold out one hand
toward everyone
in blessing, and say:

May the almighty and merciful God
bless and protect us:

ALL ▶ all make
the sign
of the cross

The Confiteor

WEEKLY PRAYER

With a Reading from the Gospel for Sunday, March 25, 2001

 Reminder: The Psalm for Late Lent is on page 30 in *Blessed Be God!*

■ INTRODUCTION

Today's reading is a story that Jesus told. It is a favorite of Christians everywhere, so you may know it by heart. Listen again to the story of the wasteful boy and his forgiving father.

■ A PSALM FOR LATE LENT

 turn to page 246

■ READING

Luke 15:11–20, 22, 24

Listen to the words of the holy gospel according to Luke:

Jesus told this story: Once a man had two sons. The younger son said to his father, "Give me my share of the property." So the father divided his property between his two sons. The younger son packed up everything he owned and left for a foreign *(FOR-in)* country. He had spent everything, when a bad famine spread through that whole land. He went to work for a man in that country, and the man sent him out to take care of his pigs. He would have been glad to eat what the pigs were eating, but no one gave him a thing.

Finally, he came to his senses and said, "My father's workers have plenty to eat, and here I am, starving to death! I will go to my father and say to him, 'Father, I have sinned against God in heaven and against you. I am no longer good enough to be called your son. Treat me like one of your workers.'"

The younger son got up and started back to his father. But when he was still a long way off, his father saw him and felt sorry for him. He ran to his son and hugged and kissed him. His father said to the servants, "Hurry and bring the best clothes and put them on him. Give him a ring for his finger and sandals for his feet. This son of mine was dead, but has now come back to life. He was lost and has now been found."

The gospel of the Lord.

■ REFLECTION

What does this story mean to me? Why is this a good story for Lent?

■ CLOSING

Let us remember these intentions:

Forgiving Lord,
    we have sinned against you
    and against each other.
We have wasted the gifts you have given us.
We don't deserve to be called your children.
But forgive us and open your arms
    to welcome us.
We ask this through Christ our Lord. **Amen.**

Let us pray with the words that Jesus taught us:
Our Father . . .

249

MONDAY PRAYER

March 26, 2001

▶ Reminders: Please use October's Meal Prayer (the Angelus), on page 49, and the End of the Day Prayer on page 25.

■ INTRODUCTION

Today we celebrate the Annunciation of the Lord, when the Son of God became a human person. We are happy that the Son of God loved us enough to become one of us. We are happy that first Mary, and then many other people, accepted Jesus.

■ A PSALM FOR LATE LENT

▶ turn to page 246

■ READING

Luke 1:26–32, 34–35, 38

Listen to the words of the holy gospel according to Luke:

God sent the angel Gabriel to the town of Nazareth *(NAZ-uh-reth)* in Galilee *(GAL-uh-lee)* with a message for a virgin named Mary. She was engaged to Joseph from the family of King David. The angel greeted Mary and said, "You are truly blessed! The Lord is with you."

Mary was confused by the angel's words and wondered what they meant. Then the angel told Mary, "Don't be afraid! God is pleased with you, and you will have a son. His name will be Jesus. He will be great and will be called the Son of God Most High."

Mary asked the angel, "How can this happen? I am not married!"

The angel answered, "The Holy Spirit will come down to you, and God's power will come over you. So your child will be called the holy Son of God."

Mary said, "I am the Lord's servant! Let it happen as you have said."

The gospel of the Lord.

■ REFLECTION

The Annunciation is the beginning of the story of Jesus. Easter is its completion. How much do we remember about the life and work of Jesus?

■ CLOSING

Let us remember these intentions:

Loving God, you give us your finest grace,
 your greatest blessing.
You give us yourself.
In Christ you share our life.
In Christ you share our suffering.
In Christ you redeem us.
All glory to you now and for ever. **Amen.**

Mother Mary, in Christ we are your children.
Pray for us.
Let us all say: **Hail Mary, full of grace . . .**

Let us pray with the words that Jesus taught us:
Our Father . . .

TUESDAY PRAYER

March 27, 2001

▶ Reminder: The Psalm, Meal and End of the Day Prayers for Late Lent are on pages 30 to 32 in *Blessed Be God!*

■ INTRODUCTION

Today we remember Margaret Clitherow, who lived in England when Catholics were forbidden to practice their faith. Margaret bravely hid priests in her house, and allowed others to secretly gather there for the eucharist. When she was arrested and condemned to death, her husband cried out that "they would murder the best wife within the kingdom and the best Catholic."

On March 25, 1586, the feast of the Annunciation, Margaret became the first English woman to give her life for the Catholic faith during the reign *(rayn)* of Queen Elizabeth the First.

■ A PSALM FOR LATE LENT

▶ turn to
page 246

■ READING

John 9:1–3, 5–7

Listen to the words of the holy gospel according to John:

As Jesus walked along, he saw a man who had been blind since birth. Jesus' disciples asked, "Teacher, why was this man born blind? Was it because he or his parents sinned?"

"No, it wasn't!" Jesus answered. "But you will see God work a miracle for him. While I am in the world, I am the light for the world." After Jesus said this, he spit on the ground. He made some mud and smeared it on the man's eyes. Then he said, "Go and wash off the mud in Siloam *(SIL-oh-ahm)* Pool." The man went and washed in Siloam. When he had washed off the mud, he could see.

The gospel of the Lord.

■ REFLECTION

Why does God allow bad things to happen to people? Do I blame God for my problems?

■ CLOSING

My brothers and sisters,
during Lent God invites us to be renewed
in our thoughts and actions
and to open our hearts to others.

Lord, be with those who believe in you.
Lord, have mercy.
Christ, be with those who take up their cross
and follow you.
Christ, have mercy.
Lord, be with those who hope
in your resurrection.
Lord, have mercy.

Let us remember these intentions:

Let us pray with the words that Jesus taught us:
Our Father . . .

WEDNESDAY PRAYER

March 28, 2001

■ INTRODUCTION

Many people give their homes a spring cleaning during Lent. They also try to put their lives in order through the prayer of Lent.

Perhaps we can plan a time to clean our desks and lockers and give the cupboards a scrubbing. The principal, coach or librarian might like some help with their cupboards, too. It can be a sign of the new beginning that comes to each of us at Easter.

■ A PSALM FOR LATE LENT

turn to
page 246

■ READING

John 9:8–12

Listen to the words of the holy gospel according to John:

The [neighbors of the man born blind], and the people who had seen him begging wondered if he really could be the same man. Some of them said he was the same beggar, while others said he only looked like him. But he told them, "I am that man."

"Then how can you see?" they asked.

He answered, "Someone named Jesus made some mud and smeared it on my eyes. He told me to go and wash it off in Siloam (SIL-oh-ahm) Pool. When I did, I could see."

"Where is he now?" they asked.

"I don't know," he answered.

The gospel of the Lord.

■ REFLECTION

How does learning more about Jesus open our eyes? What could the pool of water in the story mean for us? If someone asked me where Jesus is now, what would I answer?

■ CLOSING

My brothers and sisters,
    during this season of Lent
  let us admit that we are sinners,
    express our sorrow,
  and ask God to forgive us.

Lord, we ask your forgiveness for all our sins.
  Lord, have mercy.
Christ, we turn our hearts toward you.
  Christ, have mercy.
Lord, we ask your blessing on us during Lent.
  Lord, have mercy.

Let us remember these intentions:

Let us pray with the words that Jesus taught us:
Our Father . . .

252

THURSDAY PRAYER

March 29, 2001

■ INTRODUCTION

Today we continue reading the story of the man who received sight from Jesus. This story is important for all who are preparing for baptism, and for all of us who will renew our baptism at Eastertime.

The man was happy about his wonderful gift. His parents and friends were happy. But some people were not pleased. They knew that Jesus was working signs that showed God's power. Some thought he was the Messiah, but some thought he was just a fake. Many people were just confused.

■ A PSALM FOR LATE LENT

turn to
page 246

■ READING

John 9:13–17

Listen to the words of the holy gospel according to John:

The day when Jesus made the mud and healed the man was a Sabbath. So the people took the man to the religious leaders. They asked him how he was able to see, and he answered, "Jesus made some mud and smeared it on my eyes. Then after I washed off the mud, I could see."

Some of the leaders said, "This man Jesus does not come from God. If he did, he would not break the law of the Sabbath."

Others asked, "How could someone who is a sinner work such a miracle?"

They asked the man, "What do you say about this one who healed your eyes?"

"He is a prophet!" the man told them.

The gospel of the Lord.

■ REFLECTION

What could the cured man see that some of the religious leaders could not? In what way are we like the man in the story? In what way are we like the people who saw it all happening?

■ CLOSING

My brothers and sisters,
   during this season of Lent
   let us admit that we are sinners,
   express our sorrow,
   and ask God to forgive us.

Lord, we ask your forgiveness for all our sins.
   Lord, have mercy.
Christ, we turn our hearts toward you.
   Christ, have mercy.
Lord, we ask your blessing on us during Lent.
   Lord, have mercy.

Let us remember these intentions:

Let us pray with the words that Jesus taught us:
Our Father . . .

253

FRIDAY PRAYER

March 30, 2001

■ INTRODUCTION

The story we are reading from the gospel of John tells us what Jesus did long ago. But it also tells us what Jesus is doing today. Jesus is still active in the events of daily life.

We are like the man who had been blind. When we begin to follow Jesus we begin to see things that we had not noticed before. We begin to understand things that we had not paid attention to before. This is the mystery of our growth in Christ.

■ A PSALM FOR LATE LENT

➤ turn to
page 246

■ READING

John 9:18, 23–25, 28–29, 31, 33

Listen to the words of the holy gospel according to John:

The leaders would not believe that the man had once been blind. They had already agreed that no one was to have anything to do with anyone who said Jesus was the Messiah.

The leaders called the man back and said, "Swear by God to tell the truth! We know that Jesus is a sinner."

The man replied, "I don't know if he is a sinner or not. All I know is that I used to be blind, but now I can see!"

The leaders said, "You are his follower! We are followers of Moses. We are sure that God spoke to Moses, but we don't even know where Jesus comes from."

The man replied, "We know that God listens only to people who love and obey him. Jesus could not do anything unless he came from God."

The gospel of the Lord.

■ REFLECTION

Why do some people believe in Jesus today and some do not? Are we able to discuss and explain our faith to other people? What has my faith in Jesus helped me to see?

■ CLOSING

My brothers and sisters,
    during this season of Lent
  let us admit that we are sinners,
    express our sorrow,
  and ask God to forgive us.

Lord, we ask your forgiveness for all our sins.
  Lord, have mercy.
Christ, we turn our hearts toward you.
  Christ, have mercy.
Lord, we ask your blessing on us during Lent.
  Lord, have mercy.

Let us remember these intentions:

Let us pray with the words that Jesus taught us:
Our Father . . .

WEEKLY PRAYER

With a Reading from the Gospel for Sunday, April 1, 2001

■ INTRODUCTION

The end of Lent is not far off. But it is not too late to do something special. Lent is the time to try harder, to be more sensitive to others and to listen to the word that God speaks in our hearts.

After we listen to a reading from the Bible, we should sit quietly for a minute, to allow God's word to take root in us. The word of God deserves prayerful listening.

■ A PSALM FOR LATE LENT

➤ turn to
page 246

■ READING

John 8:3–7, 9–11

Listen to the words of the holy gospel according to John:

[The leaders brought a sinful woman to Jesus.] They made her stand in the middle of the crowd. Then they said, "Teacher, this woman was caught with a man who wasn't her husband. The Law of Moses teaches that a woman like this should be stoned to death! What do you say?"

Jesus simply bent over and started writing on the ground with his finger. Finally, he stood up and said, "If any of you have never sinned, then go ahead and throw the first stone at her!" The people left one by one, beginning with the oldest. Finally, Jesus and the woman were there alone.

Jesus stood up and asked her, "Where is everyone? Isn't there anyone left to accuse you?"

"No, sir," the woman answered. Then Jesus told her, "I am not going to accuse you either. You may go now, but don't sin any more."

The gospel of the Lord.

■ REFLECTION

Why did the people leave instead of punishing the woman? What does this story teach us about judging others? How is this gospel like the sacrament of reconciliation?

■ CLOSING

My brothers and sisters,
during this season of Lent
let us admit that we are sinners,
express our sorrow,
and ask God to forgive us.

Lord, we ask your forgiveness for all our sins.
Lord, have mercy.
Christ, we turn our hearts toward you.
Christ, have mercy.
Lord, we ask your blessing on us during Lent.
Lord, have mercy.

Let us remember these intentions:

Let us pray with the words that Jesus taught us:
Our Father . . .

MONDAY PRAYER

April 2, 2001

■ INTRODUCTION

Today we remember Saint Francis of Paola. He began an order of Franciscan monks who dedicate their lives to prayer. They live very simply and own nothing.

The kings of France found his advice so good and wise that they made him stay in France for 25 years. They even built a monastery for him. He died there on Good Friday in 1507.

■ A PSALM FOR LATE LENT

turn to
page 246

■ READING

John 11:1, 3, 17, 21, 23–27

Listen to the words of the holy gospel according to John:

A man by the name of Lazarus was sick in the village of Bethany. He had two sisters, Mary and Martha. The sisters sent a message to the Lord and told him that his good friend Lazarus was sick. When Jesus got to Bethany, he found that Lazarus had already been in the tomb four days.

Martha said to Jesus, "Lord, if you had been here, my brother would not have died. Yet even now I know that God will do anything you ask."

Jesus told her, "Your brother will live again!" Martha answered, "I know that he will be raised to life on the last day, when all the dead are raised."

Jesus then said, "I am the one who raises the dead to life! Everyone who has faith in me will live, even if they die. And everyone who lives

because of faith in me will never die. Do you believe this?"

"Yes, Lord!" she replied, "I believe that you are Christ, the Son of God. You are the one we hoped would come into the world."

The gospel of the Lord.

■ REFLECTION

Do we believe that Jesus is the Messiah, the Son of God, with power over life? What difference does this belief make in my life?

■ CLOSING

My brothers and sisters,
    during Lent God invites us to be renewed
        in our thoughts and actions
    and to open our hearts to others.

Lord, be with those who believe in you.
    Lord, have mercy.
Christ, be with those who take up their cross
    and follow you.
    Christ, have mercy.
Lord, be with those who hope
    in your resurrection.
    Lord, have mercy.

Let us remember these intentions:

Let us pray with the words that Jesus taught us:
Our Father . . .

TUESDAY PRAYER

April 3, 2001

■ INTRODUCTION

We began to read the story of Lazarus yesterday. This gospel is sometimes used for a Sunday in Lent. It is easy to understand the importance of this story as we prepare for Easter.

This story is taken from the gospel according to John, so we can expect that it will have many meanings for us. John calls each miracle of Jesus a "sign." People who believe in Jesus try to read these signs that have been handed down to us.

■ A PSALM FOR LATE LENT

➤ turn to
   page 246

■ READING

John 11:32, 35–36, 38–40

Listen to the words of the holy gospel according to John:

Mary [the sister of Lazarus] went to where Jesus was. Then as soon as she saw him, she knelt at his feet and said, "Lord, if you had been here, my brother would not have died."

Jesus started crying, and the people said, "See how much he loved Lazarus."

Jesus was still terribly upset. So he went to the tomb, which was a cave with a stone rolled against the entrance. Then he told the people to roll the stone away. But Martha said, "Lord, you know that Lazarus has been dead four days, and there will be a bad smell."

Jesus replied, "Didn't I tell you that if you had faith, you would see the glory of God?"

The gospel of the Lord.

■ REFLECTION

Have I ever cried for someone who has died? Is it hard to imagine Jesus crying? What does that tell us about his feelings for his friends?

■ CLOSING

My brothers and sisters,
   during Lent God invites us to be renewed
      in our thoughts and actions
   and to open our hearts to others.

Lord, be with those who believe in you.
   Lord, have mercy.
Christ, be with those who take up their cross
   and follow you.
   Christ, have mercy.
Lord, be with those who hope
   in your resurrection.
   Lord, have mercy.

Let us remember these intentions:

Let us pray with the words that Jesus taught us:
Our Father . . .

257

WEDNESDAY PRAYER

April 4, 2001

■ INTRODUCTION

Today we will learn more about Jesus and his friends. When they were sad, he was sad with them. Jesus comforted Mary and Martha, and he cried with them because their brother Lazarus was dead. At times when life seems dark or fearful, it is good to remember that Jesus loves us as he loved his friends in Bethany. He wants to comfort us and bring us life.

■ A PSALM FOR LATE LENT

turn to
page 246

■ READING

John 11:41–44

Listen to the words of the holy gospel according to John:

After the stone had been rolled aside [from the tomb of Lazarus], Jesus looked up toward heaven and prayed, "Father, I thank you for answering my prayer. I know that you always answer my prayers."

When Jesus had finished praying, he shouted, "Lazarus, come out!" The man who had been dead came out. His hands and feet were wrapped with strips of burial cloth, and a cloth covered his face.

Jesus then told the people, "Untie him and let him go."

The gospel of the Lord.

■ REFLECTION

Can I say with confidence, "Father, I know that you always answer my prayers"? How can we "untie" other people and free them?

■ CLOSING

My brothers and sisters,
   during Lent God invites us to be renewed
     in our thoughts and actions
   and to open our hearts to others:

Lord, be with those who believe in you.
   Lord, have mercy.
Christ, be with those who take up their cross
   and follow you.
   Christ, have mercy.
Lord, be with those who hope
   in your resurrection.
   Lord, have mercy.

Let us remember these intentions:

Let us pray with the words that Jesus taught us:
Our Father . . .

THURSDAY PRAYER

April 5, 2001

■ INTRODUCTION

As we move toward the last week of Lent it is good to renew our efforts to pray well. When the followers of Jesus asked him to teach them to pray, he gave them the "Our Father." That prayer shows us how to speak to God as a parent, not as a faraway emperor. It shows us how to ask God for what we need.

Jesus listed five things to ask God for. He did not include money or fame or an easy life. In today's reading Jesus tells us that once we know what to ask for, we should keep "bothering" God with our prayers.

■ A PSALM FOR LATE LENT

➤ turn to
page 246

■ READING

Luke 11:5–9

Listen to the words of the holy gospel according to Luke:

Jesus said to his disciples, "Suppose one of you goes to a friend in the middle of the night and says, 'Let me borrow three loaves of bread. A friend of mine has dropped in, and I don't have a thing for him to eat.' And suppose your friend answers, 'Don't bother me! The door is bolted, and my children and I are in bed. I cannot get up to give you something.'

"He may not get up and give you the bread, just because you are his friend. But he will get up and give you as much as you need, simply because you are not ashamed to keep on asking.

"So I tell you to ask and you will receive, search and you will find, knock and the door will be opened for you."

The gospel of the Lord.

■ REFLECTION

Have I ever given up when God did not answer my prayers the way I wanted? Am I loyal to God, my friend? Do I continue to pray both in good times and bad?

■ CLOSING

My brothers and sisters,
    during Lent God invites us to be renewed
  in our thoughts and actions
    and to open our hearts to others.

Lord, be with those who believe in you.
  Lord, have mercy.
Christ, be with those who take up their cross
  and follow you.
  Christ, have mercy.
Lord, be with those who hope
  in your resurrection.
  Lord, have mercy.

Let us remember these intentions:

Let us pray with the words that Jesus taught us:
Our Father . . .

FRIDAY PRAYER
April 6, 2001

■ INTRODUCTION

At sundown tomorrow, the Jewish feast of Passover begins. As Jews begin their most sacred days of prayer, Christians too are preparing for their holiest days of the year. On April 8, we will hear the story of Jesus' last Passover with his followers.

Today's reading tells of a woman who showed her love for Jesus in a very unusual way.

■ A PSALM FOR LATE LENT

▶ turn to page 246

■ READING

John 12:1–7

Listen to the words of the holy gospel according to John:

Six days before Passover, Jesus went back to Bethany, where he had raised Lazarus from death. A meal had been prepared for Jesus. Martha was doing the serving, and Lazarus himself was there.

Mary took a very expensive bottle of perfume and poured it on Jesus' feet. She wiped them with her hair, and the sweet smell of the perfume filled the house.

A disciple named Judas Iscariot *(iss-KA-ree-ut)* was there. He was the one who was going to betray Jesus, and he asked, "Why wasn't this perfume sold for three hundred silver coins and the money given to the poor?" Judas did not really care about the poor. He asked this because he carried the moneybag and sometimes would steal from it.

Jesus replied, "Leave her alone! She has kept this perfume for the day of my burial. You will always have the poor with you, but you won't always have me."

The gospel of the Lord.

■ REFLECTION

Mary's gift to Jesus was unusual. Has anyone ever made fun of me for the gifts I have given to God? Have I ever made fun of people from other traditions who do not worship God the same way I do?

■ CLOSING

My brothers and sisters,
    during Lent God invites us to be renewed
in our thoughts and actions
    and to open our hearts to others.

Lord, be with those who believe in you.
    Lord, have mercy.
Christ, be with those who take up their cross
    and follow you.
    Christ, have mercy.
Lord, be with those who hope
    in your resurrection.
    Lord, have mercy.

Let us remember these intentions:

Let us pray with the words that Jesus taught us:
Our Father . . .

WEEKLY PRAYER

With a Reading from the Gospel for Sunday, April 8, 2001

■ INTRODUCTION

On Sunday, April 8, we bless palms and we hear the reading of the passion of Jesus. So that is why it is called both "Passion Sunday" and "Palm Sunday."

Carrying branches on the Sunday before Easter unites us with all people who have ever welcomed Jesus as the Messiah.

■ A PSALM FOR LATE LENT

▶ turn to
page 246

■ READING

Luke 19:28, 29–38

Listen to the words of the holy gospel according to Luke:

Jesus went on toward Jerusalem. He sent two of his disciples on ahead. He told them, "Go into the next village, where you will find a young donkey that has never been ridden. Untie the donkey and bring it here. If anyone asks why you are doing that, just say, 'The Lord needs it.'"

They went off and found everything just as Jesus had said. While they were untying the donkey, its owners asked, "Why are you doing that?"

They answered, "The Lord needs it."

Then they led the donkey to Jesus. They put some of their clothes on its back and helped Jesus get on. And as he rode along, the people spread clothes on the road in front of him. When Jesus was starting down the Mount of Olives, his large crowd of disciples were happy and praised God because of all the miracles they had seen. They shouted,

"Blessed is the king who comes in the name of the Lord! Peace in heaven and glory to God."

The gospel of the Lord.

■ REFLECTION

What did it mean to put a coat on the ground before Jesus? How do I show honor to Jesus?

■ CLOSING

As we prepare to keep the Three Days of Easter, let us all say:
Holy God: **Holy God!**
Holy mighty One: **Holy mighty One!**
Holy immortal One, have mercy on us:
Holy immortal One, have mercy on us!

Let us remember these intentions:

O God,
grant us your forgiveness and mercy
as we celebrate the death, burial
and resurrection of Jesus.
We ask this through Christ our Lord. **Amen.**

Let us pray with the words that Jesus taught us:
Our Father . . .

MONDAY PRAYER

April 9, 2001

Reminder: You may want to make copies of the Psalm, Meal Prayer and End of the Day Prayers for Early Eastertime, on pages 270 to 272.

■ INTRODUCTION

It is a custom to clean the house and the class-room before Easter. We can give the classroom a scrubbing. We can do to our rooms what we have been doing to our hearts. We throw out the trash, fix up what is still useful and make every-thing more beautiful.

Let us try to keep our Lenten promises dur-ing this last week of the season.

■ A PSALM FOR LATE LENT

 turn to page 246

■ READING

Luke 22:1–6

Listen to the words of the holy gospel according to Luke:

The Festival of Thin Bread, also called Passover, was near. The [religious leaders] were looking for a way to get rid of Jesus, because they were afraid of what the people might do. Then Satan entered the heart of Judas Iscariot *(iss-KA-ree-ut),* who was one of the twelve apostles.

Judas went to talk with the [religious leaders] and the officers of the temple police about how he could help them arrest Jesus. They were very pleased and offered to pay Judas some money. He agreed and started looking for a good chance to betray Jesus when the crowds were not around.

The gospel of the Lord.

■ REFLECTION

What could have made Judas turn against Jesus? Do I know anyone who has turned against a friend? Has anyone ever turned against me or talked behind my back? How might Jesus have felt about what Judas was doing?

■ CLOSING

As we prepare to keep the Three Days of Easter, let us all say:
Holy God: **Holy God!**
Holy mighty One: **Holy mighty One!**
Holy immortal One, have mercy on us:
Holy immortal One, have mercy on us!

Let us remember these intentions:

O God,
grant us your forgiveness and mercy
as we celebrate the death, burial
and resurrection of Jesus.
We ask this through Christ our Lord. **Amen.**

Let us pray with the words that Jesus taught us:
Our Father . . .

TUESDAY PRAYER

April 10, 2001

■ INTRODUCTION

Soon many Christians around the world will begin their most solemn holy days—Holy Thursday evening until Easter Sunday.

In our reading today, Jesus and the disciples make arrangements for the feast of Passover. On that day Jews eat a meal called a seder *(SAY-der)*. They share special foods, including wine and thin, unleavened bread. This meal recalls the time when God rescued them from slavery in Egypt, and led them to freedom.

■ A PSALM FOR LATE LENT

➤ turn to
page 246

■ READING

Luke 22:7–13

Listen to the words of the holy gospel according to Luke:

The day had come for the Festival of Thin Bread, and it was time to kill the Passover lambs. So Jesus said to Peter and John, "Go and prepare the Passover meal for us to eat."

But they asked, "Where do you want us to prepare it?"

Jesus told them, "As you go into the city, you will meet a man carrying a jar of water. Follow him into the house and say to the owner, 'Our teacher wants to know where he can eat the Passover meal with his disciples.' The owner will take you upstairs and show you a large room ready for you to use. Prepare the meal there."

Peter and John left. They found everything just as Jesus had told them, and they prepared the Passover meal.

The gospel of the Lord.

■ REFLECTION

If the eucharist is our Passover meal, who prepares that meal for us? What saving act of God does our Passover meal recall? In what way is Jesus like the lamb that is the Passover sacrifice?

■ CLOSING

As we prepare to keep the Three Days of Easter, let us all say:
Holy God: **Holy God!**
Holy mighty One: **Holy mighty One!**
Holy immortal One, have mercy on us:
Holy immortal One, have mercy on us!

Let us remember these intentions:

O God,
grant us your forgiveness and mercy
as we celebrate the death, burial
and resurrection of Jesus.
We ask this through Christ our Lord. **Amen.**

Let us pray with the words that Jesus taught us:
Our Father . . .

■ INTRODUCTION

Each day of April brings new signs of life in and on the earth. As the sun's rays become stronger, leaves and buds start to grow on the bare branches of the trees. We may even find the broken eggshells of newly hatched birds. How many signs of new life can we find? We can bring some into our classroom.

They remind us that Jesus rose from the tomb just as the creatures of the earth are rising from the death of winter. The signs of spring can help us look forward to Easter during these final days of Lent.

■ A PSALM FOR LATE LENT

➤ turn to page 246

■ READING

Luke 22:14–16, 19–20

Listen to the words of the holy gospel according to Luke:

When the time came for Jesus and the apostles to eat [the Passover meal], he said to them, "I have very much wanted to eat this Passover meal with you before I suffer. I tell you that I will not eat another Passover meal until it is finally eaten in God's kingdom."

Jesus took some bread in his hands and gave thanks for it. He broke the bread and handed it to his apostles. Then he said, "This is my body, which is given for you. Eat this as a way of remembering me!"

After the meal he took another cup of wine in his hands. Then he said, "This is my blood. It is poured out for you, and with it God makes his new agreement."

The gospel of the Lord.

■ REFLECTION

Why did Jesus give us this sacrament of his body and his blood? Do I celebrate the eucharist with respect and gratitude?

■ CLOSING

As we prepare to keep the Three Days of Easter, let us all say:
Holy God: **Holy God!**
Holy mighty One: **Holy mighty One!**
Holy immortal One, have mercy on us:
Holy immortal One, have mercy on us!

Let us remember these intentions:

O God,
    grant us your forgiveness and mercy
      as we celebrate the death, burial
    and resurrection of Jesus.
We ask this through Christ our Lord. **Amen.**

Let us pray with the words that Jesus taught us:
Our Father . . .

◼ INTRODUCTION

At his last Passover meal with his disciples, Jesus gave to his disciples, and to us, the bread and wine that are his body and blood. Tonight many Christians remember and celebrate that mystery.

Tonight is also the sixth evening of the Jewish Passover. As Jews and Christians gather on these most sacred days of remembrance, let us pray that God will open for all of us new roads toward freedom and faith.

◼ A PSALM FOR LATE LENT

➤ turn to page 246

◼ READING

Luke 22:39–46

Listen to the words of the holy gospel according to Luke:

[After the Passover supper] Jesus went out to the Mount of Olives, as he often did, and his disciples went with him. When they got there, he told them, "Pray that you won't be tested."

Jesus walked on a little way before he knelt down and prayed. "Father, if you will, please don't make me suffer by having me drink from this cup. But do what you want, and not what I want."

Then an angel from heaven came to help him. Jesus was in great pain and prayed so sincerely that his sweat fell to the ground like drops of blood.

Jesus got up from praying and went over to his disciples. They were asleep and worn out from being so sad. He said to them, "Why are you asleep? Wake up and pray that you won't be tested."

The gospel of the Lord.

◼ CLOSING

As we prepare to keep the Three Days of Easter, let us all say:
Holy God: **Holy God!**
Holy mighty One: **Holy mighty One!**
Holy immortal One, have mercy on us:
Holy immortal One, have mercy on us!

Let us remember these intentions:

O God,
   grant us your forgiveness and mercy
      as we celebrate the death, burial
   and resurrection of Jesus.
We ask this through Christ our Lord. **Amen.**

Let us pray with the words that Jesus taught us:
Our Father . . .

A Blessing before Easter Break

Shortly before dismissal, the students gather so that the teacher will be able to bless each one.

TEACHER

May the Lord's face shine on us,
   and may the Lord guide our feet
      into the way of peace.
Blessed be the name of the Lord,
   now and for ever.

ALL

Amen.

TEACHER

Let us put ourselves into the hands of the Lord,
   and pray that God will bless us
      and our families
   during the coming holy days.
May each of us help to make our homes
   places of joy, love, peace and safety.
May we be generous and considerate,
   helping others keep the celebration
      of the dying and rising
   of our Lord and Savior, Jesus Christ.

Please respond "Amen" as I bless each of you.

▶ the teacher goes to each student in turn,
   places a hand on the student's head
   or shoulder, and says:

N., go with God.

ALL

Amen.

▶ when these individual blessings are
   completed, prayer continues:

TEACHER

My dear friends and students
   may almighty God give you light and joy.
And, until we gather here again,
   may God bless all of us:

ALL

▶ all make
   the sign
   of the cross

▶ end with a hymn, such as
   "Lord, who throughout these forty days"
   (page 156 in the *Hymnal for Catholic Students*)
   or "Shalom chaverim" (page 177)

EARLY EASTERTIME

Easter Sunday, April 15, to Friday, May 11

EARLY EASTERTIME 2001

■ ABOUT THE SEASON

Christ is risen! Alleluia! The simplicity and sacrifice of Lent are over. We can relax and enjoy the glory of Jesus and the share he has given us in the resurrection. The natural world reflects this joy.

Eastertime is about new life. We celebrate new life

LOOKING AHEAD

with the symbols of eggs, rabbits, chicks, flowers, green grass and butterflies. We rejoice that new members of our parish entered the life of our church when they were baptized and confirmed at the Easter Vigil. All of us nourish the life of God when we share in the Easter sacrament of the eucharist. And so we sing over and over, "alleluia," "praise God."

■ CAN WE BRING IN SOME EASTER SYMBOLS TO DECORATE THE ROOM AND PRAYER CENTER? Two important Easter symbols are water and light. We can place a bowl of Easter water and an Easter candle on the table in the prayer center. We can talk about ways to make the classroom "sing" of the resurrection, just as we will sing with our alleluias.

■ WE HAVE SPOKEN MANY TIMES THIS YEAR OF JESUS AS THE "LIGHT OF THE WORLD." During Advent we lighted candles on the wreath to show that the Savior brings God's light into the world's darkness. Light is a sign of grace, peace and life.

During Christmastime we used the words of Simeon, who called Jesus the "light of revelation." We used many lights to celebrate the coming of Christ. We put lights on trees and in windows.

Now, during Eastertime, we celebrate Jesus again with symbols of light. The paschal candle, the giant candle that is lighted during this season whenever we celebrate in the church, shows that Jesus lives. His light was not put out with death but shines now because of his resurrection.

The sun rises each morning, bright and strong. It too is a sign of the resurrection of Jesus. The sun has always been recognized as a sign of God's warmth, love and life-giving power. What would we do without it? Let us think about this as we enjoy the longer and warmer days and as we see the plants and flowers that the sun seems to be calling out of the earth.

■ EASTER IS NOT JUST ONE DAY. It is a whole season, just as Lent is a season. In fact, Easter is even longer than Lent! Lent lasts for 40 days, but Eastertime is 50 days long. The Easter season will last until Pentecost, June 3. So we can plan a variety of Eastertime events in the classroom. All of us can take even longer to celebrate Easter than we took during Lent to prepare for it.

■ THE DAILY READINGS DURING EASTERTIME ARE FILLED WITH GOOD NEWS. They tell of excited disciples running to tell one another of the risen Jesus. They tell of Jesus traveling along the road to the town of Emmaus. At first when Jesus joins his followers they do not recognize him. But then Jesus opens up the words of the scriptures to help them understand. Jesus blesses and breaks bread, and he gives it to his disciples to eat. They recognize him in these actions. Their hearts and minds are opened to a deeper faith.

■ PREPARATION FOR EARLY EASTERTIME

If you do not use the student booklet *Blessed Be God!* you may want to make copies of the Psalm, Meal Prayer and End of the Day Prayer for Early Eastertime. They are found on pages 270, 271 and 272. The class will use them from Easter Monday, April 16, to Friday, May 11.

■ THE FIRST THING TO DO AFTER EASTER BREAK IS TO RESTORE THE ALLELUIA TO YOUR PRAYERS! For classes that "buried the alleluia" with a ritual of

bells and song, there is another ritual to raise it from its "tomb." That ritual is described on page 273. And even if you did not put away the "alleluia," you can still welcome it back with joy and lots of music.

▪ PERHAPS SOME OF YOUR CLASSMATES CELE-BRATED THE EASTER SACRAMENTS OF BAPTISM, CONFIRMATION AND EUCHARIST. If so, it is important to share your joy with them. On page 274 there is a ritual of welcome for those who have been newly baptized or received into the church. It can be used at any convenient time.

▪ BECAUSE EASTER COMES IN MID-APRIL, WE WILL SOON TURN OUR CALENDARS TO MAY. During that month many people remember Mary, the Mother of God, in their prayer. There is a ceremony on page 289 for blessing and crowning an image of Mary. You may wish to use the Meal Prayer for Late Eastertime (page 303) during May. It is the *Regina Caeli,* which means "Queen of Heaven."

▪ HAVE YOU NOTICED THE LARGE CANDLE IN THE CHURCH? It was brought there during the Easter Vigil. It is called the paschal candle, and it represents the light of the risen Christ shining for all believers to see.

You can have a candle in your prayer area, too. The candle is an important symbol of the Easter season. You might use the same large candle that was used at Christmastime. The Daily, Weekly and End of the Day Prayers tell just when to light this candle and when to put it out. There are simple acclamations for the class to learn.

▪ SUGGESTED HYMNS: "O sons and daughters" (page 170 in the *Hymnal for Catholic Students)* is a beautiful carol from France. Remember that carols are songs for dancing. That is why they are so much fun to sing. They can make you want to move your feet to their rhythm. "That Easter day with joy was bright" (page 192 in the hymnal) is a carol that can

be sung as a round. Other songs for the Easter season are suggested on page 301.

You can get into the happy spirit of Eastertime by using musical instruments when you sing your prayer. Rhythm instruments, such as bells, finger cymbals, drums and tambourines, can be used in almost any song.

■ THE SCHOOL OF RELIGION

The readings for Weekly Prayer are from the gospel of John. They tell us how the risen Jesus strengthened the faith of his disciples and gave the church a mission to "catch," like fish, the whole world.

▪ IF SOME MEMBERS OF THE SCHOOL OF RELIGION WERE BAPTIZED or received into the church at Easter, celebrate the blessing after initiation (on page 274) with them. This might be done by the entire community or by individual classes. You might want to invite their parents to participate.

▪ MANY STUDENTS OF THE SCHOOL OF RELIGION LIKE TO HONOR MARY DURING MAY. You might place flowers before an icon of Mary, say the rosary (see page 348), or hold a "May Crowning" procession (see page 289).

▪ IF YOUR FAMILIES USED THE PRAYERS you brought home during Lent, they might like to continue to pray together. The Psalm for Early Eastertime, the Meal Prayer and the End of the Day Prayer can be copied for them or a copy of *Blessed Be God!* can be sent home.

A PSALM FOR EARLY EASTERTIME

▶ all make
the sign
of the cross

Psalm 118: 1–2, 13–14, 22–24

LEADER Christ is risen like the sun, alleluia!
ALL **The light of Christ shines
over the whole world, alleluia!**

▶ light a candle,
and then say:

LEADER This is the day the Lord made.
ALL **Let us rejoice and be glad.**

SIDE A Give thanks, the Lord is good,
"God is lasting love!"
Now let Israel say,
"God is lasting love!"

SIDE B I was pushed to falling,
but the Lord gave me help.
My strength, my song is the Lord,
who has become my savior.

SIDE A The stone the builders rejected
has become the cornerstone.

SIDE B This is the work of the Lord,
how wonderful in our eyes.

LEADER This is the day the Lord made.
ALL **Let us rejoice and be glad.**

**Glory to the Father, and to the Son,
and to the Holy Spirit:
as it was in the beginning, is now,
and will be for ever. Amen. Alleluia.**

▶ turn back to Daily Prayer or
Weekly Prayer for today

270

EARLY EASTERTIME

MEAL PRAYER

LEADER Let us offer God praise and thanksgiving:

ALL ▶ all make
the sign
of the cross

LEADER Christ is risen, alleluia!
ALL **Christ is truly risen, alleluia!**
LEADER Jesus says to us:
"I am the living bread
that came down from heaven.
Whoever eats of this bread
will live forever."

ALL **Loving God, give us the daily bread
that is your Son, Jesus,
who is our resurrection and our life,
now and for ever. Amen.**

▶ these words can be sung
to the tune "Bread of life"
(page 134 in the *Hymnal for Catholic Students*)

I am the Bread of life.
You who come to me shall not hunger
and who believe in me shall not thirst.
No one can come to me
unless the Father beckons.
And I will raise you up,
and I will raise you up,
and I will raise you up
on the last day.

▶ all make
the sign
of the cross

John 6

271

EARLY EASTERTIME

END OF THE DAY PRAYER

> all make
> the sign
> of the cross

LEADER   Christ is risen like the sun, alleluia!

ALL   **The light of Christ shines
over the whole world, alleluia!**

> light a candle,
> and then say:

LEADER   Loving God, Creator of the universe,
     we thank you for calling us
     to be members of your holy people,
     and we say:

ALL   **Amen.**

LEADER   Lord Jesus Christ,
     we thank you for forgiving our sins
     and for sharing with us your risen life,
     and we say:

ALL   **Amen.**

LEADER   Holy Spirit of God,
     fill us with your love
     and guide us in the way of peace,
     and we say:

ALL   **Amen.**

LEADER
> hold out one hand
> toward everyone
> in blessing, and say:

     Wherever we go,
     may we live in the light of Christ:

ALL
> all make
> the sign
> of the cross

> at the end of prayer,
> put out the candle

Welcoming the Alleluia

Do this on the day you return to class after Easter break, before prayer and before you use any Easter songs or greetings.

Make sure the banner is still where you put it 40 days earlier. Decorate the place with flowers and pennants and other signs of Easter. Bells, noisemakers and instruments should be there as well.

Everyone first comes together in class.

all make
the sign
of the cross

READER   Matthew 27:57–60
Listen to the words of the holy gospel according to Matthew:

That evening a rich disciple named Joseph went and asked for Jesus' body. Pilate gave orders for it to be given to Joseph, who took the body and wrapped it in a clean linen cloth. Then Joseph put the body in his own tomb that had been cut into solid rock and had never been used. He rolled a big stone against the entrance to the tomb and went away.

The gospel of the Lord.

LEADER
Let us go forth in silence and in peace.

Form a procession that goes from the classroom to the place you buried the banner. Bring the shovel or key or whatever you will need to open the box. Move silently to the place of burial.

When you are there, the reader reads the following gospel:

READER   Matthew 28:1–7
Listen to the words of the holy gospel according to Matthew:

It was almost daybreak on Sunday when Mary Magdalene *(MAG-duh-lin)* and the other Mary went to see the tomb. Suddenly a strong earthquake struck, and the Lord's angel came down from heaven. He rolled away the stone and sat on it. The angel looked as bright as lightning, and his clothes were white as snow. The guards shook from fear and fell down, as though they were dead.

The angel said to the women, "Don't be afraid! I know you are looking for Jesus, who was nailed to a cross. He is not here! God has raised him to life, just as Jesus said he would. Come, see the place where his body was lying. Now hurry! Tell his disciples that he has been raised to life and is on his way to Galilee. Go there, and you will see him."

The gospel of the Lord.

Dig up or unlock the box. Hold up the alleluia banner. Everyone shouts "alleluia!" and then the whole group should clap, cheer, ring bells and make a joyful noise.

Sing an Easter song with lots of alleluias, such as the song you sang when you buried the alleluia. Move to the place where the banner is to be hung and then to the classroom, singing and ringing bells all the time.

A Blessing after Initiation

This blessing is for students initiated or received into the Catholic community at the Easter Vigil or during the Easter season. The blessing is also appropriate at any time of the year after confirmation or first communion.

A large candle should be in a central place. The newly initiated or received gather near it. One or more of them prepare the announcement, such as, "At the Easter Vigil I was initiated into the church through baptism, confirmation and first eucharist." Or, "Last Sunday, we celebrated the sacrament of confirmation."

Begin and end with an Easter song.

 all make
the sign
of the cross

LEADER
Christ is risen like the sun, alleluia!

ALL
The light of Christ shines over the whole world, alleluia!

 light
the candle

NEWLY INITIATED/RECEIVED:
Friends and classmates,
   I (we) bring you good news
      and invite you to share in my (our) joy.
This is my (our) announcement:

_____

_____

_____

all may clap
as a sign of good wishes

READER   Ephesians 3:19–21
Listen to the words of the apostle Paul:

I want you to know all about Christ's love, although it is too wonderful to be measured. Then your lives will be filled with all that God is.

I pray that Christ Jesus and the church will forever bring praise to God. His power at work in us can do far more than we dare ask or imagine.

The word of the Lord.

LEADER
Let us hold out a hand in blessing.

all hold out a hand
toward the newly initiated/received in
blessing, while the leader says:

May God give you strength
   and fill you with love
      so that you may live faithfully
   your new life in Christ.
We ask this through Christ our Lord.

ALL
Amen.

all make
the sign
of the cross

MONDAY PRAYER

April 16, 2001

> Reminders: Raise the Alleluia before prayer today. The Prayers for Early Eastertime are on pages 34 to 36 of *Blessed Be God!*

■ INTRODUCTION

Happy Easter Monday! At the Easter Vigil people were baptized and given white clothes to wear. They were dressed like the angels in today's reading. They too announce the good news that Jesus is risen.

Many people wear something bright at Easter as a reminder of baptism and even of angels!

■ A PSALM FOR EARLY EASTERTIME

> turn to page 270

■ READING

Luke 24: 1–8

Listen to the words of the holy gospel according to Luke:

Very early on Sunday morning the women went to the tomb, carrying the spices that they had prepared. When they found the stone rolled away from the entrance, they went in. But they did not find the body of the Lord Jesus, and they did not know what to think.

Suddenly two men in shining white clothes stood beside them. The women were afraid and bowed to the ground. But the men said, "Why are you looking in the place of the dead for someone who is alive? Jesus isn't here! He has been raised from death. Remember that while he was still in Galilee, he told you, 'The Son of Man will be handed over to sinners who will nail him to a cross. But three days later he will rise to life.'" Then they remembered what Jesus had said.

The gospel of the Lord.

■ REFLECTION

Why didn't the women expect Jesus to rise from the dead? I have not seen the empty tomb. Why do I believe in the resurrection?

■ CLOSING

Let us remember these intentions:

Gracious God,
    through the announcement
        of the holy women
    you bring the good news of your love
        to all the peoples of the earth.
Strengthen us to carry that good news
        in our lives, in our hearts and in our words.
We ask this through Christ our Lord. **Amen.**

Let us pray with the words that Jesus taught us:
Our Father . . .

> sing "alleluia"

May we live in the light of Christ. Amen.

> put out the candle

TUESDAY PRAYER

April 17, 2001

■ INTRODUCTION

Today is Tuesday of the Easter Octave. An octave is an eight-day celebration. This is a week of great rejoicing!

All of the gospels tell us that the women disciples were the first to discover that Jesus had risen. Today's reading tells about a disciple and friend of Jesus whose name was Mary.

■ A PSALM FOR EARLY EASTERTIME

➤ turn to page 270

■ READING

John 20:11–16

Listen to the words of the holy gospel according to John:

Mary Magdalene (*MAG-duh-lin*) stood crying outside the tomb. She was still weeping, when she stooped down and saw two angels inside. They were dressed in white and were sitting where Jesus' body had been. One was at the head and the other was at the foot. The angels asked Mary, "Why are you crying?"

She answered, "They have taken away my Lord's body! I don't know where they have put him."

As soon as Mary said this, she turned around and saw Jesus standing there. But she did not know who he was. Jesus asked her, "Why are you crying? Who are you looking for?"

She thought he was the gardener and said, "Sir, if you have taken his body away, please tell me, so I can go and get him."

Then Jesus said to her, "Mary!"
She turned and said to him, "Teacher."

The gospel of the Lord.

■ REFLECTION

The resurrection gospels often mention white clothing. What might this symbolize? What are some ways that clothing is used as a symbol? What does the way I dress mean to me?

■ CLOSING

Let us remember these intentions:

Gracious God,
    through the announcement
        of the holy women
    you bring the good news of your love
        to all the peoples of the earth.
Strengthen us to carry that good news
    in our lives, in our hearts and in our words.
We ask this through Christ our Lord. **Amen.**

Let us pray with the words that Jesus taught us:

Our Father . . .

sing "alleluia"

May we live in the light of Christ. **Amen.**

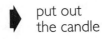
put out the candle

WEDNESDAY PRAYER

April 18, 2001

■ INTRODUCTION

Today is Easter Wednesday. All of our readings this week remind Christians that Jesus is risen from the dead.

In our world there are many signs of resurrection. New grass, green buds, eggs and flowers remind us of the resurrection of nature after the death of winter. We can bring some of these symbols to brighten our classroom. They can help us celebrate the joy of our new life in the risen Christ.

■ REFLECTION

Why did no one believe the women? How would I feel if I had such good news and no one believed me? Why is it difficult to explain our beliefs to other people?

■ CLOSING

Let us remember these intentions:

■ A PSALM FOR EARLY EASTERTIME

turn to
page 270

■ READING

Luke 24:9–12

Listen to the words of the holy gospel according to Luke:

Mary Magdalene *(MAG-duh-lin),* Joanna, Mary the mother of James, and some other women were the ones who had gone to the tomb. When they returned, they told the eleven apostles and the others what had happened. The apostles thought it was all nonsense, and they would not believe.

But Peter ran to the tomb. And when he stooped down and looked in, he saw only the burial clothes. Then he returned, wondering what had happened.

The gospel of the Lord.

Gracious God,
  through the announcement
    of the holy women
  you bring the good news of your love
    to all the peoples of the earth.
Strengthen us to carry that good news
    in our lives, in our hearts and in our words.
We ask this through Christ our Lord. **Amen.**

Let us pray with the words that Jesus taught us:
Our Father . . .

sing
"alleluia"

May we live in the light of Christ. **Amen.**

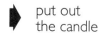
put out
the candle

THURSDAY PRAYER

April 19, 2001

■ INTRODUCTION

Today is Easter Thursday. A lot of work goes into celebrating Easter. Our parents and relatives prepared baskets and eggs. People of the parish put banners and flowers in the church to express our joy in Christ's resurrection. The choir *(KWI-er)* has learned new songs. So much of the Easter celebration is prepared for us. Is there something we can do to share our joy with others?

■ A PSALM FOR EARLY EASTERTIME

▶ turn to
page 270

■ READING

Luke 24:36–39, 41, 45–48

Listen to the words of the holy gospel according to Luke:

While Jesus' disciples were talking about what had happened, Jesus appeared and greeted them. They were frightened and terrified because they thought they were seeing a ghost.

But Jesus said, "Why are you so frightened? Why do you doubt? Look at my hands and my feet and see who I am! Touch me and find out for yourselves. Ghosts don't have flesh and bones as you see I have." The disciples were so glad and amazed that they could not believe it.

Then Jesus helped them understand the Scriptures. He told them, "The Scriptures say that the Messiah must suffer, then three days later he will rise from death. They also say that all people of every nation must be told in my name to turn to God, in order to be forgiven. So

beginning in Jerusalem, you must tell everything that has happened."

The gospel of the Lord.

■ REFLECTION

How did Jesus help the disciples' faith? Has Jesus opened my mind to the meaning of the scriptures?

■ CLOSING

Let us remember these intentions:

Gracious God,
    through the announcement
      of the holy women
    and the preaching of the apostles,
    you bring the good news of your love
      to all the peoples of the earth.
Strengthen us to carry that good news
    in our lives, in our hearts and in our words.
We ask this through Christ our Lord. **Amen.**

Let us pray with the words that Jesus taught us:

Our Father . . .

 sing
"alleluia"

May we live in the light of Christ. **Amen.**

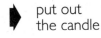 put out
the candle

278

FRIDAY PRAYER

April 20, 2001

■ INTRODUCTION

Today is Easter Friday. The celebration of Easter goes on for 50 days. The fiftieth day is Pentecost. Our Easter celebration prepares us for the coming of the Holy Spirit on that day.

In the days after the resurrection, many disciples saw Jesus. Today's reading from the gospel of Mark tells of those events and what they meant to the disciples.

■ A PSALM FOR EARLY EASTERTIME

▶ turn to
page 270

■ READING

Mark 16:9–15

Listen to the words of the holy gospel according to Mark:

Very early on the first day of the week, after Jesus had risen to life, he appeared to Mary Magdalene *(MAG-duh-lin)*. She left and told his friends, who were crying and mourning *(MORN-ing)*. Even though they heard that Jesus was alive and that Mary had seen him, they would not believe it.

Later, Jesus appeared in another form to two disciples, as they were on their way out of the city. But when these disciples told what had happened, the others would not believe.

Afterwards, Jesus appeared to his eleven disciples as they were eating. He scolded them because they were too stubborn to believe the ones who had seen him after he had been raised to life. Then he told them, "Go and preach the good news to everyone in the world."

The gospel of the Lord.

■ REFLECTION

The faith of the apostles grew day by day. Do I understand the word of God any better now than I did when I was younger?

■ CLOSING

Let us remember these intentions:

Loving and glorious God,
    we praise you with Easter joy
    because Christ is our redeemer.
Christ has broken the power of sin
    and healed an injured world.
Christ has made us whole again.
Bless our celebrations and our joy.
We ask this through Christ our Lord. **Amen.**

Let us pray with the words that Jesus taught us:

Our Father . . .

▶ sing
"alleluia"

May we live in the light of Christ. **Amen.**

▶ put out
the candle

WEEKLY PRAYER

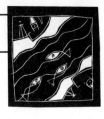

With a Reading from the Gospel for Sunday, April 22, 2001

▶ Reminders: If you buried the alleluia, raise it before prayer today. See page 273.
  The Psalm for Early Eastertime is on page 34 in *Blessed Be God!*

■ INTRODUCTION

Easter is too important to last only one day, so the church gives us seven weeks to celebrate and sing and be joyful. During these beautiful spring days, the world itself seems to shout "alleluia."

Jesus is risen and he is with the church, to teach and guide it until the end of time. Let us all join joyfully in the world's "alleluia."

■ A PSALM FOR EARLY EASTERTIME

▶ turn to
  page 270

■ READING

John 20:19–23

Listen to the words of the holy gospel according to John:

On the evening of that same Sunday the disciples locked themselves in a room. Suddenly, Jesus appeared in the middle of the group. He greeted them and showed them his hands and his side. When the disciples saw the Lord, they became very happy.

After Jesus had greeted them again, he said, "I am sending you, just as the Father has sent me." Then he breathed on them and said, "Receive the Holy Spirit. If you forgive anyone's sins, they will be forgiven. But if you don't forgive their sins, they will not be forgiven."

The gospel of the Lord.

■ REFLECTION

What is Jesus sending the disciples to do? Do I find it easier to forgive others or to hold back my forgiveness?

■ CLOSING

Let us remember these intentions:

Loving and glorious God,
  we praise you with Easter joy
  because Christ is our redeemer.
Christ has broken the power of sin
  and healed an injured world.
Christ has made us whole again.
Bless our celebrations and our joy.
We ask this through Christ our Lord. **Amen.**

Let us pray with the words that Jesus taught us:

Our Father . . .

▶ sing
  "alleluia"

May we live in the light of Christ. **Amen.**

▶ put out
  the candle

MONDAY PRAYER

April 23, 2001

➤ Reminder: If this is the first day after Easter break and you buried the alleluia, raise it before prayer. See page 273.

■ INTRODUCTION

Today we begin the second week of Easter by reading Matthew's account of the morning of the resurrection.

■ A PSALM FOR EARLY EASTERTIME

➤ turn to
page 270

■ READING

Matthew 28:1–3, 5–6, 8–10

Listen to the words of the holy gospel according to Matthew:

It was almost daybreak on Sunday when Mary Magdalene *(MAG-duh-lin)* and the other Mary went to see the tomb. Suddenly a strong earthquake struck, and the Lord's angel came down from heaven. He rolled away the stone and sat on it. The angel looked as bright as lightning, and his clothes were white as snow. The angel said to the women, "Don't be afraid! I know you are looking for Jesus, who was nailed to a cross. He isn't here! God has raised him to life, just as Jesus said he would."

The women were frightened and yet very happy, as they hurried from the tomb and ran to tell his disciples. Suddenly Jesus met them and greeted them. They went near to him, held on to his feet, and worshiped him. Jesus said to them, "Don't be afraid! Tell my followers to go to Galilee. They will see me there."

The gospel of the Lord.

■ REFLECTION

Jesus told his followers to return to their homes in Galilee—and they would see him there. What can that message mean to us?

■ CLOSING

Let us remember these intentions:

Gracious God,
   through the announcement
     of the holy women
   and the preaching of the apostles,
   you bring the good news of your love
     to all the peoples of the earth.
Strengthen us to carry that good news
   in our lives, in our hearts and in our words.
We ask this through Christ our Lord. **Amen.**

Let us pray with the words that Jesus taught us:
Our Father . . .

➤ sing
"alleluia"

May we live in the light of Christ. **Amen.**

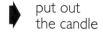

➤ put out
the candle

TUESDAY PRAYER

April 24, 2001

■ INTRODUCTION

Today we remember Mark Rey, a 17th-century priest who was given the name Fidelis *(fee-DAY-lis)*. The name means "faithful," and it suited him well. He was a faithful preacher of the gospel, even when it put him in great danger. He also cared for homeless people and brought the sick into his own home.

■ A PSALM FOR EARLY EASTERTIME

▶ turn to
page 270

■ READING

Luke 24:13–17, 19–23

Listen to the words of the holy gospel according to Luke:

Two of Jesus' disciples were going to the village of Emmaus *(em-MAY-us)*, which was about seven miles from Jerusalem *(juh-ROO-suh-lem)*. As they were talking and thinking about what had happened, Jesus came near and started walking along beside them. But they did not know who he was. Jesus asked them, "What were you talking about as you walked along?"

They answered: "Those things that happened to Jesus from Nazareth *(NAZ-uh-reth)*. By what he did and said he showed that he was a powerful prophet. Then [he was] arrested and sentenced to die on a cross. We had hoped that he would be the one to set Israel free! But it has already been three days since all this happened.

"Some women in our group surprised us. They had gone to the tomb early in the morning, but did not find the body of Jesus. They came back, saying that they had seen a vision of angels who told them that he is alive."

The gospel of the Lord.

■ REFLECTION

How does Jesus walk with his friends today? What do I tell Jesus when I talk with him?

■ CLOSING

Let us remember these intentions:

Loving and glorious God,
    we praise you with Easter joy
    because Christ is our redeemer.
Christ has broken the power of sin
    and healed an injured world.
Christ has made us whole again.
Bless our celebrations and our joy.
We ask this through Christ our Lord. **Amen.**

Let us pray with the words that Jesus taught us:

Our Father . . .

▶ sing
"alleluia"

May we live in the light of Christ. **Amen.**

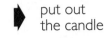
▶ put out
the candle

282

WEDNESDAY PRAYER

April 25, 2001

■ INTRODUCTION

Today is the feast of Saint Mark the evangelist. He traveled with Peter to Rome. He also traveled with Paul and Barnabas to bring the good news to many towns. The first of the four gospels to be written down is named for Mark. It begins, "This is the good news of Jesus Christ." The word gospel means "good news."

Today's reading continues the story of the two disciples who went home in sadness after Jesus died on the cross. They met Jesus on the road, but they did not recognize him.

■ A PSALM FOR EARLY EASTERTIME

➤ turn to
page 270

■ READING

Luke 24:25–29

Listen to the words of the holy gospel according to Luke:

Jesus asked the two disciples, "How can you be so slow to believe all that the prophets said? Didn't you know that the Messiah would have to suffer before he was given his glory?" Jesus then explained everything written about himself in the Scriptures, beginning with the Law of Moses and the Books of the Prophets.

When the two of them came near the village where they were going, Jesus seemed to be going farther. They begged him, "Stay with us! It's already late, and the sun is going down." So Jesus went into the house to stay with them.

The gospel of the Lord.

■ REFLECTION

It's hard to think that suffering and glory go together. Why is that? Am I willing to pay the price in discipline and hard work for things that are important?

■ CLOSING

Let us remember these intentions:

Loving and glorious God,
   we praise you with Easter joy
   because Christ is our redeemer.
In the mystery of his dying and rising
   we learn the good news of your mercy.
Let our voices join with his
   as we sing of your endless glory.
We praise you through Christ our Lord. **Amen.**

Let us pray with the words that Jesus taught us:

Our Father . . .

sing
"alleluia"

May we live in the light of Christ. **Amen.**

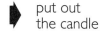
put out
the candle

THURSDAY PRAYER

April 26, 2001

■ INTRODUCTION

The story of the disciples traveling to Emmaus *(em-MAY-us)* tells us something about the mystery of Christ's presence. He is present to us in many ways. The two disciples in the story recognized him in their talk about the scriptures and in the breaking of the bread. This story tells us that Jesus is present with us whenever we talk and pray together about the meaning of Christ's death and resurrection.

■ A PSALM FOR EARLY EASTERTIME

➤ turn to
page 270

■ READING

Luke 24:28–32

Listen to the words of the holy gospel according to Luke:

When the two disciples came near the village where they were going, Jesus seemed to be going farther. They begged him, "Stay with us! It's already late, and the sun is going down." So Jesus went into the house to stay with them.

After Jesus sat down to eat, he took some bread. He blessed it and broke it. Then he gave it to them. At once they knew who he was, but he disappeared. They said to each other, "When he talked with us along the road and explained the Scriptures to us, didn't it warm our hearts?"

The gospel of the Lord.

284

■ REFLECTION

What helped the disciples recognize Jesus? Do I hear the voice of Christ when the scriptures are proclaimed? Do I recognize him when we celebrate the eucharist?

■ CLOSING

Let us remember these intentions:

Loving and gracious God,
    we praise you with Easter joy
    because Christ is our redeemer.
Through the eucharist we live the risen life
    and share the mission of your Son.
Keep us faithful to Jesus,
    who is always with us.
We ask this through Christ our Lord. **Amen.**

Let us pray with the words that Jesus taught us:

Our Father . . .

 sing
"alleluia"

May we live in the light of Christ. **Amen.**

 put out
the candle

FRIDAY PRAYER

April 27, 2001

■ INTRODUCTION

It seems that whenever the disciples see the risen Jesus, at first they do not know who he is. They think he is a stranger or even a ghost! But his words and his actions give him away. Perhaps these stories tell us how to know Jesus when we meet him on the roads we travel.

■ A PSALM FOR EARLY EASTERTIME

turn to
page 270

■ READING

Luke 24:33–39, 46–48

Listen to the words of the holy gospel according to Luke:

The two disciples got right up and returned to Jerusalem [where they] found the eleven apostles and the others gathered together. And they learned from the group that the Lord was really alive and had appeared to Peter. Then the disciples from Emmaus *(em-MAY-us)* told what happened on the road and how they knew he was the Lord when he broke the bread.

While Jesus' disciples were talking about what had happened, Jesus appeared and greeted them. They were frightened and terrified because they thought they were seeing a ghost. But Jesus said, "Why are you so frightened? Ghosts don't have flesh and bones as you see I have."

He told them, "The Scriptures say that the Messiah must suffer, then three days later he will rise from death. They also say that all people of every nation must be told in my name to turn to

God, in order to be forgiven. So beginning in Jerusalem, you must tell everything that has happened.

The gospel of the Lord.

■ REFLECTION

Does Jesus have "flesh and bones" today? Why is it so important to understand the Bible?

■ CLOSING

Let us remember these intentions:

Loving and glorious God,
   we praise you with Easter joy
   because Christ is our redeemer.
Christ has broken the power of sin
    and healed an injured world.
Christ has made us whole again.
Bless our celebrations and our joy.
We ask this through Christ our Lord. **Amen.**

Let us pray with the words that Jesus taught us:

Our Father . . .

sing
"alleluia"

May we live in the light of Christ. **Amen.**

put out
the candle

WEEKLY PRAYER

■ INTRODUCTION

Many stories in the gospels tell of Jesus appearing to the disciples after his resurrection. Each visit strengthened the disciples' faith that Jesus had truly risen, and that he was truly the Messiah. Jesus is still present to his disciples. He shares a meal with us and opens our minds to the meaning of the scriptures.

■ A PSALM FOR EARLY EASTERTIME

turn to
page 270

■ READING

John 21:3–6, 9, 12

Listen to the words of the holy gospel according to John:

Simon Peter said, "I'm going fishing!" The others said, "We'll go with you." They went out in their boat. But they didn't catch a thing that night.

Early the next morning Jesus stood on the shore, but the disciples did not realize who he was. Jesus shouted, "Friends, have you caught anything?" "No!" they answered. So he told them, "Let your net down on the right side of your boat, and you will catch some fish."

They did, and the net was so full of fish that they could not drag it up into the boat.

When the disciples got out of the boat, they saw some bread and a charcoal fire with fish on it. Jesus said, "Come and eat!" But none of the disciples dared ask who he was. They knew he was the Lord.

The gospel of the Lord.

286

■ REFLECTION

How does Jesus feed his people today? Why do some say that the fish in the net symbolize all Christian people? How did the disciples recognize that it was Jesus?

■ CLOSING

Let us remember these intentions:

Loving and glorious God,
   we praise you with Easter joy
   because Christ is our redeemer.
Through the eucharist we live the risen life
   and share the mission of your Son.
Keep us faithful to Jesus,
   who is always with us.
We ask this through Christ our Lord. **Amen.**

Let us pray with the words that Jesus taught us:
Our Father . . .

sing
"alleluia"

May we live in the light of Christ. **Amen.**

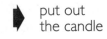
put out
the candle

MONDAY PRAYER

April 30, 2001

■ INTRODUCTION

Tomorrow is May Day! May Day is Halloween in reverse. Instead of collecting treats from neighbors, we can bring them treats. Surprise someone with flowers or a picture or a hug.

At Easter we rejoice that we are joined to the risen Christ through the sacraments of baptism, confirmation and eucharist. These sacraments make us part of the body of Christ, the church. During Eastertime we prayerfully study Christ's action in our lives. This is called "mystagogy" *(MIS-tuh-go-jee)*. This week's readings will help us in this study.

■ A PSALM FOR EARLY EASTERTIME

turn to
page 270

■ READING

John 6:5, 7–9, 11–12

Listen to the words of the holy gospel according to John:

When Jesus saw the large crowd coming toward him, he asked Philip, "Where will we get enough food to feed all these people?" Philip answered, "Don't you know that it would take almost a year's wages just to buy only a little bread for each of these people?" Andrew spoke up and said, "There is a boy here who has five small loaves of barley bread and two fish. But what good is that with all these people?"

Jesus took the bread in his hands and gave thanks to God. Then he passed the bread to the people, and he did the same with the fish, until everyone had plenty to eat. The people ate all they wanted, and Jesus told his disciples to gather up the leftovers, so that nothing would be wasted.

The gospel of the Lord.

■ REFLECTION

What does this story tell us about the eucharist? How does the eucharist join us to the church? Do I receive the eucharist with love and attention?

■ CLOSING

Let us remember these intentions:

Loving and glorious God,
    we praise you with Easter joy
    because Christ is our redeemer.
Through the eucharist we live the risen life
    and share the mission of your Son.
Keep us faithful to Jesus,
    who is always with us.
We ask this through Christ our Lord. **Amen.**

Let us pray with the words that Jesus taught us:
Our Father . . .

sing
"alleluia"

May we live in the light of Christ. **Amen.**

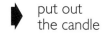
put out
the candle

287

■ INTRODUCTION

Today is the first of May, or May Day. There are many customs about this day. People show love and friendship with baskets of flowers and cookies. In Hawaii, necklaces of flowers, called leis *(LAY-eez)*, are worn. On this day the church honors Saint Joseph the Worker, who supported the holy family in Nazareth *(NAZ-uh-reth)*. This day begins the month which honors Mary as "Queen of Heaven."

Today's reading tells of the days after Jesus was raised to heaven, when his followers were waiting for the coming of the Holy Spirit. It is the last time Mary is mentioned in the Bible.

■ A PSALM FOR EARLY EASTERTIME

➤ turn to
page 270

■ READING

Acts 1:12–14

Listen to the words of the Acts of the Apostles:

The Mount of Olives was about half a mile from Jerusalem. The apostles who had gone there were Peter, John, James, Andrew, Philip, Thomas, Bartholomew *(bar-THAL-uh-mew)*, Matthew, James the son of Alphaeus *(al-FAY-us)*, Simon, known as the Eager One, and Judas the son of James. After the apostles returned to the city, they went upstairs to the room where they had been staying.

The apostles often met together and prayed with a single purpose in mind. The women and

Mary the mother of Jesus would meet with them, and so would his brothers.

The word of the Lord.

■ REFLECTION

Why did the followers of Jesus spend so much time together? What might they have talked about during this time? Do I pray when I know there will be a change in my life?

■ CLOSING

Let us remember these intentions:

Loving and glorious God,
    we praise you with Easter joy
    because Christ is our redeemer.
Through Christ we offer you our lives,
    with Christ we are your children,
    in Christ we bear your name.
Bless our celebrations and our joy.
We ask this through Christ our Lord. **Amen.**

Let us pray with the words that Jesus taught us:
Our Father . . .

➤ sing
"alleluia"

May we live in the light of Christ. **Amen.**

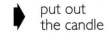

➤ put out
the candle

A May Blessing of an Image of Mary

Use a statue or other image of Mary. A crown of flowers can be prepared to fit on the image. The blessing can begin in one spot (such as a classroom) and move to another (such as the church). Students might carry drawings, flags or pennants, or flowers to put into a vase near the statue. See that any ladders are safe and that lighted candles are out of the way.

 all make
the sign
of the cross

LEADER
Christ is risen, alleluia!

ALL
Christ is truly risen, alleluia!

LEADER
Lord God, you have given us life
    and guided us on our journey.
Be with us as we honor Mary
    in song and prayer.

 all sing a song about Mary
and walk in procession
to the image

READER   Revelation 12:1, 5
Listen to the words of the book of Revelation:

Something important appeared in the sky. It was a woman whose clothes were the sun. The moon was under her feet, and a crown made of twelve stars was on her head.

The woman gave birth to a son, who would rule all the nations with an iron rod. He was taken to God and placed on his throne.

The word of the Lord.

LEADER   adapted from the *Book of Blessings*
My friends,
    today we bless God
    and we honor the Mother of God.
I invite you now
        to hold out your hand in blessing.

 all hold out a hand toward the
image of Mary in blessing,
and the leader says:

Loving God,
    in Mary you have given your church
        a sign of the glory to come.
May those who honor this image of Mary
    look to her as a model of holiness
        for all your people.
We ask this through Christ our Lord.

ALL
Amen.

 crown the image
or honor it with flowers

LEADER
We turn to you for protection,
    holy Mother of God.
Listen to our prayers
    and help us in our needs.
Save us from every danger,
    glorious and blessed Virgin.

ALL

 all make
the sign
of the cross

May 2, 2001

■ INTRODUCTION

Today we remember Saint Athanasius *(ath-uh-NAY-shus)*, a bishop and teacher of the early church. Athanasius lived in Egypt.

When some Christians began to teach that Jesus was not divine, Athanasius was asked to go to the town of Nicea *(nye-SEE-uh)*, where a great council would discuss this question. The council decided to make the faith more clear by writing it in the form of a prayer. You have joined in that prayer many times. It is called the Nicene *(nye-SEEN)* Creed. The church says it every Sunday. Some time today you may want to see how much of it you know by heart.

■ A PSALM FOR EARLY EASTERTIME

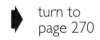

turn to
page 270

■ READING

John 6:27–29, 32–33, 35

Listen to the words of the holy gospel according to John:

Jesus said to the people, "Don't work for food that spoils. Work for food that gives eternal life. The Son of Man will give you this food, because God the Father has given him the right to do so."

"What exactly does God want us to do?" the people asked. Jesus answered, "God wants you to have faith in the one he sent."

Jesus then told them, "My Father is the one who gives you the true bread from heaven. And the bread that God gives is the one who came down from heaven to give life to the world. I am the bread that gives life! No one who comes to me will ever be hungry. No one who has faith in me will ever be thirsty."

The gospel of the Lord.

■ REFLECTION

What could it mean when Jesus calls himself "the bread that gives life"? What could it mean to have faith in Jesus and never be thirsty again?

■ CLOSING

Let us remember these intentions:

Loving and glorious God,
   we praise you with Easter joy
   because Christ is our redeemer.
Through the eucharist we live the risen life
   and share the mission of your Son.
Keep us faithful to Jesus,
   who is always with us.
We ask this through Christ our Lord. **Amen.**

Let us pray with the words that Jesus taught us:

Our Father . . .

sing
"alleluia"

May we live in the light of Christ. **Amen.**

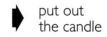

put out
the candle

290

THURSDAY PRAYER

May 3, 2001

■ INTRODUCTION

Today is the feast of the apostles Philip and James. Apostles are important signs that the church has received the true teaching of Jesus. This teaching has been handed down to us from the people who learned these teachings from Jesus himself.

■ A PSALM FOR EARLY EASTERTIME

turn to
page 270

■ READING

Acts 8:26–27, 29–31, 35, 37–38

Listen to the words of the Acts of the Apostles:

The Lord's angel said to Philip, "Go south along the desert road that leads from Jerusalem to Gaza." So Philip left.

An important Ethiopian *(ee-thee-OH-pee-un)* official happened to be going along that road in his chariot *(CHAIR-ee-ut)*. The Spirit told Philip to catch up with the chariot. Philip ran up close and heard the man reading aloud from the book of Isaiah. Philip asked him, "Do you understand what you are reading?"

The official answered, "How can I understand unless someone helps me?" So Philip began at this place in the Scriptures and explained the good news about Jesus.

The official said, "Look! Here is some water. Why can't I be baptized?" He ordered the chariot to stop. Then they both went down into the water, and Philip baptized him.

The word of the Lord.

■ REFLECTION

Do you think a person can come to know Jesus without knowing the Bible? What connections can you see between this story and the story of the disciples on the road to Emmaus?

■ CLOSING

Let us remember these intentions:

Loving and glorious God,
    we praise you with Easter joy
    because Christ is our redeemer.
Through baptism we receive the risen life
    and share the mission of your Son.
Keep us faithful to Jesus,
    who is always with us.
We ask this through Christ our Lord. **Amen.**

Let us pray with the words that Jesus taught us:
Our Father . . .

sing
"alleluia"

May we live in the light of Christ. **Amen.**

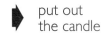
put out
the candle

291

FRIDAY PRAYER

May 4, 2001

■ INTRODUCTION

During this week, our readings have been about a claim that Jesus made. It was so unusual, so strange, that many turned away from him. Even today many people find it too hard to believe. It is the claim that Jesus is present in the bread and wine of the eucharist *(YOU-kuh-rist),* and that those who share in the eucharist share in his eternal life.

■ A PSALM FOR EARLY EASTERTIME

▶ turn to
page 270

■ READING

John 6:48, 50, 51, 66–69

Listen to the words of the holy gospel according to John:

Jesus told the people, "I am the bread that gives life! The bread from heaven has come down, so that no one who eats it will ever die. My flesh is the life-giving bread that I give to the people of this world."

Because of what Jesus said, many of his disciples turned their backs on him and stopped following him. Jesus then asked his twelve disciples if they were going to leave him. Simon Peter answered, "Lord, there is no one else that we can go to! Your words give eternal life. We have faith in you, and we are sure that you are God's Holy One."

The gospel of the Lord.

■ REFLECTION

What does it mean that Jesus is the "bread that gives life"? Why do some people turn away from Jesus today? Do our actions show we believe Jesus is "God's Holy One"?

■ CLOSING

Let us remember these intentions:

Loving and glorious God,
    we praise you with Easter joy
    because Christ is our redeemer.
Through the eucharist we live the risen life
    and share the mission of your Son.
Keep us faithful to Jesus,
    who is always with us.
We ask this through Christ our Lord. **Amen.**

Let us pray with the words that Jesus taught us:
Our Father . . .

▶ sing
"alleluia"

May we live in the light of Christ. **Amen.**

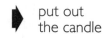
▶ put out
the candle

WEEKLY PRAYER

With a Reading from the Gospel for Sunday, May 6, 2001

Reminder: You may want to make copies of the Psalm for Late Easter. It is on page 302.

■ INTRODUCTION

On Sunday, May 6, we hear the Easter gospel in which Jesus speaks of himself as the shepherd of God's people.

A good shepherd stays close to the sheep and pays attention to them. This way the shepherd can protect them from falling down rocky hillsides or being attacked by wolves. The shepherd knows where the best pastures are and where there is clean water to drink. The sheep could not survive without the shepherd's care, and so they learn to recognize the special sound of their own shepherd's call.

This is a week to rejoice that God has given us Jesus as our savior and our shepherd.

■ A PSALM FOR EARLY EASTERTIME

turn to
page 270

■ READING

John 10:27–30

Listen to the words of the holy gospel according to John:

Jesus said to his disciples:

"My sheep know my voice, and I know them. They follow me, and I give them eternal life, so that they will never be lost. No one can snatch them out of my hand. My Father gave them to me, and he is greater than all others. No one can snatch them from his hands, and I am one with the Father."

The gospel of the Lord.

■ REFLECTION

What could possibly snatch us away from Jesus? How well do we know Jesus, our shepherd? Is there something that I think Jesus does not know about me? How can I tell him?

■ CLOSING

Let us remember these intentions:

Loving and glorious God,
we praise you with Easter joy
because Christ is our redeemer.
We pray that divisions among peoples be ended,
and that all become united
in the flock of Jesus, the Good Shepherd.
We ask this through Christ our Lord. **Amen.**

Let us pray with the words that Jesus taught us:
Our Father . . .

sing
"alleluia"

May we live in the light of Christ. **Amen.**

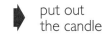

put out
the candle

MONDAY PRAYER

May 7, 2001

■ INTRODUCTION

This week's readings are from the Acts of the Apostles. This book of the Bible tells about the days and years just after the resurrection of Jesus. It was written by the author of the gospel of Luke, and it is sometimes called a "travel story." In Luke's gospel Jesus travels from Galilee to Jerusalem. In the Acts of the Apostles the church of Jesus travels from Jerusalem to Rome, the center of the world of that time.

■ A PSALM FOR EARLY EASTERTIME

➤ turn to page 270

■ READING

Acts 1:3–5

Listen to the words of the Acts of the Apostles:

For forty days after Jesus had suffered and died, he proved in many ways that he had been raised from death. He appeared to his apostles and spoke to them about God's kingdom.

While he was still with them, he said, "Don't leave Jerusalem yet. Wait here for the Father to give you the Holy Spirit, just as I told you he has promised to do. John baptized with water, but in a few days you will be baptized with the Holy Spirit."

The word of the Lord.

■ REFLECTION

Why did the apostles need the Holy Spirit? Why should Christians wait for the Holy Spirit before beginning their ministry? How do we know if we have been "baptized with the Holy Spirit"?

■ CLOSING

Let us all say:
Christ, our light and our salvation!
Christ, our light and our salvation!

You are the sun that shines on everyone,
 the day that knows no ending:
Christ, our light and our salvation!

You are the springtime of the universe
 and the savior of the world:
Christ, our light and our salvation!

Let us remember these intentions:

Let us pray with the words that Jesus taught us:
Our Father . . .

➤ sing
 "alleluia"

May we live in the light of Christ. **Amen.**

➤ put out
 the candle

TUESDAY PRAYER

May 8, 2001

■ INTRODUCTION

This is World Red Cross Day. Since 1864 this society has provided emergency food and medical care for people all over the world. In times of war they care for people without choosing sides. The red cross on the white banner tells people where to turn for help.

■ A PSALM FOR EARLY EASTERTIME

 turn to page 270

■ READING

Acts 2:1–4, 6–7, 11

Listen to the words of the Acts of the Apostles:

On the day of Pentecost all the Lord's followers were together in one place. Suddenly there was a noise from heaven like the sound of a mighty wind! It filled the house where they were meeting. Then they saw what looked like fiery tongues moving in all directions, and a tongue came and settled on each person there. The Holy Spirit took control of everyone, and they began speaking whatever languages the Spirit let them speak.

When they heard this noise, a crowd gathered. But they were surprised, because they were hearing everything in their own languages. They were excited and amazed, and said: "Don't all these who are speaking come from Galilee *(GAL-uh-lee)*? Yet we all hear them using our own languages to tell the wonderful things God has done."

The word of the Lord.

■ REFLECTION

Why are wind and fire good symbols of the Holy Spirit? What are some other stories from the Bible that use these symbols?

■ CLOSING

Let us all say:
Christ, our light and our salvation!
Christ, our light and our salvation!

You are the sun that shines on everyone,
  the day that knows no ending:
Christ, our light and our salvation!

You are the springtime of the universe
  and the savior of the world:
Christ, our light and our salvation!

Let us remember these intentions:

Let us pray with the words that Jesus taught us:
Our Father . . .

 sing "alleluia"

May we live in the light of Christ. **Amen.**

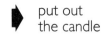 put out the candle

■ INTRODUCTION

When the Holy Spirit came to the disciples on Pentecost, they began to preach boldly. Peter told the crowd that Jesus had been raised from death, and that he was with his followers now in his Spirit. This is the heart of all Christian teaching. It is the message that our parents, teachers and pastors have handed on to us. It is a message that never changes.

■ A PSALM FOR EARLY EASTERTIME

turn to
page 270

■ READING

Acts 2:1, 14, 22–24, 33

Listen to the words of the Acts of the Apostles:

On the day of Pentecost, Peter stood with the eleven apostles and spoke in a loud and clear voice to the crowd. "Now, listen to what I have to say about Jesus from Nazareth. God proved that he sent Jesus to you by having him work miracles, wonders, and signs. All of you know this. Evil men put him to death on a cross. But God set him free from death and raised him to life. Death could not hold him in its power.

"Jesus was taken up to sit at the right side of God, and he was given the Holy Spirit, just as the Father had promised. Jesus is also the one who has given the Spirit to us, and that is what you are now seeing and hearing."

The word of the Lord.

■ REFLECTION

Are we able to say what we believe in a "loud and clear voice"? Does the good news of Jesus still fill our church with excitement?

■ CLOSING

Let us all say:
Christ, our light and our salvation!
Christ, our light and our salvation!

You are the sun that shines on everyone,
    the day that knows no ending:
Christ, our light and our salvation!

You are the springtime of the universe
    and the savior of the world:
Christ, our light and our salvation!

Let us remember these intentions:

Let us pray with the words that Jesus taught us:
Our Father . . .

sing
"alleluia"

May we live in the light of Christ. **Amen.**

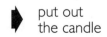
put out
the candle

THURSDAY PRAYER

May 10, 2001

■ INTRODUCTION

The warm sunny days of May multiply the flowers and deepen the green of leaves and grass. May is a good month for poets and for picnics. The beauty of nature is reflected in the spirit of Eastertime.

We are counting the 50 Days of Easter, just as the Jewish people are counting 50 days from Passover to the feast of Weeks. Fifty days are about one-seventh of the year, just as the Sabbath is one-seventh of the week.

■ A PSALM FOR EARLY EASTERTIME

turn to
page 270

■ READING

Acts 2:37–39, 41–42

Listen to the words of the Acts of the Apostles:

When the people heard [what Peter said], they were very upset. They asked Peter and the other apostles, "Friends, what shall we do?"

Peter said, "Turn back to God! Be baptized in the name of Jesus Christ, so that your sins will be forgiven. Then you will be given the Holy Spirit. This promise is for you and your children. It is for everyone our Lord God will choose, no matter where they live."

On that day about three thousand believed his message and were baptized. They spent their time learning from the apostles, and they were like family to each other. They also broke bread and prayed together.

The word of the Lord.

■ REFLECTION

Have I ever heard something and wanted to act on it right away? What does the phrase "no matter where they live" mean? How are the members of my parish "like family to each other"?

■ CLOSING

Let us all say:
Christ, our light and our salvation!
Christ, our light and our salvation!

You are the sun that shines on everyone,
 the day that knows no ending:
Christ, our light and our salvation!

You are the springtime of the universe
 and the savior of the world:
Christ, our light and our salvation!

Let us remember these intentions:

Let us pray with the words that Jesus taught us:
Our Father . . .

sing
"alleluia"

May we live in the light of Christ. **Amen.**

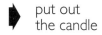
put out
the candle

297

FRIDAY PRAYER

May 11, 2001

■ INTRODUCTION

On Friday, Saturday and Sunday of this week, farmers and gardeners watch their fields, ready to protect their plants from a late frost. A very old legend names the "Three Freezing Saints" as the culprits on these three days of danger. They are Saints Mamertus *(muh-MER-tus)*, Pancras *(PAN-krus)* and Servatus *(ser-VAH-tus)*.

After May 13th, the legend says, the weather will be kind, and new plants can be set out.

■ A PSALM FOR EARLY EASTERTIME

turn to
page 270

■ READING

Acts 2:43–47

Listen to the words of the Acts of the Apostles:

Everyone was amazed by the many miracles and wonders that the apostles worked. All the Lord's followers often met together, and they shared everything they had. They would sell their property and possessions and give the money to whomever needed it.

Day after day they met together in the temple. They broke bread together in different homes and shared their food happily and freely, while praising God. Everyone liked them, and each day the Lord added to their group others who were being saved.

The word of the Lord.

298

■ REFLECTION

How does this picture of Christian life compare with life in our class? our school? our parish? How can I help my family live this way? What does it mean that they "broke bread together in different homes"?

■ CLOSING

Let us all say:
Christ, our light and our salvation!
Christ, our light and our salvation!

You are the sun that shines on everyone,
the day that knows no ending:
Christ, our light and our salvation!

You are the springtime of the universe
and the savior of the world:
Christ, our light and our salvation!

Let us remember these intentions:

Let us pray with the words that Jesus taught us:
Our Father . . .

sing
"alleluia"

May we live in the light of Christ. **Amen.**

put out
the candle

LATE
EASTERTIME

Sunday, May 13 to Sunday, June 3

LATE EASTERTIME 2001

■ ABOUT THE SEASON

Easter came quite late this year. Springtime is almost over and the days are sunny and warm. The gardens have provided flowers to decorate the "May altars" we have prepared to honor Mary, the Mother of God. We do not need our sweaters or raincoats as

LOOKING AHEAD

much and in many places, softball and T-ball practice have already begun.

May has been full of life and beauty and activity. And for some of us or our friends, it has been the time for confirmation and first communion. We have seen an Eastertime filled with natural joy and wonders, as well as God's message of resurrection and new life. There are many reasons for us to sing "alleluia!"

May is generous with days of celebration. Sunday, May 13, is Mother's Day. On Thursday, May 24, we will celebrate the Ascension of the Lord (although in some states, it is kept on the following Sunday). Monday, May 29, is Memorial Day, when our nation remembers those who have died in war. And then the feast of the Visit of Mary to her cousin Elizabeth, on May 31, will bring May to an end.

■ WE CELEBRATE THE COMING OF THE HOLY SPIRIT AT PENTECOST ON SUNDAY, JUNE 3, WHICH ENDS THE EASTER SEASON. The nine days before Pentecost are a time of preparation. It is a time for each of us to prepare our hearts and perhaps our world, too, for the coming of the Spirit.

The risen Jesus helped his disciples realize that he would always be with them. He spoke to them of the coming of the Holy Spirit, who would be God's everlasting presence. The disciples were to wait for the coming of the Spirit and then do as the Spirit guided them. The Holy Spirit brings God's gifts of love, unity and wisdom.

The Holy Spirit has been with each of us and with our class during this school year. Through the power of that Spirit we have been able to care about each

other and grow in respect for each other. In the power of that Spirit we have been able to grow in our love of God and in our ability to see Christ in others. In the power of that Spirit we have prayed and worked for people in need.

The book of Isaiah tells about the Spirit that will rest upon God's servants. Isaiah says it will be a spirit of understanding, wisdom and insight, of counsel and strength, and of knowledge and the fear of the Lord.

When people prepare for the sacrament of confirmation, they learn about the gifts of the Spirit. These gifts are promised to all who join Jesus in doing the work of God.

■ OUR READINGS FOR DAILY PRAYER ARE TAKEN FROM THE ACTS OF THE APOSTLES. We follow the adventures of the first Christians as they spread the good news and learn to live with both persecution and acceptance.

There are readings about the first martyr, Saint Stephen, and about the missionary team of Paul and Barnabas. All these readings focus on the role of the Holy Spirit. The Acts of the Apostles is often called the "gospel of the Holy Spirit."

■ PREPARATION FOR LATE EASTERTIME

We have a new Psalm, a new Meal Prayer and a new End of the Day Prayer. They are on pages 302, 303 and 304. If you do not use the booklet *Blessed Be God!* you may want to make copies for the class.

■ IS THE PRAYER CENTER STILL FRESH AND BEAUTIFUL FOR EASTERTIME? Does it have signs of new life and resurrection? Do we have a bowl of fresh water there to help us remember the Easter sacrament of baptism?

A drop of perfume or scented oil can be added to the Easter water to remind us of chrism. Chrism is a

fragrant oil that is put on our heads after we are baptized and when we are confirmed. Chrism makes us a new Christ, because the word "Christ" means "anointed one."

▪ DURING MAY, MANY PEOPLE REMEMBER MARY, THE MOTHER OF GOD, IN THEIR PRAYER. Our Meal Prayer, the *Regina Caeli*, brings Mary into our Easter celebration. There is also a ceremony on page 289 for blessing and crowning an image of Mary.

If you have placed an image of Mary in the prayer center, you might replace it with a different one for the final days of May. Find a picture that you have not seen before. There are many beautiful pictures and carvings of Mary from every part of the church's history, and from every country where the gospel has been preached.

▪ THE ASCENSION OF THE LORD: In some parts of our country, the Ascension is celebrated on Sunday, June 3. In other states, the Ascension is kept as usual on Thursday, May 24. The Daily Prayer on page 315 can be used on May 24, whether or not we celebrate the Ascension that day.

Where it is celebrated on a Thursday, Ascension is a holy day of obligation. This means that Catholics gather to celebrate the eucharist on that day. If we will celebrate Mass during school on that Thursday, we may want to skip or shorten Daily Prayer.

▪ THE END OF THE SCHOOL YEAR is not far away! If your classes end before June 1, don't forget the Blessing before Summer Vacation, on page 331.

▪ SUGGESTED HYMNS: "Shout for joy" (page 178 in the *Hymnal for Catholic Students*) is a carol. "The Lord, the Lord, the Lord is my shepherd" (page 194 in the hymnal) is an African American spiritual that can be sung with tambourines, sleigh bells and clapping. See the other suggestions for Eastertime, found on page 269.

A fine song for the end of Eastertime is "Lord, you give the great commission" (page 156 in the

hymnal). "Sing with all the saints in glory" (page 184 in the hymnal) uses the same melody.

A song for the Ascension is "Alleluia, sing to Jesus" (page 106 in the hymnal). Sing this hymn like a dance, with one strong beat in each measure.

To prepare for Pentecost, sing "O breathe on me, O breath of God" (page 162 in the hymnal). This Irish melody can be sung as a round. The Holy Spirit is sometimes called "God's breath." That is what the Latin word *spiritus* means.

■ THE SCHOOL OF RELIGION

The readings for Weekly Prayer follow the Sunday gospels. We hear about Jesus' gift and command of love, about the promised Spirit, about our unity in Christ, and finally, about the coming of the Holy Spirit on Pentecost.

You may want to use the prayer for Ascension Day (page 315) no matter what day you meet between May 21 and May 27.

▪ MANY STUDENTS LIKE TO HONOR MARY DURING MAY. You might place flowers before an icon of Mary, say the rosary or hold a "May Crowning" procession (see page 289).

▪ WHETHER THE FINAL CLASS ENDS WITH A PARTY OR NOT, DON'T FORGET THE BLESSING BEFORE SUMMER VACATION. It is found on page 331. You might be able to take *Blessed be God!* home for the summer if you have been using it in class. You and your families can pray together during the summer and ask God's blessings on this wonderful season.

A PSALM FOR LATE EASTERTIME

> all make
> the sign
> of the cross

Psalm 23:1–6

LEADER Christ is risen like the sun, alleluia!

ALL **The light of Christ shines
over the whole world, alleluia!**

> light a candle,
> and then say:

LEADER The Lord is my shepherd, all that I need,
giving me rest in green and pleasant fields,

ALL **reviving my life by finding fresh water,
guiding my ways with a shepherd's care.**

SIDE A Though I should walk in death's dark valley,
I fear no evil with you by my side.
Your shepherd's staff comforts me.

SIDE B You spread my table in sight of my foes,
anoint my head, my cup runs over.
You tend me with love always loyal.
I dwell with you, Lord, as long as I live.

LEADER The Lord is my shepherd, all that I need,
giving me rest in green and pleasant fields,

ALL **reviving my life by finding fresh water,
guiding my ways with a shepherd's care.**

**Glory to the Father, and to the Son,
and to the Holy Spirit:
as it was in the beginning, is now,
and will be for ever. Amen. Alleluia.**

> turn back to
> Daily Prayer or Weekly Prayer
> for today

LATE EASTERTIME

LEADER   Let us offer God praise and thanksgiving:

ALL   ▶   all make
            the sign
            of the cross

LEADER   Christ is risen, alleluia!
ALL   **Christ is truly risen, alleluia!**

LEADER   O Queen of heaven, rejoice:
ALL   **Alleluia.**

LEADER   For he to whom you once gave birth:
ALL   **Alleluia.**

LEADER   Has risen as he promised:
ALL   **Alleluia.**

LEADER   Pray for us to God:
ALL   **Alleluia.**

LEADER   Rejoice and be glad, O Virgin Mary, alleluia.
ALL   **For the Lord has truly risen, alleluia.**

LEADER   God, through the resurrection of your Son,
           our Lord Jesus Christ,
        you gave joy to the world.
      Now through the prayer of his mother,
          the Virgin Mary,
        may we gain the joys of everlasting life.
      We ask this in the name of Jesus the Lord.
ALL   **Amen.**

  all make
       the sign
       of the cross

The *Regina Caeli*, from *A Book of Prayers*

LATE EASTERTIME

END OF THE DAY PRAYER

> all make
> the sign
> of the cross

LEADER Christ is risen like the sun, alleluia!

ALL **The light of Christ shines
over the whole world, alleluia!**

> light a candle,
> and then say:

LEADER Come, Holy Spirit,
fill the hearts of your faithful.

ALL **And kindle in them the fire of your love.**

LEADER Send forth your Spirit
and they shall be created.

ALL **And you will renew the face of the earth.**

LEADER Gracious God,
send your Spirit into the church
to strengthen the hearts of all who believe.
And send your Spirit into the world
to fulfill the work of the gospel.
We ask this through Christ our Lord.

ALL **Amen.**

LEADER ▶ hold out one hand
toward everyone
in blessing, and say:

May we live in the light of Christ:

ALL ▶ all make
the sign
of the cross

> ▶ at the end of prayer,
> put out the candle

WEEKLY PRAYER

With a Reading from the Gospel for Sunday, May 13, 2001

 Reminder: The Psalm for Late Eastertime is on page 37 in *Blessed Be God!*

■ INTRODUCTION

May is one of the most beautiful months. In most places, bright flowers and green leaves are everywhere. The world seems filled with life.

This is a good time for Mother's Day, because mothers are people who give life. They try to see that their children are fed, healed, comforted and protected. No one is a perfect mother, but most do the best they can.

This week we can give thanks for our mothers, stepmothers, grandmothers, godmothers, aunts, and anyone who is like a mother to us.

■ A PSALM FOR LATE EASTERTIME

 turn to page 302

■ READING

John 13: 31, 33–35

Listen to the words of the holy gospel according to John:

After Judas had gone, Jesus said, "My children, I will be with you for a little while longer. Then you will look for me, but you won't find me. I tell you just as I told the people, 'You cannot go where I am going.'

"But I am giving you a new command. You must love each other, just as I have loved you. If you love each other, everyone will know that you are my disciples."

The gospel of the Lord.

■ REFLECTION

Have I made these words of Jesus a rule that I always keep? Would someone who saw us know by our love that we are disciples of Jesus?

■ CLOSING

Let us all say:
Christ, our light and our salvation!
Christ, our light and our salvation!

You are the sun that shines on everyone,
    the day that knows no ending:
Christ, our light and our salvation!

You are the springtime of the universe
    and the savior of the world:
Christ, our light and our salvation!

Let us remember these intentions:

Let us pray with the words that Jesus taught us:
Our Father . . .

 sing "alleluia"

May we live in the light of Christ. **Amen.**

 put out the candle

MONDAY PRAYER

May 14, 2001

■ INTRODUCTION

Today is the feast of Saint Matthias *(muth-EYE-us)*. He was chosen as an apostle to take the place of Judas, who betrayed Jesus. We will read about his election today.

It was important to the early church to bring the number of apostles back to 12. Jews traced their family connections to the tribes that descended from the 12 sons of Jacob. Therefore 12 became a symbol of the complete or entire community.

■ A PSALM FOR LATE EASTERTIME

turn to
page 302

■ READING

Acts 1:15–17, 21, 24–26

Listen to the words of the Acts of the Apostles:

One day there were about one hundred twenty of the Lord's followers meeting together, and Peter stood up to speak to them.

He said, "My friends, Judas was one of us and had worked with us, but he brought the mob to arrest Jesus. So we need someone else to help us tell others that Jesus has been raised from death."

Then they all prayed, "Lord, you know what everyone is like! Show us the one you have chosen to be an apostle and to serve in place of Judas." They drew names, and Matthias *(muh-THI-us)* was chosen to join the group of the eleven apostles.

The word of the Lord.

■ REFLECTION

Do most people I know pray before an election? How are leaders of the church chosen in our own day?

■ CLOSING

Let us remember these intentions:

Loving and glorious God,
we praise you with Easter joy
because Christ is our redeemer.
Through him apostles have been called,
and sent to the whole world.
We welcome those who bring your good news.
We pray for them and listen to their teaching.
Call on us, one day, to become apostles, too.
We ask this through Christ our Lord. **Amen.**

Let us pray with the words that Jesus taught us:

Our Father . . .

sing
"alleluia"

May we live in the light of Christ. **Amen.**

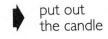
put out
the candle

TUESDAY PRAYER

May 15, 2001

■ INTRODUCTION

Today we remember a married couple, Saints Isidore and Maria. They lived near the city of Madrid, in Spain, in the twelfth century. Although they were poor, Maria and Isidore always shared what they had with those in greater need. Isidore did farm labor, praying as he worked on the land each day. Today let us join Isidore the Farmer and his wife Maria in thanking God for the good earth and its bounty.

Perhaps one way we can celebrate this day would be to plant something bright or tasty.

■ A PSALM FOR LATE EASTERTIME

turn to
page 302

■ READING

Acts 5:14–21

Listen to the words of the Acts of the Apostles:

Many men and women started having faith in the Lord. Then sick people were brought out to the road and placed on cots and mats. It was hoped that Peter would walk by, and his shadow would fall on them and heal them. A lot of people living in the towns near Jerusalem *(juh-ROO-suh-lem)* brought those who were sick or troubled by evil spirits, and they were all healed.

The [officials] became jealous. They arrested the apostles and put them in the city jail. But that night an angel from the Lord opened the doors of the jail and led the apostles out. The angel said, "Go to the temple and tell the people everything about this new life." So they went into the temple before sunrise and started teaching.

The word of the Lord.

■ REFLECTION

Why does it surprise us that those who are close to Jesus could heal others, as Jesus did? Why were the officials jealous? How does jealousy usually affect people my age? Has jealousy ever led me to be unjust?

■ CLOSING

Let us remember these intentions:

O God, from the beginning,
    the earth has produced plants of every kind.
During this growing season,
    give us seeds and soil, sunshine and rain,
    so there may be food for us
    and for all your creatures.
We ask this through Christ our Lord. **Amen.**

Let us pray with the words that Jesus taught us:
Our Father . . .

sing
"alleluia"

May we live in the light of Christ. **Amen.**

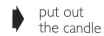
put out
the candle

WEDNESDAY PRAYER

May 16, 2001

■ INTRODUCTION

In today's reading we will meet Stephen. He was one of seven men chosen to handle the business affairs of the Christian community. Stephen spoke both Greek and Hebrew, and he was probably an important man in town.

■ A PSALM FOR LATE EASTERTIME

▶ turn to
page 302

■ READING

Acts 6:1–2, 3, 5, 6, 8

Listen to the words of the Acts of the Apostles:

A lot of people were now becoming followers of the Lord. But some of the ones who spoke Greek started complaining about the ones who spoke Aramaic *(ar-uh-MAY-ick)*. They complained that the Greek-speaking widows were not given their share when the food supplies were handed out each day.

The twelve apostles called the whole group of followers together and said, "My friends, choose seven men who are respected and wise and filled with God's Spirit. We will put them in charge of these things."

This suggestion pleased everyone, and they began by choosing Stephen. Then the apostles prayed and placed their hands on the men to show that they had been chosen to do this work. God gave Stephen the power to work great miracles and wonders among the people.

The word of the Lord.

■ REFLECTION

Is it surprising that people who are committed to Jesus can still argue about such things as food? How are disagreements settled among my friends? Do I try to cooperate and settle things fairly in my family?

■ CLOSING

Let us remember these intentions:

Loving and glorious God,
    we praise you with Easter joy
    because Christ is our redeemer.
Through him apostles have been called,
    and sent to the whole world.
We welcome those who bring your good news.
We pray for them and listen to their teaching.
Call on us, one day, to become apostles, too.
We ask this through Christ our Lord. **Amen.**

Let us pray with the words that Jesus taught us:

Our Father . . .

▶ sing
"alleluia"

May we live in the light of Christ. **Amen.**

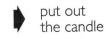
▶ put out
the candle

308

THURSDAY PRAYER

May 17, 2001

■ INTRODUCTION

Today we continue the story of Stephen. When his enemies complained to the officials, Stephen was arrested. In a fine speech he explained that Jesus was the Messiah promised by God. Many did not believe him, and they were upset that Stephen would mislead people. The punishment for false teaching was death by stoning.

Our reading begins at the end of his speech.

■ A PSALM FOR LATE EASTERTIME

▶ turn to
page 302

■ READING

Acts 7:54–60

Listen to the words of the Acts of the Apostles:

When the council members heard Stephen's speech, they were angry and furious. But Stephen was filled with the Holy Spirit. He looked toward heaven, where he saw our glorious God and Jesus standing at his right side. Then Stephen said, "I see heaven open and the Son of Man standing at the right side of God!"

The council members shouted and covered their ears. At once they all attacked Stephen and dragged him out of the city. Then they started throwing stones at him. As Stephen was being stoned to death, he called out, "Lord Jesus, please welcome me!" He knelt down and shouted, "Lord, don't blame them for what they have done." Then he died.

The word of the Lord.

■ REFLECTION

How is the death of Stephen like the death of Jesus? Why is it sometimes difficult to accept the message that prophets bring?

■ CLOSING

Let us remember these intentions:

Loving and glorious God,
we praise you with Easter joy
because Christ is our redeemer.
Through him apostles have been called,
and sent to the whole world.
We welcome those who bring your good news.
We pray for them and listen to their teaching.
Call on us, one day, to become apostles, too.
We ask this through Christ our Lord. **Amen.**

Let us pray with the words that Jesus taught us:

Our Father . . .

▶ sing
"alleluia"

May we live in the light of Christ. **Amen.**

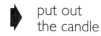
▶ put out
the candle

FRIDAY PRAYER

May 18, 2001

■ INTRODUCTION

On this day 81 years ago, Karol Wojtyla *(KAR-ul voy-TEE-wuh)* was born in Poland. He studied in drama school and in the seminary. He became a priest and then a bishop. In 1978 Bishop Wojtyla was elected our 263rd pope. He chose the name John Paul II. Let us remember Pope John Paul in our prayers today.

■ A PSALM FOR LATE EASTERTIME

▶ turn to
page 302

■ READING

Acts 8:1–4

Listen to the words of the Acts of the Apostles:

Some faithful followers of the Lord buried Stephen and mourned very much for him.

At that time the church in Jerusalem *(juh-ROO-suh-lem)* suffered terribly. All of the Lord's followers, except the apostles, were scattered everywhere in Judea *(joo-DEE-uh)* and Samaria *(suh-MAIR-ee-uh)*. Saul started making a lot of trouble for the church. He went from house to house, arresting men and women and putting them in jail.

The Lord's followers who had been scattered went from place to place, telling the good news.

The word of the Lord.

■ REFLECTION

Where in our world today are people being persecuted for their beliefs? How do people of different ethnic or religious groups treat each other in my school? my neighborhood? Have I ever been treated badly because of what I believe?

■ CLOSING

Let us remember these intentions:

Loving and glorious God,
    we praise you with Easter joy
    because Christ is our redeemer.
Through him apostles have been called,
    and sent to the whole world.
We welcome those who bring your good news.
We pray for them and listen to their teaching.
Call on us, one day, to become apostles, too.
We ask this through Christ our Lord. **Amen.**

Let us pray with the words that Jesus taught us:

Our Father . . .

sing
"alleluia"

May we live in the light of Christ. **Amen.**

put out
the candle

310

WEEKLY PRAYER

With a Reading from the Gospel for Sunday, May 20, 2001

■ INTRODUCTION

Have you ever wanted to see God, just to know for sure that God has not forgotten about you? Jesus knew that his followers would sometimes be lonely and discouraged. So he promised to be with them. He promised them his Spirit, and he promised them his peace. Today's reading strengthens us for the times when God may seem far away.

■ A PSALM FOR LATE EASTERTIME

➤ turn to
page 302

■ READING

John 14:23–24, 25–27, 29

Listen to the words of the holy gospel according to John:

Jesus said, "If anyone loves me, they will obey me. Then my Father will love them, and we will come to them and live in them. But anyone who doesn't love me, won't obey me.

"I have told you these things while I am still with you. But the Holy Spirit will come and help you, because the Father will send the Spirit to take my place. The Spirit will teach you everything and will remind you of what I said while I was with you.

"I give you peace, the kind of peace that only I can give. It isn't like the peace that this world can give. So don't be worried or afraid.

"I am telling you this before I leave, so that when it does happen, you will have faith in me."

The gospel of the Lord.

■ REFLECTION

Jesus says that he and the Father will make a home with those who keep his word. Can I imagine God living with me? Am I prepared?

■ CLOSING

Let us all say:
Christ, our light and our salvation!
Christ, our light and our salvation!

You are the sun that shines on everyone,
  the day that knows no ending:
Christ, our light and our salvation!

You are the springtime of the universe
  and the savior of the world:
Christ, our light and our salvation!

Let us remember these intentions:

Let us pray with the words that Jesus taught us:
Our Father . . .

➤ sing
"alleluia"

May we live in the light of Christ. **Amen.**

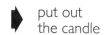

➤ put out
the candle

MONDAY PRAYER

May 21, 2001

■ INTRODUCTION

In today's reading we learn more about Saul. At first, he believed that those who followed Jesus were turning away from the true God. But after he had a vision of Jesus he became a Christian. We know him as Saint Paul.

■ A PSALM FOR LATE EASTERTIME

 turn to page 302

■ READING

Acts 9:1–9

Listen to the words of the Acts of the Apostles:

Saul kept on threatening to kill the Lord's followers. He even went to the high priest and asked for letters to their leaders in Damascus. He did this because he wanted to arrest and take to Jerusalem any man or woman who had accepted the Lord's Way. When Saul had almost reached Damascus, a bright light from heaven suddenly flashed around him. He fell to the ground and heard a voice that said, "Saul! Saul! Why are you so cruel to me?"

"Who are you?" Saul asked.

"I am Jesus," the Lord answered. "I am the one you are so cruel to. Now get up and go into the city, where you will be told what to do."

The men with Saul stood there speechless. They had heard the voice, but they had not seen anyone. Saul got up from the ground, and when he opened his eyes, he could not see a thing. Someone then led him by the hand to Damascus, and for three days he was blind.

The word of the Lord.

■ REFLECTION

Why did Jesus say, "You are cruel to me," instead of, "You are cruel to my people"? What is the meaning of Saul's blindness? Have I ever done something cruel because I was blind to truth?

■ CLOSING

Let us remember these intentions:

Loving and glorious God,
  we praise you with Easter joy
  because Christ is our redeemer.
Through him you heal our blindness
  so that we may see you in every person
    and delight in the wonders of your world.
Open our eyes
  to the goodness of our friends
    and to the harm we sometimes do.
We ask this through Christ our Lord. **Amen.**

Let us pray with the words that Jesus taught us:

Our Father . . .

 sing "alleluia"

May we live in the light of Christ. **Amen.**

put out
the candle

TUESDAY PRAYER

May 22, 2001

■ INTRODUCTION

Today's reading tells us more about the early Christians. They spoke about Jesus in meeting places and among neighbors.

We, too, share our enthusiasm for Jesus. We should not be ashamed to let others know that we live according to the word we have received.

■ A PSALM FOR LATE EASTERTIME

▶ turn to page 302

■ READING

Acts 9:10, 11, 13–15, 17–18, 20

Listen to the words of the Acts of the Apostles:

The Lord spoke to Ananias *(an-uh-NYE-us)* in a vision. "Get up and go to the house of Judas on Straight Street. When you get there, you will find a man named Saul from the city of Tarsus."

Ananias replied, "Lord, a lot of people have told me about the terrible things this man has done to your followers in Jerusalem *(juh-ROO-suh-lem)*. Now the [leaders] have given him the power to come here and arrest anyone who worships in your name."

The Lord said to Ananias, "Go! I have chosen him to tell foreigners *(FOR-in-erz)*, kings, and the people of Israel about me." Ananias left and went into the house where Saul was staying. Ananias placed his hands on him and said, "Saul, the Lord Jesus has sent me. He wants you to be able to see and to be filled with the Holy Spirit." Suddenly something like fish scales fell from Saul's eyes, and he could see. He got up

and was baptized. Soon he went to the Jewish meeting places and started telling people that Jesus is the Son of God.

The word of the Lord.

■ REFLECTION

How is the story of Saul's conversion like the stories of Jesus curing blind people? Has anyone helped me as Ananias helped Saul?

■ CLOSING

Let us remember these intentions:

Loving and glorious God,
   we praise you with Easter joy
   because Christ is our redeemer.
Through baptism we live the risen life
   and share the mission of your Son.
Keep us faithful to Jesus,
   who is always with us.
We ask this through Christ our Lord. **Amen.**

Let us pray with the words that Jesus taught us:
Our Father . . .

▶ sing "alleluia"

May we live in the light of Christ. **Amen.**

▶ put out the candle

313

WEDNESDAY PRAYER

May 23, 2001

■ INTRODUCTION

All the people brought up as Jews knew what the disciples meant when they called Jesus the Messiah. People of other religions were called Gentiles *(JEN-tilez)*. Some Gentiles had studied Moses and the prophets and they knew about the Messiah too. Many Gentiles listened to the disciples and became followers of Jesus.

■ A PSALM FOR LATE EASTERTIME

 turn to
page 302

■ READING

Acts 11:19–23, 25–26

Listen to the words of the Acts of the Apostles:

Some of the Lord's followers had been scattered because of the terrible trouble that started when Stephen was killed. But they told the message only to the Jews. Some of the followers went to Antioch and started telling Gentiles *(JEN-tilez)* the good news about the Lord Jesus. The Lord's power was with them, and many people turned to the Lord and put their faith in him. News of what was happening reached the church in Jerusalem. Then they sent Barnabas *(BAR-nuh-bus)* to Antioch *(AN-tee-ock)*. When Barnabas got there and saw what God had been kind enough to do for them, he was very glad.

Barnabas went to Tarsus to look for Saul. He found Saul and brought him to Antioch, where they met with the church for a whole year and taught many of its people. There in Antioch the Lord's followers were first called Christians.

The word of the Lord.

■ REFLECTION

When I have good news, whom do I tell first? What does the title "Christian" mean? What does the title "Catholic" mean?

■ CLOSING

Let us remember these intentions:

Loving and glorious God,
    we praise you with Easter joy
    because Christ is our redeemer.
Through him apostles have been called,
    and sent to the whole world.
We welcome those who bring your good news.
We pray for them and listen to their teaching.
Call on us, one day, to become apostles, too.
We ask this through Christ our Lord. **Amen.**

Let us pray with the words that Jesus taught us:

Our Father . . .

 sing
"alleluia"

May we live in the light of Christ. **Amen.**

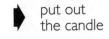 put out
the candle

314

THURSDAY PRAYER

May 24, 2001

Reminder: On page 316 there is an End of the Day Prayer for Ascension Day.

■ INTRODUCTION

Today is the fortieth day of the Easter season. It is a day of great joy!

We do not see Jesus with our eyes, but he is still with us. Or perhaps we do see Jesus whenever we look at another person.

■ A PSALM FOR LATE EASTERTIME

turn to
page 302

■ READING

Acts 1:3–4, 8–11

Listen to the words of the Acts of the Apostles:

For forty days after Jesus had suffered and died, he proved in many ways that he had been raised from death. He appeared to his apostles and spoke to them about God's kingdom.

While he was still with them, he said, "Don't leave Jerusalem yet. Wait here for the Father to give you the Holy Spirit, just as I told you he has promised to do. But the Holy Spirit will come upon you and give you power. Then you will tell everyone about me everywhere in the world."

After Jesus had said this and while they were watching, he was taken up into a cloud. They could not see him, but as he went up, they kept looking up into the sky.

Suddenly two men dressed in white clothes were standing there beside them. They said, "Why are you standing here and looking up into the sky? Jesus has been taken to heaven. But he will come back in the same way that you have seen him go."

The word of the Lord.

■ REFLECTION

This feast reminds us to see Jesus in others. How do we do this? Am I ready to do this?

■ CLOSING

Let us remember these intentions:

Lord God, make us joyful
  in the ascension (*uh-SEN-shun*)
    of your Son Jesus.
May we follow him one day
  into the new creation,
    the kingdom of your glory.
We ask this through Christ our Lord. **Amen.**

Let us pray with the words that Jesus taught us:
Our Father . . .

sing
"alleluia"

May we live in the light of Christ. **Amen.**

put out
the candle

The Ascension of the Lord

> all make
> the sign
> of the cross

LEADER Christ is risen like the sun, alleluia!
  ALL **The light of Christ shines
      over the whole world, alleluia!**

> light a candle,
> and then say:

LEADER Jesus is taken up to heaven!
    May he come again to rule over us,
        now and for ever.
  ALL **Amen.**

LEADER Jesus sits at God's right hand!
    May he watch over his people with love,
        now and for ever.
  ALL **Amen.**

LEADER Jesus gives us his gospel and his mission!
    May he give us a share in his glory,
        now and for ever.
  ALL **Amen.**

LEADER ▶ hold out one hand
      toward everyone
      in blessing, and say:

    May we live in the light of Christ.

  ALL ▶ all make
      the sign
      of the cross

      ▶ put out
        the candle

➤ Reminder: Monday is Memorial Day. If your class meets that day you may want to use Weekly Prayer on page 318.

■ INTRODUCTION

Pentecost is the fiftieth and final day of Eastertime. Then we celebrate the coming of the Holy Spirit just as Jesus promised his followers before he ascended to heaven. The nine days before that feast are spent in prayer and preparation.

■ A PSALM FOR LATE EASTERTIME

➤ turn to
page 302

■ READING

Acts 13:1, 2–5

Listen to the words of the Acts of the Apostles:

The church at Antioch *(AN-tee-ock)* had several prophets and teachers. While they were worshiping the Lord and fasting, the Holy Spirit told them, "Appoint Barnabas and Paul to do the work for which I have chosen them." Everyone prayed and fasted for a while longer. Next, they placed their hands on Barnabas and Paul to show that they had been appointed to do this work. Then everyone sent them on their way.

After Barnabas and Paul had been sent by the Holy Spirit, they sailed to the island of Cyprus *(SYE-prus).* They arrived and began to preach God's message in the Jewish meeting places. They also had John as a helper.

The word of the Lord.

■ REFLECTION

How did Barnabas and Paul know what God called them to do? How do I know what God wants me to do? What is the meaning of the ceremony of laying hands on the two men?

■ CLOSING

Please respond to each petition:
"Come, Holy Spirit."

That the Spirit of wisdom may guide the leaders of our church, let us pray to the Lord:
Come, Holy Spirit.

That the Spirit of knowledge may open the scriptures to us, let us pray to the Lord:
Come, Holy Spirit.

That the Spirit of courage will strengthen those who are suffering, let us pray to the Lord:
Come, Holy Spirit.

Let us also remember these intentions:

Let us pray with the words that Jesus taught us:
Our Father . . .

➤ sing
"alleluia"

May we live in the light of Christ. **Amen.**

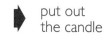

➤ put out
the candle

WEEKLY PRAYER

With a Reading from the Gospel for Sunday, May 27, 2001

■ INTRODUCTION

With his resurrection, Jesus entered the glory that belongs to him as Son of God. Into that glory he will welcome each of us one day. This week we celebrate the Ascension *(uh-SEN-shun)* of Jesus. But Eastertime is not over. It lasts the full 50 days until Pentecost.

The disciples prayed and wondered during those 50 days as they waited for the coming of the Holy Spirit. Today's reading tells us how close Jesus is to his disciples.

■ A PSALM FOR LATE EASTERTIME

▶ turn to
page 302

■ READING

John 17:20–21, 25–26

Listen to the words of the holy gospel according to John:

Jesus prayed, "Father, I am not praying just for these followers. I am also praying for everyone else who will have faith because of what my followers will say about me. I want all of them to be one with each other, just as I am one with you and you are one with me. I also want them to be one with us. Then the people of this world will believe that you sent me.

"Good Father, the people of this world don't know you. But I know you, and my followers know that you sent me. I told them what you are like, and I will tell them even more. Then the love that you have for me will become part of them, and I will be one with them."

The gospel of the Lord.

■ REFLECTION

Do we talk about our faith with our friends? Do I have friends who seem close to God? How does Jesus help us become closer to him?

■ CLOSING

Let us all say:
Christ, our light and our salvation!
Christ, our light and our salvation!

You are the sun that shines on everyone,
 the day that knows no ending:
Christ, our light and our salvation!

You are the springtime of the universe
 and the savior of the world:
Christ, our light and our salvation!

Let us remember these intentions:

Let us pray with the words that Jesus taught us:
Our Father . . .

 sing
 "alleluia"

May we live in the light of Christ. **Amen.**

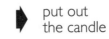
 put out
 the candle

318

TUESDAY PRAYER

May 29, 2001

■ INTRODUCTION

At sundown last night, the Jewish Feast of Weeks, or Shavuot *(shah-voo-OAT)* began. This feast is held 50 days after Passover. On Sunday, June 3, Christians will celebrate Pentecost, the feast held 50 days after Easter. Once again, people all over the world are giving thanks to God for the gift of the Holy Law and the gift of the Holy Spirit.

■ A PSALM FOR LATE EASTERTIME

➤ turn to page 302

■ READING

Acts 14:8–11, 14–15

Listen to the words of the Acts of the Apostles:

In Lystra *(LIS-truh)* there was a man who had been born with crippled feet and had never been able to walk. The man was listening to Paul speak, when Paul saw that he had faith in Jesus and could be healed. So he looked straight at the man and shouted, "Stand up!" The man jumped up and started walking around.

When the crowd saw what Paul had done, they yelled out, "The gods have turned into humans and have come down to us!" When the two apostles found out about this, they tore their clothes in horror and ran to the crowd, shouting, "We are humans just like you. Please give up all this foolishness. Turn to the living God, who made the sky, the earth, the sea, and everything in them."

The word of the Lord.

■ REFLECTION

Idols are things or persons we treat as if they were God, even though of course they aren't. Do we sometimes make idols of athletes? money? actors or singers? computers? teachers? designer clothes? Do I have any idols?

■ CLOSING

Please respond to each petition:
"Come, Holy Spirit."

That the Spirit of understanding may do away with hatred, let us pray to the Lord:
Come, Holy Spirit.

That the Spirit of knowledge may teach us to live as Christians, let us pray to the Lord:
Come, Holy Spirit.

That the Spirit of courage may help people give up addictions, let us pray to the Lord:
Come, Holy Spirit.

Let us also remember these intentions:

Let us pray with the words that Jesus taught us:
Our Father . . .

➤ sing "alleluia"

May we live in the light of Christ. **Amen.**

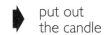
➤ put out the candle

■ INTRODUCTION

Today we remember Saint Joan of Arc, a patron of France. As a teenager, Joan heard the voices of saints telling her to lead the French army against its enemies. She led the troops to victory but was betrayed. Her enemies tried to get her to deny that she had spoken with the saints. But Joan remained faithful to the call of God. She was burned to death in 1431.

■ A PSALM FOR LATE EASTERTIME

turn to
page 302

■ READING
Acts 14:19–23

Listen to the words of the Acts of the Apostles:

Some people came and turned the crowds against Paul. They hit him with stones and dragged him out of the city, thinking he was dead. But when the Lord's followers gathered around Paul, he stood up and went back into the city.

The next day Paul and Barnabas went to Derbe. They preached the good news in Derbe and won some people to the Lord. They encouraged the followers and begged them to remain faithful. They told them, "We have to suffer a lot before we can get into God's kingdom."

Paul and Barnabas chose some leaders for each of the churches. Then they fasted and prayed that the Lord would take good care of these leaders.

The word of the Lord.

■ REFLECTION

Why did Paul and Barnabas keep going even when their work was so difficult? Do I persevere when things get hard?

■ CLOSING

Please respond to each petition:
"Come, Holy Spirit."

That the Spirit of counsel may protect mothers and their children, let us pray to the Lord:
Come, Holy Spirit.

That the Spirit of courage may lead us to new adventures, let us pray to the Lord:
Come, Holy Spirit.

That the Spirit of awe may bring people joy, let us pray to the Lord:
Come, Holy Spirit.

Let us also remember these intentions:

Let us pray with the words that Jesus taught us:
Our Father . . .

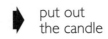
sing
"alleluia"

May we live in the light of Christ. **Amen.**

put out
the candle

THURSDAY PRAYER

May 31, 2001

■ INTRODUCTION

Mary learned that her cousin Elizabeth was going to have a baby. So Mary visited her. Today we celebrate that visit. Elizabeth's child was John the Baptist. Mary's child was Jesus. That is why Elizabeth told Mary she was so blessed.

■ A PSALM FOR LATE EASTERTIME

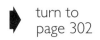
turn to
page 302

■ READING

Luke 1:39–42, 45–48

Listen to the words of the holy gospel according to Luke:

Mary hurried to a town in the hill country of Judea. She went into Zechariah's *(zek-uh-RYE-uhz)* home, where she greeted Elizabeth. When Elizabeth heard Mary's greeting, her baby moved within her.

The Holy Spirit came upon Elizabeth. Then in a loud voice she said to Mary: "God has blessed you more than any other woman! He has also blessed the child you will have. The Lord has blessed you because you believed that he will keep his promise." Mary said:

"With all my heart I praise the Lord,
   and I am glad because of God my Savior.
He cares for me, his humble servant.
From now on, all people will say
   God has blessed me."

The gospel of the Lord.

■ REFLECTION

What promise did God keep? Mary brought Jesus to Elizabeth and to her baby. Do I bring Jesus to the people who know me?

■ CLOSING

Please respond to each petition:
"Come, Holy Spirit."

That the Spirit of understanding may teach us
   to love one another, let us pray to the Lord:
Come, Holy Spirit.

That the Spirit of love may teach us
   to forgive one another, let us pray to the Lord:
Come, Holy Spirit.

That the Spirit of courage may strengthen us
   to do the right thing, let us pray to the Lord:
Come, Holy Spirit.

Let us also remember these intentions:

Let us pray with the words that Jesus taught us:
Our Father . . .

sing
"alleluia"

May we live in the light of Christ. **Amen.**

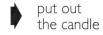
put out
the candle

FRIDAY PRAYER

June 1, 2001

■ INTRODUCTION

Today we remember Saint Justin, a teacher and a philosopher *(fi-LAHS-ah-fer)*. This word means "a lover of wisdom." When Justin began to study Christianity, he saw that it is much more than a way of looking at life; it is a way of living. Justin died for his faith in the year 165.

■ A PSALM FOR LATE EASTERTIME

➤ turn to
page 302

■ READING

Acts 19: 1–6

Listen to the words of the Acts of the Apostles:

Paul traveled across the hill country to Ephesus *(EF-uh-sus),* where he met some of the Lord's followers. He asked them, "When you put your faith in Jesus, were you given the Holy Spirit?"

"No!" they answered. "We have never even heard of the Holy Spirit." "Then why were you baptized?" Paul asked. They answered, "Because of what John taught."

Paul replied, "John baptized people so that they would turn to God. But he also told them that someone else was coming, and that they should put their faith in him. Jesus is the one that John was talking about." After the people heard Paul say this, they were baptized in the name of the Lord Jesus. Then Paul placed his hands on them. The Holy Spirit was given to them, and they spoke unknown languages and prophesied *(PRAH-fuh-side)*.

The word of the Lord.

■ REFLECTION

What gifts does the Holy Spirit bring? Why do we need these gifts? What gifts does the church most need today?

■ CLOSING

Please respond to each petition:
"Come, Holy Spirit."

That the Spirit of awe will lead us to
care for the earth, let us pray to the Lord:
Come, Holy Spirit.

That the Spirit of justice will guide
all our actions, let us pray to the Lord:
Come, Holy Spirit.

That the Spirit of faithfulness will keep us
true to God's word, let us pray to the Lord:
Come, Holy Spirit.

Let us also remember these intentions:

Let us pray with the words that Jesus taught us:
Our Father . . .

➤ sing
"alleluia"

May we live in the light of Christ. **Amen.**

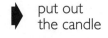
➤ put out
the candle

322

WEEKLY PRAYER

With a Reading from the Gospel for Sunday, June 3, 2001

■ INTRODUCTION

Sunday, June 3, is Pentecost, a great day in our Christian year. It is the fiftieth day of Easter. On Pentecost we remember that Jesus keeps his promises. He said he would send the Holy Spirit to unify and strengthen his followers, and he did just that.

The Holy Spirit is the church's "Advocate" *(AD-vo-ket)*. An advocate speaks up for us and takes our side. It should give us courage to know that we have God as our advocate.

■ A PSALM FOR LATE EASTERTIME

turn to
page 302

■ READING

John 20:19–23

Listen to the words of the holy gospel according to John:

The disciples were afraid of the leaders, and on the evening of that same Sunday they locked themselves in a room. Suddenly, Jesus appeared in the middle of the group. He greeted them and showed them his hands and his side. When the disciples saw the Lord, they became very happy.

After Jesus had greeted them again, he said, "I am sending you, just as the Father has sent me." Then he breathed on them and said, "Receive the Holy Spirit. If you forgive anyone's sins, they will be forgiven. But if you don't forgive their sins, they will not be forgiven."

The gospel of the Lord.

■ REFLECTION

What is Jesus sending the disciples to do? What is the result when we forgive others? What is the result when we do not forgive?

■ CLOSING

Please respond to each petition:
"Come, Holy Spirit."

That the Spirit of knowledge may open the scriptures to us, let us pray to the Lord:
Come, Holy Spirit.

That the Spirit of courage will strengthen those who are suffering, let us pray to the Lord:
Come, Holy Spirit.

That the Spirit of awe may teach us habits of prayer, let us pray to the Lord:
Come, Holy Spirit.

Let us also remember these intentions:

Let us pray with the words that Jesus taught us:
Our Father . . .

sing "alleluia"

May we live in the light of Christ. **Amen.**

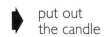
put out the candle

323

EARLY SUMMER

Monday, June 4, to the End of the School Year

ORDINARY TIME EARLY SUMMER 2001

■ ABOUT THE SEASON

Eastertime spills over into June this year, with its warm and sunny weather. Many spring flowers have finished blooming, leaving the rich, green world ready for the hot sun of summer. Vacation time cannot be far away!

LOOKING AHEAD   It seems strange for the church to call this "Ordinary Time," because it is so special to us. But remember that "ordinary" does not mean "dull." Ordinary food can be very nourishing. Ordinary clothes are usually the most comfortable. Ordinary jobs can be very important. And ordinary people make our world a very good place to live.

Actually, these weeks can be called "Ordinal Time." The word "ordinal" means that the Sundays are counted: the first Sunday, the tenth Sunday, the fourteenth Sunday, and so on. Ordinary things are things we usually can count on.

■ OUR DAILY READINGS BEGIN WITH THE STORIES OF SOME OF THE HOLY WOMEN MENTIONED IN THE HEBREW SCRIPTURES. We will hear about Shiphrah and Puah, the prophet Miriam, and a brave mother whose name we do not know. These women are known for their courage, wisdom and holiness.

Readings for the last week describe the reign of God in our lives. They are taken from the book of the prophet Isaiah.

■ THIS BOOK PROVIDES A WEEK OF UNDATED PRAYERS FOR USE DURING THE LAST WEEK OF SCHOOL. Use them whenever those last five days come for you. This book provides dated prayers for June 4 through June 10. You can plan additional prayers if you need them. This is how you can do it:

Continue to use the Psalm, the Meal Prayer and the End of the Day Prayer for Early Summer. Let different students write introductions to as many days as you need. Look up the saints and events that are listed below, or tell about important things happening in the news or in your own families.

You may choose your own readings from the Bible or look back in this book to find readings you want to hear again. Use the Reflection printed on the same page, or write your own. Use the Closing of June 4, or any other that you like.

Remember that prayers for the last week of school are provided on pages 338 to 342. Weekly Prayer with a Reading from the Gospel for Sunday, June 17, the feast of the Body and Blood of Christ, is on page 343.

■ CALENDAR FOR THE REMAINDER OF JUNE:

Monday, June 11
Saint Barnabas, an early missionary and companion of Paul. His story is in the Acts of the Apostles.

Tuesday, June 12
Anne Frank, diary writer and martyr of the Holocaust.

Wednesday, June 13
Saint Anthony of Padua, Franciscan preacher. A wonder worker and patron of Italy.

Thursday, June 14
Saint Basil, whose grandparents, parents, two brothers and one sister are also saints.

Friday, June 15
Amos, the shepherd who was drafted by God to be a prophet.

Sunday, June 17
Solemnity of the Body and Blood of Christ, a day to thank God for the gift of the eucharist.

Monday, June 18
Dr. Sally Ride becomes the first American woman in space in 1983; a day to celebrate our home planet.

Tuesday, June 19
Saint Romuald, who was such a wise teacher that people traveled from miles around to listen to him.

Wednesday, June 20
Saint Alban, the first English martyr. He died for hiding a priest from Roman soldiers.

Thursday, June 21
Summer solstice, a day to enjoy the sunshine. Since the beginning of this year, our planet has safely traveled almost 243 million miles in its journey around the sun.

Friday, June 22
Solemnity of the Sacred Heart of Jesus, a day to draw closer to God's love and care.

Sunday, June 24
Solemnity of the Birth of John the Baptist and Midsummer Day. Traditional celebrations include cookouts, campfires, songs and dancing.

Monday, June 25
In 1988 the American bishops spoke out about the dangers of nuclear weapons.

Tuesday, June 26
Dom Virgil Michel, a Benedictine monk who brought a love of liturgy to Minnesota. It spread from there to the whole country.

Wednesday, June 27
John Gerard, an underground priest who had many daring escapes in Elizabethan England.

Thursday, June 28
Saint Irenaeus, a bishop who died for his faith about the year 203.

Friday, June 29
Saints Peter and Paul, two great saints who helped form the early church.

■ PREPARATION FOR EARLY SUMMER

You may want to make copies of the new Psalm, Meal Prayer and End of the Day Prayer for Early Summer. These are found on pages 328, 329 and 330. If you are using *Blessed Be God!* you will find these prayers on pages 40 to 42.

■ THE DAILY PRAYERS PLANNED FOR THE LAST WEEK OF SCHOOL ARE ON PAGES 338 TO 342. The Closing for these days is a litany of thanksgiving. During the second to last week of school, the class should be asked to list some of the good things that have happened during the school year so that these things can be included in this litany.

This is a good time to look back and see the fine things that have happened.

We have grown. We have changed. We have learned many things. Now is the time to reflect on these things, appreciate them and say "thank you" for them. There may be many people who deserve our thanks.

■ THERE IS A BLESSING OF STUDENTS FOR THE TEACHER TO USE WHEN THE CLASS IS DISMISSED FOR THE LAST TIME. If you are going to exchange cards or have some other way of saying good-bye to each other, you may want to do all of this at the same time. Talk this over with the teacher. The Blessing before Summer Vacation is on page 331.

■ SUGGESTED HYMNS: "Lord, you give the great commission" (page 156 in the *Hymnal for Catholic Students*) is a good choice for early summer.

At this time of year you may prefer to sing favorite hymns rather than learn new ones. You might have a "hymn sing." Sing all the sacred songs you've learned since September. This gathering just for the joy of singing to the Lord is a wonderful ending of the year. Talk this over with the teacher.

The conclusion to the Meal Prayer for Early Summer can be sung. The melody is on page 173 in the *Hymnal for Catholic Students*. It is easy to learn and easy to remember.

A PSALM FOR EARLY SUMMER

> ▶ all make
> the sign
> of the cross

Psalm 104: 1–2, 13–15

LEADER Lord, open my lips.
    ALL **And my mouth will proclaim your praise.**

LEADER I will bless you, Lord my God!
    ALL **You fill the world with awe.**

SIDE A You dress yourself in light,
in rich, majestic light.
You drench the hills
with rain from high heaven.
You nourish the earth
with what you create.

SIDE B You make grass grow for cattle,
make plants grow for people,
food to eat from the earth
and wine to warm the heart,
oil to glisten on faces
and bread for bodily strength.

LEADER I will bless you, Lord my God!
    ALL **You fill the world with awe.**

**Glory to the Father, and to the Son,
and to the Holy Spirit:
as it was in the beginning, is now,
and will be for ever. Amen. Alleluia.**

> ▶ turn back to
> Daily Prayer or Weekly Prayer
> for today

EARLY SUMMER

LEADER   Let us offer God praise and thanksgiving:

ALL ▶ all make
the sign
of the cross

LEADER   Let us pray.

Lord, the lover of life,
   you feed the birds of the skies
   and dress the lilies of the field.
We bless you for all your creatures
   and for the food we are about to receive.
We humbly pray that in your goodness
   you will provide
   for our brothers and sisters
   who are hungry.
We ask this through Christ our Lord.

ALL   **Amen.**

▶ the following words
can be sung to the melody for
"Praise God from whom all blessings flow":

Be present at our table, Lord.
Be here and everywhere adored.
Thy creatures bless and grant that we
May feast in Paradise with thee. Amen.

▶ all make
the sign
of the cross

EARLY SUMMER

END OF THE DAY PRAYER

> all make
> the sign
> of the cross

LEADER Let us praise and glorify God
      for the beauty of our summer world.

      For sunshine that warms the day, we pray:

ALL **Glory to you, O Lord.**

LEADER For rain that makes the grass sparkle,
      we pray:

ALL **Glory to you, O Lord.**

LEADER For bright mornings and free afternoons,
      we pray:

ALL **Glory to you, O Lord.**

LEADER For our good mother earth,
      we pray:

ALL **Glory to you, O Lord.**

> other praises
> may be added

LEADER Lord our God, you create us out of the earth
      and ask us to care for it.
    Give us strength like your own,
      and fill us with knowledge
      that we may know the majesty of your works
      and praise your holy name.
    We ask this through Christ our Lord.

ALL **Amen.**

LEADER ▶ hold out one hand
      toward everyone
      in blessing, and say:

    May the almighty and merciful God
      bless and protect us:

ALL ▶ all make
      the sign
      of the cross

A Blessing before Summer Vacation

Shortly before their final dismissal of the school year, the students gather so that the teacher can bless each one of them.

TEACHER
May the Lord's face shine on us,
   and may the Lord guide our feet
      into the way of peace.
Blessed be the name of the Lord,
   now and for ever.

ALL
Amen.

TEACHER
Let us put ourselves into the hands of the Lord,
   and pray that God will bless us
      and our families
   during the wonderful months of summer.
May each of us help to make our home
   a place of relaxation, joy, love,
      peace and safety.
May we be generous and considerate,
   not thinking only about ourselves
   but helping others enjoy the blessings
      of the summertime.

Please respond "Amen" as I bless each of you.

> the teacher goes to each student in turn,
> places a hand on the student's head
> or shoulder, and says:

N., go with God.

ALL
Amen.

> when these individual blessings
> are completed, prayer continues:

TEACHER
Lord God,
   this class has shared many things this year.
We were linked by common tasks
   and time together.

Those ties are broken now.
We say good-bye and end our year.

Lord, bless each of these,
   my students and friends,
      especially those I will not see again.
Keep each of us in your care
   during the coming summer
   and throughout our lives.
Guide our steps and strengthen our hearts
   until we gather once again in your kingdom.
We ask this through Christ our Lord.

ALL
Amen.

TEACHER
Let us end this year as we began it,
   with the sign of the cross.

ALL

> all make
> the sign
> of the cross

> sing a song of praise, such as
> "God who stretched the spangled heavens"
> (page 130 in the *Hymnal for Catholic Students*) or "Shalom chaverim" (page 177)

MONDAY PRAYER

June 4, 2001

■ INTRODUCTION

In the Bible God's wisdom is often pictured as a woman who goes about the city inviting everyone to her home. The symbol of Sophia *(so-FEE-uh)*, or Holy Wisdom, reminds us that God is gentle and attractive. God seeks us out and offers us welcome.

This week's readings from the Hebrew scriptures tell about women who were "lovers of wisdom." Today we hear the story of two brave midwives. A midwife helps women who are having babies.

■ A PSALM FOR EARLY SUMMER

turn to page 328

■ READING

Exodus 1:9, 11, 15–21

Listen to the words of the book of Exodus:

The king told the Egyptians, "There are too many of those Israelites in our country, and they are becoming more powerful than we are." The Egyptians put slave bosses in charge of the people of Israel and tried to wear them down with hard work. Finally the king called in Shiphrah *(SHIF-rah)* and Puah *(POO-ah)*, the two women who helped the Hebrew mothers when they gave birth. He told them, "If a Hebrew woman gives birth to a girl, let the child live. If the baby is a boy, kill him!"

But the two women were faithful to God and did not kill the boys, even though the king had told them to. The king called them in again and asked, "Why are you letting those baby boys live?"

They answered, "Hebrew women have their babies much quicker than Egyptian women. By the time we arrive, their babies are already born." God was good to the two women because they truly respected him, and he blessed them with children of their own.

The word of the Lord.

■ REFLECTION

Why did people in power persecute the Hebrews? How did Shiphrah and Puah show courage? How did they show wisdom? What does this story tell about the value of each life?

■ CLOSING

Let us remember these intentions:

God of grace and wisdom,
    you continually raise up good people
    who show with their lives
    that they follow a holy and loving God.
Let our lives be as true as our faith.
We ask this through Christ our Lord. **Amen.**

Let us pray with the words that Jesus taught us:
Our Father . . .

 sing "alleluia"

TUESDAY PRAYER

June 5, 2001

■ INTRODUCTION

When the Hebrew people were slaves in Egypt, a law was passed that all the boy babies were to be killed. The brave midwives, Shiphrah *(SHIF-rah)* and Puah *(POO-ah)* would not do this. One of the babies they saved was Moses. His mother and sister hid him in a basket near the river, where an Egyptian princess rescued him. Moses' sister, Miriam, became a prophet. She was there when her brother, Moses, led the Hebrews in their great escape.

■ A PSALM FOR EARLY SUMMER

▶ turn to
page 328

■ READING

Exodus 14:21–23, 27, 31; 15:20–21

Listen to the words of the book of Exodus:

Moses stretched his arm over the sea, and the LORD sent a strong east wind that blew all night until there was dry land where the water had been. The sea opened up, and the Israelites walked through on dry land with a wall of water on each side.

The Egyptian chariots and cavalry went after them. Moses stretched out his arm, and at day-break the water rushed toward the Egyptians. They tried to run away, but the LORD drowned them in the sea.

Because of the mighty power the LORD had used against the Egyptians, the Israelites worshiped him and trusted him and his servant Moses. Miriam the sister of Aaron [and Moses] was a prophet. So she took her tambourine *(tam-boo-REEN)* and led the other women out to play their tambourines and to dance. Then she sang to them:

"Sing praises to the LORD
for his great victory!
He has thrown the horses and their riders
into the sea."

The word of the Lord.

■ REFLECTION

What do music and dance add to liturgy? The prophets of Israel led the people in prayer and gave advice. Who does those things in our church?

■ CLOSING

Let us remember these intentions:

God of grace and wisdom,
you continually raise up good people
who show with their lives
that they follow a holy and loving God.
Let our lives be as true as our faith.
We ask this through Christ our Lord. **Amen.**

Let us pray with the words that Jesus taught us:
Our Father . . .

 sing
"alleluia"

WEDNESDAY PRAYER

June 6, 2001

▶ Reminder: If next week is not the last week of school, you will need to prepare additional weekly prayers. Suggestions are on pages 326 and 327.

■ INTRODUCTION

Today's reading tells about Deborah, one of the judges of Israel. Before the Israelites were united under one king, they were ruled by judges. Judges settled disputes, gave moral leadership, and commanded armies when it was necessary.

■ A PSALM FOR EARLY SUMMER

▶ turn to page 328

■ READING

Judges 4:4–9

Listen to the words of the book of Judges:

Deborah was a prophet and a leader of Israel during those days. She would sit under Deborah's Palm Tree in the hill country of Ephraim *(EF-rum),* where Israelites would come and ask her to settle their legal cases.

One day Deborah sent word for Barak *(BAH-rak)* to come and talk with her. When he arrived, she said, "I have a message for you from the LORD God of Israel! You are to get together an army of ten thousand men and lead them to Mount Tabor.

"The LORD will trick Sisera *(SIS-uh-ruh)* into coming out to fight you at the river. They will have their chariots, but the LORD has promised to help you defeat them."

"I'm not going unless you go!" Barak told her.

"All right, I'll go!" she replied. "But I'm warning you that the LORD is going to let a woman defeat Sisera, and no one will honor you for winning the battle."

The word of the Lord.

■ REFLECTION

How did Deborah show courage and wisdom? Why did Deborah think it might bother Barak when she got the honor for victory? Who did Deborah think should really get credit for the victory?

■ CLOSING

Let us remember these intentions:

God of grace and wisdom,
    you continually raise up good people
    who show with their lives
    that they follow a holy and loving God.
Let our lives be as true as our faith.
We ask this through Christ our Lord. **Amen.**

Let us pray with the words that Jesus taught us:

Our Father . . .

▶ sing "alleluia"

THURSDAY PRAYER

June 7, 2001

> Reminder: Ask the class to write down things that have happened this year that they are thankful for. Use these ideas in the Closing each day of the last week of school.

■ INTRODUCTION

Today we learn the story of Judith. It is the story of a victory won by the Jews through the actions of a woman.

An enemy has surrounded Judith's town and the people are starving. The elders of the town promise to surrender if, after five days, the Lord has not worked a miracle to save them. Judith gives the elders a lesson about courage and about the Lord.

■ A PSALM FOR EARLY SUMMER

> turn to
> page 328

■ READING

Judith 8:10–12, 14, 15–17

Listen to the words of the book of Judith:

Judith said to the elders, "Listen to me, rulers of the people! What you have said to the people today is not right. You have promised to surrender the town to our enemies unless the Lord turns and helps us within so many days. Who are you to put God to the test today?

"You cannot plumb the depths of the human heart or understand the workings of the human mind. How do you expect to search out God, who made all these things, and find out his mind or comprehend his thought? No, my brothers, do not anger the Lord our God. For if he does not choose to help us within these five days, he has power to protect us within any time he pleases, or even to destroy us in the presence of our enemies.

"Do not try to bind the purposes of the Lord our God, for God is not like a human being, to be threatened. God is not like a mere mortal, to be won over by pleading. Therefore, while we wait for deliverance, let us call upon God to help us, and he will hear our voice, if it pleases him."

The word of the Lord.

■ REFLECTION

How did Judith show wisdom and courage? Have I ever tried to bargain with God? What does this story tell us about prayer?

■ CLOSING

Let us remember these intentions:

God of grace and wisdom,
    you continually raise up good people
    who show with their lives
    that they follow a holy and loving God.
Let our lives be as true as our faith.
We ask this through Christ our Lord. **Amen.**

Let us pray with the words that Jesus taught us:
Our Father . . .

> sing
> "alleluia"

335

FRIDAY PRAYER

June 8, 2001

■ INTRODUCTION

This week we have heard of wise and holy women who were midwives, prophets, leaders and teachers. Today's reading tells of a wise mother who strengthened her children in a time of persecution *(per-sih-KYU-shun)*. Foreign *(FOR-in)* kings who defeated Israel were trying to destroy the people's faith by forcing them to give up their religious practices.

■ A PSALM FOR EARLY SUMMER

▶ turn to
page 328

■ READING

2 Maccabees 7:1, 20–23

Listen to the words of the second book of Maccabees *(MACK-ah-bees):*

Seven brothers and their mother were arrested and were being compelled by the king, under torture with whips, to eat pork, which was forbidden. The mother was especially admirable and worthy of honor. Although she saw her seven sons die within a single day, she bore it with good courage because of her hope in the Lord.

Filled with a noble spirit, she reinforced her woman's reasoning with a man's courage, and said to them, "It was not I who gave you life and breath, nor I who set in order the elements within each of you. Therefore the Creator of the world, who shaped the beginning of humankind and devised the origin of all things, will in his mercy give life and breath back to you again, since you now forget yourselves for the sake of his laws."

The word of the Lord.

■ REFLECTION

What customs are important expressions of my faith? Have I ever been mocked for religious behavior? Have I ever made fun of others for their religious or ethnic customs? How did the mother show courage? How did she show wisdom?

■ CLOSING

Let us remember these intentions:

God of grace and wisdom,
　you continually raise up good people
　who show with their lives
　that they follow a holy and loving God.
Let our lives be as true as our faith.
We ask this through Christ our Lord. **Amen.**

Let us pray with the words that Jesus taught us:

Our Father . . .

▶ sing
"alleluia"

336

WEEKLY PRAYER

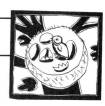

With a Reading from the Gospel for Sunday, June 10, 2001

■ INTRODUCTION

On Sunday, June 10, the church celebrates the Holy Trinity. God's life is a mystery too great for us to understand. We can only know what God has shown us through divine actions, divine revelation, and by being with us. We try to put what we know into words. Then we try to speak about God and to speak to God.

One of our oldest traditions has been to call God by the name of the Father, Son and Holy Spirit. These are the three persons of the Holy Trinity. And yet we know that there is only one God. This is hard to understand with the mind. But our hearts can take hold of it.

■ A PSALM FOR EARLY SUMMER

turn to
page 328

■ READING

John 16: 12–15

Listen to the words of the holy gospel according to John:

Jesus said to his disciples: "I have much more to say to you, but right now it would be more than you could understand. The Spirit shows what is true and will come and guide you into the full truth. The Spirit does not speak on his own. He will tell you only what he has heard from me, and he will let you know what is going to happen.

"The Spirit will bring glory to me by taking my message and telling it to you. Everything that the Father has is mine. That is why I have

said that the Spirit takes my message and tells it to you."

The gospel of the Lord.

■ REFLECTION

Do I expect the Holy Spirit to share God's truth with me? Do we ever pray for the truth?

■ CLOSING

Let us remember these intentions:

The response is: "We praise you."

Holy Trinity, one God:
   We praise you.
God our Father, endless in mercy:
   We praise you.
Son of God, savior of the world:
   We praise you.
Holy Spirit, strength of God's people:
   We praise you.

O holy, undivided Trinity,
   one God in three Persons:
for sharing your life with us,
   we praise and bless you
   now and for ever. **Amen.**

Let us pray with the words that Jesus taught us:
Our Father . . .

sing
"alleluia"

MONDAY PRAYER

Last Monday of the School Year

> Reminder: For the Closing today, select three or more things for which you are thankful from the list you made last week.

■ INTRODUCTION

Most of us look forward to summer the way we look forward to heaven! We expect to spend time with our friends doing wonderful things. Maybe God renews our excitement for heaven by giving us a taste of it each summer.

The prophet Isaiah (*eye-ZAY-uh*) wrote about what God's kingdom would be like. In our readings this last week of the school year, we will hear about Isaiah's dreams.

■ A PSALM FOR EARLY SUMMER

> turn to
> page 328

■ READING
Isaiah 65:17–18, 19–20

Listen to the words of the prophet Isaiah:

The LORD says this:
  "I am creating new heavens and a new earth;
  everything of the past will be forgotten.
  Celebrate and be glad for ever!
  I will celebrate with Jerusalem
    and all of its people;
  there will be no more crying
    or sorrow in that city.
  No child will die in infancy;
    everyone will live to a ripe old age."

The word of the Lord.

■ REFLECTION

Are there parts of the past year that I would like to forget? What have we learned from the difficulties that we faced? What memories do I want to keep?

■ CLOSING

Please respond, "Thank you, Lord our God."

Generous God,
  you have blessed us during this school year.
We thank you for these things:

For_____,
  let us thank the Lord:
Thank you, Lord our God.

> repeat this pattern
> two or more times

We thank you, Lord,
  for the gift of your kingdom
  and for the promise of summer.
Be with us each day.
We ask this through Christ our Lord. **Amen.**

Let us pray with the words that Jesus taught us:

Our Father . . .

> sing
> "alleluia"

338

TUESDAY PRAYER

Last Tuesday of the School Year

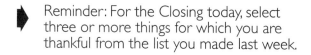

Reminder: For the Closing today, select three or more things for which you are thankful from the list you made last week.

■ INTRODUCTION

When we think of summer's freedom, it makes us happy. Then we will not have to get up early or sit quietly in a classroom.

The prophet Isaiah lived in a time of war and bitterness and disorder. When he thought about happy times to come, he mentioned the harmony and peacefulness that the nation longed for.

■ A PSALM FOR EARLY SUMMER

turn to
page 328

■ READING

Isaiah 11:6–9

Listen to the words of the prophet Isaiah:

The LORD says this:
   "Leopards will lie down with young goats,
      and wolves will rest with lambs.
   Calves and lions will eat together
      and be cared for by little children.
   Cows and bears will share the same pasture;
      their young will rest side by side.
   Lions and oxen will both eat straw.
   Little children will play near snake holes.
   They will stick their hands
      into dens of poisonous snakes
         and never be hurt.
   Nothing harmful will take place
      on the LORD's holy mountain."

The word of the Lord.

■ REFLECTION

Isaiah says that in God's kingdom all creatures are at peace. How can we work toward that day? Do I know any peacemakers?

■ CLOSING

Please respond, "Thank you, Lord our God."

Generous God,
   you have blessed us during this school year.
We thank you for these things:

For_____,
   let us thank the Lord:
Thank you, Lord our God.

repeat this pattern
two or more times

We thank you, Lord,
   for the gift of your kingdom
   and for the promise of summer.
Be with us each day.
We ask this through Christ our Lord. **Amen.**

Let us pray with the words that Jesus taught us:

Our Father . . .

sing
"alleluia"

WEDNESDAY PRAYER
Last Wednesday of the School Year

▶ Reminder: For the Closing today, select three or more things for which you are thankful from the list you made last week.

■ INTRODUCTION

In today's reading Isaiah tells us that animals will share in the peace and freedom of God's kingdom. This is a good day to think about all kinds of animals, especially our pets. They depend on our love and care. They reward us with their friendship. They don't care if our room is clean or if our socks don't match, as long as we talk to them when we come home.

Today let us thank God for all creatures, wild and tame, large and small. What would God's world be like without them?

■ A PSALM FOR EARLY SUMMER

▶ turn to page 328

■ READING

Isaiah 65: 22, 24–25

Listen to the words of the prophet Isaiah:

The LORD says this:
"My chosen people will live
    to be as old as trees,
and they will enjoy
    what they have earned.
I will answer their prayers
    before they finish praying.
Wolves and lambs will graze together;
    lions and oxen will feed on straw.
Snakes will eat only dirt!

They won't bite or harm anyone
    on my holy mountain."
The word of the Lord.

■ REFLECTION

What does it mean that "wolves and lambs will eat together" and "lions will eat straw"? What are my images for a world where every creature is safe and no creature is a threat? What do I fear? How do I fight that fear?

■ CLOSING

Please respond, "Thank you, Lord our God."

Generous God,
    you have blessed us during this school year.
We thank you for these things:

For_____,
    let us thank the Lord:
Thank you, Lord our God.

▶ repeat this pattern two or more times

We thank you, Lord,
    for the gift of your kingdom
    and for the promise of summer.
Be with us each day.
We ask this through Christ our Lord. **Amen.**

Let us pray with the words that Jesus taught us:

Our Father . . .

▶ sing "alleluia"

THURSDAY PRAYER

Last Thursday of the School Year

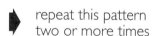 Reminder: For the Closing today, select three or more things for which you are thankful from the list you made last week.

■ INTRODUCTION

As the school year draws to a close and the bright weather makes us eager to be outdoors, it is hard to believe that the church calls these days "Ordinary Time."

But of course we do not mean this time is dull or boring. We are given the gift of life, and we are as bright and alive as God can make us. There is nothing ordinary about that!

■ A PSALM FOR EARLY SUMMER

▶ turn to page 328

■ READING

Isaiah 40:25–26, 29–31

Listen to the words of the prophet Isaiah:

The holy God asks,
"Who compares with me?
Is anyone my equal?"
Look at the evening sky!
Who created the stars?
Who gave them each a name?
Who leads them like an army?
The LORD is so powerful
that none of the stars are ever missing.
The LORD gives strength
to those who are weary.
Even young people get tired,
then stumble and fall.

But those who trust the LORD
will find new strength.
The word of the Lord.

■ REFLECTION

Why do many people think of God when they look at the night sky? What other parts of nature make me think about God? Do we trust the Lord when we "stumble and fall"?

■ CLOSING

Please respond, "Thank you, Lord our God."

Generous God,
you have blessed us during this school year.
We thank you for these things:

For_____,
let us thank the Lord:
Thank you, Lord our God.

 repeat this pattern two or more times

We thank you, Lord,
for the gift of your kingdom
and for the promise of summer.
Be with us each day.
We ask this through Christ our Lord. **Amen.**

Let us pray with the words that Jesus taught us:

Our Father . . .

▶ sing "alleluia"

FRIDAY PRAYER
Last Friday of the School Year

> Reminder: For the Closing today, select three or more things for which you are thankful from the list you made last week.

■ INTRODUCTION

The time is coming when we end one thing and begin another. We end our school year with thanks to God for all the year has brought us. And we begin our summer vacation with confidence that God is with us.

We will try to turn to God in prayer each day, remembering the forms of prayer that we have learned this year. Words and silence, songs and sorrows, thunderstorms and family meals—all things are meeting places with God, who loves us.

■ A PSALM FOR EARLY SUMMER

> turn to page 328

■ READING

Isaiah 12: 4–5

Listen to the words of the prophet Isaiah:
> When the Lord comes you will say,
> "Our LORD, we are thankful,
>   and we worship only you.
> We will tell the nations how glorious you are
>   and what you have done.
> Because of your wonderful deeds
>   we will sing your praises
>   everywhere on earth."

The word of the Lord.

■ REFLECTION

What are my plans for the summer? What ways can we think of to continue to sing God's praises everywhere during the weeks of summertime?

■ CLOSING

Please respond, "Thank you, Lord our God."

Generous God,
    you have blessed us during this school year.
We thank you for these things:

For_____,
    let us thank the Lord:
Thank you, Lord our God.

> repeat this pattern two or more times

We thank you, Lord,
    for the gift of your kingdom
    and for the promise of summer.
Be with us each day.
We ask this through Christ our Lord. **Amen.**

Let us pray with the words that Jesus taught us:

Our Father . . .

> sing "alleluia"

WEEKLY PRAYER

With a Reading from the Gospel for Sunday, June 17, 2001

■ INTRODUCTION

Sunday, June 17, is the festival of the Body and Blood of Christ. Let us take this week to thank God for the gift of the Mass.

At Mass, we listen to God's word. We pray for the world and for the church, and we give thanks to God with bread and wine. Then, united with God and with one another, we share the bread and wine. They are the body and blood of Christ. Christians have promised to do this every Sunday until the end of time.

■ A PSALM FOR EARLY SUMMER

➤ turn to
page 328

■ READING

Luke 9:12–17

Listen to the words of the holy gospel according to Luke:

Late in the afternoon the twelve apostles came to Jesus and said, "Send the crowd to the villages and farms around here. They need to find a place to stay and something to eat. There is nothing in this place. It is like a desert!"

Jesus answered, "You give them something to eat." But they replied, "We have only five small loaves of bread and two fish. If we are going to feed all these people, we will have to go and buy food." There were about five thousand men in the crowd.

Jesus said to his disciples, "Have the people sit in groups of fifty." They did this, and all the people sat down. Jesus took the five loaves and

the two fish. He looked up toward heaven and blessed the food. Then he broke the bread and fish and handed them to his disciples to give to the people.

Everyone ate all they wanted. What was left over filled twelve baskets.

The gospel of the Lord.

■ REFLECTION

The gift of the eucharist is one sign of God's love for us. How can we show our love for others this summer? In what other ways does God feed us each day?

■ CLOSING

Let us remember these intentions:

Loving God,
   through the bread and wine of the eucharist
   you give us a share in the life, death,
      and resurrection of your Son, Jesus.
Guide us by his Holy Spirit
   and lead us faithfully
      into the heavenly banquet.
We ask this through Christ our Lord. **Amen.**

Let us pray with the words that Jesus taught us:

Our Father . . .

sing
"alleluia"

343

Teacher's Farewell to the Classroom

The classroom is a sacred space, made so by the life and growth it has sheltered. When the last book is boxed and the last desk is scrubbed, take a few minutes to bless the classroom and to break your ties to it.

Use a class list and prepare some burning charcoal in a bowl for incense or use a bowl of holy water.

In the name of the Father,
    and of the Son,
    and of the Holy Spirit. Amen.

Lord, open my lips.
And my mouth will proclaim your praise.

O God,
    you call me to be a teacher,
    sharing in children's wonder at your world
        and at the power of your love.
The children are gone now,
    and my job is finished.

> be quiet
> for a minute or two

Merciful God,
    you know the hopes of August
    and the reality of June.
You know my regret and contrition
    for hopes not realized,
    things not done,
    needs not met,
    errors, angers and injuries.

> be quiet
> for a minute or two

Redeeming God,
    in your mercy, forgive and cleanse me.
Let this incense (holy water)
    be a sign of release and purification.
Bless and renew this room.
Make it a safe and nurturing shelter
    for students and teachers yet to come.

> bless the room
> with incense or holy water

Loving God,
    I thank you for the bright spirits
        of my students.
They have taught me much.
Surround them with safety and love.
Be with them on their journey.
Let the memory of the months spent in
    this room always bring them joy.

> read the list of your students,
> commending each to God

Gracious God,
    be forgiving of my failure!
Be glorified in my success!
Turn my face toward the future,
    and renew my energy for what is yet to be.

"I have not yet reached my goal,   Philippians 3:12
    and I am not perfect.
But Christ has taken hold of me.
So I keep on running and struggling
    to take hold of the prize."

In the name of the Father,
    and of the Son,
    and of the Holy Spirit. Amen.

A Farewell Blessing for a Friend

Sometimes a student or a teacher leaves before the school year is over. A blessing can be part of your goodbye.

Prepare a gift that will help your friend remember all of you. It can be as simple as a booklet of drawings, a picture of the class, or a card that everyone has signed. You may want to invite your friend's parents or other relative. If you share songs or something good to eat, use this blessing just before your friend's departure.

 all make
the sign
of the cross

LEADER   Psalm 121:3–8
God is ever watchful and always near.

ALL
God is ever watchful and always near.

LEADER
Gracious and loving God,
you have prepared a new place
   for our sister/brother _____
where she/he may continue to grow in wisdom
   and in love for you.
Be with _____ on her/his journey.
Send your Son as light for her/his path,
   your Spirit as strength for new beginnings.
Bless this gift as a sign
   of our friendship and best wishes.
We ask this through Christ our Lord.

ALL
Amen.

 give the gift
you have prepared

LEADER
In joy God gathered us together.
In peace God now leads us along separate paths.
Let us ask God to bless _____

 all extend their hands
in blessing

LEADER
May almighty God keep you from harm
   and bless you with every good gift:

ALL
Amen.

LEADER
May God's word abide in your heart
   bringing you comfort and wisdom:

ALL
Amen.

LEADER
May your path be clear and joyous
   and your heart strengthened by lasting
   friendships:

ALL
Amen.

LEADER
And may God bless all of us:

 all make
the sign
of the cross

Prayers for Sad Days

These are prayers for sad days and other times of trouble. Each one can be memorized and used when it is needed by students. To pray as a group, you can begin with the sign of the cross, then read one of the passages from scripture, and end with the prayer and sign of the cross.

It also can be good to sing a hymn. If someone is sick or has died, a fine song is "Blest are they" (page 112 in the Hymnal for Catholic Students) *or "Sing with all the saints in glory" (page 184 in the hymnal).*

A song for times of war or times of violence is "O God of love, O King of peace" (page 168 in the hymnal).

In times of trouble, a fitting song is "The Lord, the Lord, the Lord is my shepherd" (page 194 in the hymnal).

Psalm 18:28

O my God,
   you brighten the darkness about me.

Psalm 27:13–14

I believe that I shall see the goodness
    of the Lord
   in the land of the living.
Wait for the Lord.
Be strong, and let your heart take courage.
Wait for the Lord!

Psalm 28:6

Blessed be the Lord
   who hears my cry.

Psalm 91:14–16

I deliver all who cling to me,
raise the ones who know my name,
answer those who call me,
stand with those in trouble.
These I rescue and honor,
satisfy with long life,
and show my power to save.

Isaiah 41:10

Do not fear, for I am with you.
Do not be afraid, for I am your God;
   I will strengthen you, I will help you,
   I will hold you in my hand.

Prayer

Most holy and most merciful God,
   strength of the weak,
   rest for the weary,
   comfort of the sorrowful,
   our refuge in every time of need:
Grant us strength and protect us.
Support us in all dangers,
   and carry us through all trials.
We ask this through Christ our Lord. **Amen.**

 all make
the sign
of the cross

Prayers for the Sick

Theotokos

Holy Mary, Mother of God,
   pray for all who are sick,
   especially _____ .

Mother of Mercy,	**pray for them.**
Mother of Light,	**pray for them.**
Mother of the Savior,	**pray for them.**
Mother of the Good Shepherd,	**pray for them.**
Mother of the Church,	**pray for them.**

Lord God, through the prayers of Mary,
   our Mother,
bring your healing presence
   to all who are sick, injured or troubled.
We ask this through Christ our Lord. **Amen.**

You see our troubles, Lord;
   you know our suffering.
In your mercy strengthen all the sick
   especially _____ .
Ease their pain,
   heal their bodies,
   brighten their loneliness and
   calm their fears.
Let them know you are always near,
   their healer and redeemer.
**In the name of the Father,
   and of the Son,
   and of the Holy Spirit. Amen.**

Isaiah 40:29 – 31

The Lord gives strength to those who are weary,
Even young people get tired,
   then stumble and fall.
But those who trust the Lord
   will find new strength.
They will be strong like eagles
   soaring upward on wings;
they will walk and run without getting tired.

Psalm 10:12, 14

Arise, God, and act;
do not ignore the weak.
You observe our trouble and grief,
and at the right time
take things in hand.

Prayer of Saint Augustine *(adapted)*

Watch, O Lord, with those who wake,
   or watch or weep tonight.
Tend your sick ones.
Rest your weary ones.
Bless your dying ones.
Soothe your suffering ones.
Pity your afflicted ones,
   for your love's sake, O Lord Christ. **Amen.**

The Rosary

The rosary helps us think about events in God's plan of salvation. During this prayer, the Hail Mary is repeated many times. That way we invite the Blessed Mother to pray along with us.

A full rosary has 150 beads divided into sets of ten. The 150 beads remind us of the 150 psalms. As we pray each set of ten beads, or "decade," we think about one mystery in the plan of God. The fifteen mysteries of the rosary are listed on this page. Today, most rosaries have five decades.

The Joyful Mysteries

1. **The Annunciation.** Mary learns that she will become the mother of God.
2. **The Visitation.** Mary and Elizabeth visit and tell about God's wonders.
3. **The Nativity.** Jesus is born in a stable.
4. **The Presentation.** Mary and Joseph take the infant Jesus to the Temple, and they meet Simeon and Anna.
5. **The Finding of Jesus in the Temple.** Mary and Joseph lose Jesus, then find him teaching.

The Sorrowful Mysteries

1. **The Agony in the Garden.** Jesus prays about the suffering he will go through.
2. **The Scourging at the Pillar.** Soldiers whip Jesus.
3. **The Crowning with Thorns.** Soldiers mock Jesus.
4. **The Carrying of the Cross.** Jesus goes through the streets of Jerusalem to Calvary.
5. **The Crucifixion.** Jesus is crucified and dies on the cross.

The Glorious Mysteries

1. **The Resurrection.** God raises Jesus from death to life.
2. **The Ascension.** Jesus enters into divine glory.
3. **The Sending of the Holy Spirit.** The church is filled with God's courage and guidance.
4. **The Assumption of Mary.** She is the first to share in the resurrection of Jesus.
5. **The Coronation of Mary.** The Mother of God becomes queen of heaven.

Saying the Rosary in School

In school we usually say one decade. First the mystery is announced, then we say the Our Father, and then we say ten Hail Marys. We end with the Glory to the Father. Prayers for saying a decade are on the next page.

If you will say five decades of the rosary, introduce it with the Apostles' Creed, the Our Father and three Hail Marys. Then say five decades. When you are finished with five decades, say the Hail, Holy Queen (which is on the next page).

Because there are many Hail Marys, we should not say them as slowly as we would say a psalm. As we become used to saying the Hail Marys, we give our thoughts to the mystery. However, we cannot rush the words, or we will not be praying together or with dignity.

Praying a Decade of the Rosary

▶ all make
the sign
of the cross

LEADER
While we say one decade of the rosary, we will
think about _____.

▶ choose one
of the mysteries
and read it to the class

Our Father, who art in heaven,
　hallowed be thy name;
　thy kingdom come;
　thy will be done on earth as it is in heaven.

ALL
Give us this day our daily bread;
　and forgive us our trespasses
　as we forgive those who trespass against us;
　and lead us not into temptation,
　but deliver us from evil. Amen.

LEADER
Hail Mary, full of grace,
　the Lord is with you!
Blessed are you among women,
　and blessed is the fruit of your womb, Jesus.

ALL
Holy Mary, Mother of God,
　pray for us sinners,
　now and at the hour of our death. Amen.

▶ repeat the
Hail Mary
nine more times

LEADER
Glory to the Father, and to the Son,
　and to the Holy Spirit:

ALL
As it was in the beginning, is now,
　and will be for ever. Amen.

▶ it is good to end the rosary with a song,
such as "Magnificat" (page 158 in the
Hymnal for Catholic Students) or "Immaculate
Mary" (page 140 in the hymnal)

Hail, Holy Queen

▶ this prayer is said
after praying five decades
of the rosary:

Hail, holy Queen, mother of mercy,
　hail, our life, our sweetness, and our hope.
To you we cry, the children of Eve;
　to you we send up our sighs,
　mourning and weeping in this land of exile.

Turn, then, most gracious advocate,
　your eyes of mercy toward us;
　lead us home at last
　and show us the blessed fruit
　　of your womb, Jesus:
O clement, O loving, O sweet Virgin Mary.

▶ all make
the sign
of the cross

A Blessing of Gifts

Gather around the food, clothing or other gifts you have collected. If this is not possible, place a portion of the gifts where they can be seen. Fill in the blank lines in the blessing with a description of the gifts.

To begin and end, sing a song of thanksgiving, such as "Now thank we all our God" (page 158 in the Hymnal for Catholic Students*) or "Let all things now living" (page 150 in the hymnal).*

 all make
the sign
of the cross

LEADER
Blessed be the name of the Lord,
> now and for ever.

ALL
Amen.

READER   Joel 2:20–22, 26
Listen to the words of the prophet Joel:

The LORD works wonders
> and does great things.
So tell the soil to celebrate
> and wild animals to stop being afraid.
Grasslands are green again;
fruit trees and fig trees
> are loaded with fruit.
My people, you will eat until you are satisfied.
Then you will praise me
> for the wonderful things I have done.

The word of the Lord.

LEADER
Loving God,
> in your goodness you have given us
> the food, clothing and shelter
> > that we need for life.
You have given us a family and friends
> to care for us.
Now, because it is our turn to care for others,
> we have gathered:

_____

_____.

 extend your hand
toward the gifts
in blessing, and say:

Merciful God, bless these gifts
> and bless the people who will receive them.
Do not let these gifts
> be a cause of embarrassment
> but a cause of joy and a sign of our respect.
We ask this through Christ our Lord.

ALL
Amen.

 all make
the sign
of the cross

A Blessing of Food for Sharing

Place the basket or platter of food (fruit, cookies or anything simple) where it can be seen. After the ritual, the food will be shared by everyone as a simple meal of friendship.

To begin, sing a song of thanksgiving, such as "In the Lord I'll be ever thankful" (page 142 in the Hymnal for Catholic Students) *or "Now thank we all our God" (page 158 in the hymnal).*

 all make the sign
of the cross

LEADER
Blessed be the name of the Lord,
   now and for ever.

ALL
Amen.

LEADER
Bless, O Lord, this fruit of your good earth
   and the work of human hands.
It comes to us through your grace
   and the loving care of many people.
As we eat this food,
   make us joyful today.
For this food is a sign of your greatest gift:
   your Son Jesus who redeems us in faith
   and your Holy Spirit who unites us in hope.
Let this gathering be a taste of your kingdom,
   where all things are transformed by love.

We ask this through Christ our Lord.

ALL
Amen.

 all make the sign
of the cross

Subject Index

The introductions to most Daily or Weekly Prayers touch on the liturgical season or the day's scripture reading. These are not indexed here: The annual scheme of readings is outlined beginning on page x.

This index covers the church festivals, saints' days, national days and other observances that are the subjects of the introductions to Daily or Weekly Prayer. For example, Mardi Gras is the subject of the introduction to prayer for February 27. Note that days ranked as feasts and solemnities on the church's calendar are in **bold type**.

Abel, January 2
Agatha, St., February 5
All Saints, November 1
All Souls, November 2
Ambrose, St., December 7
Andrew Kim Taegon, St., September 20
Andrew, St., November 30
Annunciation of the Lord, March 26
Anthony Claret, St., October 24
Anthony of Egypt, St., January 17
Ascension of the Lord, May 24
Ash Wednesday, February 28
Athanasius, St., May 2
Augustine, St., August 28
Baptism of the Lord, January 8
Barbara, St., December 4
Birth of Mary, September 8
Body and Blood of Christ, June 17
Boscardin, Bertilla, St., October 20
Butler, Alban, October 10
Candlemas, February 2
Carnival, February 25–27
Catechetical Sunday, September 17
Catholic Schools Week, January 28–February 2
Chair of Peter, February 22
Chapman, John, September 26
Christ the King, November 26
Conversion of St. Paul, January 25
Damasus, St., December 11
Day, Dorothy, November 29
Death of John the Baptist, August 29
Dedication of the Lateran Basilica, November 9
Easter Octave, April 15–22
Easter Sunday, April 15
Edwards, Jonathan, October 5
Elizabeth Ann Seton, St., January 4
Elizabeth of Hungary, St., November 17

Epiphany of the Lord, January 7
Erasmus, Desiderius, October 27
Fidelis, St., April 24
Frances Cabrini, St., November 13
Francis of Paola, St., April 2
Frances of Rome, St., March 9
Francis de Sales, St., January 24
Francis of Assisi, St., October 4
Genevieve, St., January 3
Guardian Angels, October 2
Halloween, October 31
Hanukkah, December 21
Holy Cross, September 14
Holy Trinity, June 10
Ignatius, St., October 17
Immaculate Conception of Mary, December 8
Isaac Jogues and John de Brébeuf, SS., October 19
Isidore and Maria, SS., May 15
Jerome Emiliani, St., February 8
Joan of Arc, St., May 30
John Bosco, St., January 31
John Chrysostom, St., September 13
John Neumann, St., January 5
John of the Cross, St., December 14
Jones, Absalom, February 13
Joseph of Cupertino, St., September 18
Joseph, St., Husband of Mary, March 19
Joseph the Worker, May 1
Justin, St., June 1
King, Martin Luther, Jr., January 15
Leo, St., November 10
Louise de Marillac, St., March 15
Lucy, St., December 13
Luke, St., October 18
Mardi Gras, February 27
Margaret Clitherow, St., March 27
Mark, St., April 25
Martin de Porres, St., November 3
Matthew, St., September 21
Matthias, St., May 14
Michael, Gabriel and Raphael, archangels, September 29
Mother's Day, May 13
Nicholas, St., December 6
O Antiphons, December 18–23
Our Lady of Guadalupe, December 12
Our Lady of Sorrows, September 15
Palm Sunday/Passion Sunday, April 6, 8
Paul Miki, St., February 6

Parks, Rosa, December 1
Passover, April 6
Pentecost novena, May 25–June 2
Pentecost, June 3
Perpetua and Felicity, SS., March 7
Philip and James, SS., May 3
Polycarp, St., February 23
Presentation of Mary, November 21
Presentation of the Lord, February 2
Presidents' Day, February 19
Pulaski, Casimir, October 11
Purim, March 8
Ramadan, November 27
Roque Gonzalez, St., November 15
Rosh Hashanah, September 29
Salmon, Ben, February 15
Sergius, St., September 25
Shavuot, May 29
Sukkot, October 13
Thanksgiving, November 23
Three Freezing Saints, May 11–13
Timothy and Titus, SS., January 26
Triduum, April 12–15
Turibius, St., March 23
Tyndale, William, October 6
Valentine, St., February 14
Vincent de Paul, St., September 27
Vincent Pallotti, St., January 22
Visit of Mary and Elizabeth, May 31
Week of Prayer for Christian Unity, January 18–25
Wenceslaus, St., September 28
Wojtyla, Karol, May 18
World Day of Prayer, March 2
World Red Cross Day, May 8
Yom Kippur, October 9

352